FRENCH

for

Oral and Written Review

FRENCH
for
Oral and Written Review
SECOND EDITION

Charles Carlut   *Walter Meiden*

THE OHIO STATE UNIVERSITY

HOLT, RINEHART AND WINSTON

New York   San Francisco   Toronto   London

PERMISSIONS

Jean Cocteau: Excerpt from *Les Enfants terribles*, by permission of Editions Gallimard. (F)

Colette: Excerpt from *La Maison de Claudine*, by permission of Librairie Hachette and of Mr. Maurice Goudeket. (J)

Marguerite Duras: Excerpt from *Moderato cantabile*, by permission of Les Editions de Minuit. (IF)

Alain Robbe-Grillet: Excerpts from *Instantanés*, by permission of Les Editions de Minuit. (E)

Antoine de Saint-Exupéry: Excerpt from *Terre des hommes*, by permission of Editions Gallimard. (D)

André Pieyre de Mandiargues: Excerpt from *Feu de braise* by permission of Editions Bernard Grasset.

Simone de Beauvoir: Excerpt from *La Force de l'âge* by permission of Editions Gallimard.

Jean Tardieu: Excerpt from *Un Mot pour un autre* by permission of Editions Gallimard.

Library of Congress Cataloging in Publication Data

Carlut, Charles
 French for oral and written review.

 Includes index.
 1. French language—Grammar—1950–   I. Meiden,
Walter E., joint author.   II. Title.
PC2112.C3 1976   448'.2'421   75–20021
ISBN 0–03–089726–2

Printed in the United States of America

1   090   98

Table of Contents

Preface to the Second Edition

In preparing the second edition of *French for Oral and Written Review* we have tried to retain all the favorable features of the first edition and to improve and update the work as follows:

(1) Certain rules have been reworded to make them clearer.

(2) Occasionally additional notes have been added to afford explanations of less common grammatical points which were not mentioned in the first edition.

(3) In the exercises, **tu** or **vous** is indicated at the beginning of sentences containing a second person pronoun or adjective, where this is not indicated elsewhere in the sentence.

(4) Some of the exercises have been rewritten in part and shortened. Where possible, words which have become very common in France during this decade have been introduced into the sentences.

(5) *Textes* 5 to 8 have been replaced by new selections. *Texte* 5 shows another aspect of Saint-Exupéry; *Textes* 6–8 are by authors who are well known in contemporary France.

ACKNOWLEDGMENTS

We would like to thank the various French teachers who have sent us suggestions of how to improve the first edition of this text and those who participated in the formal survey of the book conducted by Holt, Rinehart and Winston, Inc. We are very grateful to Dr. Mary Lynne Flowers of the University of Kentucky, to Dr. Diane Birchbickler of the Ohio State University, and to Miss Marie-Claire Charton of Mrs. Porter's School for their detailed reactions to various points in the text.

Charles Carlut
Walter Meiden

Preface to the First Edition

This text is designed to review all the common elements of French grammar, both orally and in written form. To that end it provides taped pattern practice, all-French exercises, and English-to-French translations on the various phases of the French language. Ways of expressing certain problem words are studied, and the verb is systematically reviewed. In addition, there are eight twentieth century texts edited for grammatical analysis.

The organization of the chapters

In general, each chapter deals with a specific grammatical topic. The chapters are divided into short sections, each one of which takes up a particular aspect of the subject. At the end of a certain number of sections treating related topics, there are short oral and written exercises which afford practice on the material of the preceding paragraphs. Finally, some three or four problem words are explained, and the chapter ends with a verb review.

This type of organization affords great flexibility: it allows teachers who so desire to assign a limited amount of grammar each day with reading from other texts; it permits those using the book in a pure grammar review course to adjust the number of sections and exercises to the needs of the class; topics can easily be omitted without disturbing the unity of the whole. For those wishing exercises which offer practice on all aspects of a grammatical topic, there are *exercices d'ensemble* at the end of most chapters.

Inductive presentation of grammar

To encourage students to arrive at grammatical generalizations inductively, each section is set up as follows:

(1) question on grammatical point
(2) examples to illustrate the point
(3) answer to the question in form of a generalization

It is hoped that this presentation will induce the students to work out the answers to the questions by studying the examples given.

The Pattern Practice

Taped pattern practice exercises complete each group of written exercises except where the topic at hand does not lend itself to oral drill. In the text itself, the existence of these pattern practice exercises is indicated only by a model sentence illustrating the type of responses desired. The entire drill does not appear because of the desirability of having the student prepare the pattern practice orally in the language laboratory without seeing it in print. However, for the use of the teacher and for those classes whose instructor wishes the student to have the script of the taped material for home study, there is a *Pattern Practice Manual* which contains all the sentences which the student may hear in the laboratory. The pattern practice exercises may be handled in various ways, e.g.:

METHOD 1: The students do not see the printed form of the drills, but they listen to them in the language laboratory and then later go over them in the class hour.

METHOD 2: The students first prepare the exercises at home from the *Pattern Practice Manual*, next listen to and repeat them in the language laboratory, and finally practice them during the class hour.

METHOD 3 (where the school has no laboratory facilities): The students prepare the exercises at home from the *Pattern Practice Manual*, then in class they reproduce them orally without reference to the manual.

However the students prepare the pattern practice, it is suggested that a part of each recitation hour be devoted to the laboratory material and that the students be required to repeat the exercises without looking at the printed manual during the class hour. It is important for the teacher to insist on rapid and accurate responses, for in that case the students tend to prepare the lesson in such a way as to make such responses.

The Problem Words

Each chapter treats ways of expressing some three or four English words which habitually cause trouble because usages in the two languages are different. Although these words constitute a vocabulary rather than a syntactical problem, they would seem properly a part of a review of French, for the ability to express them correctly is at

least as important in speaking and writing as a knowledge of points
of grammar.

The words presented are among those most frequently misused by
students in their compositions and French translations. No attempt
has been made to give every possible way of expressing such words,
but rather to focus the attention of the reader on the commonest
difficulties inherent in them. Often there comes into consideration
also the fact that the spoken and written language express such words
in different ways.

The PROBLEM WORDS are presented at the end of each chapter and
in alphabetical order partly so as to be easily available for reference
and partly so that where it is found desirable, they may be studied
independently of the grammar and could even be used as part of the
subject-matter of a separate conversation or composition course.

The Texts

Eight texts from twentieth century French literature afford the
students the opportunity to study French grammar as used by contemporary writers. These passages have been edited with comments
and questions in order to guide the students in their study. Only a
limited number of possible points of grammar are taken up in any
one selection, since the authors desire to present different grammatical material in each text wherever possible.

If the detailed study of the texts is begun early in the course, many
points of grammar not yet learned through work on the chapters will
arise in the texts. But it is sometimes advantageous to meet a new
grammatical phenomenon for the first time in a text. To introduce
and discuss such a topic before the student has encountered it in his
more organized study has the advantage of acquainting him with it
in advance and of preparing him to understand it more fully when
he meets it in the more formal discussion.

Naturally, instructors so desiring may use the "Textes" for purposes other than grammatical study. They lend themselves to conversation, to literary comment, to a study of style, etc.

Ways in which the book may be adjusted
to fit the needs of different types of courses

Where the number of recitations in a course is limited, parts of the
book may be omitted without affecting the study of the parts that
are assigned, for each chapter is an independent unit. No chapter

depends on what has been learned in any preceding chapter. Therefore, the chapters may be studied in any order, and any group of sections which terminates in exercises based on them may be omitted
without affecting the rest of the study.

For the shorter grammar course, the PROBLEM WORDS, the "Exercices d'ensemble" at the end of the chapters, Chapter 17 dealing with
Problem Prepositions, and the "Textes" could be omitted at the dis-
cretion of the instructor.

Some schools which are on the shorter quarter system take up the
majority of the chapters of *French for Oral and Written Review* in their
grammar review course and use the rest of them as the grammatical
portion of one or more conversation-composition courses.

For the course where reading material is considered especially desirable, the "Textes" could be given an important role. They could be
assigned at every second chapter, if the teacher wished to distribute
them equally throughout the course.

For the course where an emphasis on the proper use of words is
paramount, the core of the study could be built around the PROBLEM
WORDS and, where necessary, certain grammatical sections might be
omitted.

To the Student

Grammar is an organized study of the usages of the various aspects
of a language. This study usually consists of a series of principles or
rules.

A rule is simply a statement of usage in a generalized form.

To formulate a rule to govern any French grammatical construction, one looks for as many examples as possible of this construction
in both written and spoken French, and, after carefully examining
how the construction is expressed, one tells how it is expressed in
generalized form.

In a small way, you should try to make your own rules by studying
the examples of the constructions found in this book.

To that end, each section of a chapter begins with a question on
some type of French construction. There follow examples of the construction. Study these examples carefully in light of the question
which precedes them. From what you observe, try to derive a generalization which will answer the question and which will then constitute your own rule for that construction. To permit you to check

the accuracy of your generalization, the answer to the question follows the examples. This answer is likewise in form of a generalization and constitutes a rule.

It is not necessary to learn these rules verbatim, but it is valuable to understand the principle at hand and to be able to state it accurately and clearly as a generalization.

Naturally, a knowledge of French grammar will not be of much use to you unless you can apply it in speaking and writing. For that reason, each grammatical unit is followed by oral and written exercises which will give you the opportunity to apply what you have learned in the unit. Practice the oral exercises and work out the written exercises as your teacher directs. If you have access to a laboratory, listen carefully to the tapes and repeat with the indicated changes during the intervals of silence until you can say the pattern in question without hesitation. If you do not have a laboratory, go over the exercises in the *Pattern Practice Manual* again and again until you can say them rapidly and without hesitation.

But a knowledge of grammatical principles and the ability to apply them will not alone give you a mastery of French, even if you learn to say the patterns automatically. In addition, you must know how to use the common words of the language properly.

In English and French, there are a certain number of common words and ideas which are expressed in several ways in each language, but their usages do not correspond. Let us consider two examples:

EXAMPLE 1: The French word **temps**

Je n'ai pas beaucoup de **temps**.	*I don't have much* time.
Le **temps** est splendide aujourd'hui.	*The* weather *is marvelous today.*

In each sentence, we find the French word **temps**. But English expresses **temps** of the first sentence by *time*, of the second sentence by *weather*.

EXAMPLE 2: The English word *time*

Je n'ai pas beaucoup de **temps**.	*I don't have much* time.
Je vous ai appelé trois **fois**.	*I called you three* times.
Quelle **heure** est-il?	*What* time *is it?*
Que faites-vous en ce **moment**?	*What are you doing at this* time?
A cette **époque**-là, j'étais très jeune.	*At that* time *I was very young.*
Vous êtes-vous amusé à cette soirée?	Did you have a good time *at that party?*

In each sentence, English has used the same word — *time*. But French has used successively **temps, fois, heure, moment,** and **époque** to express the English word *time*, and in the last sentence it uses the verb **s'amuser** to convey the idea of *having a good time*.

It is very important to know when French uses one word and when another to express a given English word, for often the various French words that express the same English word cannot be interchanged. To teach you how to deal with such words, there is at the end of each lesson a group of some three or four "problem words". Through the examples, explanations, and exercises, familiarize yourself with all aspects of the words given.

A thorough knowledge of the forms of the most used tenses of regular and irregular verbs is essential if you wish to speak and write French correctly. For that reason, two verbs are reviewed at the end of each lesson. On pages 281–283 you are shown how you can organize your knowledge of the verb by deriving its tenses from the five principal parts.

FRENCH

for

Oral and Written Review

CHAPTER 1

Interrogatives

I. Interrogative Adjectives

An interrogative adjective is one which modifies a noun and asks a question. In English the interrogative adjectives are *which* and *what*.

1. What are the French interrogative adjectives and how are they used before a noun?

Quel livre lisez vous?	Which *book are you reading?*
Quelles leçons préparent-ils?	Which *lessons are they preparing?*
Quel homme! **Quels** beaux enfants!	What *a man!* What *good-looking children!*

The interrogative adjectives are:

	MASCULINE	FEMININE
Singular	quel	quelle
Plural	quels	quelles

Interrogative adjectives precede their noun and its modifiers directly and agree with it in gender and number.

The interrogative **quel** is also used in an exclamation and is then the equivalent of the English *what . . . !* or *what a . . . !*

NOTE: The interrogative adjective *Whose . . . ?* is usually expressed by **De qui . . . ?** Ex.: **De qui** portez-vous la cravate? (or) Vous portez la cravate **de qui?** (Whose *tie are you wearing?*)

In sentences in which the French equivalent of *Whose . . . ?* is used with a form of **être**, it is expressed by **De qui . . . ?** except when *Whose . . . ?* denotes possession. Ex.: **De qui** est-il le fils? (Whose *son is he?*) **De qui** est ce livre? (Whose *book is that?* = Who *is the author* of *that book?*)

But when *Whose . . . +* **être** . . . indicates possession, **A qui . . . ?** is used. Ex.: **A qui** est cette radio? (Whose *radio is that?*)

2. Under what circumstances is the interrogative *quel* used before some form of the verb *être?*

Quelle est la règle la plus difficile?   Which *is the most difficult rule?*
Quels sont ces hommes en noir?   Who *are these men in black?*

NOTE: It is also possible to say: «**Qui** sont ces hommes en noir?» But by using **Quels** the nature of the question is changed slightly to mean: *What sort of . . .*

The interrogative adjective is used before a form of the verb **être** to ask which of a number of possible answers is the case and to ask the nature of a person or thing.

A. *Remplacez les tirets par la forme convenable de l'adjectif interrogatif.*

1. _____ est la vraie raison de votre départ? 2. Dans _____ rue habitent vos amis? 3. _____ est votre acteur préféré? 4. _____ pays étrangers avez-vous visités? 5. _____ sont les plus belles villes des États-Unis? 6. _____ professeur! 7. _____ heure est-il? 8. _____ sont les dernières nouvelles?

B. *Traduisez en français.*

1. (*tu*) What dress do you want to wear? 2. Which is the best car this[1] year? 3. (*vous*) What are your favorite[2] songs? 4. (*tu*) What programs interest you the most? 5. What a catastrophe! 6. What is that girl's telephone number[3]? 7. (*tu*) What animals do you prefer, dogs[4] or cats[4]?

---

[1] **de cette année** [2] The normal position for descriptive adjectives in French is treated fully on pages 20–21. [3] **numéro de téléphone** [4] Use the proper form of the definite article with these nouns.

Pattern 1

YOU HEAR   Je regarde les photos de notre voyage en Europe.
YOU SAY   Quelles photos regardez-vous?

Pattern 2

YOU HEAR   Paris est la capitale de la France.
YOU SAY   Quelle est la capitale de la France?

II. Interrogative Pronouns

An interrogative pronoun is one that asks a question. In English, the interrogative pronouns are *who? whose? whom? which? what? which one?*

3. What interrogative pronoun is used in French to refer to persons?

Qui a ouvert la porte?   Who *opened the door?*
Qui avez-vous vu?   Whom *did you see?*
Avec **qui** êtes-vous sorti?   *With* whom *did you go out?*

In French, **qui** is the interrogative pronoun which refers to persons.

NOTE: For **qui** as the subject, the longer form **qui est-ce qui** may be used; for **qui** as the object, the longer form **qui est-ce que** may be used. But since the longer forms sometimes entail a change in word order, students are advised to use the shorter forms for the present.

4. When *qui* is the object of the sentence, what word order is used when the subject of the sentence is a pronoun? a noun?

Qui voyez-vous?   Whom *do you see?*
Qui Jacques voit-il?   Whom *does Jack see?*

When **qui** is the direct object of the sentence, note the word order:

Qui + VERB + PRONOUN SUBJECT
Qui + NOUN SUBJECT + VERB + PRONOUN SUBJECT

5. Which interrogative pronouns are used to refer to things in French?

Qu'est-ce qui est sur la table?   What *is on the table?*
Que faites-vous?   } What *are you doing?*
Qu'est-ce que vous faites? }
Avec **quoi** avez-vous ouvert la boîte?   *With* what *did you open the box?*

The four French interrogative pronouns referring to things are **qu'est-ce qui, que, qu'est-ce que** and **quoi.** Their use depends on their function in the sentence.

6. When is que and when qu'est-ce que used as the object of the sentence to refer to a thing?

Que voyez-vous?
Qu'est-ce que vous voyez? } *What do you see?*

Que fait Françoise?
Qu'est-ce que Françoise fait? } *What does Frances do?*

When the direct object is a thing, either **que** or **qu'est-ce que** may be used, but notice the difference in word order:

Que + VERB + SUBJECT	and	**Qu'est-ce que** + SUBJECT + VERB

7. What are the various uses of the word quoi?

De **quoi** parlez-vous?   *Of what are you speaking?*

—Ah! je vois quelque chose.   *"Oh, I see something."*
—**Quoi?**   *"What?"*

Je ne sais pas **quoi** faire.   *I don't know what to do.*

Quoi!
Comment! } Vous partez?   *What! You're leaving?*

The word **quoi** is used to refer to a thing after a preposition, it is used when asking: "*What?*" alone, it is often used instead of **que** before an infinitive, especially in a negative sentence, and it is used to express the exclamatory *What!* **Comment!** may also be used to express *What!*

—Allez chercher le dossier du can-   *"Go and get the candidate's file."*
didat.
—**Comment?**   *"What?"*

In English, when we do not hear or do not understand what someone has said, we normally ask: "*What?*" The French normally ask «**Comment?**» rather than «**Quoi?**» under such circumstances. However, «**Quoi?**» is often used by children who have not yet learned the amenities and by certain uneducated people.

8. How can the interrogative pronouns be presented in graphic tabular form?

FUNCTION	PERSONS	THINGS
SUBJECT	qui	qu'est-ce qui
OBJECT	qui	$\begin{cases} \text{que} \\ \text{qu'est-ce que} \end{cases}$
AFTER PREPOSITION	qui	quoi

C. *Remplacez le mot anglais par son équivalent français.*

1. (*Whom*) avez-vous vu en allant à la bibliothèque?   2. De (*what*) avez-vous parlé pendant mon absence?   3. A (*whom*) donc écrivez-vous toutes ces lettres?   4. (*What*) doit-on faire dans ce cas? 5. (*What*) vous trouvez de si difficile dans ce devoir?   6. (*Who*) me montrera le chemin?   7. De (*whom*) est le roman que vous avez acheté?   8. (*What*) vous intéresse le plus dans ce livre?   9. (*What*) vous aimeriez faire maintenant?   10. (*What*) est sur votre bureau? 11. Je vais vous faire un petit cadeau. (*What?*)

D. *Traduisez en français.*

1. Who took my ball pen?   2. (*vous*) We don't have any[1] vase.   In what do you want me to put these flowers?   3. (*tu*) What makes you laugh?   4. (*tu*) What did you learn in[2] class today?   5. (*tu*) With whom are you going to the movies?   6. (*vous*) What are you going to read?   7. (*tu*) Whom did your brother meet[3] at the station? 8. (*vous*) He seems[4] angry. What did you say to him?   9. Whom will Maurice and Marie see?   10. (*tu*) "I'd like to tell you something." "What?"   11. (*vous*) Who told you that it was a good book? 12. (*tu*) What! You're crying?

---
[1] de   [2] en   [3] Use a form of **aller chercher**.   [4] Use a form of **avoir l'air**.

PATTERN PRACTICE: **qui** used as the subject

Pattern 3

    YOU HEAR   Jeanne arrive demain.
    YOU SAY   Qui arrive demain?

PATTERN PRACTICE: **qui** used as the object

Pattern 4

     YOU HEAR   J'ai interrogé les élèves après la classe.
     YOU SAY   Qui avez-vous interrogé après la classe?

Pattern 5

     YOU HEAR   Les ouvriers attendent leur patron.
     YOU SAY   Qui les ouvriers attendent-ils?

PATTERN PRACTICE: **qu'est-ce qui**

Pattern 6

     YOU HEAR   Un livre est sur la table.
     YOU SAY   Qu'est-ce qui est sur la table?

PATTERN PRACTICE: **que** used as the object

Pattern 7

     YOU HEAR   Marie fait son travail.
     YOU SAY   Que fait Marie?

PATTERN PRACTICE: **qu'est-ce que** used as the object

Pattern 8

     YOU HEAR   Sylvie a écrit un roman pendant ses vacances.
     YOU SAY   Qu'est-ce que Sylvie a écrit pendant ses vacances?

9. When is a form of *lequel* used to ask *which one* in French? What are the forms of *lequel*?

J'ai trois stylos. **Lequel** voulez-vous?   *I have three fountain pens.* Which one *do you want?*

Laquelle de ces personnes parle français?   Which one *of these persons speaks French?*

The interrogative *which one*, referring to a definite object already mentioned or mentioned immediately after *which one of* is expressed by the following:

	MASCULINE	FEMININE
Singular	**lequel**	**laquelle**
Plural	**lesquels**	**lesquelles**

These pronouns contract with **à** and **de** forming: **auquel, auxquels, auxquelles; duquel, desquels, desquelles.**

10. When must *qui, que* or *qu'est-ce que* be used to express *which one*?

Que préférez-vous, le français ou l'italien? ⎫
Qu'est-ce que vous préférez, le ⎬ Which one *do you prefer, French or Italian?*
français ou l'italien? ⎭

When asking a question about something which has not yet been mentioned, *which one* must be expressed by **qui . . . ?** (referring to persons), or **que . . . ?** or **qu'est-ce que . . . ?** (referring to things) except that *which one of* + THE OBJECT is expressed by a form of **lequel de** + THE OBJECT.

E. *Remplacez les tirets par la forme convenable de* **lequel.** *Faites les contractions nécessaires.*

1. ____ de vous deux veut bien me prêter sa voiture?   2.—Votre ami est très original. —De ____ parlez-vous?   3. —Voyez-vous ces deux dames? — ____?   4. ____ de ses filles va épouser Henri? 5. Tous ces exercices sont bons, mais ____ sont les plus utiles?

F. *Traduisez en français.*

1. These watches are[1] expensive; I do not know which one to buy. 2. "There will be many difficulties." "Which?"   3. Which of the two roads[2] must we take?   4. (*vous*) Which do you prefer, tea[3] or coffee[3]?   5. (*tu*) I like Italian films a great deal[4]. Which ones do you prefer?   6. (*vous*) There are several programs this afternoon. Which one do you wish to see?

---

[1] Use a form of **coûter cher.**   [2] **routes**   [3] Either the definite or the partitive article is possible, depending on the meaning.   [4] The adverb comes immediately after the verb.

PATTERN PRACTICE: forms of **lequel**

Pattern 9

YOU HEAR   Voici trois stylos. Je veux celui-ci.
YOU SAY   Voici trois stylos. Lequel voulez-vous?

11. When does French use a variation of *quel est* . . . to express *what is* . . . or *what are* . . .?

Quelle est la capitale de la Belgique?	What is *the capital of Belgium?*
Quels sont les produits les plus importants de ce pays?	What are *the most important products of that country?*

When *what is* . . . or *what are* . . . ask 'which of a number of possibilities,' French uses **quel est** . . . or some variation of it.

12. How does French express *what is* . . . or *what are* . . . when asking a definition?

Qu'est-ce que la philosophie?	What is *philosophy?*
Qu'est-ce que c'est que le communisme?	What is *communism?*
Qu'est-ce que c'est que les mathématiques?	What are *mathematics?*

When *what is* . . . or *what are* . . . ask for a definition of a word, French uses either **qu'est-ce que** . . . or **qu'est-ce que c'est que** . . . with that word.

G. *Remplacez les tirets par l'équivalent de* what is *ou* what are *selon le cas.*

1. ____ un héros?   2. ____ les présidents des États-Unis les plus connus?   3. ____ la biologie?   4. ____ votre fleur favorite?   5. ____ le meilleur système de gouvernement?

H. *Traduisez en français.*

1. What is the longest river in[1] the United States?   2. What is the Louvre?   3. What are the qualities of a good teacher?   4. What is democracy?   5. (*vous*) What is the aim of your work?

---
[1] Not «dans»

PATTERN PRACTICE: asking for a definition with **Qu'est-ce que** . . .?

Pattern 10

YOU HEAR   le capitalisme
YOU SAY   Qu'est-ce que le capitalisme?

PATTERN PRACTICE: asking for a definition with **Qu'est-ce que c'est que . . .?**

Pattern 11

>YOU HEAR   le capitalisme
>YOU SAY   Qu'est-ce que c'est que le capitalisme?

EXERCICES D'ENSEMBLE

I. *Remplacez les mots anglais par leur équivalent français.*

1. (*Which*) jeune fille Jacques veut-il épouser? 2. (*Who*) est là?
3. (*Which one*) aimez-vous le mieux, votre secrétaire ou la mienne?
4. (*What*) nous ferons cet après-midi? 5. Chez (*whom*) passerez-vous le week-end? 6. (*What*) l'empêche de venir? 7. (*What*) dites-vous? 8. (*What*) sont les fruits les plus nourrissants? 9. Avec (*whom*) allez-vous jouer au bridge? 10. (*Who*) est ce monsieur à la barbe blanche? 11. (*What is*) un mythe? 12. (*What*) vous me donnerez en échange? 13. (*What*) regardez-vous? 14. Avec (*what*) a-t-il fait cette réparation? 15. (*Whom*) êtes-vous allé voir? 16. Nous ne savons pas (*what*) faire.

J. *Traduisez en français.*

1. "What is the smallest state in[1] the United States?" "What?"[2]
2. (*tu*) What are you going to do now? 3. What is a computer?
4. Who has just gone out? 5. To whom shall we give our old sofa?
6. Which are the most useful languages? 7. (*vous*) What sort of plays do you like to see? 8. Whom did the policeman arrest? 9. (*tu*) What are you speaking of? 10. (*vous*) What makes you believe that?
11. Who is at the door? 12. (*vous*) What did your friends do last evening? 13. What is making that noise? 14. To whom did Michelle lend her necklace? 15. (*tu*) "What did you learn during your trip?" "Which one?" 16. What! Paul isn't here?

---

[1] Not «dans»   [2] This "What?" indicates that the second speaker did not hear or understand the question.

Problem Words

1. actually

(**a**) When *actually* = *really*

Avez-vous **réellement** vu l'accident? ⎫
Avez-vous **vraiment** vu l'accident? ⎬ *Did you* actually *see the accident?*
                                      ⎭

When *actually* means *really*, it may be expressed by **vraiment, véritablement,** or **réellement,** depending on the sentence.

(**b**) When *actually* = *as a matter of fact*

Il caresse vos chats, mais **en fait** ⎫
   il ne les aime pas beaucoup.   ⎪ *He pets your cats, but* actually *he*
Il caresse vos chats, mais **à vrai dire,** ⎬ *doesn't like them very much.*
   il ne les aime pas beaucoup.   ⎭

When *actually* means *as a matter of fact* and contradicts what seems to be the case, it may be expressed by **en fait** or **à vrai dire.**

CAUTION: DO NOT use «actuellement» for *actually*. It means *at present.*

2. advice

(**a**) How to say *a piece of advice*

Donnez-moi **un conseil.**   *Give me* a piece of advice.

The singular **un conseil** means *some advice* or *a piece of advice.*

(**b**) How to say *advice*

J'ai toujours écouté **les conseils** de   *I always listened to* the advice *of my*
   mon vieux maître.   *old teacher.*

The word *advice* is expressed by the plural form, **les conseils.**

CAUTION: The French word **avis** means *opinion.* Do NOT use it for *advice.*

3. again

(**a**) The prefix **re-** + VERB = *again*

Voulez-vous **relire** cette phrase?   *Will you* read *that sentence* again?
Je te **retéléphonerai** tout de suite. *I'll* telephone *you* again *right away.*

In negative sentences, *not . . . again* is often expressed by **ne . . . plus,** but it may also be expressed by **ne re- +** VERB **+ pas** when **re- +** VERB exists.

(b) encore, encore une fois, de nouveau and **à nouveau** = *again*

Mon avocat m'a parlé **de nouveau** à ce sujet.	*My lawyer talked to me on that matter again.*
Écoutons **encore** ce disque.	*Let's listen to that record again.*
Faites cela **encore une fois.**	*Do that again.*

In affirmative sentences, *again* is expressed by **encore, encore une fois, de nouveau** and occasionally by **à nouveau.**

(c) In negative sentences **ne . . . plus** = *again*

Je **ne** le ferai **plus.**	*I will not do it again.*

In negative sentences, *not . . . again* is often expressed by **ne . . . plus,** but it may also be expressed by **ne . . . re- +** VERB when **re- +** VERB exists.

4. agree

(a) When *agree to* = *consent to*

Monsieur Pommier **a consenti à** venir parler devant notre groupe. Monsieur Pommier **a accepté de** venir parler devant notre groupe.	*Mr. Pommier has agreed to come and speak to our group.*

When *agree to* means *consent to*, it may be expressed by **consentir à** or by **accepter de.**

(b) When *agree* = *be in agreement*

Ma femme et moi **sommes d'accord** sur l'éducation de nos enfants.	*My wife and I agree on the bringing-up of our children.*

When *agree* means *be in agreement*, it may be expressed by **être d'accord.**

(c) When *agreed* = *OK*

—Voulez-vous venir à six heures?	*"Do you want to come at six o'clock?"*
—**C'est entendu.**	*"Agreed."*

The English *agreed*, indicating assent, may be rendered by: **c'est entendu** or by: **entendu,** or: **d'accord.**

(d) When *agree* is a grammatical term

L'adjectif **s'accorde** avec le nom   *The adjective* agrees *with the noun it* qu'il modifie.   *modifies.*

Grammatical agreement is expressed by forms of the verb **s'accorder**.

CAUTION: Do NOT use «agréer» for *agree*. French use **agréer** only in special situations, and it normally means *accept*.

K. *Remplacez les mots anglais par leur équivalent français.*

1. Jacques est (*again*) en retard. 2. Est-ce que le participe passé (*agrees*) avec le sujet? 3. Vos (*advice*) sont toujours très utiles. 4. Il paraît que Marcel est (*actually*) très malade. 5. Le patron (*agreed to*) vous voir ce soir après cinq heures. 6. Je vous répète (*again*) que vous regretterez cette action. 7. (*Actually*), j'aimerais mieux ne pas aller voir cet opéra. 8. (*Advice*) ne servent à rien à la plupart des gens. 9. Il faut (*begin the lesson again*). 10. —Voulez-vous venir me chercher à midi? —(*Agreed*). 11. Je (*agree*) avec vous sur la politique actuelle.

L. *Traduisez en français. Attention aux mots en italique.*

1. (*vous*) Copy that exercise *again*. 2. He *agreed* to write a letter of recommendation for me. 3. (*tu*) Do you want me to give you a a piece of good *advice?* 4. John says he works hard, but *actually* he wastes a great deal of time. 5. (*vous*) You should follow my *advice*. 6. Jack told me that he would not smoke *again*. 7. (*vous*) We all *agree* that you must leave immediately. 8. (*tu*) Did you *actually* go to the movies yesterday evening? 9. (*tu*) Tell me *again* what you want. 10. Does the present participle *agree* with the noun it modifies? 11. I heard that noise *again* last night. 12. (*vous*) You don't see them? Look *again*.

Verb Review

Review the verbs **parler** and **finir** according to the outline on page 283.

CHAPTER 2

Adjectives

An adjective is a word that modifies a noun or pronoun. Ex.: the *green* house; the *tall* tree; the *interesting* letter. The house is *green*. The trees were *tall*. The letter will be *interesting*.

I. The Formation of Adjectives

In English, adjectives have one form only. In French, they usually have four forms: masculine singular, feminine singular, masculine plural, feminine plural.

PLURAL OF ADJECTIVES

1. How do most French adjectives form their masculine plural?

       petit   petit**s**

Most French adjectives form their masculine plural by adding **-s** to the masculine singular.

2. What about the masculine plural of adjectives whose masculine singular ends in -s, -x or -z?

       gris   gris
       heureu**x**   heureu**x**

Adjectives whose masculine singular ends in **-s, -x** or **-z** do not change in the masculine plural.

3. What about the masculine plural of adjectives whose masculine singular ends in -eau?

       nouv**eau**   nouv**eaux**

Adjectives whose masculine singular ends in **-eau** add **-x** to form the masculine plural.

4. What about the masculine plural of adjectives whose masculine singular ends in -al?

national   nationaux

Most adjectives whose masculine singular ends in **-al** change the **-al** to **-aux** in the masculine plural.

5. How is the feminine plural of adjectives formed?

petite	petites
grise	grises
nouvelle	nouvelles
nationale	nationales

Feminine adjectives normally form their plural by adding **-s** to the feminine singular form.

A. *Écrivez le pluriel de l'adjectif indiqué.*

1. des chats (gris) 2. de (nouveau) livres 3. de (grand) événements 4. des enfants très (gentil) 5. deux (gros) garçons 6. des docteurs (distingué) 7. de (riche) touristes 8. de (mauvais) livres 9. des hôtels (élégant) 10. de (vieux) amis 11. des amis (loyal) 12. de (beau) musées

FEMININE OF ADJECTIVES

English adjectives have no feminine form. French adjectives have a special feminine form. The forms of the examples that follow are given in this order:

masculine singular; feminine singular;
masculine plural; feminine plural.

6. How do most adjectives form their feminine singular and plural?

petit	petite	petits	petites
fermé	fermée	fermés	fermées

Most adjectives form their feminine singular by adding **-e** to the masculine singular form.

7. What about adjectives whose masculine form ends in unaccented -e?

| difficile | difficile | difficiles | difficiles |

Adjectives whose masculine form ends in unaccented **-e** do not change in the feminine.

8. What about certain adjectives whose masculine form ends in -e- + consonant?

premier	première	premiers	premières
étranger	étrangère	étrangers	étrangères
complet	complète	complets	complètes

Certain adjectives whose masculine form ends in **-e- +** CONSONANT place a grave accent (`) over this **-e-** as well as adding the regular **-e** to form the feminine.

9. What about adjectives whose masculine form ends in -f?

| actif | active | actifs | actives |
| neuf | neuve | neufs | neuves |

Adjectives whose masculine form ends in **-f** change the **-f** to **-ve** in the feminine.

10. What about adjectives whose masculine form ends in -x?

| nombreux | nombreuse | nombreux | nombreuses |
| heureux | heureuse | heureux | heureuses |

Adjectives whose masculine form ends in **-x** change the **-x** to **-se** in the feminine.

11. What about adjectives whose masculine form ends in -el, -eil, -ien, -as, and -os?

quel	quelle	quels	quelles
pareil	pareille	pareils	pareilles
ancien	ancienne	anciens	anciennes
bas	basse	bas	basses
gros	grosse	gros	grosses

Adjectives whose masculine form ends in **-el, -eil, -ien, -as** and **-os** double the final consonant before adding **-e.**

12. What are the irregular feminine forms of the adjectives *blanc, bon, doux, épais, faux, frais, gentil, grec, long, public,* and *sec?*

blanc	**blanche**	blancs	**blanches**	*white*
bon	**bonne**	bons	**bonnes**	*good*
doux	**douce**	doux	**douces**	*soft, sweet*
épais	**épaisse**	épais	**épaisses**	*thick*
faux	**fausse**	faux	**fausses**	*false*
frais	**fraîche**	frais	**fraîches**	*fresh*
gentil	**gentille**	gentils	**gentilles**	*nice*
grec	**grecque**	grecs	**grecques**	*Greek*
long	**longue**	longs	**longues**	*long*
public	**publique**	publics	**publiques**	*public*
sec	**sèche**	secs	**sèches**	*dry*

B. *Écrivez la forme féminine de l'adjectif indiqué.*

1. une leçon (difficile)   2. des femmes (actif)   3. la semaine (dernier)   4. deux robes (pareil)   5. une (long) histoire   6. les familles (nombreux)   7. des souliers (usé)   8. la maison (blanc)   9. des chansons (italien)   10. les populations (natif)   11. des années (heureux)   12. une armoire (massif)   13. une nuit (frais)   14. des jeunes filles (sérieux)

PATTERN PRACTICE: the feminine of adjectives

Pattern 1

> YOU HEAR   Le bureau est grand. Et la lampe?
> YOU SAY   La lampe est grande aussi.

13. What are the masculine and feminine singular and plural forms of the adjectives *beau, fou, mou, nouveau* and *vieux,* and when is the second masculine form used?

MASCULINE			Plural		
(before consonant)	*(before vowel)*	FEMININE	MASCULINE	FEMININE	
beau	**bel**	belle	beaux	belles	*beautiful*
fou	**fol**	folle	fous	folles	*foolish*
mou	**mol**	molle	mous	molles	*soft*
nouveau	**nouvel**	nouvelle	nouveaux	nouvelles	*new*
vieux	**vieil**	vieille	vieux	vieilles	*old*

Some adjectives have two masculine singular forms, one of which is used when the word it directly precedes begins with a consonant, the other when the word it directly precedes begins with a vowel or a mute **h.** In the plural, they have only one form for the masculine and one for the feminine.

C. *Écrivez la forme convenable de l'adjectif indiqué.*

1. de (vieux) rues   2. la (nouveau) mode   3. un très (beau) homme
4. le (nouveau) an   5. une vitesse (fou)   6. une personne un peu
(mou)   7. de (vieux) souvenirs   8. les (beau) quartiers   9. un
(vieux) oncle   10. de (vieux) dames   11. un (beau) arbre

PATTERN PRACTICE: **beau, nouveau** and **vieux**

Pattern 2

   YOU HEAR   J'ai visité une ville.
   YOU SAY   J'ai visité une belle ville.

Pattern 3

   YOU HEAR   J'ai acheté un costume.
   YOU SAY   J'ai acheté un nouveau costume.

Pattern 4

   YOU HEAR   Nous avons vu cette ville.
   YOU SAY   Nous avons vu cette vieille ville.

II. Comparison of Adjectives

In English, adjectives are compared with *more* or *less* (comparative degree) and *most* and *least* (superlative degree) if they have more than two syllables.

POSITIVE	COMPARATIVE	SUPERLATIVE
beautiful	*more* beautiful	*most* beautiful
interesting	*less* interesting	*least* interesting

French adjectives are compared in somewhat the same way.

14. How are French adjectives compared?

POSITIVE	COMPARATIVE	SUPERLATIVE
cher	**plus** cher	**le plus** cher
difficile	**moins** difficile	**le moins** difficile

The comparative form of the French adjective is formed by placing **plus** (*more*) or **moins** (*less*) before the positive form. The superlative form is reached by placing the definite article (**le, la, les**) before the comparative form.

15. How are the adjectives *bon, mauvais,* **and** *petit* **compared?**

POSITIVE	COMPARATIVE	SUPERLATIVE
bon	**meilleur**	**le meilleur**
mauvais	{ **plus mauvais** { **pire**	{ **le plus mauvais** { **le pire**
petit	{ **plus petit** { **moindre**	{ **le plus petit** { **le moindre**

The adjective **bon** is always compared irregularly, the adjectives **mauvais** and **petit** have a regular and irregular comparative form. The form **moindre** is ordinarily used in the superlative and means *slightest.*

16. How is *than* **expressed in French?**

> Les hivers sont plus froids **que** les étés.

After a comparative, *than* is expressed by **que.**

BUT

> Nous avons **plus de vingt** pages à lire.
> Vous avez **moins de dix** minutes pour y arriver.

After **plus** and **moins** before a numeral *than* is expressed by **de.**

17. When the superlative form of an adjective follows its noun, what is the sign of the superlative?

> Le russe est la langue **la plus difficile** à apprendre.

When the superlative form of an adjective follows its noun, the definite article must always directly precede **plus** or **moins.**

18. What preposition regularly follows the French superlative?

La France et la Russie sont les pays les plus grands **d'**Europe.	*France and Russia are the largest countries in Europe.*
Quel est le meilleur élève **de** la classe?	*Who is the best pupil in the class?*

In English, the superlative is usually followed by *in.* But in French, **de** is regularly used after the superlative.

19. How is the *as . . . as* **comparative expressed in French?**

Jacques est **aussi** consciencieux **que**   *Jacques is* as *conscientious* as *Paul.*
   Paul.
Le français n'est **pas aussi** difficile   *French is* not as *hard* as *Latin.*
   que le latin.

The comparison with *as . . . as* is called the comparative of equality. In French this comparative is formed with **aussi . . . que.** In present day French, the negative is expressed by **pas aussi . . . que.**

D. *Remplacez les adjectifs indiqués entre parenthèses par le comparatif ou le superlatif de l'adjectif, selon le cas.*

1. Robert est l'élève (vif) de la classe.   2. Est-ce que les hommes sont (curieux) que les femmes?   3. La campagne de Normandie est (vert) que celle de Provence.   4. L'étoile du Berger est (brillant) des étoiles.   5. Les automobiles françaises sont (petit) que les américaines.   6. Quels sont les livres (intéressants) de votre bibliothèque?   7. Prenez ce fauteuil. Il est (confortable) que celui-là.   8. Je trouve les poires (savoureux) que les pommes.   9. Mon chien est mon (bon) ami.   10. Le tennis est bien (fatigant) que le ping-pong.   11. Les (beau) années sont souvent celles de la jeunesse.   12. Il travaille plus et pourtant ses résultats sont (mauvais) que l'année dernière.

E. *Remplacez les mots anglais par leur équivalent français.*

1. Voici les meilleurs élèves (*in*) la classe.   2. Il habite la plus belle maison (*in*) la ville.   3. Je vais vous montrer le timbre le plus rare (*in*) ma collection.   4. Nous avons moins (*than*) cent dollars pour faire le voyage.   5. Qui est plus occupé (*than*) le président?   6. Ce chien est (*as*) méchant (*as*) un loup.   7. Les routes sont (*as*) bonnes en France (*as*) en Angleterre.   8. Les prix des repas ne sont pas (*as*) élevés en Espagne (*as*) en Italie.

F. *Traduisez en français.*

1. What is the largest city in Canada?   2. He refuses to read even the most interesting books.   3. I have never more than five dollars with[1] me.   4. Le Mont Blanc is the highest mountain in Europe.   5. He has nothing, but he is as happy as a king.   6. His closest friends do not understand his attitude.   7. A conversation[2] class is too large if there are more than twelve students.   8. Bridge requires

_____
[1] **sur**   [2] **classe de conversation**

more attention than poker. 9. It is easier to preach than to put into practice what one preaches. 10. (*vous*) I waited for you more than half an hour. 11. Motorcycles are more dangerous than cars. 12. The shortest answers are sometimes the best. 13. He allows[3] himself to be stopped by the slightest difficulty. 14. The richest people are often the least generous.

---

[3] Use a form of **se laisser arrêter.**

PATTERN PRACTICE : various aspects of the comparison of adjectives

Pattern 5

YOU HEAR   L'anglais est facile. Et l'histoire?

YOU SAY   L'histoire est plus facile que l'anglais.

Pattern 6

YOU HEAR   Shakespeare est un grand écrivain de la littérature anglaise.

YOU SAY   Shakespeare est le plus grand écrivain de la littérature anglaise.

Pattern 7

YOU HEAR   Madame Aubert a vingt chapeaux.

YOU SAY   Madame Aubert a plus de vingt chapeaux.

Pattern 8

YOU HEAR   Ce fauteuil est confortable. Et cette chaise?

YOU SAY   Cette chaise est aussi confortable que ce fauteuil.

III. Position of Adjectives

In English, adjectives precede their nouns. Ex.: *bad* weather, *disagreeable* work.

20. What is the normal position of a descriptive adjective in French?

Il m'a fait une proposition **intéressante.**
C'est une maison **blanche.**
Quelles sont les couleurs du drapeau **français?**
Voulez-vous du pain **grillé?**

In French, descriptive adjectives normally follow their nouns. They distinguish the object under consideration from others of its kind. Adjectives of color, nationality, religion, and past participles almost always follow their noun.

21. Why are descriptive adjectives sometimes placed before their noun?

> Il a été victime d'un **terrible** accident.
> M. Garet est un **excellent** professeur.
> Chenonceaux est un **magnifique** château de la Renaissance.
> Elle oubliait la **triste soirée** de la veille.

Many descriptive adjectives may precede their noun for stylistic effect. In such cases, the adjective, which usually indicates a quality inherent in the noun, adorns its noun rather than distinguishing it from other objects of its kind.

22. When an adjective has both a literal and a figurative meaning, where is the adjective usually placed to denote its figurative meaning?

une **porte** <u>étroite</u>	une **mer** <u>profonde</u>
une <u>étroite</u> **amitié**	un <u>profond</u> **sentiment**
une **boisson** <u>amère</u>	un **chat** <u>maigre</u>
un <u>amer</u> **reproche**	un <u>maigre</u> **salaire**

Certain adjectives are sometimes placed before and sometimes after their noun. They usually have a literal meaning when they follow their noun and take on a figurative meaning when they precede the noun.

23. What is the meaning of the following adjectives when they precede and when they follow their noun?

MEANING WHEN PRECEDING NOUN	ADJECTIVE	MEANING WHEN FOLLOWING NOUN
former	**ancien**	*old, ancient*
fine, good (referring to a person)	**brave**	*brave* (but usually the word **courageux** is used instead)
certain (*one of many*)	**certain**	*certain* (*sure*)
dear, beloved	**cher**	*dear, expensive*
last (*of a series*)	**dernier**	*last* (used with time element to indicate the one just passed)
different, various	**différent**	*different* (*unlike*)
same	**même**	*very*
many different kinds	**nombreux**	*many of the same kind*
poor (*unfortunate*)	**pauvre**	*poor* (*not rich*) (ordinarily used with **très**)

next *(in a series)*	**prochain**	*next* (used with time element to indicate one about to come)
own	**propre**	*clean*
darned, confounded	**sacré**	*sacred*
ugly, bad	**sale**	*dirty*
only	**seul**	*alone*
mere	**simple**	*simple in character*
real	**vrai**	*true*

24. What is the position of limiting adjectives in French?

    deux leçons   **ces** journaux   **son** père
    quelles difficultés   **plusieurs** personnes   **quelques** amis

Numerals, both cardinal and ordinal, and demonstrative, interrogative, possessive and indefinite adjectives regularly precede their noun. These are called LIMITING ADJECTIVES, for they limit the meaning of the noun.

25. What about the position of the short, common descriptive adjectives?

    une **autre** femme   un **beau** rêve   une **bonne** solution
    une **grande** ville   un **jeune** enfant   une **jolie** maison
    une **longue** histoire   un **mauvais** tour   une **petite** bouche

A number of commonly used short adjectives regularly precede their noun. The most common of these are: **autre, bon, gentil, grand, gros, haut, jeune, joli, long, mauvais, méchant, meilleur, moindre, nouveau, petit, vieux,** and **vilain.**

NOTE: The superlative of most of these adjectives is formed by **le (la, les)** + **plus** + ADJECTIVE. The superlative forms of these particular adjectives only may either precede or follow the noun. Ex.: C'est **la plus longue** rue de la ville. (or) C'est la rue **la plus longue** de la ville.

G. *Mettez l'adjectif à la position convenable, en faisant l'accord de l'adjectif.*

1. (rouge) une fleur 2. (inestimable) des trésors 3. (difficile) une leçon 4. (mauvais) une route 5. (anglican) l'église 6. (gentil) un garçon 7. (social) les conflits 8. (bruyant) une salle 9. (insupportable) des enfants 10. (noir) le drapeau 11. (usé) des souliers 12. (profond) un puits 13. (absolu) un monarque 14. (réussi) un spectacle 15. (vert) des volets 16. (secondaire) les écoles 17. (indien) des étoffes

H. *Traduisez en français. Faites attention à l'accord et à la position de l'adjectif.*

1. Send her some[1] flowers.   2. We saw a terrible[2] accident.   3. There are American tourists in every country in[3] the world.   4. There is a real hero.   5. There are still certain[4] difficulties.   6. We want a free country.   7. Those fine people don't have any luck.   8. It was a somber[2] story.   9. High[5] mountains separate those two countries.   10. (*tu*) You always make the same mistakes.   11. There is a slight difference between those two words.   12. (*vous*) Take[6] a course with that excellent[2] professor.   13. Paul has a bad cold.   14. A hostile crowd was in[7] the square.   15. I like illustrated magazines.   16. (*vous*) Have you seen those elegant[2] models?   17. Numerous[8] foreigners study here.   18. I should like a good warm meal.   19. That book made a deep impression on the students.   20. (*vous*) Next week you will write your last résumé.

---

[1] Use a form of **quelque**.   [2] Consider this as an adjective used to adorn its noun for stylistic effect, as described in §21.   [3] **du**   [4] Do not use the partitive or any substitute for it here.   [5] Use a form of **haut**. Place **de** in front of **haut**.   [6] Use a form of **suivre**.   [7] **sur**
[8] Place **de** in front of this adjective.

PATTERN PRACTICE : the position of adjectives

Pattern 9

YOU HEAR   Cet homme est intelligent.
YOU SAY   C'est un homme intelligent.

EXERCICE D'ENSEMBLE

I. *Traduisez en français. Attention aux adjectifs.*

1. (*vous*) I should like to thank you for your marvelous[1] gift.   2. I find her much prettier than her sister.   3. (*tu*) Will you finish your studies next month?   4. That vicious[2] animal ought to be tied up.   5. (*vous*) Have you noticed the deep-seated uneasiness which exists[3] in this country?   6. The most expensive products are not always the best.   7. The young people were exchanging tender[1] smiles and ardent glances.   8. (*vous*) You sent me some beautiful carnations.   9. This interesting[1] hypothesis has been condemned by experience.

---

[1] Consider this adjective as being used to adorn its noun for stylistic effect.   [2] Use a form of **méchant**.   [3] Use a form of **régner**.

10. Public opinion favors that change. 11. We made the trip more than ten years ago. 12. Certain⁴ pupils do not work enough. 13. (*tu*) I like your nice apartment. 14. (*vous*) I am your humble¹ servant. 15. The Italians are one of the most musical peoples in the world. 16. They are richer than we, but are they happier? 17. Tomorrow we will discuss this grave¹ affair. 18. (*vous*) Do you write to your former teacher from time to time? 19. (*tu*) My examinations are harder than yours. 20. They served us a meager meal.

---

¹ Consider this adjective as being used to adorn its noun for stylistic effect. ⁴ Do not use the partitive or any substitute for it here.

Problem Words

5. become

(**a**) When *become* is followed by a NOUN

Jacques **est devenu** officier.   *Jack* became an officer.

The verb *become* is **devenir,** and when a noun follows *become,* the French usually employ a form of **devenir.**

(**b**) When *become* is followed by an ADJECTIVE

Ne **vous fâchez** pas si je vous dis   *Don't* become angry *if I tell you that.*
  cela.
Le patron **s'est impatienté** en vous   *The boss* became impatient *while*
  attendant.   *waiting for you.*

French often uses the reflexive form of a verb where English uses *become* + ADJECTIVE.

(**c**) How to express *became* in certain idiomatic expressions

Tout à coup **il a fait** très **chaud.**   *Suddenly it* became *very* warm.
Vers onze heures **j'ai eu** très **som-** *About eleven o'clock* I became *very*
  meil.   sleepy.

The English *became* + ADJECTIVE is often expressed in French by using the simple past or the compound past of the verb. This is especially true in the case of idiomatic expressions with **avoir** and **faire.**

CAUTION: Avoid using **devenir** + ADJECTIVE. To express *become* + ADJECTIVE, French occasionally does use **devenir** + ADJECTIVE, but far more often it uses a reflexive verb or a past tense of **avoir** or **être**.

6. better

(**a**) When *better* is an adjective

Je cherche une **meilleure** solution.   *I am looking for a* better *solution.*

As an adjective, *better* is normally expressed by **meilleur.**

Ces peintures sont **mieux** que les autres.   *These paintings are* better *than the others.*

However, when the adjective *better* is used after a form of **être**, French sometimes uses **mieux**. In such cases, a form of **meilleur** could also be used.

(**b**) When *better* is an adverb

Jacques lit **mieux** que Jean.   *Jack reads* better *than John.*

The adverb *better* is expressed by **mieux.**

(**c**) How to say *much better*

Le livre est **bien meilleur** que le film.
Le livre est **beaucoup mieux** que le film.   *The book is* much better *than the film.*

After forms of **être**, *much better* may be expressed by **bien meilleur, bien mieux** or **beaucoup mieux**. But the French do not say «beaucoup meilleur».

Cet élève comprend { **bien** / **beaucoup** } **mieux** l'algèbre maintenant.   *This pupil understands algebra* much better *now.*

As an adverb, *much better* is either **beaucoup mieux** or **bien mieux.**

CAUTION: When expressing *better* in French, determine whether it is used as an adjective or an adverb. Do NOT use «meilleur» as an adverb.

CAUTION: Do NOT use «beaucoup meilleur» for *much better*. This combination does not exist in French.

7. bring

(**a**) How to say *bring a thing*

Apportez-moi ce livre.   Bring *me that book.*

When it is a question of *bringing a thing*, French usually employs a form of **apporter.**

(**b**) How to say *bring a person*

Est-ce que je pourrais **amener** mon   *Could I* bring *my husband?*
  mari?

When it is a question of *bringing a person*, a form of **amener** is used. But **amener** is also used for taking a person somewhere.

CAUTION: Do NOT use «apporter» when it is a question of bringing a *person*.

8. can

(**a**) When *can = be able*

Vous ne **pouvez** pas porter cela tout   *You* can*not carry that all alone. Let me*
  seul. Laissez-moi vous aider.   *help you.*

The English *can* (*= be able*) is ordinarily expressed by **pouvoir.**

(**b**) When *can = may*

Vous **pouvez** partir si vous voulez.   *You* $\left\{ \begin{array}{l} can \\ may \end{array} \right.$ *leave if you wish.*

Careful speakers of English distinguish between *can* and *may*. In French, the verb **pouvoir** is used for both ideas.

(**c**) When to use **je peux** and when **je puis**

Je peux vous accompagner demain.   I can *go with you tomorrow.*
Puis-je vous voir à huit heures?   Can I *see you at eight o'clock?*

The **je** form of the present tense of **pouvoir** is both **peux** and **puis**. In non-interrogative sentences **je peux** is normally used. When an interrogative sentence has inverted word order, **puis-je** is used, but this form is mainly literary.

(d) When *can = know how to*

Est-ce que Thérèse **sait** conduire?   Can *Theresa drive?*

When *can = know how to*, French often uses a form of **savoir** rather than of **pouvoir**.

J. *Remplacez les mots anglais par leur équivalent français.*

1. Il a fallu à Georges plusieurs années d'études pour (*become*) pharmacien.   2. N'hésitez pas à (*bring*) votre frère; nous serons très heureux de faire sa connaissance.   3. La représentation des *Femmes savantes* était bien, mais celle du *Misanthrope* était (*better*).   4. Les programmes du dimanche sont (*much better*) que ceux de la semaine. 5. (*Can*) -vous me dire l'heure?   6. Quand la lumière s'est éteinte, tout le monde (*became frightened*[1]).   7. Les résultats de cet étudiant sont (*better*) ce trimestre.   8. Finis tes études avant de te marier, ce serait (*much better*).   9. (*Can*) -on traverser l'Atlantique en moins de six heures?   10. Prenez plutôt cette route; elle est (*better*) que l'autre. 11. On (*becomes tired*) à faire toujours la même chose.   12. Claude nous (*brings*) toujours des chocolats quand il vient nous voir. 13. François a beaucoup souffert ces derniers jours, mais maintenant il se sent (*better*).   14. Les repas dans ce petit bistrot sont (*much better*) que dans les autres restaurants du quartier.

---
[1] Use a form of **avoir peur.**

K. *Traduisez en français. Attention aux mots en italique.*

1. The climate of the Riviera would be *much better* for them.   2. (*vous*) *Could* you explain this problem to me?   3. Henry *became* interested in that writer after hearing his lecture[1].   4. (*tu*) If these stamps interest you, I'll *bring* you my collection next week.   5. The day[2] was warm, but it *became* cold as soon as the sun set.   6. (*vous*) Can your fiancée play the[3] piano?   7. (*vous*) It is in Paris that you will find the *best* perfumes.   8. Mr. Borel *became* one of the directors of the company[4].   9. *Can* I *bring* my friend Roger to the next meeting

---
[1] Not «lecture»   [2] **journée**   [3] Not «le»   [4] **société**

of our club?   10. Pierrette finally *brought* us the snapshots of her family.   11. (*vous*) *Bring* me what you have just written.   12. (*tu*) *Can* you typewrite?

Verb Review

Review the verbs **dormir** and **perdre** according to the outline on page 283.

CHAPTER 3

Adverbs

An adverb is a word that modifies a verb, an adjective or another adverb. Ex.: He writes *clearly*. They have a *very* difficult lesson. He speaks *somewhat* slowly.

I. Formation of Adverbs

1. How are adverbs usually formed from adjectives?

rapide	rapide**ment**	sérieux	sérieuse**ment**
vrai	vrai**ment**	naturel	naturelle**ment**

Many French adverbs are formed by adding **-ment** to the masculine form of adjectives that end in a vowel and to the feminine form of adjectives whose masculine form ends in a consonant.

NOTE: A certain number of adverbs have an **-é-** before **-ment.** The most common of these are: **aveuglément, commodément, conformément, énormément, obscurément, précisément, profondément.**

To the adjective **gentil** corresponds the adverb **gentiment,** to **bref** the adverb **brièvement.** The adjective **bon** has not only the very common adverb **bien** (meaning *well*) but also **bonnement** (*simply*).

A certain number of adjectives do not have a corresponding adverbial form. Such adjectives may be used adverbially in a phrase. For instance, **charmant** and **amusant** have no adverbial form. But one can say: Elle a agi **d'une façon charmante.** Il a parlé **d'une façon amusante.**

2. How are adverbs formed from adjectives ending in *-ant* and *-ent*?

suffisant	suffis**amment**	récent	réc**emment**

Adjectives in **-ant** and **-ent** usually have adverbial forms in **-amment** and **-emment.** These suffixes are both pronounced [amã].

But the adjective **lent** has the corresponding adverb **lentement.**

29

3. **Which adjectives have irregular adverbial forms?**

bon **bien**   meilleur **mieux**   petit **peu**   mauvais **mal**

NOTE: The masculine singular form of a few adjectives is sometimes used as an adverb, often with only a few verbs. Ex.: Il a crié **fort.** Parlez **haut.** Elle parle trop **bas.** Ça coûte **cher.** Ces fleurs sentent **bon.** Il a tenu **ferme.**

The word **vite** is both an adjective (=*quick*) and an adverb (=*quickly*). The form "vitement" does not exist. Distinguish between **sentir bon/mauvais** (*smell good/bad*) and **se sentir bien/mal** (feel *good/bad*). Ex.: Cette viande sent **mauvais.** (*That meat smells* bad.) Je me sens **bien.** (*I feel* good.)

A. *Écrivez les adverbes qui correspondent aux adjectifs suivants.*

1. clair   2. heureux   3. rare   4. évident   5. faux   6. constant
7. discret   8. patient   9. profond   10. ardent   11. bruyant
12. mauvais   13. triste   14. bon   15. sage   16. savant   17. tendre
18. violent   19. élégant

PATTERN PRACTICE: formation of adverbs

Pattern 1

YOU HEAR   Il est poli. Il répond . . .
YOU SAY   Il est poli. Il répond poliment.

II. Position of Adverbs

4. **What is the usual position of the adverb in a sentence with a simple verb?**

Jean sait **aussi** le français.   *John* also *knows French.*

The adverb usually follows a simple verb directly.

5. **What is the position of most common adverbs in sentences with compound tenses?**

Nous avons **beaucoup** travaillé.   *We worked* a great deal.
Il a **bien** compris la phrase.   *He understood the sentence* well.
Vous n'avez pas **encore** remis votre devoir.   *You have not* yet *handed in your exercise.*

In sentences with compound tenses, most common adverbs not ending in **-ment** are placed between the auxiliary verb and the past participle and after **pas**. But sometimes the position of these adverbs is changed because the speaker wishes to stress a certain word. Also, see §7.

6. Where are adverbs in -*ment* placed?

Nous avons soulevé ce poids **facile-ment**.	*We lifted this weight* easily.
Il a **complètement** oublié mon nom.	*He* completely *forgot my name.*
Vous avez **probablement** envoyé cette lettre.	*You* probably *sent this letter.*
Nous avons marché **lentement** jusqu'à la poste.	*We walked* slowly *up to the post office.*

Some adverbs in **-ment** come between the auxiliary verb and the past participle, some follow the past participle directly and some follow the noun object of the sentence. The length of the adverb in **-ment** does not determine its position in sentences with compound tenses. The position of each adverb in **-ment** must be learned.

7. What is the position of adverbs of place and time?

Jean est venu me voir **hier**.	*John came to see me* yesterday.
Aujourd'hui, nous avons parlé avec votre mère.	Today *we spoke with your mother.*
M. Dupont est arrivé **ici** après un long voyage.	*Mr. Dupont arrived* here *after a long trip.*

The adverbs of time and place **aujourd'hui, hier, demain, autrefois, tôt, tard, ici, là, ailleurs** and **partout** never come between the auxiliary verb and the past participle. They normally follow the past participle, but not always directly. The adverbs of time **aujourd'hui, hier, demain,** and **autrefois** often begin the sentence.

8. When a sentence begins with *peut-être, aussi* (therefore), or *à peine*, what word order follows?

Peut-être est-il déjà parti. ⎱ **Peut-être** qu'il est déjà parti. ⎰	*Perhaps he has already left.*
Aussi a-t-il perdu ses amis.	*Therefore he lost his friends.*
A peine est-il parti que les autres ont commencé à parler.	*Scarcely did he leave when the others began to speak.*

After **peut-être** and **à peine** when placed at the beginning of the sentence, the subject and the verb are inverted. After **peut-être** this construction is normally found only in written literary style. In conversational French, the usual word order is **peut-être que** + SUBJECT + VERB.

When **aussi** has the meaning of *therefore*, it must come first in its clause, and it is usually followed by inverted word order. For that reason, **aussi** meaning *also* must NEVER come first in a sentence.

However, **Aussi** . . . = *So/Therefore* is literary. To express this idea in conversation, a word such as **Alors** or **Et alors** would be used. Ex.: **Alors** il a perdu ses amis. (So *he lost his friends.*)

B. *Introduisez les adverbes indiqués pour qu'ils modifient le verbe en italique.*

MODEL: (vite) Il *a fermé* la porte. **Il a vite fermé la porte.**

1. (trop) Il *travaille;* il se rendra malade.   2. (toujours) Le vice *est* puni et la vertu aussi.   3. (attentivement) *Avez*-vous *lu* cette page? 4. (immédiatement) Pourquoi *est*-il *parti* après la conférence? 5. (peut-être) Vous *devriez* voir un docteur.   6. (déjà) Il *a raconté* cette histoire aux enfants.   7. (follement) Elle l'*a aimé* dans sa jeunesse.   8. (continuellement) Le pauvre *se plaint* de ses douleurs. 9. (à peine) Je dois m'en aller; j'*ai* le temps de manger.   10. (lentement) Ils *se sont promenés* le long de la rivière.   11. (demain) Je vous *enverrai* la lettre.   12. (tôt) Marie *est arrivée* à la maison.   13. (enfin) Il *s'est arrêté* de parler.

C. *Traduisez en français.*

1. He would have liked to see me at[1] length tomorrow.   2. (*vous*) You received him well at your house.   3. (*tu*) Have you read a good book recently?   4. I often wonder what John was writing. 5. (*tu*) What did you do recently?   6. He spoke brilliantly.   7. (*vous*) You have scarcely arrived, and you already wish to leave.   8. It rained so much[2] that I could[3] not come.   9. Man always seeks happiness.   10. So[4] he often finds what he wants.   11. We haven't received any[5] news from him; perhaps he is dead.

---

[1] **longuement**   [2] **tellement**   [3] Use a form of the **passé composé.**   [4] Write first in conversational, then in literary French.   [5] *any news from him* = **de ses nouvelles**

PATTERN PRACTICE: the position of adverbs

Pattern 2

YOU HEAR   Nous comprenons le professeur. (bien)
YOU SAY   Nous comprenons bien le professeur.

Pattern 3

YOU HEAR   Ce matin j'ai travaillé. (beaucoup)
YOU SAY   Ce matin j'ai beaucoup travaillé.

III. Negative Adverbs

9. What is the normal position of the *ne . . . pas* in a negative statement with a simple verb?

Je **ne** parle **pas** allemand.   Ce jeune homme **ne** me salue **pas.**
Il **ne** me donnera **pas** ce livre.   Paul **ne** le lui montrera **pas.**

The word order is:

SUBJECT* + **ne** + PRONOUN OBJECT** + VERB + **pas**

10. What is the position of *ne . . . pas* in interrogative sentences with a simple verb?

Ne parle-t-il **pas** allemand?   Paul **ne** le lui montrera-t-il **pas?**
Ne me donnera-t-il **pas** ce livre?   Ce jeune homme **ne** vous salue-t-il **pas?**

In sentences with a pronoun-subject, negative interrogative order is:

Ne + PRONOUN OBJECT** + VERB + PRONOUN SUBJECT + **pas** + following words

In questions with a noun-subject, negative interrogative word order is:

NOUN SUBJECT* + **ne** + PRONOUN OBJECT** + VERB + PRONOUN SUBJECT + **pas** + following words

* that is, the subject with all its modifiers
** The pronoun-object comes here if there is one. Many sentences do not have a pronoun-object.

11. What is the position of *ne . . . pas* in sentences with compound verbs?

Je n'ai **pas** parlé allemand.   N'avez-vous **pas** parlé allemand?
Il **ne** m'a **pas** donné ce livre.   Paul **ne** le lui a-t-il **pas** montré?

In sentences with verbs in compound tenses, the auxiliary verb only is regarded as the verb as far as the position of negative words is concerned. In other words, the word order in §§9–10 is followed, but **pas** comes directly after the auxiliary verb.

D. *Mettez les phrases suivantes au négatif.*

1. Je partirai avant son retour. 2. Il lui a donné beaucoup d'argent. 3. Êtes-vous allé en Europe l'année dernière? 4. Pourquoi venez-vous me voir? 5. Je suis sûr que tout s'arrangera. 6. Il a cru ce que vous avez dit. 7. Se décidera-t-il à venir? 8. Les questions de grammaire m'intéressent.   9. Aimeriez-vous faire une promenade avec Lucie?

E. *Traduisez en français.*

1. This news[1] did not surprise me a great deal. 2. Isn't it difficult to learn Russian? 3. He doesn't go to[2] Florida[3] every winter. 4. These events do not worry me. 5. (*tu*) Didn't this painter make your portrait? 6. He didn't continue his work. 7. Doesn't the Rhone[3] cross Lyons[3]? 8. (*vous*) Didn't you buy that car last year? 9. Didn't Denis get up at six o'clock?

---

[1] Use the singular to indicate *piece of news*.   [2] **en**   [3] The French spelling is slightly different.

PATTERN PRACTICE: the position of **pas** in compound tenses

Pattern 4

    YOU HEAR   Avez-vous vu le film?
    YOU SAY   Non, je n'ai pas vu le film.

12. What other negative combinations are there?

ne . . . aucun	*no, not any*	**ne . . . plus**	*no longer, no more*
ne . . . guère	*scarcely*	**ne . . . point**	*not at all*
ne . . . jamais	*never*	**ne . . . que**	*only*
ne . . . ni . . . ni	*neither . . . nor*	**ne . . . rien**	*nothing*
ne . . . personne	*no one*		

In addition to **ne . . . pas** these are the negative combinations often used in French.

13. What word order is used with these combinations?

Je **ne** le vois **jamais**.   N'avez-vous **jamais** visité la Suisse?
Il **ne** vient **plus** ici.   Paul **n**'a-t-il **jamais** vu son oncle?

In all negative sentences, **ne** comes exactly where it would if used with **pas**. (See §§9–11)

The negatives **guère, jamais, plus,** and **point** follow the same rules for position as **pas**. (See §§9–11)

In sentences with simple tenses, **personne** and **rien** come where they would in the corresponding English sentence.

Je **n**'ai vu **personne**.   Il **n**'a **rien** compris.

In compound tenses, **personne** follows the past participle, whereas **rien** comes between the auxiliary and the past participle.

Il **n**'a vu **que** trois élèves.   Nous **n**'avons écrit **que** dix pages.

The **que** of the **ne . . . que** combination follows the entire verb.

Aucun étudiant **ne** travaille.   Nous **n**'avons trouvé **aucune** trace
                                                de lui.

The negative **aucun** is an adjective and comes directly before its noun.

Nous **n**'avons trouvé **ni** livres **ni** papier.

The negative adverbs **ni . . . ni,** precede their noun immediately. If these nouns are indefinite, they follow **ni . . . ni** without any article. (See page 174, §9)

14. When negative words are used in a sentence without a verb, what happens to *ne*?

—Qui a-t-il trouvé?   —Quand le ferez-vous?
—**Personne.**   —**Jamais.**

—Puis-je boire du café,   —Combien de fautes avez-vous trou-
  docteur?   vées?
—Non, **plus** de café.   —**Aucune.**

When negative words are used in a sentence without a verb, the **ne** disappears.

F. *Traduisez en français.*

1. I like the movies very much, but I no longer have the time to[1] go there.   2. He has neither money nor friends.   3. Who knocked at the door? No one.   4. In any case, I didn't hear anything.   5. (*tu*) I know no one who can[2] do what you ask.   6. No gift gave[3] me so much pleasure.   7. He asked me for some stamps, but I didn't have any at all.   8. (*vous*) When will I be able to see[4] you again? Never.   9. She saw no one in the corridor.   10. I looked for[5] a long time, but I found nothing.   11. No one has ever done anything for him.   12. There are only twelve pupils in the class.   13. (*vous*) Neither you nor I know[6] anything about it[7].   14. We read only half of the book last week.

---

[1] **d'**   [2] The subjunctive is required. See p. 148, §10.   [3] Use a form of **faire**.   [4] Use a form of **revoir**. Whenever possible, French expresses *again* by using the prefix **re-** + the verb.   [5] Either omit or express by **pendant**.   [6] This verb must be in the first person plural.   [7] **en**

PATTERN PRACTICE: negative combinations

Pattern 5

YOU HEAR   Est-ce que Marie est allée en France?
YOU SAY   Non, Marie n'est jamais allée en France.

Pattern 6

YOU HEAR   Qui parle anglais en classe?
YOU SAY   Personne ne parle anglais en classe.

Pattern 7

YOU HEAR   Qui avez-vous cherché cet après-midi?
YOU SAY   Je n'ai cherché personne cet après-midi.

Pattern 8

YOU HEAR   J'ai trouvé votre stylo.
YOU SAY   Je n'ai rien trouvé.

Problem Words

9. change

(a) How to say *a change*

Avez-vous remarqué **un change-ment** en entrant?   *Did you notice* a change *when you came in?*

Ces dernières années il y a eu de   *In these last few years there have been*
grands **changements** dans le   *great* changes *in the world.*
monde.

The ordinary French word for *change* is **le changement.**

CAUTION: Do NOT use «le change» for *change*. The French **le change**
is used for financial transactions, in expressions such as **le cours du
change** (*the rate of exchange*), **l'office des changes** (*office dealing with
foreign exchange*), **agent de change** (*stock broker*), etc.

(**b**) How to say *small change*

Je n'aime pas avoir toute cette **mon-**   *I don't like to have all this* change *in
naie dans ma poche.*   my pocket.*

When *change* = *small change*, French uses **la monnaie.**

(**c**) How to say that *something changes*

Cécile **a** beaucoup **changé** depuis   *Cecilia has changed a great deal since
l'année dernière.*   last year.*

The English *to change* is expressed by **changer.**

(**d**) When **changer** has a direct object

J'ai changé mes projets de voyage   *I* changed my travel plans *the last
au dernier moment.*   minute.*

The verb **changer** + OBJECT means *to alter something.*

(**e**) When **changer de** is used

Tous les combien **change**-t-on **de**   *How often do they* change towels *in this
serviettes dans cet hôtel?*   hotel?*

The expression **changer de quelque chose** means *to replace things
of the same kind.*

(**f**) When **se changer** is used

Vous êtes tout mouillé; allez vite   *You're all wet; quick, go and* change
vous changer.   your clothes.*

The reflexive **se changer** = *change one's clothes.*

(g) When to use **échanger**

Je voudrais **échanger** ma moto   *I'd like* to exchange *my motorcycle for*
   contre une voiture.   *a car.*

The verb **échanger** means *exchange*, and *to exchange one thing for another* is **échanger une chose contre une autre.**

10. character

(a) How to say a *character* (in a literary work)

Combien de **personnages** y a-t-il   *How many* characters *are there in that*
   dans cette pièce?   *play?*

A *character* in a literary work is **un personnage.**

(b) How to speak of *a person's character*

Georges est intelligent, mais je   *George is intelligent, but I don't care*
   n'aime pas beaucoup son **carac-**   *much for his* character.
   tère.

One's personal attributes or one's *character* is **le caractère.**

CAUTION: Do NOT use «le caractère» to indicate *a character* in a novel or a play.

11. day (morning, evening)

(a) The ordinary way of saying *day*

Nous avons passé trois **jours** à Rome.   *We spent three* days *in Rome.*

The common word for *day* is **jour,** for *morning* is **matin,** for *evening* is **soir.**

(b) When the **-ée** forms are used

Toute la **journée** nous avons visité   *The whole* day *we visited churches and*
   des églises et des musées.   *museums.*

But **la journée** is used to indicate *day* when the speaker wishes to emphasize the duration of the time during the day and what happened during that time. The same distinction applies to **la matinée** and **la soirée,** but **la soirée** has the additional meaning of *evening gathering* or *evening party.*

(c) When **tous les jours** and when **toute la journée** is used

Note the following:

toute la journée = *the whole day*	**tous les jours** = *every day*
toute la matinée = *the whole morning*	**tous les matins** = *every morning*
toute la soirée = *the whole evening*	**tous les soirs** = *every evening*

G. *Remplacez les mots anglais par leur équivalent français.*

1. Pierre a cessé de fumer, mais cela influe sur son (*character*). 2. Il faut comprendre que les gens (*change*). 3. J'ai peu dormi cette nuit et j'ai eu sommeil (*the whole day*). 4. Avec quelques (*changes*), notre salle de séjour serait beaucoup mieux. 5. Pour réussir, une pièce ne doit pas avoir trop de (*characters*). 6. C'est ennuyeux de (*change clothes*) juste pour leur dire bonjour et au revoir. 7. En hiver il fait sombre à six heures (*in[1] the evening*). 8. Il serait bon de (*exchange*) nos vues sur la question. 9. J'ai toujours (*change*) sur moi quand je prends l'autobus. 10. J'ai passé (*the whole evening*) à rédiger cette composition. 11. Suzanne a la manie de tout (*change*) au dernier moment. 12. Jean a si mauvais (*character*) qu'on ne peut rien lui dire sans qu'il se fâche. 13. La traversée en bateau a duré cinq (*days*). 14. Qu'est-ce qui a pu (*change*) Paul comme cela? 15. A midi je prends mon repas au restaurant, (*in[2] the evening*) je dîne chez moi. 16. Va (*change*) souliers si tu veux aller à la pêche. 17. Roland organise (*an evening party*) la semaine prochaine.

---

[1] How is *in* expressed after the time of day? See pages 240–241.   [2] How is *in* expressed with units of time? See pages 240–241.

H. *Traduisez en français. Attention aux mots en italique.*

1. I spoke of it to Daniel two *days* ago. 2. That author had to make many *changes* in his book in order to have[1] it published. 3. At Christmas everyone *exchanges* gifts. 4. Who are the main *characters* in[2] that play? 5. (*tu*) Where did you spend the *day?* 6. (*vous*) Do you have any *change* to buy a newspaper? 7. Which *characters* of Molière have

---

[1] **le faire publier**   [2] *in the* = **du**

become most famous?   8. The Carrels³ will come to play bridge tomorrow *evening*.   9. Mrs. Clair has *changed* chauffeurs⁴ again. 10. How can a person *change* in that way?   11. I must *change clothes* in order to go out this *evening*.

---

³ In French, proper names do not take an **-s** in the plural.   ⁴ Use the singular form.

Verb Review

Review the verbs **recevoir** and **avoir** according to the outline on page 283.

CHAPTER 4
Personal Pronouns

A pronoun is a word that takes the place of a noun. The subject pronouns are: *I, you, he, she, it, we,* the object pronouns are: *me, you, him,* etc.

I. Object Pronouns and Their Uses

1. What are the direct object pronouns?

Jean **me** voit.
Jacques **la** vend.
Je l'achète.

Louise **nous** appelle.
Mes amis **vous** connaissent.
Nous **les** trouverons.

The direct object pronouns are:

me	*me*		**nous**	*us*
te	*you*		**vous**	*you*
le	*him, it*		**les**	*them*
la	*her, it*			

NOTE: When the forms **me, te, se, le** or **la** precede a verb beginning with a vowel or a mute **h,** they elide, becoming **m', t', s',** or **l'.**

2. What are the indirect object pronouns?

Gilbert **me** montre sa voiture.
Anne **lui** explique la leçon.
Jacques **te** parlera demain.

Brigitte **nous** téléphonera.
Gérard **vous** indiquera la route.
Vous **leur** obéirez.

The indirect object pronouns are:

me	*to me*		**nous**	*to us*
te	*to you*		**vous**	*to you*
lui	{ *to him* / *to her*		**leur**	*to them*

The reflexive pronoun **se** may be either a direct or indirect object and means: (*to*) *himself, herself, itself, themselves, oneself.* As a reciprocal pronoun **se** means (*to*) *each other.*

A. *Remplacez les tirets par le pronom qui convient au sens.*

1. Qu'est-ce que Paul vous a fait? Cessez de _____ tourmenter.
2. Quand il arrivera, dites _____ de venir _____ voir. 3. Jean est
heureux que vous _____ ayez promis ce voyage. 4. Entrez donc, je
suis seul et vous ne _____ dérangez pas. 5. Regardez bien ces gens,
car vous ne _____ reverrez plus. 6. Ils sont partis avant que j'aie pu
_____ parler. 7. J'aurais voulu _____ demander où ils allaient.

B. *Traduisez en français.*

1. (*tu*) Do you like spring? Yes, I prefer it to the other seasons.
2. (*vous*) My boys have arrived. I will ask them if they know your
children and if they saw them on the way. 3. We'll tell them to write
him at once. 4. (*vous*) I will give you that magazine.

PATTERN PRACTICE: single pronoun objects

Pattern 1

> YOU HEAR   Est-ce que Robert lit le livre?
> YOU SAY   Oui, il le lit.

Pattern 2

> YOU HEAR   Jacques écrira à Roger.
> YOU SAY   Jacques écrira à Roger et il nous écrira aussi.

Pattern 3

> YOU HEAR   Est-ce que vous parlerez à Jacques?
> YOU SAY   Oui, je lui parlerai.

Pattern 4

> YOU HEAR   Avez-vous mis le livre sur le bureau?
> YOU SAY   Oui, je l'ai mis sur le bureau.

Pattern 5

> YOU HEAR   Est-ce que vous me voyez?
> YOU SAY   Oui, je vous vois.

3. When is *y* used as the place pronoun *there*, and when is the adverb *là* used?

> —Allez-vous à Paris? —J'**y** vais demain.
> —Je vais en classe. —**Y** serez-vous à neuf heures?
> —Où est Georges? —Il est **là**, derrière vous.

The pronoun **y** is used to express *there* when the place has been
previously mentioned. The adverb **là** points out, usually when the
place has not been previously mentioned.

4. When is *en* used as a pronoun object instead of *le, la* and *les*?

Il voit **sa sœur** souvent.	*He sees his sister often.*
Il **la** voit souvent.	*He sees her often.*

Il achète **des fleurs** dans la rue.	*He buys some flowers in the street.*
Il **en** achète dans la rue.	*He buys some in the street.*

Il a trouvé **trois amis** au café.	*He found three friends in the café.*
Il **en** a trouvé trois au café.	*He found three of them in the café.*

The pronoun **en** replaces a noun object when that object is indefinite in nature. A noun object is indefinite when it is modified by a partitive construction, by a numeral, by adverbs of quantity, etc.

For practical purposes, one can say that **en** is used whenever in the English sentence the pronoun object is rendered by *some* or by *of them.*

C. *Remplacez les tirets par* **le, la, les, y** *ou* **en**, *selon le cas.*

1. —Comment trouvez-vous sa maison? —Je ＿＿ trouve superbe.
2. —Voyez-vous des taxis dans la rue? —Oui, nous ＿＿ voyons.
3. —Combien d'enfants ont-ils? —Ils ＿＿ ont cinq. 4. —Il est parti pour Bordeaux. —Qu'est-ce qu'il va ＿＿ faire? 5. —Combien de courses avez-vous à faire? —Nous ＿＿ avons beaucoup.
6. —Georges a-t-il un but dans la vie? —Oui, il ＿＿ a plusieurs.
7. —Vous me dites que vous allez en France. ＿＿ allez-vous bientôt? 8. —Connaissez-vous cette femme? —Oui, et je ＿＿ plains.

D. *Traduisez en français.*

1. I have many friends and I see them every week. 2. (*vous*) I should like to spend a few days in the country. Do you want to go there with me? 3. (*tu*) Do you want some tea? Yes, I'll take some.
4. When will he arrive in Paris? He has already arrived there.
5. (*vous*) How many brothers do you have? I have two[1]. 6. Are there many students in that class? Yes, there are many[2]. 7. The telephone book is there, under the desk.

---

[1] In French, one must say *two of them*.   [2] In French, one must say *many of them*.

PATTERN PRACTICE: y, en and **le, la, les.**

Pattern 6

YOU HEAR	Allez-vous en classe?
YOU SAY	Oui, j'y vais.

Pattern 7

    YOU HEAR   Est-ce que Robert a beaucoup d'argent?
    YOU SAY   Oui, il en a beaucoup.

Pattern 8

    YOU HEAR   Est-ce que Suzanne a trouvé ses affaires?
    YOU SAY   Oui, elle les a trouvées.

Pattern 9

    YOU HEAR   Est-ce que vous avez trouvé des amis?
    YOU SAY   Oui, j'en ai trouvé.

II. Position of Object Pronouns

5. Where do object pronouns come in relation to the verb?

Je **le** donne à Jean.	Je ne **la** vois pas.	Donnez-**le** à Marc.
Il **en** a trouvé.	Ne **me le** dites pas.	Allez-**y.**

Pronoun objects come immediately before the verb except in the affirmative imperative, in which case they follow the verb and are appended to it by a hyphen.

6. Where do object pronouns come when the sentence contains an auxiliary verb followed by an infinitive?

Jacques veut **vous** voir.	Qui peut **me le** dire?
Vous devez **en** chercher.	Nous commencerons à **le** faire.
Qui a refusé de **lui** parler?	Ils vont **y** aller.

When there is a pronoun object in a sentence which has a verb followed by an infinitive, the pronoun object normally precedes the infinitive. This is because in most cases, it is the infinitive which governs the pronoun object.

NOTE: When the main verb governs a pronoun object, that pronoun object precedes it. Ex.: Je l'ai laissé partir. **Vous** a-t-il vu sortir?

7. Where do y and en come in relation to other pronoun objects?

Je **lui en** ai donné.	Donnez-**lui-en.**	Il **y en** a dans le couloir.
Il **vous en** a montré.	Montrez-**m'en** trois.	Donnez-**leur-en.**

The pronouns **y** and **en** follow all other object pronouns and in that order.

8. What is the order of pronoun objects other than y and en?

Georges **me le** montre.   Montrez-**le-moi.**
Ils **nous les** expliquent.   Expliquez-**les-nous.**

When there are two object pronouns other than **y** or **en,** the *l*-form comes nearest the verb.

Je **le lui** indique.   Indiquez-**la-leur.**

When there are two *l*-forms, they come in alphabetical order, that is, **le, la** and **les** always precede **lui** and **leur.**

E. *Remplacez les expressions en italique par des pronoms compléments.*

1. —Expliquera-t-il aux élèves la théorie de la relativité? —Non, il n'expliquera pas *aux élèves la théorie de la relativité.* 2. —Portez ce paquet à mon cousin. —Je porterai *ce paquet à votre cousin* quand j'aurai le temps. 3. —Êtes-vous allé voir ce film? —Oui, je suis allé voir *ce film.* 4. —Voulez-vous montrer vos tableaux à notre ami? —Oui, je veux bien montrer *mes tableaux à notre ami.* 5. —Prêtez-moi les notes de votre cours. —Je vous rendrai *les notes* la semaine prochaine. 6. —Donnez ce rapport au directeur. —Je donnerai *ce rapport au directeur.* 7. —Est-ce qu'il a annoncé son mariage à ses parents? —Oui, il a annoncé *son mariage à ses parents.* 8. —Puis-je demander des renseignements à cet agent? —Oui, vous pouvez demander *des renseignements à cet agent.* 9. —Ne voulez-vous pas raconter votre accident à ces journalistes? —Non, je ne veux pas raconter *cet accident aux journalistes.* 10. —Voulez-vous m'acheter un journal? —Oui, je vous achèterai un *journal.* 11. Les enfants aiment les jouets à Noël, mais il ne faut pas donner *aux enfants* trop *de jouets.*

F. *Traduisez en français.*

1. (*tu*) Here are some oranges. If you see your brother, give him some. 2. (*vous*) Your first French[1] class must[2] have been interesting. Describe it to us. 3. (*tu*) I have seven books. I will bring them to you tomorrow. 4. (*vous*) Where are your magazines? Show them to him at once. 5. (*vous*) Did you hear the news[3]? Do not tell it to them. 6. She spoke of it to him. 7. (*tu*) Those rules are not difficult. The teacher will explain them to you tomorrow. 8. (*vous*) You have grapefruit[4]? Send me some this afternoon. 9. (*vous*) Do you

---

[1] **classe de français**   [2] **a dû être**   [3] Use the singular form.   [4] *grapefruit* is plural.

have that article? Do you want to read it to me?   10. (*vous*) Give it to us tomorrow.   11. (*tu*) Do you know[5] any interesting stories? Tell us some.

---

[5] Use a form of **connaître**.

PATTERN PRACTICE: the position and order of object pronouns

Pattern 10

YOU HEAR	Je vais acheter cette voiture.
YOU SAY	Je vais l'acheter.

Pattern 11

YOU HEAR	Ouvrez la porte.
YOU SAY	Ouvrez-la.

Pattern 12

YOU HEAR	N'ouvrez pas la fenêtre.
YOU SAY	Ne l'ouvrez pas.

Pattern 13

YOU HEAR	Est-ce que Jean donne le livre à Robert?
YOU SAY	Oui, il le lui donne.

Pattern 14

YOU HEAR	Est-ce que Roger vous donnera le livre?
YOU SAY	Oui, il me le donnera.

Pattern 15

YOU HEAR	Donnez le livre à Marie.
YOU SAY	Donnez-le-lui.

Pattern 16

YOU HEAR	Ne montrez pas ce journal à Louise.
YOU SAY	Ne le lui montrez pas.

Pattern 17

YOU HEAR	Donnez-moi le couteau.
YOU SAY	Donnez-le-moi.

Pattern 18

YOU HEAR	Ne me donnez pas cette assiette.
YOU SAY	Ne me la donnez pas.

III. Disjunctive Pronouns

9. What are the disjunctive pronouns?

moi	*me*		**nous**	*us*
toi	*you*		**vous**	*you*
lui	*him*		**eux**	*them, (m.)*
elle	*her*		**elles**	*them, (f.)*

soi   *oneself*

10. What are the seven commonest uses of the disjunctive pronouns?

The disjunctive pronoun is always used in an emphatic position.

> (a) Nous sommes allés en France avec **eux.**

The disjunctive pronoun is used after prepositions.

> (b) Jean et **lui** sont partis ce matin.
> **Eux** et **moi** avons l'intention de la voir.
> Vous les avez vus les deux, Maurice et **lui?**

The disjunctive pronoun is used as a part of a compound subject or object.

> (c) **Moi,** je vais y aller.
> **Lui,** il n'en sait rien.
> **Eux** seuls peuvent le faire.

The disjunctive pronoun is used to emphasize the subject of the sentence or when the subject is separated from the verb.

(d) Mes frères sont plus grands que **moi.**   Je suis aussi intelligent qu'**eux.**
Vous parlez mieux que **lui.**   Vous êtes aussi riche qu'**elle.**

The disjunctive pronoun is used after **que** meaning *as* or *than* in comparisons.

> (e) C'est **moi.**   C'est **lui.** $\begin{cases} \text{C'est} \\ \text{Ce sont} \end{cases}$ **eux.**

The disjunctive is used after **ce** + a form of the verb **être.**

(f) —Qui est là? —**Lui.**   —Qui partira le premier? —**Toi.**

The disjunctive is used alone, in answer to questions.

(g) **moi**-même   **lui**-même   **eux**-mêmes   **soi**-même

The disjunctive is used when compounded with **-même** (*self*).

11. When is *soi* ordinarily used as a disjunctive?

Là, on ne pense qu'à **soi.**   Il est si bon de rester chez **soi.**

Chacun travaille pour **soi.**   Il ne faut pas être trop content de
                                         soi.

La télévision en **soi** n'est pas   Ça va de **soi.**
mauvaise.

The disjunctive **soi** is most often used in a sentence where an indefinite subject such as **on** or **chacun** or one introduced by an impersonal expression is its antecedent and in the fixed expressions **en soi** and **de soi.**

G. *Remplacez le mot anglais par le pronom disjoint convenable.*

1. Je crois qu'ils finiront par se marier, (*she*) et Pierre.   2. Regardez ce que cet enfant a fabriqué (*himself*).   3. Pierre va aller avec (*me*) au bureau.   4. (*As for me*), maintenant, je m'en moque[1].   5. Ah! qu'on est bien chez (*oneself*[2]).   6.—Les voilà. —Qui? —(*They*).   7. Tu es ingrat après tout ce qu'ils ont fait pour (*you*).   8. Chacun parle de (*himself*).   9. (*You*), tu as toujours eu de la chance!   10. Vous pouvez continuer sans (*me*).   11. C'est (*he*) qui m'a raconté votre aventure.   12. Qui a cassé le vase? —Ce n'est pas (*I*).   13. Est-ce qu'elle est aussi amusante que (*he*)?   14. Dans un moment de danger, pense-t-on à (*himself*)?

----

[1] In this sense, the expression means: *I don't care.*   [2] French tends not to use the **–même** form unless it is absolutely needed for clarity.

H. *Traduisez en français.*

1. (*vous*) Would you like to work for him?   2. His friend and he can go to the movies this evening.   3. I found out[1] this news[2] through them.   4. (*tu*) You must do your exercises yourself.   5. They[3] are the ones who are happy[4] at his return.   6. (*vous*) You have a better

----

[1] Use a form of **apprendre.**   [2] Use the singular noun.   [3] lit.: *It is they who*   [4] **contents de**

car than he.   7. Who will go to that meeting? She and I.   8. He is much more patient than they.

PATTERN PRACTICE: disjunctive pronouns

Pattern 19

    YOU HEAR   Marie et Jean-Jacques suivent le même cours.
    YOU SAY   Marie et lui suivent le même cours.

Pattern 20

    YOU HEAR   Nous partons avec Suzanne.
    YOU SAY   Nous partons avec elle.

12. What pronoun construction replaces de + <u>noun</u>?

(a) noun-person

Je parle **de ma soeur.**	Je parle **d'elle.**
Il se souvient **de son grand-père.**	Il se souvient **de lui.**
J'ai besoin **d'amis.**	J'**en** ai besoin.

In general, one may say that **de** + NOUN (person) is replaced by **de** + DISJUNCTIVE PRONOUN. However, **en** sometimes replaces this construction, especially when the person in question is indefinite.

(b) noun-thing

Je parle **de mon travail.**	J'**en** parle.
Il se souvient **de ses voyages.**	Il s'**en** souvient.
Ils ont besoin **d'argent.**	Ils **en** ont besoin.

The construction **de** + NOUN (thing) is regularly replaced by **en**.

13. What pronoun construction replaces à + noun?

(a) noun-person after verbs which take an indirect object

Jacques a raconté son aventure **à l'agent.**	Jacques **lui** a raconté son aventure.
Vous ressemblez **à vos frères.**	Vous **leur** ressemblez.
Ils obéissent **à leur mère.**	Ils **lui** obéissent.

When **à** + NOUN (person) follows a non-reflexive verb which takes an indirect object, the construction is replaced by the indirect object pronouns. In French, in addition to the common verbs such as **dire, raconter, demander,** etc., a number of other verbs such as **obéir à, ressembler à** and **plaire à** take an indirect object.

(**b**) noun-person after reflexive verbs and after certain non-reflexive verbs which are followed by **à** but which do not take an indirect object

Je m'intéresse **à cet enfant.**	Je m'intéresse **à lui.**
Nous pensons **à Marie.**	Nous pensons **à elle.**
Faites attention **à l'agent.**	Faites attention **à lui.**

When **à** + NOUN (person) follows any reflexive verb and certain other verbs, the most common of which are **penser à** and **faire attention à,** the construction is replaced by **à** + DISJUNCTIVE PRONOUN.

(**c**) noun-things

Je réponds **à la lettre.**	J'y réponds.
Nous pensons **à nos études.**	Nous **y** pensons.
Qui s'intéresse **aux langues?**	Qui s'**y** intéresse?

When **à** + NOUN (thing) follows a verb, it is generally replaced by **y.**

I. *Remplacez l'expression en italique par le pronom convenable.*

1. La police s'est emparée *de ces criminels.*   2. Nous ressemblons *à nos parents.*   3. Je me chargerai *de ce problème.*   4. Croyez-vous *à cette histoire?*   5. Essayez de ne plus penser *à ces imbéciles.*   6. Je m'intéresse beaucoup *à la politique.*   7. A-t-on besoin *d'argent* pour s'amuser?   8. Ne vous adressez pas *à cet homme.*   9. Il a dit *à sa mère* ce qu'il voulait.   10. Obéissez *aux agents.*   11. Nous avons parlé *des Français.*   12. Vous souvenez-vous *de ce monsieur?*   13. Je me souviens bien *de sa voiture.*   14. Ne vous fiez pas *à ces statistiques.*   15. Faites attention *au signal.*   16. Faites attention *à ces gens.*

J. *Traduisez en français.*

1. (*tu*) Why don't you ever speak of him? 2. (*vous*) She is rather strange, but you will get accustomed to her. 3. (*vous*) You are very kind to take an interest in us. 4. I received the letter and I answered it. 5. When the teacher asked me a question yesterday, I answered him. 6. His father is easy-going, but it is necessary to obey him. 7. Unfortunately, I have a lot of work, but I wasn't thinking of it. 8. (*tu*) It's Maurice. Were you thinking of him?

PATTERN PRACTICE: replacing **à** and **de** + NOUN (person and thing)

Pattern 21

YOU HEAR   Je pense à mon frère.
YOU SAY   Je pense à lui.

EXERCICE D'ENSEMBLE

K. *Traduisez en français.*

1. (*vous*) These books are too heavy. Don't take[1] them to them. 2. (*vous*) Tell them what happened to you. 3. Who will get[2] the first prize? I. 4. (*tu*) Do you like tea? Yes, I prefer it to coffee. 5. (*vous*) You have only one car; we have two. 6. (*tu*) Can you do this problem yourself? 7. Helen is my best friend. I speak of her with pleasure. 8. They[3] are the ones who gave us this picture. 9. Are there many pupils in this class? Yes, there are many. 10. (*tu*) Do you remember them? 11. They too[4] can leave now. 12. His brother is not as ambitious as he. 13. (*tu*) Do you want to go to Europe with me? 14. Since they are late, let's leave without them. 15. (*vous*) Are you going to France, or are you coming back from there? 16. (*vous*) You and I agree on this point. 17. (*vous*) You like exotic countries, but do you go there from time to time? 18. (*vous*) They want to know the truth; tell it to them. 19. They should[5] be there, but I do not see them. 20. *He* can do that, not I.

---

[1] Use a form of **apporter**. [2] Use a form of **avoir**. [3] lit.: *It is they* [4] Put *too* in this place in the sentence. [5] Use a form of **devoir**.

Problem Words

12. early

(**a**) When *early* means *early in a certain period of time*

Est-ce que vous vous couchez **tôt?** ⎫
Est-ce que vous vous couchez **de** ⎬ *Do you go to bed* early?
bonne heure? ⎭

Ne venez pas trop **tôt.**   *Don't come too* early.

Both **tôt** and **de bonne heure** mean *early* in a given period of time.

(**b**) When *early = ahead of time*

Il y aura beaucoup de monde; il   *There will be a lot of people there; it is*
vaut mieux arriver **en avance.**   *better to arrive* early.

But *early,* meaning *ahead of time,* is expressed by **en avance,** which is the opposite of **en retard.**

Sometimes **d'avance** and **à l'avance** are also used to express *early = ahead of time,* but it is rather difficult to indicate just when one of these expressions is used rather than the other.

13. end

(**a**) When *end* is the opposite of *beginning*

C'est **la fin** de la leçon.   *It is* the end *of the lesson.*

The word **la fin** means *end* when it implies the opposite of *beginning*.

(**b**) When *end* means *tip* or *extremity*

Ne touchez pas **le bout** de ce fil.   *Don't touch* the end *of this wire.*
Il y a un cinéma au **bout** de la rue.   *There is a movie at* the end *of the street.*

The French uses **le bout** to express *end* meaning *tip* or *extremity*.

(**c**) How to say *at the end of* + PERIOD OF TIME

A la fin du mois il ne me reste jamais   At the end of *the month I don't ever*
rien.   *have anything left.*
Au bout de trois mois M. Roux a   At the end of three *months, Mr. Roux*
donné sa démission.   *resigned.*
Au bout de quelques semaines j'en   At the end of some *weeks I had enough*
ai eu assez.   *(of it).*

French expresses *at the end of the* + PERIOD OF TIME by **à la fin de** + DEFINITE ARTICLE + PERIOD OF TIME. On the other hand, when the period of time is accompanied by a numeral or by some other adjective indicating quantity, **au bout de** . . . is used.

14. escape

(a) When *escape* means *avoid*

Le criminel a réussi à **échapper** à la police.

The criminal succeeded in escaping *the police.*

The non-reflexive form **échapper à** is used to indicate that one has avoided or escaped someone or something that one has not yet confronted.

(b) When *escape* means *get out of*

Ce voleur réussit toujours à **s'échapper de** prison.

That thief always succeeds in escaping from *prison.*

The reflexive form **s'échapper de** is used to indicate that one has succeeded in getting away from a person or thing that one has confronted.

In the first example, the thief evaded the police, therefore, never came in contact with them, whereas in the second he was in prison and got out of it.

15. every

(a) How to express *every* by **chaque**

Chaque fois que je vois Paul, il me parle de ses ennuis.

Every time I see Paul, he talks to me of his troubles.

The adjective **chaque** means *every* or *each.*

(b) How to express *every* by **tous les** . . .

Tous les matins nous sortons de bonne heure et **tous les soirs** nous rentrons tard.

Every morning we leave early and every evening we return home late.

The English *every* is frequently expressed by **tous les** + UNIT OF TIME (**toutes les** + UNIT OF TIME). This formula is more common with units of time than **chaque,** although **chaque** is not incorrect.

(c) How to say *everyone*

Tout le monde est parti.   Everyone *has left.*

The pronoun *everyone* is expressed by **tout le monde,** which is singular and which must be followed by a singular verb.

CAUTION: Do NOT use a plural verb after **tout le monde.**

(d) How to say *everything*

Tout est perdu.   Everything *is lost.*
J'ai **tout** oublié.   *I've forgotten* everything.

The pronoun *everything* is expressed by **tout.** In the compound tenses, **tout** comes between the auxiliary and the past participle.

(e) How to say *everything that*

Tout ce qui est sur la table est à   Everything that *is on the table is*
  Jean.   *John's.*
Donnez-moi **tout ce que** vous pou-   *Give me* everything that *you can.*
  vez.

In French, *everything* used as the subject of its clause = **tout ce qui;** *everything* used as the object of its clause = **tout ce que.**

CAUTION: The indefinite **ce** must come between **tout** and the relative pronoun. Do NOT write «tout qui» or «tout que».

L. *Remplacez les mots anglais par leur équivalent français.*

1. Sauve qui peut! Un lion (*has escaped from*) sa cage. 2. Il me reste tant de travail à faire que je n'en vois pas (*the end*). 3. Je préfère travailler le soir; je n'aime pas me lever (*early*). 4. Voilà le menu; commande (*everything that*) tu veux. 5. (*Everyone laughed*) quand Pierre a raconté ses aventures. 6. (*At the end*) du deuxième acte, la situation semblait inextricable. 7. Jacques fait une période militaire (*every summer*). 8. Nous avons eu de la chance de (*escape*) cette épidémie. 9. (*Everything that*) vous dites est très juste. 10. Vous arrivez trop (*early*), Jacques n'est pas encore rentré. 11. —Où se trouve le bureau de tabac? —(*At the end*) de la rue, à droite. 12. Il y aura un cadeau pour (*every*) invité. 13. Saluez (*everyone*) de ma part. 14. Il vaudrait mieux arriver (*early*) au théâtre; sinon, nous ne trouverons plus de places. 15. Leurs enfants aiment (*everything that*) fait du bruit.

M. *Traduisez en français. Attention aux mots en italique.*

1. Nicole likes *everything that* is beautiful. 2. The airplane will not wait for us; it is better to arrive *early* than[1] to be late. 3. At the *end* of the book I finally understood what the author meant. 4. *Every* time that he gets angry, he regrets it. 5. We are invited for seven o'clock; we must not arrive too *early*. 6. If I am caught[2], I'll do *everything* to[3] *escape*. 7. At the *end* of two weeks at the university, Jack dropped his courses. 8. Paul and Anne-Marie see each other *every* day. 9. She is hurt[4] because they put her at the *end* of the table. 10. *Everyone* knows that. 11. That teacher is remarkable; he knows absolutely *everything*. 12. Is *everyone* there? 13. (*vous*) I don't know how you can *escape* his anger. 14. I heard *everything*.

---

[1] than to be = **que d'être**   [2] **pris**   [3] **pour**   [4] **vexée**

Verb Review

Review the verbs **être** and **aller** according to the outline on page 283.

CHAPTER 5

Participles

A participle has properties of both a verb and an adjective. English and French have a present and a past participle.

Verb	Present Participle	Past Participle
(*speak*) parler	(*speaking*) **parlant**	(*spoken*) **parlé**
(*finish*) finir	(*finishing*) **finissant**	(*finished*) **fini**
(*lose*) perdre	(*losing*) **perdant**	(*lost*) **perdu**
(*drink*) boire	(*drinking*) **buvant**	(*drunk*) **bu**

Syntactically, the past participle offers almost no problems in spoken French and only the problem of agreement in written French.

The present participle is somewhat more complex, since French often expresses an English present participle by some construction other than the French present participle.

I. The Past Participle

1. With what auxiliaries are French verbs conjugated in the compound tenses?

1. most verbs

Nous **avons donné** un livre à l'élève.
Robert **a vu** un film intéressant.
Les étudiants **avaient** beaucoup **travaillé**.

2. intransitive verbs of motion

Vous **êtes venu** trop tard.
Nous **sommes arrivés** vers trois heures.
J'**étais parti** quand mon ami est arrivé chez moi.

3. reflexive verbs

La voiture **s'est arrêtée** devant notre porte.
Nous **nous sommes échappés** par la fenêtre.
Je ne **m'étais** pas **rasé** ce matin-là.

56

Most verbs are conjugated with the auxiliary **avoir**. Ordinarily, intransitive verbs of motion are conjugated with **être**. All reflexive verbs are conjugated with **être**.

A. *Remplacez les tirets par l'auxiliaire convenable pour former le passé composé.*

1. Qui ____ ouvert la porte pour laisser rentrer le chat? 2. Pourquoi vous ____ -vous caché quand je ____ arrivé? 3. Le président ____ reçu le nouvel ambassadeur aujourd'hui. 4. Cette pièce était ennuyeuse; je ____ parti après le premier acte. 5. Le chauffeur s'____ arrêté brusquement pour éviter un accident. 6. ____ -vous monté sur la Tour Eiffel? 7. A Paris nous nous ____ promenés le long de la Seine. 8. Il était trois heures du matin quand Jacques ____ rentré. 9. Ils ont une belle pelouse et ils ____ interdit aux enfants de jouer dessus.

B. *Traduisez en français en faisant bien attention à l'auxiliaire des verbes au passé composé.*

1. (*vous*) I recommend this hotel to you—we stayed there a month. 2. I was so tired that I did not wake up early enough to go to[1] class. 3. I have finished my exercises and now I can go out. 4. (*tu*) You'll be sick; you were warm, and you drank some ice water. 5. Henry did not remember[2] his date with Pierrette. 6. After his retirement, he went back to[3] his little village. 7. (*vous*) What have you learned up to now[4]? 8. Many children were[5] born during the last war. 9. The little boys sat down in[6] the first row at the movies.

---

[1] **en**   [2] Use a form of **se souvenir de.**   [3] **dans**   [4] **ici**   [5] What tense will this verb be in? What will be the tense of the auxiliary?   [6] *in the* = **au**

PATTERN PRACTICE: the use of auxiliaries in compound tenses

Pattern 1

YOU HEAR   Je vais en France.

YOU SAY   Je suis allé en France.

2. When and how does the past participle of a verb conjugated with *avoir* agree?

Le père a **mené** ses enfants au cirque.	(No agreement. Why?)
Il **les** a **menés** au cirque.	(Agreement. Why?)
Les enfants qu'il a **menés** au cirque sont les siens.	(Agreement. Why?)
Quels enfants a-t-il **menés** au cirque?	(Agreement. Why?)

The past participle of a verb conjugated with **avoir** is invariable unless a direct object precedes the verb. The past participle of a verb conjugated with **avoir** agrees with the preceding direct object in gender and number.

3. Does the past participle of a verb conjugated with *avoir* agree with a preceding *en*?

Nous avons **mené** des enfants au cirque.	(No agreement. Why)?
Nous **en** avons **mené** au cirque.	(No agreement. Why?)

The past participle of a verb conjugated with **avoir** does not ordinarily agree with a preceding **en**.

C. *Remplacez l'infinitif par la forme convenable du participe passé.*

1. Où sont ces belles photos que vous avez (prendre)? 2. Nous avons (entendre) une bonne chanteuse. 3. —Avez-vous (voir) ma femme? —Oui, je l'ai (voir) il y a un instant. 4. Qui est la personne que vous avez (saluer)? 5. Quelles fleurs avez-vous (choisir)? 6. —Où sont les gâteaux? En avez-vous (acheter)? 7. —Je n'en ai pas (voir) sur le buffet.

D. *Traduisez en français.*

1. (*tu*) You have told me an interesting story. 2. (*vous*) Where is the person that you introduced to me? 3. (*vous*) What beautiful gifts you bought! 4. (*vous*) I didn't receive your letter. When did you send it? 5. I like his book. Has he written others[1]? 6. (*tu*) You wish some stamps? I bought some yesteday.

---

[1] d'autres

PATTERN PRACTICE: the agreement of the past participle

Pattern 2

YOU HEAR	J'ai peint la maison.
YOU SAY	Je l'ai peinte.

Pattern 3

YOU HEAR	Quel tableau avez-vous peint? (Quelle chambre . . .)
YOU SAY	Quelle chambre avez-vous peinte?

Pattern 4

YOU HEAR   L'édifice qu'il a construit est superbe.   (La maison . . .)
YOU SAY   La maison qu'il a construite est superbe.

4. Which common intransitive verbs of motion are conjugated with être? When and how does the past participle of an intransitive verb of motion conjugated with être agree?

Jacqueline était déjà **revenue** quand **nous**   (Agreement. Why?)
    sommes **partis**.
Mes camarades sont **morts** pendant la guerre.   (Agreement. Why?)
Ils sont **allés** à Paris pour les fêtes de Noël.   (Agreement. Why?)

The common intransitive verbs of motion conjugated with **être** are: **aller, arriver, descendre, devenir, entrer, monter, mourir, naître, partir, passer, rentrer, rester, retourner, revenir, sortir, tomber** and **venir**.

The past participle of an intransitive verb of motion conjugated with **être** always agrees in gender and number with the subject of its clause.

The past participle of a verb of motion conjugated with **être** always agrees with the subject of the sentence in gender and number.

5. In matters of agreement, is the pronoun vous considered singular or plural?

Vous êtes **tombé(e)(s)**, n'est-ce pas?   (Agreement. Why?)

The pronoun **vous** may be singular or plural, masculine or feminine. The past participle of a verb agrees according to whether **vous** refers to one or more than one person, and whether these persons are masculine or feminine. When **vous** refers to both masculine and feminine nouns the masculine plural agreement is used.

E. *Remplacez l'infinitif par la forme convenable du participe passé.*

1. Les élèves étaient déjà (partir) quand leur professeur est (arriver). 2. Marie est (sortir) sans se retourner.   3. Nous sommes (tomber) dans un piège.   4. Mes chers amis, vous êtes (arriver) trop tôt. 5. Pourquoi ne sont-ils pas (venir)?   6. Êtes-vous déjà (monter) sur la Tour Eiffel, Jacqueline?

F. *Traduisez en français.*

1. He had said that he would come back, and he came back. 2. (*vous*) Did you come[1] back home to[2] rest? 3. Our friends became important men. 4. Those who stayed all[3] died. 5. (*vous*) When did your sisters arrive?

---

[1] *come back home* = **rentrer**   [2] either **pour** or no preposition at all   [3] Put this word between the auxiliary and the past participle.

6. When and how does the past participle of a reflexive or reciprocal verb agree?

A reflexive verb is one in which the reflexive object refers back to the subject of the sentence. Ex.: *I* see *myself* in the mirror. *She* washes *herself*.

A reciprocal verb is one whose reciprocal object has the connotation of *each other*. Ex.: *They* see *each other* every week. *We* spoke to *each other* yesterday.

In French, reflexive and reciprocal verbs have the same pronominal forms and follow the same rules for agreement.

French reflexive objects may be

(a) direct objects

Elle **s'**est coupée.	*She cut* herself.
Ils **se** sont lavés.	*They washed* themselves.

(b) indirect objects

Elles **se** sont parlé.	*They spoke* to each other.
Elle **s'**est coupé le doigt.	*She cut her finger* (lit.: *She cut the finger* to herself).

(c) inherent objects

Some reflexive pronouns are neither direct nor indirect in function but simply an integral part of the verb. We may call the verbs with which they are used INHERENTLY REFLEXIVE VERBS.

Elle **s'**est souvenue de son rendez-vous.	*She remembered her appointment.*
Nous **nous** sommes échappés.	*We escaped.*
Elles **se** sont doutées de ce qui se passait.	*They suspected what was happening.*

Let us now examine the agreement of such verbs.

Votre femme et la mienne **se sont vues** hier.	(Agreement. Why?)
Nous **nous sommes levés** à dix heures.	(Agreement. Why?)
Janine **s'est souvenue** de mon adresse.	(Agreement. Why?)
Nos amis **se sont parlé** longtemps.	(No agreement. Why?)
Les enfants **se sont lavé** les mains.	(No agreement. Why?)

The past participle of a reflexive or reciprocal verb agrees with the reflexive object unless it is an indirect object. In that case, the past participle remains invariable. (In other words, the past participle of a reflexive verb agrees with the reflexive object when it is direct or inherent but not when it is indirect.)

G. *Écrivez la forme convenable du participe passé.*

1. Nous nous sommes (lever) à six heures, nous avons déjeuner, puis nous nous sommes (dire) au revoir.   2. Lucile s'est (habiller) mais elle ne s'est pas (brosser) les dents.   3. Ces enfants se sont-ils (laver) les oreilles comme il faut?   4. Ils se sont (raconter) leurs souvenirs pendant des heures.   5. Elle s'est beaucoup (amuser) à ce bal.   6. Nous nous sommes (apercevoir) qu'il était tard.   7. Sylvie s'est (marier) il y a deux mois.   8. Vous[1] êtes-vous (rendre) compte de votre erreur, Charlotte?   9. Comment vous êtes-vous (faire) mal, vous deux?   10. Nous nous sommes (revoir) avec plaisir.

[1] lit.: *Did you render account to yourself of your error?* What is the function of the reflexive pronoun in this sentence?

H. *Traduisez en français.*

1. We met each other on[1] the street and then we spoke to each other.   2. They rushed into the store.   3. Why didn't they speak to each other?   4. She cut her finger yesterday.   5. Finally we all[2] found[3] each other again.   6. We were mistaken.   7. They blamed each other for the accident.   8. They related their adventures to each other.   9. (*vous*) You made fun of me, both[4] of you.

[1] **dans**   [2] Place directly after the auxiliary.   [3] *find again* = **retrouver**   [4] **vous deux**

II. The Present Participle

7. How is the present participle formed?

First Person Plural Present	PRESENT PARTICIPLE	First Person Plural Present	PRESENT PARTICIPLE
donnons	donnant	dormons	dormant
finissons	finissant	lisons	lisant
perdons	perdant	prenons	prenant
buvons	buvant	voyons	voyant

The present participle is formed by adding **-ant** to the stem of the verb which is derived by taking away the **-ons** from the first person plural present.

8. What three verbs have irregular present participles?

être	**étant**	avoir	**ayant**	savoir	**sachant**

Être, avoir and **savoir** have irregular present participles.

9. What is the nature of the present participle?

Voyant la porte ouverte, je suis entré.	*Seeing the open door, I entered.*
Beaucoup de gens, **profitant** de leur week-end, étaient à la plage.	*Many people were at the beach, taking advantage of their weekend.*

The present participle is a verbal adjective, that is, it partakes both of the nature of an adjective and of a verb. As an adjective, it modifies some noun or pronoun in the sentence; as a verb, it indicates action or mode of being and may be followed by whatever types of constructions other forms of the same verb are followed.

10. When and with what does the present participle agree?

Les Michaud ont de la chance d'avoir des enfants si **obéissants.**	*The Michauds are lucky to have such obedient children.*

When the **-ant** form of the verb is used entirely as an adjective, it agrees in gender and number with the noun it modifies.

In that case, it has none of the functions of a verb, that is, it does not indicate action or mode of being, and it cannot govern an object or be followed by constructions which could follow it when used as a verb.

Les enfants, **obéissant** à leurs parents, sont allés se coucher.	*The children, obeying their parents, went to bed.*

When the **-ant** word is used as a present participle, it is invariable.

As a present participle, the **-ant** word is an adjective in that it is identified with some noun or pronoun in the sentence, and it is a verb in that it tells what someone is or is doing and may be followed by whatever types of constructions other forms of the same verb are followed.

11. The present participle is sometimes used without *en*, at other times with *en* or *tout en*. To what does it refer when used without *en*? when used with *en*?

De bonne heure ce matin il a rencontré **Marie sortant**** de la bibliothèque.	*Early this morning he met Marie* leaving *the library.*
De bonne heure ce matin **il** a rencontré Marie **en sortant** de la bibliothèque.	*Early this morning* he *met Marie* on leaving *the library.*

When the present participle is used without **en,** it generally refers to the nearest noun or pronoun. When it is used with **en** or with **tout en,** its action regularly refers to the subject of the sentence.

12. How does the use of *en* or *tout en* with the present participle influence its relation to the action of the main verb in respect to time?

Disant ces mots, <u>le pasteur</u> **s'est levé.**	Saying *these words,* <u>*the pastor*</u> arose.
En sortant de la poste, <u>notre facteur</u> **a glissé** sur le verglas.	On leaving *the post office,* <u>*our mailman*</u> slipped *on the ice.*
Tout en parlant, <u>le docteur</u> **a remis** son manteau.	While he was talking, <u>*the doctor*</u> put on *his overcoat.*
Tout en étant sévère, <u>le professeur</u> **aimait** beaucoup ses élèves.	Although he was *strict,* <u>*the teacher*</u> was *very* fond *of his pupils.*

When the present participle is used without **en,** its action is usually followed by another action. When it is used with **en,** the two actions are somewhat more simultaneous, and when it is used with **tout en,** the simultaneous nature of the action is emphasized still more.

Notice that **en** + PRESENT PARTICIPLE is expressed in English by *in, on, by,* and *while* + PRESENT PARTICIPLE and sometimes by *while, when* or *as* + CLAUSE. The expression **tout en** + PRESENT PARTICIPLE

---

* More common than **sortant** in this sentence would be **qui sortait.** The use of a **qui** clause to express the English present participle is very common in French. See page 67, §14.

is expressed in a variety of ways in English: *while* or *still* + PRESENT PARTICIPLE, *all the while* + CLAUSE, *even though* + CLAUSE, etc.

I. *Dans le devoir suivant, le mot entre parenthèses se termine en* **-ant**. *Il peut être un adjectif pur ou un participe présent. Faites l'accord du mot entre parenthèses où il y a lieu.*

1. Nous avons passé une journée (fatigant) à l'exposition. 2. (Fatiguant) tout le monde, Jeanne a recommencé son histoire. 3. Il y a dans la pièce des scènes (étonnant). 4. (Etonnant) ses amies, Madame Delom a déchiré toutes les lettres. 5. Nous avons trouvé les pauvres enfants (tremblant) de peur. 6. Le malade mangeait encore avec peine, la main (tremblant). 7. Nicole, (courant) vers la porte, a renversé la lampe. 8. Les Bérard ont l'eau (courant) dans leur ferme.

J. *Traduisez en français les phrases suivantes. La traduction française de chaque phrase comporte un participe présent — seul, avec* **en** *ou avec* **tout en**.

1. Closing her[1] eyes, Genevieve listened attentively to the music. 2. The painter hurt himself by falling from the ladder. 3. Even though he was sick, George used to read a great deal. 4. Opening the door with care[2], Bernard looked into the room. 5. On seeing that Mr. Lambert was busy, we left at once. 6. I saw Frederick while coming back from the office. 7. All the while that I was listening to her, I was thinking of something else. 8. On arriving in Paris, go to see the Jamois.

---

[1] Not the possessive adjective in French.   [2] **prudence**

PATTERN PRACTICE: using the present participle with **en**

Pattern 5

YOU HEAR   Pendant que j'attendais l'autobus, je faisais des mots croisés.
YOU SAY   En attendant l'autobus, je faisais des mots croisés.

13. How does French express the English present participle when it stresses the idea of *in the act of?*

Marc était **en train de lire** le jour-   *Mark* was reading (was in the act of
  nal.   reading) *the newspaper.*

When the English present participle stresses the idea of *in the act of*, French often uses **en train de** + INFINITIVE. This may also be expressed in English by *be busy doing something*.

14. How is the English present participle expressed after French verbs of perception, such as *voir, entendre, sentir*, etc.?

Nous avons vu Claire
- **ouvrir** la lettre.
- **qui ouvrait** la lettre.
- **en train d'ouvrir** la lettre.

We saw Clara opening the letter.

Je les entends
- **se préparer.**
- **qui se préparent.**
- **en train de se préparer.**

I hear them getting ready.

After verbs of perception, the English present participle is usually expressed in French by either a **qui** clause, an INFINITIVE, or by **en train de** + INFINITIVE. The **qui** clause and the **en train de** + INFINITIVE constructions are also used after forms of the verb **trouver**.

15. When is the English present participle expressed by à + <u>infinitive</u> in French?

Nous avons passé trois heures **à jouer** aux cartes.

We spent three hours playing *cards.*

Paul est resté au moins dix minutes **à lire** l'affiche.

Paul stood at least ten minutes reading *the announcement.*

L'enfant s'est amusé **à découper** des images.

The child amused himself cutting out *pictures.*

The English present participle is not always expressed by a French present participle. (English present participles and gerunds are expressed in a variety of ways in French. We give only two of the most common of these.)

When the English present participle expresses manner of passing time, French often uses **à** + INFINITIVE.

After forms of the verb **passer** (*to spend time*), this construction must be used rather than a present participle.

K. *Traduisez en français.*

1. We spent two hours looking at television.   2. We saw them getting[1] on the bus.   3. (*vous*) Will you spend the evening playing cards?   4. John was busy fixing his car when I came back.   5. (*tu*)

---

[1] *get on* = **monter dans**

Don't spend so much time reading detective stories.   6. (*vous*)
Don't bother me now—I'm busy working.   7. I heard Jean playing
the[2] violin.   8. We amused ourselves doing crossword puzzles.
9. I found Philip looking for his keys.   10. She sees the children
going to[3] school every morning.

---

[2] du   [3] à l'

PATTERN PRACTICE: the use of the passing time construction

Pattern 6

YOU HEAR   J'ai lu la leçon en une heure.
YOU SAY   J'ai passé une heure à lire la leçon.

Pattern 7

YOU HEAR   Maurice réparait sa moto quand je suis arrivé.
YOU SAY   Maurice était en train de réparer sa moto quand je suis
            arrivé.

Problem Words

16. expect

(a) How to say *expect a person or a material thing*

J'**attends** ma femme demain.   *I* expect *my wife tomorrow.*
Nous **attendons** une augmentation   *We* expect *a raise next month.*
  le mois prochain.

The non-reflexive **attendre** may mean *expect* when it is followed
by a direct object which is either *a person* or *a material thing*.

(b) How to say *expect an event or some other immaterial thing*

Nous nous attendons à une belle   We are expecting *a great surprise.*
  surprise.

Je ne m'attendais pas à vous voir.   I did not expect *to see you.*

The reflexive **s'attendre à** is often the equivalent of *to expect* followed by an event or some other immaterial thing.

(c) How to say *expect that* + CLAUSE

Jacques **s'attend à ce que nous**   *Jack* expects us to come.
  venions.

The expression **s'attendre à ce que** + SUBJUNCTIVE is the equivalent of *expect that* + CLAUSE.

(d) When *expect to* = *intend to*

Nous **comptons** le voir cet après-   *We* expect to *see him this afternoon.*
  midi.
J'ai l'intention de lire cet article.   *I* expect to *read that article.*

When *expect to* = *intend to*, French may express it by **compter** +
INFINITIVE or **avoir l'intention de** + INFINITIVE.

(e) How to say: *What do you expect? What do you expect me to . . .?*

Que voulez-vous, il est si jeune!   What do you expect, *he is so young!*
Où veut-il que j'aille?   Where does he expect *me to go?*

When *expect* is used to ask a question with a shrug of the shoulders
and implies inevitability, the French often use a form of **vouloir** as
in the above examples.

17. fail

(a) How to say *to fail to do something*

Il **ne s'est pas arrêté** au feu rouge.   *He* failed to stop *at the red light.*

The French have no special way of expressing *to fail to do something.*
They simply use the negative form of the main verb.

(b) How to say *not to fail to do something*

Ne manquez pas de nous **écrire** dès   Don't fail to write *us when you arrive.*
  votre arrivée.

To express *not to fail to do something*, use the negative of **manquer
de** + INFINITIVE.
  Notice that the affirmative of **manquer de** has another meaning,
as for example: **J'ai manqué de tomber** = *I almost fell.*

(c) How to say *fail an examination or a course*

Jean-Pierre **a échoué à** son examen
  de biologie.
Jean-Pierre **n'a pas réussi à** son
  examen de biologie.
                      Jean-Pierre failed his biology test.

The English *to fail an examination* is **échouer à un examen** and *fail a course* is **échouer à un cours**. But one can also say **ne pas réussir** or **ne pas être reçu à un examen**.

(d) How to say *to fail someone in a course*

Ce professeur **colle** rarement **ses**   *That teacher rarely* fails his pupils.
élèves.

To express the English *to fail someone*, the expression **coller quelqu'un** is used colloquially. More formal but not so common are: **refuser quelqu'un, ne pas recevoir quelqu'un** and **faire échouer quelqu'un**.

CAUTION: Do NOT say «échouer quelqu'un». Say either **refuser quelqu'un, faire échouer quelqu'un**, or **coller quelqu'un**.

18. feel

(a) When to use **sentir que**

Georges **a senti qu'**il valait mieux *George* felt that *it was better to leave.*
partir.

The English *to feel that* + CLAUSE = **sentir que** + CLAUSE.

(b) When to use **se sentir**

Je **me sens** vraiment mal.   *I really* feel *bad.*
Vous **sentez-vous** un peu mieux? *Do you* feel *a little better?*
Je **me sens** bien.   *I feel well.*

Forms of **se sentir** are used to express *feel* when it refers to the state of one's health; this verb is used with the adverbs **bien, mal, mieux,** etc.

CAUTION: The verb **sentir** sometimes means *to smell*. Do not confuse: **Il se sent bien.** (*He feels good.*) with: **Ça sent bon.** (*That smells good.*)

(c) How to express: *How do you feel?*

Comment **allez**-vous?	*How are you? How do you* feel?
Je **vais** bien, merci.	*I'm well, thank you.*

To ask a person how he feels in English, we normally say: *How are you?* although we sometimes say: *How do you feel?* To ask how a person is, French normally uses the verb **aller.**

19. get

(a) When *get = obtain*

J'ai pu **obtenir** un exemplaire de ce livre.	*I was able to* get *a copy of that book.*
Où est-ce que je peux **me procurer** un ordinateur?	*Where can I* get *a computer?*
Où **as**-tu **trouvé** cette machine à écrire?	*Where did you* get *that typewriter?*

When *get = obtain*, it may be expressed by **obtenir** or **se procurer** and in certain contexts by **trouver.**

(b) When *get = receive*

Avez-vous **reçu** ma lettre ce matin?	Did *you* get *my letter this morning?*

The verb **recevoir** is used to express *get* in the sense of *receive.*

Louis **a eu** une augmentation de salaire.	*Louis got a raise in pay.*
Philippe **a eu** une bonne note.	*Philip got a good grade.*

The compound past and simple past of **avoir** are often used in the sense of *got.*

(c) When *get = go and get*

Veux-tu **chercher** le journal?	*Will you* get *the paper?*
Allez **chercher** le courrier.	Get *the mail.*

When *get = go and get*, it may be expressed by **chercher** or **aller chercher.**

(d) When *get = catch* (a disease)

Jean a dû **attraper** la rougeole à l'école.	*John must have* gotten *the measles at school.*

(e) When *get = become*

Anne **se fatigue** facilement.	*Anne* gets tired *easily.*
Raymond **a** beaucoup **maigri** cette année.	Raymond *got* very *thin* this year.

Some reflexive verbs and also certain non-reflexive verbs carry with them the sense of *get +* ADJECTIVE in all tenses, some only in past tenses.

Tout à coup **il a fait** très **froid.**	*Suddenly* it got *very* cold.
J'ai eu très **sommeil** après le dîner.	*I* got *very* sleepy *after dinner.*

The compound past and the simple past of idiomatic expressions with **avoir** and **faire** are often used to express *get.*

Elle **est devenue** furieuse.	*She* got *furious.*

Normally, **devenir +** ADJECTIVE is used in the sense of *get* only when there is no verb equivalent to express that idea.

L. *Remplacez les mots anglais par leur équivalent français.*

1. Arrêtez-vous de tourner en rond, je vais (*feel*) mal. 2. Comment fait-on pour (*get*) un passeport? 3. Que (*do you expect*) qu'il fasse contre tous ces gens? 4. Je (*won't fail*) lui transmettre votre message. 5. On (*gets*) facilement des rhumes dans l'autobus. 6. Georges a l'air très fatigué; est-ce qu'il (*feels*) bien? 7. Je ne sais pas pourquoi il (*failed to come*). 8. Je (*expected*) un mot d'excuse de sa part. 9. Dans ce milieu mondain Jules (*feels*) mal à l'aise. 10. Si Jean-Paul (*fails*) son examen, il sera obligé de suivre des cours de vacances. 11. Je (*expect*) faire le voyage de Paris à Marseille en dix heures. 12. Eric était sûr de lui, mais les examinateurs le (*failed*). 13. Ma femme voudrait bien (*get*) cette recette. 14. Voudriez-vous (*get*) cette revue pour moi à la bibliothèque? 15. Ma propriétaire (*is getting*) complètement sourde.

M. *Traduisez en français. Attention aux mots en italique.*

1. I *got* good results with that machine. 2. (*tu*) Do you want me to open the window? You'll *feel* better. 3. (*vous*) Don't *fail* to telephone me tomorrow before noon. 4. (*vous*) What do you *expect* her to do for him now? 5. The most intelligent pupils can *fail* an examination. 6. I *got* an immediate reply to my letter. 7. If Monique *feels* tired, she should go to see the doctor. 8. Alain *failed* to hand in his work.

9. I did not *expect* to go to Brussels before next week.   10. (*tu*) George, I left my purse in the car. Will you *get* it, please?   11. Frances *expects* a letter from Paul.   12. I did not *expect* to be invited to the Dubois.   13. (*tu*) What did you *get* for Christmas?   14. Odette *gets* angry when people don't do everything she wishes.   15. It *got* so warm that we were able to go out without a coat.

Verb Review

Review the verbs **boire** and **connaître** according to the outline on page 283.

CHAPTER 6

Possessives

A possessive is a word which shows possession. English has possessive adjectives: *my, your, his, her, its, our, their,* and possessive pronouns: *mine, yours, his, hers, its, ours,* and *theirs.*

I. Possessive Adjectives

1. What are the French possessive adjectives?

Singular Masculine	Feminine	Plural		Singular Masculine	Feminine	Plural	
mon	ma	mes	*my*	notre	notre	nos	*our*
ton	ta	tes	*your*	votre	votre	vos	*your*
son	sa	ses	*his, her, its*	leur	leur	leurs	*their*

2. How and with what do the French possessive adjectives agree?

J'ai perdu **mon** portefeuille et **ma** montre.
I've lost my billfold and my watch.

Jacques est allé voir **son** cousin chez **sa** tante.
Jack went to see his cousin at his aunt's.

Elle a mis **son** courrier et **sa** revue sur la table.
She put her mail and her magazine on the table.

The French possessive adjectives agree in gender and number with the thing possessed. They do not agree with the possessor.

In English, the possessive adjectives agree with the possessor, not with the thing possessed.

72

3. When are mon, ton, and son used for ma, ta, and sa?

Son auto est belle.　　　　　　　　His *car is beautiful.*
Mon ancienne maison était plus　　My *former house was more convenient*
　commode que celle-ci.　　　　　　　*than this one.*

The forms **mon, ton,** and **son** are used to modify feminine singular nouns when the word immediately following these forms, whether a noun or an adjective, begins with a vowel sound.

4. How is the French usage in respect to the possessive adjective different from the English in a sentence such as the following:

Son père et sa mère sont partis ce　Her father and mother *left this morn-*
　matin.　　　　　　　　　　　　　　*ing.*

In English, the same possessive adjective may refer to two or more connected nouns, whereas in French, the proper possessive adjective must be used before each noun.

A. *Remplacez les mots anglais par l'adjectif français convenable.*[1]

1. (*My*) parents et (*my*) oncle sont partis pour le Canada. 2. (*His*) livre est en bien mauvais état. 3. Je n'ai pas beaucoup aimé (*their*) remarque à (*your*, s.) sujet. 4. As-tu passé (*your*) examen? 5. Que pensez-vous de (*my*) tableaux? 6. (*Our*) existence est ce que nous la faisons. 7. (*Your*, p.) références sont bonnes, mais (*your*) expérience est insuffisante. 8. Avez-vous vu (*their*) nouveaux chapeaux? 9. Il veut me vendre (*his*) voiture, mais elle marche mal. 10. Elle m'a montré (*her*) maison et (*her*) jardin. 11. (*Her*) adresse est inconnue.

---
[1] In this exercise, s. = singular, p. = plural.

B. *Traduisez en français.*

1. (*vous*) My parents would like to invite you to our party[1]. 2. (*tu*) Do we take my car or your motorcycle? 3. Do you know whether her brother and sister speak German? 4. (*tu*) Did you notice how[2] his voice has changed? 5. (*vous*) Would you do everything for your country? 6. My grandchildren are my greatest joy. 7. I hope that her son and daughter will have her good looks and intelligence.

---
[1] **soirée**　[2] **comme**

PATTERN PRACTICE: possessive adjectives

Pattern 1

    YOU HEAR   J'ai pris ma voiture. Les voisins ont pris . . .
    YOU SAY   J'ai pris ma voiture. Les voisins ont pris leur voiture.

II. Possessive Adjectives with Nouns

(parts of the body)

5. How, in general, does French express possession with nouns denoting parts of the body?

Marie a baissé **les** yeux.	*Marie lowered* her *eyes.*
Nous avons mal à **la** gorge.	Our *throats are sore.*
Il dort toujours **la** bouche ouverte.	*He always sleeps with* his *mouth open.*

In French, the definite article is often used with nouns denoting parts of the body, where English would use the possessive adjective. However, French normally employs the possessive adjective with parts of the body: (a) if ambiguity would result from the use of the article; (b) usually if the part of the body is modified; (c) if the part of the body is the subject of the sentence.

The exact usage of the article with parts of the body is so complicated that at this stage we shall present only a few of the most frequently used constructions. (§§6–10)

6. How is possession indicated in French when the subject of the sentence performs an action <u>with</u> a part of his body?

Marie lève **la** main.	*Marie raises* her *hand.*
Jean tourne **la** tête.	*John turns* his *head.*

When the subject of the sentence performs an action <u>with</u> a part of his body, in French that part of the body is modified by the definite article where English would use the possessive adjective.

SUBJECT + VERB + DEFINITE ARTICLE + NOUN (part of body)

C. *Traduisez en français.*

1. (*vous*) Raise your hand. 2. Jack closed his eyes. 3. (*vous*) Be careful! Don't move[1] your arm. 4. She opened her mouth but didn't say anything. 5. The teacher shrugged his shoulders.

----

[1] Use a form of **bouger.**

PATTERN PRACTICE: the subject of the sentence performs an action
with a part of his body

Pattern 2

YOU HEAR Nous levons la main. (le bras)
YOU SAY   Nous levons le bras.

Pattern 3

YOU HEAR J'ai levé la main et les autres élèves aussi . . .
YOU SAY   J'ai levé la main et les autres élèves aussi ont levé la main.

7. How is possession indicated in French when the subject of the sentence performs an action <u>on</u> some part of his body?

Marie **se** lave **la** figure.   *Marie washes* her *face.*
Je **me** suis cassé **la** jambe.   *I broke* my *leg.*
Jean, tu **t'**es brossé **les** dents ce   *John, did you brush* your *teeth this*
  matin?   *morning?*

When the subject of the sentence performs an action <u>on</u> a part of his body, in French that part of the body is modified by the definite article where English would use the possessive adjective, and the reflexive pronoun is used with the verb.

SUBJECT + REFLEXIVE PRONOUN + VERB + DEFINITE ARTICLE + NOUN (part of body)

NOTE: This reflexive pronoun is the indirect object.

D. *Traduisez en français.*

1. I rub my back every morning. 2. John broke his arm. 3. They brushed their hair. 4. I cut my finger yesterday. 5. (*tu*) Wash your face.

PATTERN PRACTICE: sentences where an action is performed on a
part of the subject's body

Pattern 4

    YOU HEAR   Marie se lave les mains. (Je)
    YOU SAY   Je me lave les mains.

Pattern 5

    YOU HEAR   Jacques se lave les oreilles. (la figure)
    YOU SAY   Jacques se lave la figure.

**8. How is possession expressed in French when the subject of the sentence
performs an action on <u>a part of someone else's body</u>?**

Marie **lui** lave **la** figure.   *Marie washes* his *face.*
L'infirmière **me** frotte **le** dos tous les   *The nurse rubs* my *back every morning.*
  matins.

When the subject of the sentence performs an action on <u>someone
else's</u> body, that part of the body is modified by the definite article
where English would use a possessive adjective, and an indirect object pronoun is used with the verb.

$$\text{SUBJECT} + \begin{matrix} \text{INDIRECT} \\ \text{OBJECT} \\ \text{PRONOUN} \end{matrix} + \text{VERB} + \begin{matrix} \text{DEFINITE} \\ \text{ARTICLE} \end{matrix} + \text{NOUN (part of body)}$$

NOTE: Compare the above with what happens when a noun showing
possession modifies the part of the body in the English sentence:

Marie lave **la figure <u>de Jean</u>.**   *Marie washes* <u>John</u>'s *face.*
L'infirmière frotte **le dos <u>du malade</u>.** *The nurse rubs* <u>the patient's</u> *back.*

E. *Traduisez en français.*

1. I rub his back every morning. 2. Michael twisted her arm.
3. (*vous*) Wash her face. 4. He shook my hand. ·5. We cut their hair.

PATTERN PRACTICE: action performed by the subject on a part of
someone else's body

Pattern 6

    YOU HEAR   Marie lave la figure du malade.
    YOU SAY   Marie lui lave la figure.

9. When a part of the body is the subject of the English sentence, how does French express possession?

Il a les cheveaux bruns.   His hair is *dark*.
J'ai mal **à la gorge.**   My throat is *sore.*

Whenever possible, the French avoid having a part of the body as the subject of the sentence. Generally, they use the verb **avoir** with the part of the body as the object of the sentence. The part of the body is often modified by the definite article.

F. *Traduisez en français.*

1. Your eyes are blue.   2. Her skin is soft.   3. My head aches.
4. My feet are sore.   5. Do your eyes hurt?   6. His finger hurts.

PATTERN PRACTICE: **avoir** + ARTICLE + NOUN (part of body)

Pattern 7

YOU HEAR   J'ai mal aux yeux. (pieds)
YOU SAY   J'ai mal aux pieds.

10. How does French express attitude or manner of being of a part of the body?

Il est entré **la tête baissée.**   *He entered* with his head down.
Bernard aime lire **les pieds sur le**   *Bernard likes to read* with his feet on
  bureau.   the desk.

French expresses attitude or manner of a part of the body simply by modifying the part of the body by the definite article. English often uses the preposition *with* in such cases.

G. *Traduisez en français.*

1. He eats with his elbows on the table.   2. The little boy stood in front of the teacher with his hands in his[1] pockets.   3. Marie was sitting there with her face in her arms.   4. Her husband, with his hand in[2] the air, tried to stop a taxi.   5. Micheline was watching[3] me with her eyes almost closed.   6. The poor old lady was in front of me with her hand stretched out.

---

[1] Use the article. French sometimes but not always uses the article with a piece of clothing where English uses the possessive adjective.   [2] **en l'air**   [3] Use a form of **observer.**

III. Possessive Pronouns

11. What are the French possessive pronouns?

	SINGULAR		PLURAL		
	Masculine	*Feminine*	*Masculine*	*Feminine*	
	le mien	la mienne	les miens	les miennes	*mine*
	le tien	la tienne	les tiens	les tiennes	*yours*
	le sien	la sienne	les siens	les siennes	*his, hers*
	le nôtre	la nôtre	les nôtres	les nôtres	*ours*
	le vôtre	la vôtre	les vôtres	les vôtres	*yours*
	le leur	la leur	les leurs	les leurs	*theirs*

12. How do the possessive pronouns agree? How are they used?

Vos leçons sont faciles; **les miennes** sont plus difficiles.	*Your lessons are easy;* mine *are more difficult.*
Elle expliquera cela à son père; je l'expliquerai **au mien**.	*She will explain it to her father; I will explain it to* mine.

Possessive pronouns, like possessive adjectives, agree in gender and number with the object possessed rather than the possessor. Possessive pronouns regularly take the place of nouns modified by a possessive adjective. Notice that the possessive pronouns contract with **à** and **de**.

H. *Remplacez les pronoms possessifs anglais par l'équivalent français*[1].

1. Il aime sa maison; j'aime (*mine*).   2. Je me souviens de mon premier bal; elles se souviennent de (*theirs*, s.).   3. Quelles aventures! Je ris encore quand je pense à (*his*, p.).   4. Je m'occupe de mes affaires, occupe-toi de (*yours*).   5. J'aime bien son jardin, mais je préfère (*ours*, s.).   6. Est-ce votre chien? Non, c'est (*his*).   7. Sa robe est beaucoup moins jolie que (*yours*, s.).   8. Si vous trouvez nos enfants mal élevés, vous devriez voir (*theirs*, p.).   9. Ma voiture ne marche pas; nous prendrons (*theirs*, s.).

---

[1] In this exercise, s. = singular, p. = plural.

PATTERN PRACTICE: possessive pronouns

Pattern 8

YOU HEAR	Jean a fini ses devoirs. Avez-vous fini . . .
YOU SAY	Jean a fini ses devoirs. Avez-vous fini les vôtres?

13. What are three ways of showing possession in a sentence of the following type?

Ce livre **est à moi.**
Ce livre **m'appartient.** } *This book* is mine.
Ce livre **est le mien.**

The most common way of expressing possession after **être** is by **à** + DISJUNCTIVE PRONOUN. When the possessive pronoun is used instead, the idea of the possessor is stressed. Possession is also often expressed by using an indirect object with a form of the verb **appartenir.**

PATTERN PRACTICE: ways of showing possession

Pattern 9

YOU HEAR   Cette voiture est à moi.
YOU SAY   Cette voiture est la mienne.

Pattern 10

YOU HEAR   Ces crayons sont les leurs.
YOU SAY   Ces crayons sont à eux.

(In this pattern practice drill, forms of **le leur** should be replaced by the masculine form of the disjunctive pronoun simply to duplicate the reply made on the tape.)

EXERCICES D'ENSEMBLE

I. *Traduisez en français.*

1. (*vous*) Do your duty, and I'll do mine. 2. (*vous*) Why are you shrugging your shoulders? 3. When will they finish their exercises? 4. All the pupils raised their hands[1] to answer the question. 5. (*tu*) Give her your arm; that will please[2] her . 6. She always has a headache. 7. (*vous*) If that coat is yours, leave it here. 8. He broke his arm. 9. (*vous*) Listen to him talk about his trip. 10. (*tu*) If your feet hurt, rest. 11. (*vous*) I remember your sister and his. 12. (*tu*) I have something for you; close your eyes. 13. She broke her leg for the third time. 14. (*vous*) I do not want to see your snapshots now. 15. (*tu*) Is this new[3] car yours? 16. This dictionary is mine; I need it. 17. (*vous*) You are going to hurt him if you twist his arm. 18. (*tu*) It is perhaps your opinion, but not mine.

---

[1] French uses the singular here. [2] Use a form of **faire plaisir à.** [3] Use a form of **neuf.**

19. (*vous*) Put down your hand.   20. It is his wife who cuts his hair.
21. What is there in this desk? I don't know; the desk isn't mine.
22. (*vous*) I have never seen a[4] diamond as beautiful as yours.
23. Her hairdresser will wash her hair tomorrow.   24. (*tu*) If you
haven't any ball pen, use[5] mine.   25. (*vous*) Do you have a sore
throat?

---

[4] **de**   [5] Use the proper form of **se servir de.**

Problem Words

20. go

(**a**) How to say *I'm going, I went*, etc.

—Il paraît qu'il y a un bon film au   "*It seems that there's a good film at the*
　Rex. **Tu y es allé?**   *Rex. Did you go?*"
—Oui, **j'y suis allé** hier soir.   "*Yes,* I went *last night.*"
—Moi, **j'irai** demain.   "I'll go *tomorrow.*"

In English, we often say: "Are you going?" "Yes, I'm going."
French rarely uses the verb **aller** without indicating a place to which,
and if the place has already been mentioned, they then use the adverb
y to refer to it.

But **y** is not used with the forms of the future and conditional of
aller, because then two *i*-sounds would come together.

CAUTION: In French sentences such as the English "I'm going,"
and "Did you go?", do not use the verb **aller** without indicating the
place to which or without using the adverb **y.**

(**b**) How to express certain combinations of *go* + PREPOSITION and
go + ADVERB

go back	**retourner**	*go out*	**sortir**
go back home	**rentrer**	*go through*	**traverser**
go by	**passer**	*go toward*	**se diriger vers**
go down	**descendre**	*go up*	**monter**
go in	**entrer**	*go with*	**accompagner**

The English verb *go* is used with certain prepositions and adverbs in special ways, and such combinations are expressed by separate verbs in French.

(c) When *go to = attend*

Avez-vous **assisté à la** conférence?	*Did you* go to the *lecture?*
Non, j'**ai assisté au** match de basket-ball.	*No, I* went to the *basketball game.*
En France il n'est pas obligatoire d'**assister aux** cours de la faculté tous les jours.	*In France you don't have to* go to *university classes every day.*

The verb **assister** means *go to* when *go to* is equivalent to *be present at* or *attend*. However, **assister à** may be used only with certain places and specific occasions and not with all places. For instance, "*I* go to *the university*" is rendered in French by: "Je **vais** à l'université."

The verb «assister» could not be used with **université**. Therefore, be careful when using **assister à**. In general, one can safely use **aller à** to express the idea of *being present at*.

21. happen

(a) When to use **se passer**

Qu'est-ce qui **s'est passé?**	*What* happened?
Il **s'est passé** beaucoup de choses.	*Many things* happened.
Dites-moi ce qui **s'est passé** chez les Monnier.	*Tell me what* happened *at the Monniers.*

When *happen = take place*, when there is no personal indirect object, and when the subject is impersonal and somewhat indefinite, **se passer** may be used to express *to happen*.

CAUTION: When there is a definite subject, avoid using «se passer» for *happen*.

CAUTION: When something *happens to someone*, do NOT use «se passer» for *happen*. See Section (b).

(b) When to use **arriver**

Qu'est-ce qui **est arrivé?**	*What* happened?
Dites-moi ce qui **est arrivé** chez vous.	*Tell me what* happened *at your home.*
Qu'est-ce qui **est arrivé à Simone?**	*What* happened to Simone?
Quand est-ce que **cet accident est arrivé?**	*When* did that accident happen?

Whenever *happen* may be expressed by **se passer,** it may also be expressed by **arriver.** But in addition, **arriver** may be used when there is a personal indirect object (something *happens to someone*) and when the subject is neither impersonal nor indefinite.

(c) How to say that someone *happened to do something*

J'étais là **par hasard.**	*I* happened to be *there.*
Nous **avons rencontré** Jean dans la rue **tout à fait par hasard.**	*We* happened to meet *John on the street.*

When *happen to* + VERB means *by chance*, French often uses **par hasard** or **tout à fait par hasard** with the verb.

(d) When *happen = it happens that* . . . (or *someone happens to* . . .)

Il se trouvait que j'habitais dans le même immeuble que Monsieur Martin.	*I* happened to *live in the same building as Mr. Martin.*
Il se trouve justement que Monsieur et Madame Drouet doivent venir ce soir.	It (just) happens that *Mr. and Mrs. Drouet are to come over this evening.*

When a sentence with *happen* can be begun: *It happens that* . . ., the French often express this idea by placing the proper tense of: **Il se trouve que** . . . or: **Il se trouve justement que** . . . before the main part of the sentence.

(e) How to say: *How does it happen that* . . .

Comment se fait-il que vous $\begin{cases} \text{avez} \\ \text{ayez} \end{cases}$ acheté une nouvelle voiture? How does it happen that *you bought a new car?*

Comment se fait-il que Marc $\begin{cases} \text{est} \\ \text{soit} \end{cases}$ absent? How does it happen that *Mark is absent?*

How does it happen that . . .? is expressed by **Comment se fait-il que** . . ., which is sometimes followed by the indicative, sometimes by the subjunctive.

22. hear

(**a**) How to say *to hear* (someone or something)

J'**ai entendu** un bruit en bas.　　*I* heard *a noise downstairs.*

To hear (someone or something) is expressed by the verb **entendre.** Here there is no problem, for English and French usage are the same·

(**b**) How to say *to hear of* (someone or something)

Avez-vous **entendu parler de** cette invention?　　*Have* you *heard of* that invention?

In French *to hear of* must be expressed by **entendre parler de.**

(**c**) How to say *to hear from* (someone)

Nous **avons** $\begin{cases} \textbf{eu} \\ \textbf{reçu} \end{cases}$ **des nouvelles de** notre fils ce matin.　　*We* heard from *our son this morning.*

French expresses *to hear from* by **avoir** (or **recevoir**) **des nouvelles de.**

(**d**) How to say *to hear that* . . .

Nous **avons entendu dire que** le premier ministre va démissionner.　　*We* heard that *the prime minister is going to resign.*

In French *to hear that* must be expressed by **entendre dire que.**

CAUTION: Do NOT use «entendre de» for to *hear of* nor «entendre que» for *to hear that.*

J. *Remplacez les mots anglais par leur équivalent français.*

1. Je (*heard*) de cette affaire, mais il y a déjà longtemps.　2. Je me demande ce qui (*happened*) pendant mon absence.　3. Georgette refuse absolument de (*go*) à un match de boxe.　4. Est-ce que ce sont les cloches de la cathédrale que nous (*hear*)?　5. La chose (*happened*) comme je l'avais prévu.　6. J'aime bien (*hear*) tomber la pluie. 7. Vous les (*hear*) rire?　8. Je voudrais bien savoir ce qui (*is happening*).　9. C'est ennuyeux de (*hear*) la radio du voisin tous les soirs. 10. Il (*are happening*)[1] des choses bizarres dans la maison d'en face. 11. Je (*hear*) sortir les employés. Est-ce qu'il est déjà cinq heures? 12. Daniel (*heard from*) ses cousins hier.

---

[1] In French this verb agrees with **Il.**

K. *Traduisez en français. Attention aux mots en italique.*

1. (*vous*) Did you *hear* that we will have another meeting Thursday?
2. (*tu*) There will be a football game Saturday. Do you want to *go?*
3. (*tu*) How does it *happen* that you left[1] New York?   4. (*vous*) Did you *hear* from your mother-in-law recently?   5. (*vous*) To what lycée did you *go?*   6. (*tu*) Did you *hear* of Raoul's marriage? 7. Bernard broke his leg. How did that *happen?*   8. (*vous*) If you don't *go* to the concert, I won't *go* either.   9. (*vous*) We *heard* that you *were going* to Greece this summer.   10. I *happened* to see the Benoîts[2] at the florist's.   11. It was raining, but I *went* all the same.   12. (*vous*) Come[3] to dinner; we *happen* to have a nice[4] roast duck.   13. (*tu*) If you *happen* to receive a letter from Nicolas, telephone me right away.   14. How does it *happen* that the children are not in[5] school today?   15. (*tu*) There will be a parade tomorrow. Can you *go?*

---

[1] Use a form of **quitter.**   [2] French family names do not take **-s** in the plural.   [3] French says: *come to dine.*   [4] **beau**   [5] *in school* = **à l'école**

Verb Review

Review the verbs **courir** and **craindre** according to the outline on page 283.

CHAPTER 7

The Use of Past Tenses in Narration

1. What sort of actions are expressed by the verbs in boldface type in the following passage? What is the normal function of the compound past?

Il **s'est** alors **levé** après avoir bu un verre de vin. Il **a repoussé** les assiettes et le peu de boudin[1] froid que nous avions laissé. Il **a** soigneusement **essuyé** la toile cirée de la table. Il **a pris** dans un tiroir de sa table de nuit une feuille de papier[2] quadrillé, une enveloppe jaune, un petit porte-plume de
5   bois rouge et un encrier carré d'encre violette. Quand il m'**a dit** le nom de la femme, j'**ai vu** que c'était une Mauresque[3]. J'**ai fait** la lettre. Je l'**ai écrite** un peu au hasard, mais je **me suis appliqué** à contenter Raymond parce que je n'avais pas de raison de ne pas le contenter. Puis j'**ai lu** la lettre à haute voix. Il m'**a écouté** en fumant et en hochant la tête, puis il m'**a de-**
10 **mandé** de la relire. Il **a été** tout à fait content.

Camus: L'Étranger

---

[1] black pudding   [2] paper ruled in squares   [3] Moorish woman

The COMPOUND PAST expresses a series of successive actions in conversation or in an informal narrative. Each successive action serves to forward the plot of the narrative.

The COMPOUND PAST also expresses a change of mental state. Thus, the last sentence in the above passage: **Il a été tout à fait content** means: *He was* (in the sense of *became*) *quite satisfied.*

2. What sort of actions are expressed by the italicized verbs in the following passage? What are the various functions of the imperfect?

. . . Il m'a dit: «Je *savais* bien que tu *connaissais* la vie». Je ne me suis pas aperçu d'abord qu'il me *tutoyait*. C'est seulement quand il m'a déclaré: «Maintenant, tu es un vrai copain», que cela m'a frappé. Il a répété sa phrase et j'ai dit: «Oui». Cela m'*était* égal d'être son copain et il *avait* vrai-
5   ment l'air d'en avoir envie. Il a cacheté la lettre et nous avons fini le vin.

Puis nous sommes restés un moment à fumer sans rien dire. Au dehors, tout *était* calme, et nous avons entendu le glissement d'une auto qui *passait*. J'ai dit: «Il est tard». Raymond le *pensait* aussi. Il a remarqué que le temps *passait* vite, et, dans un sens, c'*était* vrai. J'*avais* sommeil, mais j'*avais* de la peine à me lever.

10

Camus: *L'Étranger*

The IMPERFECT describes a state or action which was going on when some other action took place. The imperfect often sets a background for the principal actions. Actions in the imperfect do not take place successively; they have no beginning or end in reference to the time of the main action. They simply go on.

Let us consider the various types of imperfects in the above passage.

(a) Cela m'*était* égal d'être son copain et il *avait* vraiment l'air d'en avoir envie . . . Au dehors, tout *était* calme . . . C'*était* vrai. J'*avais* sommeil, mais j'*avais* de la peine à me lever.

The IMPERFECT is used in past descriptions. Each of these verbs describes a state of being in the past. Note that these states have neither beginning nor end, nor are they successive actions which forward a narrative.

(b) Je ne **me suis** pas **aperçu** d'abord qu'il me *tutoyait* . . . Nous **avons entendu** le glissement d'une auto qui *passait* . . . Il **a remarqué** que le temps *passait* vite.

The IMPERFECT often describes what was going on when it was interrupted by some other action.

As a rule of thumb, we can say that most past actions in which the verb has an *-ing* ending in English are expressed by the imperfect in French.

The action of each of the italicized verbs in the above passage was going on when it was interrupted by the action of the verbs in boldface type.

(c) «Je *savais* bien que tu *connaissais* la vie». . . . Raymond le *pensait* aussi.

The IMPERFECT is used to indicate a mental state in the past, for there is no beginning nor end to this state as far as the immediate actions are concerned.

Each of the above italicized verbs expresses a mental state.

3. The imperfect has still another important common function. What is the function of the imperfects in italics in the following passage?

A huit heures la cloche *annonçait* le souper. Après le souper, dans les beaux jours, on *s'asseyait* sur le perron. Mon père, armé de son fusil, *tirait* les chouettes[1] qui *sortaient* des crénaux[2] à l'entrée de la nuit. Ma mère, Lucile et moi, nous *regardions* le ciel, les bois, les derniers rayons du soleil, les premières
5 étoiles. A dix heures, on *rentrait* et l'on *se couchait*.

Les soirées d'automne et d'hiver *étaient* d'une autre nature. Le souper fini et les quatre convives revenus de la table à la cheminée, ma mère *se jetait*, en soupirant, sur un vieux lit de jour de siamoise[3] flambée; on *mettait* devant elle un guéridon[4] avec une bougie[5]. Je *m'asseyais* auprès du feu avec Lucile;
10 les domestiques *enlevaient* le couvert et *se retiraient*. Mon père *commençait* alors une promenade qui ne *cessait* qu'à l'heure de son coucher . . . Sa tête, demi-chauve, était couverte d'un grand bonnet blanc qui *se tenait* tout droit.

Chateaubriand: *Mémoires d'outre-tombe*

---

[1] owls   [2] indentures in the wall   [3] bright colored siamese cotton   [4] round table   [5] candle

Habitual or repeated past actions are expressed by the IMPERFECT. In English, such actions are usually expressed by $\left.\begin{array}{l} \textit{used to} \\ \textit{would} \end{array}\right\}$ + VERB.

4. How can an English-speaking person avoid overusing the French imperfect?

English-speaking students tend to use the French imperfect where the French would use the compound past (**passé composé**). Before expressing an action or state in the imperfect, ask yourself some questions to test whether this is the proper tense.

Use of the COMPOUND PAST (**passé composé**)

(a) Does the action advance the narrative even in the slightest degree? In that case, use the compound past rather than the imperfect.

(b) Is the action limited in time in any way? In that case, use the compound past rather than the imperfect. Even if the action takes place over twenty years or twenty centuries, if the time is limited, do not use the imperfect.

(c) Does the action state a past fact, one which does not set a background? Then use the compound past rather than the imperfect.

NOTE: The fact that the action is continued has nothing to do with whether it is imperfect or **passé composé.** All actions continue for some time — some much longer than others — but the mere fact that they continue is no criterion for the choice of tense.

Use of the IMPERFECT

(a) Does the action merely form a background for the plot by describing a state? Then use the imperfect.

(b) Is it a question of a continuing action which is interrupted by another action? In this case, put the continuing action in the imperfect.

(c) Is it a question of a past action expressed in English by $\left.\begin{array}{c} was \\ were \end{array}\right\}$ + the *-ing* form of the verb? Then use the imperfect.

(d) Is it a customary action, repeated regularly, which would be expressed in English by $\left.\begin{array}{c} would \\ used\ to \end{array}\right\}$ + verb? Then use the imperfect.

(e) Is it a question of a state of mind rather than a change of state of mind? Then use the imperfect.

There are a few other less common uses of the imperfect, but these are the principal ones.

5. What is the basic difference between actions expressed by the *passé composé* and those expressed by the imperfect?

C'*était* le 31 décembre. Je *me trouvais* seul chez moi ce soir-là. Je *lisais* dans mon bureau. Un peu avant minuit j'**ai entendu** des gens qui *chantaient* dans la rue. Ils **ont vu** de la lumière et **ont frappé** à ma fenêtre. Je ne les *connaissais* pas, mais je leur **ai ouvert** la porte. Ils *étaient* drôles, et nous **avons fêté** le Nouvel an ensemble.

Graphically, the imperfect may be represented by a straight line which indicates the flow of time. Actions above this line are going on while something else takes place. The **passé composé** (and the **passé simple**) may be represented by points in time (X) indicating the interrupting actions which take place successively.

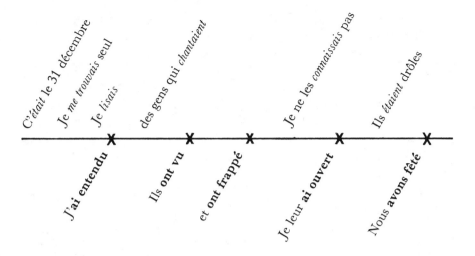

A. *Remplacez l'infinitif par la forme convenable du passé composé ou de l'imparfait, selon le cas. Expliquez oralement chaque emploi de l'imparfait.*

Il (faire) froid hier et nous n'(avoir) rien de spécial à faire. Je (vouloir) rester chez moi, mais Pierre (préférer) aller voir un de nos amis. Donc, nous y (aller). Nous (quitter) la maison à sept heures du soir et quand nous (arriver) dans la rue, il (faire) déjà sombre et il (neiger).
5 Nous (prendre) ma voiture, et nous (rouler) pendant une demi-heure. Quand notre ami nous (ouvrir) la porte, nous (entendre) des voix au salon. Nous ne (savoir) pas qui (être) là, et nous ne (vouloir) pas déranger notre ami Jacques, mais il nous (dire) d'entrer.

Pierre (s'excuser) de ne pas lui avoir téléphoné d'abord. Nous
10 (enlever) nos manteaux et nous (entrer) au salon. Il y (avoir) là plusieurs personnes que nous (connaître) et qui (parler) de musique.

Nous (être) en pleine conversation quand la sœur de mon ami (proposer) de nous montrer des diapositives. Ensuite, on nous (servir) à boire et à manger. Nous (rester) là une heure et demie. A dix
15 heures, nous (rentrer) chez nous.

B. *Traduisez en français en employant le passé composé et l'imparfait. Expliquez oralement chaque emploi de l'imparfait.*

A curious thing happened[1] to me the other day. I was[2] taking a walk

---

[1] Use a form of **arriver**.   [2] Use a form of **se promener**.

in the country with my dog. I was[3] walking along a road when I saw a man who wore an old coat. He was about[4] forty years old. When he caught[5] sight of me, he became afraid and began to run. That surprised me, and I decided to follow him. We walked rapidly[6] for[7] five minutes. Finally, he slowed[8] down and I overtook him. I asked 5 him why he was acting like that. He told me that I resembled a policeman[9] he knew and said: "I was afraid[10] when I saw you." The man spoke with an accent. I learned that he was a foreigner and that he didn't know English well. He told me that he often used[2] to go walking in the country, where he would pick up fruit[11] and would 10 eat at the farmers'[12]. We chatted a bit, and I tried to reassure him. Finally, we shook hands, and then we continued[13] on our way.

---

[1] Use a form of **arriver.**   [2] Use a form of **se promener.**   [3] Use a form of **marcher.**   [4] **environ**   [5] Use a form of **apercevoir.**   [6] **à grands pas**   [7] **pendant**   [8] *slow down* = **ralentir**   [9] **un policier**   [10] This means that he became frightened. Use a form of **avoir peur.**   [11] **des fruits**   [12] *farmer* = **le fermier**   [13] Use a form of **continuer notre route.**

PATTERN PRACTICE: certain uses of the imperfect and compound past

Pattern 1
YOU HEAR   Que faisiez-vous quand le téléphone a sonné? (lire votre lettre)
YOU SAY   Je lisais votre lettre quand le téléphone a sonné.

Pattern 2
YOU HEAR   Qu'est-ce que vous avez fait quand le professeur est arrivé? (se lever)
YOU SAY   Nous nous sommes levés quand le professeur est arrivé.

Pattern 3
YOU HEAR   Qu'est-ce que Suzanne a fait pendant que Jacques se reposait? (préparer le dîner)
YOU SAY   Suzanne a préparé le dîner pendant que Jacques se reposait.

Pattern 4
YOU HEAR   Maintenant je ne joue plus au bridge.
YOU SAY   Autrefois je jouais souvent au bridge.

Pattern 5
YOU HEAR   Quand j'étais jeune, je faisais la cour à Marie.
YOU SAY   Pendant deux ans, j'ai fait la cour à Marie.

5. When is the simple past used?

Le Tigre

Une femme *lavait* son linge dans une fontaine, à cent pas de la maison; elle *avait* avec elle un enfant de quatorze à quinze mois.

Elle **manqua** de savon, **retourna** chez elle pour en chercher, et, jugeant inutile d'emmener son enfant, le **laissa** jouer sur le gazon, près de la fon-
5 taine.

Pendant qu'elle *cherchait* son savon, elle **jeta** par la fenêtre ouverte les yeux sur la fontaine pour s'assurer si l'enfant ne *s'aventurait* pas au bord de l'eau; mais sa terreur **fut** grande lorsqu'elle **vit** un tigre sortir de la forêt, traverser le chemin, aller droit à l'enfant et poser sur lui sa large patte.
10 Elle **resta** immobile, haletante, pâle, presque morte.

Mais sans doute l'enfant **prit** l'animal féroce pour un gros chien; il lui **empoigna** les oreilles avec ses petites mains et **commença** de[1] jouer avec lui.

Le tigre ne **fut** pas en[2] reste; c'*était* un tigre d'un caractère jovial, il **joua** lui-même avec l'enfant.
15 Ce jeu effroyable **dura** dix minutes, puis le tigre, laissant l'enfant, **re-traversa** la route et **rentra** dans le bois.

La mère **s'élança, courut** tout éperdue à l'enfant, et le **trouva** riant et sans une égratignure.

Alexandre Dumas: *Le Caucase*

---

[1] Most often one finds **commencer à** + INFINITIVE, but sometimes **commencer de** + IN-FINITIVE is found in literary style.   [2] backward, reticent

The SIMPLE PAST is normally used in written French to express a series of successive actions in a literary narrative. It also sometimes states a past fact.

The SIMPLE PAST is a written tense, not used in speaking except in very formal lectures or orations. It is used in formal literary writing rather than in letters.

The SIMPLE PAST has the advantage over the COMPOUND PAST of being a single form and thus producing a smoother effect.

Notice the exact use of the simple past (**passé simple**) in the following sentences taken from the above passage:

> Elle **manqua** de savon.
> Mais sa terreur **fut** grande lorsqu'elle **vit** un tigre sortir de la forêt.
> Elle **resta** immobile, haletante, pâle, presque morte.
> Le tigre ne **fut** pas en reste; c'était un tigre d'un caractère jovial.
> Ce jeu effroyable **dura** dix minutes.

The uses of the imperfect are the same, whether the passage is written in the **passé simple** or the **passé composé**.

C. *Remplacez les infinitifs entre parenthèses par la forme convenable du passé composé ou de l'imparfait.*

(Use the compound past for successive actions unless your instructor tells you to use the simple past for such actions.)

Monsieur Grinci (être) toujours de mauvaise humeur. Pour un rien il (crier), il (gronder) et il (faire) peur à tous ceux qui l'(approcher). Il (avoir) un domestique, Jean, qui (être) bien malheureux. Mais Jean (être) aussi intelligent et (savoir) bien qu'il (falloir) obéir à son maître s'il (vouloir) garder sa place.   5

Un jour, Monsieur Grinci (rentrer) chez lui en colère et (se préparer) à dîner. La table (être) mise près d'une fenêtre qui (donner) sur la cour. Tout (être) joliment arrangé et il y (avoir) même un vase de fleurs au milieu.

Pendant que Jean (être) à la cuisine, Monsieur Grinci (goûter) la 10 soupe et la (trouver) trop chaude. Il (se mettre) encore plus en colère et la (jeter) dans la cour par la fenêtre ouverte.

Ce jour-là, Jean (être) plus calme qu'à l'ordinaire. Quand il (voir) cela, il (penser) que son maître (mériter) une leçon. Il (aller) vers la table, (prendre) l'assiette de son maître et la (jeter) dans la cour. 15 Puis, il (prendre) les services, les verres et les fleurs et (jeter) le tout par la fenêtre.

Cela (mettre) monsieur Grinci hors de lui et il (ordonner) à Jean de lui dire ce qu'il (faire).

Jean lui (répondre) tranquillement: «Monsieur, quand je vous 20 (voir) jeter la soupe par la fenêtre, je (penser) que vous (vouloir) dîner dans la cour et c'est pour cela que je (jeter) tout le reste».

Monsieur Grinci (comprendre) cette leçon. Il (sourire) quand même et, depuis ce jour, s'il ne (changer) pas de caractère, du moins il (maîtriser) ses colères.   25

D. *Traduisez en français, en employant le passé composé et l'imparfait où il y a lieu.*

(Use the compound past for successive actions unless your instructor tells you to use formal literary style. In that case, use the simple past for such actions.)

Balzac, the great French writer of the nineteenth century, had the habit of working late into the night. Most of the time he did not take the trouble to lock the door of his house.

One night as Balzac was sleeping, a thief entered the house and opened the door of the room of the writer. The latter seemed to be 5 sleeping soundly. The thief, reassured, went to Balzac's desk and began to rummage around in the drawers. Suddenly, he heard[1] a loud laugh. He turned around[2] and caught[3] sight of the writer, who was laughing heartily. The thief became frightened[4], but he was not able to keep from asking Balzac what was making him laugh. The latter answered him that it[5] amused him a great deal to see that a thief was coming in the night without light to look in a desk for money which he[6] had never been able to find even in[7] plain daylight.

---

[1] Use a form of **entendre rire très fort.** [2] Use a form of **se retourner.** [3] Use a form of **apercevoir.** [4] Use a form of **s'effrayer.** [5] **ça** [6] **lui** [7] **en plein jour**

Problem Words

23. intend

The word *intend* may be expressed in several ways. Often, but not always, these expressions may be used synonymously.

Jacques **pense** partir demain matin.	*Jack* intends to *leave tomorrow morning.*
J'ai **l'intention de** lire l'article du professeur Dugard.	*I* intend to *read Professor Dugard's article.*
La secrétaire **compte** prendre ses vacances en juillet.	*The secretary* intends *to take her vacation in July.*

The word *intend* may be expressed by **penser** + INFINITIVE, **compter** + INFINITIVE and **avoir l'intention de** + INFINITIVE.

24. introduce

How to say *introduce someone to someone*

Voulez-vous me **présenter** à Madame Leduc?	*Will you* introduce *me to Mrs. Leduc?*
Marthe m'**a présenté** à Hélène.	*Martha* introduced *me to Helen.*
Qui vous **a présenté** à Michel?	*Who* introduced *you to Michael?*

The English *introduce a person* is expressed in French by **présenter.**

CAUTION: Do NOT use the French verb «introduire» with the meaning of *introduce a person*. The verb **introduire** sometimes expresses the English *introduce* in less common connotations and also it often means *insert*.

25. a knock

How to say *a knock at the door*

On a frappé à la porte.	There was a knock *at the door.*
Avez-vous entendu frapper à la porte?	Did you hear a knock *at the door?*

French has no expression which corresponds to the English *a knock at the door*. Instead, it uses the verbal expression **frapper à la porte,** and *to hear a knock at the door* is **entendre frapper à la porte.**

CAUTION: DO NOT try to use a French noun to express the English noun *knock*.

26. know

(**a**) When *know = be acquainted with*

—**Connaissez**-vous Geneviève Leroy?	*"Do you* know *Genevieve Leroy?"*
—Oui, je la **connais** depuis longtemps.	*"Yes, I* have known *her for a long time."*

The verb **connaître** is always used to indicate *knowing a person*.

(**b**) When *know = be familiar with something*

Les jeunes **connaissent** bien les œuvres de Camus.	*Young people* know *(are well acquainted with) the works of Camus.*
Je **connais** Paris, mais je ne **connais** pas Marseille.	*I* know *Paris, but I don't* know *Marseilles.*

The verb **connaître** is used to indicate familiarity with works, places, etc.

(**c**) When *know = meet, get acquainted with*

Où **avez**-vous **connu** votre mari?	*Where did you* meet *your husband?* *Where did you* get acquainted with *your husband?* *Where did you* get to know *your husband?*

In the compound past and simple past, **connaître** sometimes means *to meet* in the sense of *to get to know* or *to get acquainted with*.

(**d**) When *know = know from memory*

Savez-vous les mois de l'année en français?	*Do you* know *the months of the year in French?*

Use **savoir** when *know = know from memory*.

(**e**) When *know = know from study*

Cet élève **sait** toujours sa leçon.	*That pupil always* knows *his lesson.*

Use **savoir** when *know = know from study*.

(**f**) When *know = be aware of*

Je **sais** où Pierre a mis son porte-   *I* know *where Peter put his billfold.*
feuille.

Use **savoir** when *know = be aware of.*

(**g**) How to say *to know how to*

Est-ce que Suzanne **sait** faire la   *Does Suzanne* know how to *cook?*
cuisine?

The verb **savoir** + INFINITIVE often means *to know how to.*

E. *Remplacez les mots entre parenthèses par leur équivalent français.*

1. Les Beaulieu (*intend to*) faire construire une nouvelle maison de campagne. 2. Tout le monde (*knows*) l'histoire de la femme du docteur. 3. Veux-tu me (*introduce*) à la jeune fille qui est assise là-bas? 4. Je (*don't know how to*) jouer d'un instrument, mais j'aime beaucoup la musique. 5. Je (*know*) parfaitement bien tout ce que vous avez dit. 6. J'habite ici depuis très longtemps; je (*know*) les plus petites rues de la ville. 7. Il (*intended to*) partir hier, mais il a manqué l'avion. 8. Vous (*know*) le russe; pouvez-vous m'aider à faire cette traduction? 9. (*Do you know how to*) conduire?

F. *Traduisez en français. Attention aux mots en italique.*

1. There was a *knock* at the door about midnight. 2. Raymond *knows* a great many very important people. 3. (*vous*) What do you *intend* to do this weekend? 4. Someone already *introduced* me to Mrs. Martel, but she probably doesn't remember me. 5. (*tu*) What[1]! You don't *know how to* swim? 6. Does Paul *intend* to spend his vacation in Corsica? 7. (*vous*) Do you *know* what happened to Mark? 8. Where did you *get to know* that artist?

---

[1] **Comment**

Verb Review

Review the verbs **croire** and **devoir** according to the outline on page 283.

CHAPTER 8

Demonstratives

A demonstrative is a word that points out. The English demonstratives are *this*, *that*, *these*, and *those*.

A demonstrative may modify a noun; in that case, it is a demonstrative adjective. Ex.: *this* book, *that* table, *those* people.

A demonstrative may take the place of a noun; in that case, it is a demonstrative pronoun. Ex.: This book is red, *that one* is green. Don't do *that*.

In French, it is important to know whether the DEMONSTRATIVE is an ADJECTIVE or a PRONOUN. If it is a pronoun, it is necessary to know which type of demonstrative pronoun it is since there are three types of demonstrative pronouns.

I. The Demonstrative Adjective

1. What are the demonstrative adjectives and how do they agree?

MASCULINE

Ce livre est bleu. **Cet** arbre est vieux.
Ces livres sont bleus. **Ces** arbres sont vieux.

FEMININE

Cette ville est grande.
Ces villes sont grandes.

The demonstrative adjectives are:

		Singular	Plural
MASCULINE	ce	used before masculine noun or adjective beginning with a consonant*	ces
	cet	used before masculine noun or adjective beginning with vowel sound	ces
FEMININE	cette	used before all feminine nouns and adjectives	ces

* That is, all consonants except mute **h.**

2. When and how do the French distinguish between *this* and *that*?

Ce professeur est excellent.	That *teacher is excellent.*
Ce professeur-**ci** est plus âgé que **ce** professeur-**là.**	This *teacher is older than* that *teacher.*
A **ce** moment-**là** il n'y avait pas beaucoup de travail.	At that *time there was not much work.*

In French there is one demonstrative adjective with several forms (**ce, cette,** etc.), in English there are two demonstrative adjectives (*this, that*).

French does not usually distinguish between *this* and *that* unless a contrast is desired. In other words, **ce** points out more definitely than **le,** but it does not make a contrast between *this* and *that*.

When two objects are mentioned and a contrast is desired, each of the nouns contrasted is preceded by a form of the demonstrative adjective, and the first noun is followed by **-ci** (to indicate *this*), the second noun is followed by **-là** (to indicate *that*). A hyphen connects **-ci** and **-là** to their nouns.

In certain time expressions referring to the past, **-là** is regularly appended to the noun modified by the demonstrative without there being any corresponding expression with **-ci.**

A. *Remplacez les tirets par un adjectif démonstratif, en mettant* **-ci** *ou* **-là** *après le nom où[1] il y a lieu.*

1. Que pensez-vous de _____ nouvelle élève? 2. J'aime bien voir _____ comédiens à la télévision. 3. _____ arbre a plus de deux cents ans. 4. Prenez _____ verre; _____ verre est pour moi. 5. A _____

[1] where it is necessary.

époque il n'y avait pas d'automobiles.   6. Ne prenez pas ＿＿ lettre;
elle est très importante.   7. Combien coûtent ＿＿ roses rouges?
8. ＿＿ journaux de sport ne sont pas très intéressants.   9. ＿＿
oiseau semble triste dans sa cage.   10. Je dois partir ＿＿ soir pour
Paris.   11. ＿＿ élèves font trop de bruit.   12. Avez-vous besoin de
＿＿ dictionnaire aujourd'hui?   13. Vous ferez ＿＿ exercices mais
pas ＿＿ exercices.   14. D'où vient ＿＿ lumière?

B. *Traduisez en français. Soulignez les démonstratifs.*

1. Who is that gentleman?   2. (*vous*) Do you like that music?   3. At
that time[1] I was only four years old.   4. (*tu*) When did you do these
exercises?   5. This car is really better than that car.   6. At that
time[2] there was no one in the street.   7. (*vous*) Have you read those
short stories?   8. That child is a real prodigy.   9. At that time[3] I
was doing the housework.   10. (*vous*) Do you know if that hotel is
comfortable?   11. (*tu*) Give me this stamp and I'll give you that
stamp.

---

[1] **époque**   [2] **heure**   [3] **moment**

PATTERN PRACTICE: demonstrative adjectives

Pattern 1

  YOU HEAR   Le livre n'est pas bon.
  YOU SAY   Ce livre n'est pas bon.

II. The Indefinite Demonstrative Pronouns

3. What are the indefinite demonstrative pronouns? When are they used? When is ça used for *cela*?

Lisez **ceci**, ne lisez pas **cela**.   *Read* this, *don't read* that.
Avez-vous vu **cela**?   *Did you see* that?
Ne fais pas **ça**.   *Don't do* that.

   The indefinite demonstrative pronouns are **ceci**, **cela**, and **ça**.
They refer to something without gender or number, such as an idea,
or they point out something indefinite. The pronoun **ça** is a shortened
and familiar form of **cela**, common in spoken style but to be avoided
in elegant written style.

The indefinite demonstrative pronouns are not normally used in good French before a form of **être**. Before a form of **être**, the demonstrative pronoun **ce** is used instead of **ça**. For example, not «Ça sera facile», but rather **Ce sera facile.**

PATTERN PRACTICE: the indefinite demonstrative pronouns

Pattern 2

YOU HEAR   Lisez cette chose.
YOU SAY   Lisez cela.

Pattern 3

YOU HEAR   Cette chose prend beaucoup de temps.
YOU SAY   Ça prend beaucoup de temps.

III. The Definite Demonstrative Pronouns

4. What are the definite demonstrative pronouns?

The definite demonstrative pronouns are:

	Singular	*Plural*
MASCULINE	**celui**	**ceux**
FEMININE	**celle**	**celles**

5. How are the definite demonstrative pronouns used?

Ces livres-ci sont meilleurs que **ceux-là.**   *These books are better than* those.

The definite demonstrative pronouns often refer to something already mentioned which has number and gender. They then agree with this antecedent in gender and number.

Celui qui travaille gagne de l'argent.   He (The one) *who works earns money.*
Ceux qui veulent peuvent partir.   Those (The ones) *who wish can leave.*

The definite demonstrative pronouns + **qui** are also used to express the English *he who, she who, the one who,* etc. In this case, the gender and number of the definite demonstrative depends on its meaning.

6. By what must the definite demonstrative pronouns be followed?

Ceux qui sont en retard sont obligés de rester après la classe.	Those who *are late are obliged to stay after class.*
J'aime mieux mes chiens que **ceux du** voisin.	*I like my dogs better than* the neighbor's (those of *my neighbor*).
Choisissez les fleurs que vous préférez. **Celles-ci** sont plus fraîches que **celles-là**.	*Choose the flowers you prefer.* These *are fresher than* those.

The definite demonstrative pronouns are always followed by **-ci, -là,** by a relative pronoun or by a preposition. They cannot be followed by **-ci** or **-là** if they are followed by either a relative pronoun or a preposition.

7. How are the former **and** the latter **expressed in French?**

Connaissez-vous ces deux dames? **Celle-ci** est anglaise; **celle-là** est polonaise.	*Do you know these two ladies?* The former *is Polish,* the latter *English.*
Je cherche des renseignements sur Jean Dubois et Pierre Petit. **Ce dernier** habite à Chartres.	*I am looking for information concerning John Dubois and Peter Petit.* The latter *lives in Chartres.*

The English *the former* and *the latter* are expressed in French by the definite demonstrative pronouns. In French *the latter* (**celui-ci,** etc.) precedes *the former* (**celui-là,** etc.). French also expresses *the latter* by a form of **ce dernier.**

C. *Remplacez les mots entre parenthèses par le pronom démonstratif convenable. Mettez* **-ci** *ou* **-là** *s'il y a lieu.*

1. (*This*) doit rester strictement entre nous. 2. —Laquelle de ces dames est Madame Delatour? —(*The one*) qui porte une robe bleue. 3. Si je découvre (*the one*) qui a fait cela, gare à lui! 4. Je l'avais dit, (*that*) devait arriver. 5. Le Rhône et la Garonne prennent leur source hors de France; (*the latter*) se jette dans l'Atlantique, (*the former*) dans la Méditerranée. 6. Ils sont partis; (*that*) me fait beaucoup de peine. 7. Savez-vous ce que veut dire (*this*)? 8. J'envie (*those*) qui peuvent aller passer l'été en France. 9. Si votre voiture ne marche pas, pourquoi ne prenez-vous pas (*your brother's*)? 10. Il y a beaucoup de robes dans le magasin, mais il faut te décider. Veux-tu (*these*) ou (*those*)?

D. *Traduisez en français. Soulignez les démonstratifs.*

1. (*vous*) That belongs to me; don't take it. 2. (*tu*) If you don't like that, leave it. 3. This gift is not the one that I had hoped for.

4. This interests me a great deal.   5. That author wrote plays and novels. The former[1] are entertaining, whereas the latter are boring. 6. Those who are not satisfied can go[2] and see the manager.   7. (*vous*) I know those girls. Go out with this one but not with that one.   8. My ideas are sometimes different from my partner's[3].   9. (*vous*) Don't think of[4] that any more.   10. I like these two lamps, especially this one.

---

[1] In French, *the latter* precedes *the former*   [2] In the sense of going to complain, *go and see* = **s'adresser à.**   [3] French says *from those of my partner*   [4] What preposition does French use with **penser** in this sense?

PATTERN PRACTICE: the definite demonstrative pronouns

Pattern 4

YOU HEAR   Avez-vous le dictionnaire de Jacques?
YOU SAY   Oui, j'ai celui de Jacques.

Pattern 5

YOU HEAR   J'ai le stylo que vous cherchez.
YOU SAY   J'ai celui que vous cherchez.

Pattern 6

YOU HEAR   Ces enfants-ci sont plus gentils que ces enfants-là.
YOU SAY   Ces enfants-ci sont plus gentils que ceux-là.

Pattern 7

YOU HEAR   L'homme qui travaille gagne de l'argent.
YOU SAY   Celui qui travaille gagne de l'argent.

IV. The Demonstrative Pronoun *ce*

When used as a demonstrative pronoun, **ce** is invariable and is usually the subject of some form of the verb **être**. It has several distinct uses. In one of its functions, we call it the *indefinite* **ce**, in another the *introductory* **ce**.

NOTE: A third function, sometimes called the *pleonastic* **ce**, will not be taken up here. Ex.: La guerre, **c'**est la ruine. Ce que Roger fait, **c'**est son affaire.

THE INDEFINITE **ce**

8. How is the English *it* expressed in French when it refers back to an idea without gender or number?

Elle nage bien. **C'**est difficile.   *She swims well. It's difficult.*

—Venez avec moi. —**C'est** impossible.	"*Come with me.*" "It's *impossible.*"
Il lit vite. **C'est** facile à voir.	*He reads rapidly.* It's *easy to see.*
Ils vont partir. **C'est** bon à savoir.	*They are going to leave.* It's *good to know.*

The *indefinite* **ce** refers back to an aforementioned idea. Since an idea has neither gender nor number, the indefinite and neuter **ce** is used to refer to such an idea. English uses *it* to refer back to an idea.

When the indefinite **ce** + a form of **être** has its meaning completed by an infinitive, the preposition **à** normally connects the infinitive to what precedes.

idea → **ce** + form of **être** + ADJECTIVE + **à** + INFINITIVE

9. When, on the other hand, is the English *it* expressed by the impersonal *il*?

Il est difficile de bien chanter.	It *is difficult to sing well.*
Il est impossible de partir avec vous.	It *is impossible to leave with you.*
Il est facile de lire vite.	It *is easy to read rapidly.*

When one would begin an English sentence with an *it* which does not refer to any previous idea, in French such a sentence is often introduced by the impersonal **il** followed by a form of **être** and an adjective. This construction is usually followed by **de** + INFINITIVE.

Il + form of **être** + ADJECTIVE + **de** + INFINITIVE

In conversational style, the French often replace the impersonal **il** by **ce**, so that **Il est difficile de bien chanter** often becomes **C'est difficile de bien chanter.** The latter is, however, less elegant.

E. *Remplacez les tirets par* **ce** *ou* **il.**

1. Jean n'est pas encore arrivé. ＿＿＿ est ennuyeux. 2. Où tout cela nous mène-t-il? ＿＿＿ est triste à penser. 3. ＿＿＿ est impossible de retourner chez elle maintenant. 4. Voilà ce que je vous ai promis. ＿＿＿ est joli, n'est-ce pas? 5. ＿＿＿ est plus facile de critiquer que de créer. 6. Savez-vous taper à la machine? ＿＿＿ est tellement utile.

F. *Traduisez en français.*

1. *(tu)* Is your father angry? It's evident.   2. It's easy to make mistakes.   3. *(vous)* What you have written surprises me, but it's interesting.   4. It is pleasant to travel.   5. It is useful to learn a foreign language.   6. Lawrence knows what he is doing. It's true.
7. John won't come back any more. It is difficult to believe.

PATTERN PRACTICE: the indefinite **ce**

Pattern 8

YOU HEAR	(facile) J'apprends à nager.
YOU SAY	J'apprends à nager. C'est facile.

Pattern 9

YOU HEAR	Apprendre une langue étrangère est difficile.
YOU SAY	Il est difficile d'apprendre une langue étrangère.

THE INTRODUCTORY **ce**

10. When is the introductory ce used?

Qui est ce garçon? **C'est mon fils.**	*Who is that boy?* He's my son.
Qui est là? **C'est lui.**	*Who is there?* It's he.
Qui sont ces personnes? **Ce** sont **mes nièces.**	*Who are those people?* They are my nieces.
C'est **Pasteur** qui a découvert un vaccin contre la rage.	It is Pasteur *who discovered a vaccine for rabies.*

The *introductory* **ce** is used before a form of the verb **être** when what follows **être** could be the subject of the sentence. After **être** normally a pronoun, a proper name, or a modified noun could be the subject of the sentence.

In such cases, the introductory **ce** is expressed in English sometimes by *it*, sometimes by *he, she,* or *they.*

NOTE: In sentences like **C'est le plus beau des mois,** the introductory **ce** is also used when a superlative form of the adjective follows a form of **être**.

11. When, on the other hand, are the subject pronouns il, elle, ils, and elles used as the subject of the verb être?

Où est <u>Marie</u>? **Elle** est en classe.	*Where is <u>Marie</u>?* She *is in class.*
Voyez-vous souvent <u>Gilbert</u>? **Il** est très intelligent.	*Do you often see <u>Gilbert</u>?* He *is very intelligent.*
Nous parlons de <u>vos enfants</u>. Sont-**ils** là?	*We are speaking of <u>your children</u>. Are they there?*

Whenever what follows a form of the verb **être** could not be the subject of the sentence, a third person subject pronoun must be used instead of the introductory **ce**. That is, whenever an adverb, an adjective, or a phrase follows **être,** it is NOT possible to use the introductory **ce**.

12. When is the personal pronoun and when is the introductory ce used with names of professions, nationalities, religions, etc., when they follow a form of être?

Il est <u>médecin.</u>	C'est <u>un médecin.</u>
Elle est <u>protestante.</u>	C'est <u>une protestante très fervente.</u>
Ils sont <u>français.</u>	Ce sont <u>des Français distingués.</u>

When the <u>unmodified</u> name of a profession, nationality, religion or any like noun is used after the verb **être,** it is considered an adjective rather than a noun. In such cases, **il, elle, ils** or **elles** are used before the form of **être**. But if such a noun is modified, it is then considered as a noun, and since it can thus be the subject of the sentence, the form of the verb **être** is preceded by the introductory **ce**.

G. *Remplacez les tirets par l'équivalent français du mot indiqué en anglais.*

1. —Où est Jacques? —(*He*) est en France.   2. Voilà Solange. (*She*) est professeur.   3. Connaissez-vous M. Dupont? (*He*) est un célèbre écrivain.   4. Est- (*she*) catholique ou protestante?   5. Ne demandez pas cela à Jacques. (*He*) n'est pas riche.   6. —Que fait son père? —(*He*) est médecin.   7.—Où est votre frère maintenant?—(*He*) est à l'armée.   8. (*It*) sont eux qui m'ont ramené à la maison.   9. —De quelle nationalité sont ces gens? —(*They*) sont allemands.   10. (*They*) sont des célibataires endurcis, mais (*they*) sont contents de leur sort.

H. *Traduisez en français.*

1. Who is this man? He is Mr. Lefranc.   2. I like this snapshot a great deal. It is very beautiful.   3. (*vous*) Look at these children; they are so cute.   4. Who took his dictionary? It wasn't[1] I.   5. I remember him; he is a teacher, isn't he?   6. Is he French or American?   7. Who is this girl? She is my sister-in-law.   8. (*vous*) Do you know Madame Dumont? She is our lawyer's second wife.

---
[1] Use present in French.

PATTERN PRACTICE: the INTRODUCTORY ce

Pattern 10

YOU HEAR   Qui est le jeune homme qui nous salue? (mon ami)
YOU SAY   C'est mon ami qui nous salue.

Pattern 11

YOU HEAR   Avez-vous vu Jean Perrot? (médecin)
YOU SAY   Il est médecin.

I. *Remplacez les mots anglais par l'équivalent français. Choisissez un des mots:* **ce, il, elle, ils, elles.**

1. Voyez-vous cette femme au chapeau rouge? (*She*) est la sœur d'Henri.   2. Je connais Pierre et sa femme; (*they*) sont des catholiques pratiquants.   3. J'aime beaucoup cet écrivain. (*He*) est mon préféré. 4.—Qui est là?—(*It*) est moi, Françoise. 5. Je n'ai pas fait ce que j'aurais dû, (*it*) est vrai.   6. Parlez plus fort, s'il vous plaît; voilà, (*it*) est mieux.   7. Je voudrais voir votre professeur. Est- (*he*) ici?   8. Qui a dit ces mensonges sur moi? Est- (*it*) Brigitte?   9. Venez tout de suite, (*it*) est très important.   10. Voyez-vous ce monsieur? Qui est- (*he*)[1]?

---

[1] Since **qui** is a pronoun, how must *he* be expressed here?

EXERCICES D'ENSEMBLE

J. *Remplacez les mots anglais par l'équivalent français.*

1. Pardonnez-nous comme nous pardonnons à (*those*) qui nous ont offensés.   2. (*It*) est un petit arbre qui a donné tous (*those*) beaux fruits.   3. Je vous présenterai mon ami. (*He*) est ingénieur.   4. Ne recommencez pas à m'ennuyer avec (*that*).   5. (*He*) est un ancien prince russe.   6. (*This*) homme de science dit qu'il pourrait créer un être humain. (*It*) est extraordinaire.   7. Je me suis trompé de route. (*It*) est évident.   8. Connaissez-vous (*those*) jeunes gens? (*They*) sont très amusants.   9. Quant à Florence, (*she*) est fâchée de n'avoir pas été invitée.   10. Je connais plusieurs Belges. (*They*) sont tous catholiques.   11. (*It*) est une triste histoire.   12. Je retrouverai (*the one*) qui m'a joué (*that*) tour.   13. (*She*) est japonaise.   14. (*The one*) que je cherche n'est pas encore arrivé.

K. *Traduisez en français.*

1. It is important to do that work.   2. I know him; he is a former

classmate.   3. I like that song a great deal.   4. She was sick, but she is[1] better.   5. (*tu*) The one who told you that lied.   6. (*tu*) You do not need two ball pens; lend me that one.   7. I want to see those who couldn't[2] come yesterday.   8. I have already seen this man somewhere.   9. (*vous*) Go[3] and see my relatives; they are very nice. 10. It is hard to understand what he is trying to explain.   11. He is a rich manufacturer.   12. (*vous*) Do you have a good specialist? Yes, he is an excellent doctor.   13. (*vous*) Take[4] her those flowers. 14. The ones[5] I prefer are the carnations.   15. Where is my brief-case? It is there, on the table.   16. (*vous*) It is clear that you are right. 17. Will he bring his radio? It's probable.   18. (*vous*) Don't say that.   19. It's a wonderful idea!   20. (*tu*) It's good to see[6] you again.

---

[1] Not a form of «être».   [2] Use the **passé composé**.   [3] **Allez voir**   [4] Use a form of **apporter**.
[5] Refers to flowers.   [6] Express *see again* by one word.

Problem Words

27. lack

(**a**) How *to lack* may be expressed by **manquer de**

Cet agent **manque de** tact.   *That policeman* lacks *tact.*

One of the commonest ways of expressing *to lack* is: SUBJECT + **manquer de** + *what is lacking*. *What is lacking* is an indefinite noun, and it therefore follows **de** without a definite article.

(**b**) How *lack* may be expressed by the impersonal **il manque . . .**

Il lui manque de la farine pour   She lacks *flour to make her cake.*
faire son gâteau.

When using the impersonal **Il manque . . .** to begin the sentence, *what is lacking* is a partitive and the person who *lacks* is the indirect object.

(**c**) How **manquer** is used when *what is lacking* is the SUBJECT

La volonté lui manque pour réussir.   He lacks the will *to succeed.*

When *what is lacking* is the SUBJECT of the sentence, it is modified by the definite article and the person who lacks is the indirect object.

28. last night

(**a**) When *last night* = *last evening*

Hier soir nous sommes allés au théâtre.   Last night *we went to the theater.*

When *last night* = *last evening*, the French say **hier soir.**

(**b**) When *last night* is *late in the night*

Il a fait très chaud **cette nuit.**   *It was very hot* last night.
Cette nuit je n'ai pas pu dormir.   Last night *I couldn't sleep.*
On a volé la banque **la nuit dernière.**   *The bank was robbed* last night.

When *last night* refers to something that happened later than the preceding evening, the French use the expression **cette nuit.** Also possible, but less common, is **la nuit dernière.**

29. late

(**a**) When *late* = *not early*

Il est **tard;** il faut partir.   *It is* late; *we must leave.*

When *late* means *not early*, use **tard.**

(**b**) When *late* = *not on time*

Il vaut mieux être en avance qu'**en retard.**   *It is better to be early than* late.

When *late* means *not on time*, use **en retard.**

30. leave

(**a**) How to say *to leave someone or something somewhere* (always with a direct object)

Nous **avons laissé Jean à la bibliothèque.**   *We* left John at the library.
Où avez-vous **laissé** votre **serviette?**   Where did *you* leave *your* briefcase?

The verb **laisser** is used when it is a question of *leaving someone or something somewhere.*

(**b**) How to say *to leave someone or something* (always with a direct object)

J'ai quitté mes amis à deux heures.   *I* left my friends *at two o'clock.*

Nous **avons quitté la maison** de   *We* left the house *early*.
bonne heure.

The verb **quitter** is used when it is a question of *leaving someone or something*.

(**c**) How to say *to leave* (never followed by a place)

Je **m'en vais.**   *I*'m leaving.
Marianne **s'en ira** demain.   *Marianne* will leave *tomorrow*.

The verb **s'en aller** means *leave* in the sense of *go away, go off*. It is not usually followed by a place.

(**d**) How to say *to leave* (for more than just a moment)

Nous **sommes partis** hier soir.   *We* left *last night*.

The verb **partir** is sometimes used to mean *leave* or *go away without indicating a place*.

Quand **partirez**-vous **de New York?**   *When* will *you* leave New York?

When **partir** indicates *leaving a place*, it must be followed by **de**.
Jacques **est parti en Espagne.**   *Jack* left for Spain.
Michel **est parti pour la Grèce.**   *Michael* left for Greece.

The idea of *leaving for* + PLACE (proper noun) is expressed by **partir pour** or **partir** + PREPOSITION OF PLACE required by the proper noun. Purists prefer **partir pour.**

In general, **partir** means *to leave* in the sense of leaving for a trip or leaving a place for a certain length of time.

(**e**) When *leave* = *go out*

Sortez par la porte de derrière.   Leave (go out) *by the back door.*
Le patron vient de **sortir.** Revenez   *The boss has just* left. *Come back in an*
dans une heure.   *hour.*

The verb **sortir** means *leave* in the sense of *go out*. It often implies leaving for a short time as contrasted with **partir,** which implies leaving for a somewhat longer time and not merely temporarily.

Qui **est sorti du bureau** tout à   *Who* left the office *just now?*
l'heure?
Les gens **sont sortis du restaurant**   *The people* left the restaurant *laughing.*
en riant.
Rentrez tout de suite **en sortant du**   *Come back home right away* after (leav-
cinéma.   ing) the movies.

To indicate *leaving a place*, use **sortir de** + *place.*

(**f**) Other uses of **sortir** = *go out*

Êtes-vous **sorti** ce matin?   Did *you* go out *this morning?*

When **sortir** is used with no indication of from what place or with whom, it often means *going out of the place* where one habitually is at a given time.

Marc **sort avec** Françoise.   *Mark* is going out with *Frances.*

To indicate *going out with* in the sense of "keeping company with," use **sortir avec.**

L. *Remplacez les mots anglais par leur équivalent français.*
1. Bernard a une décapotable et toutes les jeunes filles veulent (*go out*) avec lui. 2. Avez-vous vu ce clair de lune sur le lac (*last night*)? 3. Je regrette d'être (*late*); j'ai été pris dans un embouteillage. 4. Par ce temps, je refuse de (*leave*) la maison. 5. Excusez-moi de vous presser, mais je ne voudrais pas que vous soyez (*late*). 6. Si les Couve ne sont pas là, nous (*will leave*) notre carte de visite. 7. Il y a eu un formidable incendie (*last night*) vers deux heures du matin. 8. Il est (*late*); rentrons. 9. Les oiseaux (*are leaving*); c'est la fin de la belle saison. 10. Les chiens n'ont pas arrêté d'aboyer (*last night*). 11. Si vous (*leave*), plusieurs de nos collègues (*will leave*) aussi. 12. Comment vous arrangez-vous pour être toujours (*late*)? 13. (*Let's leave*) nos manteaux au vestiaire; nous serons plus à l'aise. 14. Avant de (*leave*) le bureau, fermez bien la porte et les fenêtres.

M. *Traduisez en français. Attention aux mots en italique.*
1. (*vous*) Take the book that I *left* on my desk. 2. The men didn't *lack* courage, but they were not able to gain ground. 3. There was a good film on[1] television at nine *last* night. 4. (*vous*) If you arrive too *late*, we won't be able to have dinner together. 5. (*tu*) Why didn't you come *last* night, Colette? 6. (*vous*) Your plants *lack* sunlight. 7. I *left* the children at the movies. 8. Gilbert *left last* night at eight o'clock. 9. Roger always goes to bed *late*. 10. Oliver doesn't *lack* ideas. 11. (*tu*) Don't *leave* without saying goodbye. 12. (*vous*) Don't fail to *leave* your address. 13. The travelers *left* at[2] dawn. 14. (*vous*) I hope you will not arrive *late*, because the bus *will leave* at one o'clock sharp.

---

[1] à la [2] à l'

Verb Review

Review the verbs **dire** and **écrire** according to the outline on page 283.

CHAPTER 9

Use of Tenses in General

I. The Present

1. What use of the simple present tense is exactly the same in French and English?

Jean **travaille** beaucoup.   *John* works *a great deal.*
Hélène **lit** un peu tous les jours.   *Helen* reads *a little every day.*

In both French and English, the SIMPLE PRESENT tense is used to state a general truth.

2. How does French express the English progressive present, that is, the present in -ing?

Jean **travaille** maintenant.   *John* is working *now.*
Hélène **lit** le journal en ce moment.   *Helen* is reading *the newspaper right now.*
Je **suis en train de corriger** mes fautes.   I am correcting *my mistakes.*

In general, French expresses the English progressive present by a simple present. But if French wishes to insist on the progressive nature of an action, it then uses a form of **être en train de** + INFINITIVE.

3. When may the French present tense express a future idea?

Demain nous **partons** pour Paris.   Tomorrow *we* leave *for Paris.*

The present is occasionally used to express an action in the immediate future when some other word in the sentence indicates futurity.

NOTE: The student should recognize this use of the present for the future but use it very sparingly, for it can be used only in certain cases.

110

4. When is the present tense used in French to express an action which would be expressed in the present perfect in English?

Nous **apprenons** le français **depuis deux ans.**	*We* have been learning *French* for *two years.*
Il y a trois jours **qu'il pleut.**	It has been raining for *three days.*
Voilà un an **que** Marc **habite** ici.	*Mark* has been living *here* for *a year.*

When an action which began in the past is still continuing in the present, French uses <u>the present tense</u> with **depuis, il y a . . . que, voici . . . que,** and **voilà . . . que.** English generally uses the progressive form of the present perfect with *for* to express the same concept.

In this type of sentence, **Il y a . . . que, Voici . . . que,** and **Voilà . . . que** normally come at the beginning of the sentence, whereas **depuis** + TIME EXPRESSION usually comes at the end of the sentence.

A. *Traduisez en français.*

1. Peter drives very well.   2. He has been going out with her for[1] a long time.   3. Lucy is talking on[2] the telephone.   4. The day after tomorrow I will give[3] them my resignation.   5. (*tu*) Leave me alone[4]; I'm working.   6. Albert has had this letter in his pocket for[5] five days.   7. We have been waiting for her for[6] an hour.   8. This evening I'll pack[3] my suitcase.   9. He has refused to see me for[7] two days.   10. Tomorrow we'll go[3] to the movies.

---

[1] Use **depuis.**   [2] *on the* = **au**   [3] Express this action by the present.   [4] **tranquille**   [5] Use **il y a . . . que.**   [6] Use **voilà . . . que.**   [7] Use **voici . . . que.**

PATTERN PRACTICE: **être en train de**

Pattern 1

YOU HEAR	Nos amis parlent de leur voyage.
YOU SAY	Nos amis sont en train de parler de leur voyage.

PATTERN PRACTICE: actions beginning in the past and continuing in the present

Pattern 2

YOU HEAR	Depuis quand les élèves sont-ils en classe? (une heure)
YOU SAY	Ils sont en classe depuis une heure.

Pattern 3

YOU HEAR   Jacques attend son frère depuis une heure.
YOU SAY   Il y a une heure que Jacques attend son frère.

II. The Future

5. In what two ways does French usually express the future?

Un de ces jours j'**achèterai** un chien.   *One of these days* I'll buy *a dog.*
Je **vais partir** bientôt pour Rome.   *Soon I*'ll leave *for Rome.*

French usually expresses the future with the FUTURE TENSE or with the present of **aller** + INFINITIVE. This normally parallels English usage, but in certain cases of an immediate future, French tends to use **aller** + INFINITIVE where English might use the future.

6. When do the French use the future tense where the present would be used in English?

Quand vous **saurez** le français, nous   When *you* know *French, we'll go to* irons en France ensemble.   *France together.*
Dès que je **recevrai** sa lettre, je   As soon as *I* receive *his letter, I'll send* vous l'enverrai.   *it to you.*
Tant que vous **parlerez** ainsi, vous   As long as *you* speak *this way, you'll* aurez des ennuis.   *have trouble.*

In French, the future is used after **quand, lorsque, dès que, aussi-tôt que,** and **tant que** if the action will take place at some future time. English uses the present in such constructions.

B. *Traduisez en français.*

1. I'll[1] inquire about that immediately.   2. We'll[2] inquire about the cost[3] of the trip next week.   3. (*vous*) When you go to Paris, send me a postcard.   4. As soon as I get my passport, we'll leave.   5. When it is warm, we'll spend the afternoon at the swimming pool.   6. (*tu*) As soon as you arrive, telephone me.   7. As long as there are men, there will be wars.   8. (*tu*) When I see you, I'll tell you what happened.

---

[1] Because it is an immediate future, French uses **aller** + INFINITIVE here.   [2] Because this is not an immediate future, French does not use «aller» + INFINITIVE here.   [3] **le prix**

PATTERN PRACTICE: **quand** and **dès que** with the future

Pattern 4

YOU HEAR   J'ai téléphoné à mon frère quand je suis arrivé à Paris.
YOU SAY   Je téléphonerai à mon frère quand j'arriverai à Paris.

III. The Conditional

7. When is the conditional used to indicate a future action?

Richard croyait que Marc le **ferait**.   *Richard thought that Mark* would do *it.*

Je lui ai demandé s'il **partirait** bientôt.   *I asked him if he* would leave *soon.*

When the main clause of a sentence is in a past tense, the CONDITIONAL is often used in the dependent clause to indicate a future action.

NOTE: English uses the same sort of construction. Compare:

He says he <u>will</u> leave.   *He said he* <u>would</u> leave.
I think it <u>will</u> rain.   *I thought it* <u>would</u> rain.

8. How is the conditional used in polite requests or questions?

Je **voudrais** un verre d'eau.   *I should like a glass of water.*
Aimeriez-vous sortir avec moi?   Would *you* like *to go out with me?*

The conditional is sometimes used to soften a statement or a question which would be somewhat direct and blunt if stated in the present tense.

NOTE: Compare the politeness of the above examples to the bluntness of the same sentences stated in the present, e.g.: *I want a glass of water. Do you want to go out with me?*

C. *Traduisez en français.*

1. I should prefer to leave at once. 2. Her parents told me that she would come today. 3. Our friends thought that we would spend the

day at their place.   4. I heard[1] that the airplane would be[2] late.
5. Claude asked Martha if she would be in class the next day.
6. (*vous*) Would you like to go to England?

---

[1] *to hear that* = **entendre dire que**   [2] *to be late* = **avoir du retard**

PATTERN PRACTICE: the conditional as the past of the future

Pattern 5

YOU HEAR   Jacques partira samedi.
YOU SAY   Roland a dit que Jacques partirait samedi.

IV. The Pluperfect, the Past Anterior, the *Passé Surcomposé*

9. What is the basic use of the pluperfect?

J'**avais fini** mon travail quand Pierre est arrivé.

I had finished my work when Peter arrived.

Colette **était** déjà **sortie** quand il a commencé à pleuvoir.

Colette had already left when it began to rain.

The PLUPERFECT indicates a past action which took place before the beginning of another past action.

PATTERN PRACTICE: the pluperfect

Pattern 6

YOU HEAR   Nous avons déjà entendu la nouvelle. Hélène nous a téléphoné.

YOU SAY   Nous avions déjà entendu la nouvelle quand Hélène nous a téléphoné.

10. What tense does French use in cases when an action begins at a certain time in the past and continues until another time in the past?

Monsieur Lenoir **travaillait depuis dix ans** quand il a découvert ce nouveau procédé.

Mr. Lenoir had been working for ten years when he discovered that new process.

Il y avait un an qu'il apprenait le   He had been learning *French* for one
français quand il est parti pour   year *when he left for Africa.*
l'Afrique.

When an action which begins in the past and continues up to a
certain point in the past is interrupted by another action, stated or
implied, the French express the first action by the IMPERFECT with
depuis or **il y avait . . . que.** In such cases, English uses the pluperfect and usually the progressive form of the pluperfect.

PATTERN PRACTICE: the imperfect with **depuis**

Pattern 7
    YOU HEAR   J'ai écrit pendant dix minutes. Mon père est rentré.
    YOU SAY   J'écrivais depuis dix minutes quand mon père est rentré.

**11. When can the French pluperfect not be used to indicate a past action which
took place before another past action?**

(a) Literary Style   (b) Conversational Style

Quand j'**eus fini** mon   **Quand** j'**ai eu fini** mon   When *I* had finished *my*
   travail, je sortis.   travail, je suis sorti.   *work, I went out.*
Dès que Louis **eut écrit**   **Dès que** Louis **a eu**   As soon as *Louis* had
   la lettre, il la mit à   **écrit** la lettre, il l'a   written *the letter, he*
   la poste.   mise à la poste.   *mailed it.*

(a) Literary Style

When a past action introduced by **quand, lorsque, dès que, aussitôt que,** or **après que** immediately precedes a second past action
which is in the simple past, the first action must be in the PAST AN-
TERIOR (**passé antérieur**). It cannot be in the pluperfect.

(b) Conversational Style

When a past action introduced by **quand, lorsque, dès que, aussitôt que,** or **après que** immediately precedes a second past action
which is in the compound past, the first action must be in the **passé
surcomposé** or in the compound past. It cannot be in the pluperfect.
(In these constructions, the **passé composé** may be used instead of
the **passé surcomposé,** but it is less exact.)

NOTE: The **passé antérieur** and the **passé surcomposé** are relatively infrequent. They are formed as follows:

> **passé antérieur** = simple past of auxiliary + past participle

> **passé surcomposé** = compound past of auxiliary + past participle

passé antérieur: j'eus parlé, je fus sorti
passé surcomposé: j'ai eu parlé, j'ai été sorti

PATTERN PRACTICE: the use of the **passé surcomposé**

Pattern 8

YOU HEAR   J'ai déjeuné et puis Jacques est venu me voir.
YOU SAY   Quand j'ai eu déjeuné, Jacques est venu me voir.

D. *Remplacez les mots anglais entre parenthèses par l'équivalent français.*

1. Quand nous avons voulu l'acheter, nos voisins (*had sold*) leur auto.
2. (*He had been trying[1] for a year*) à s'évader quand l'occasion s'est enfin présentée.   3. Dès que (*I had finished*) mon travail, je suis allé au café.   4. Jean-Paul (*had found*) une bonne place quand il a dû faire son service militaire.   5. Jacques et Paulette (*had been going out together for three weeks*) quand ils ont décidé de se marier.   6. Dès que l'écrivain (*had given[2] his lecture*), il est reparti.   7. Le suspect (*had locked the door*) quand les agents sont arrivés.   8. Il (*had been calling me for a long time*) quand je l'ai enfin entendu.   9. Quand Michel (*had visited*) le musée, il nous a rejoints au restaurant.   10. Nous (*had tried*) de le voir plusieurs fois, mais sans succès.

---

[1] Use a form of **chercher**.   [2] *give a lecture* = **faire une conférence**

E. *Traduisez en français.*

1. (*vous*) Did he ask you where you had found the billfold?   2. I had been reading for an hour when someone knocked at the door.   3. As soon as I had lost my job, I had to move.   4. We had been looking for the dog for a long time when we heard him bark in[1] the distance.   5. He had already spoken when we arrived.   6. When I had signed

---

[1] **au loin**

the letter, Mark mailed it.   7. (*vous*) Had you already left the store when it began to snow?   8. As soon as we had eaten, the waiter cleared the table.   9. Julia had been there for a half hour when her friend came to get[3] her.

---

[3] Use a form of **chercher**.

V. The Future Perfect

12. What French use of the future perfect corresponds to the English use?

J'**aurai vu** ton professeur quand tu rentreras.

I will have seen *your teacher when you get back.*

In French, as in English, the FUTURE PERFECT describes an action which will have taken place before another future action.

NOTE: The FUTURE PERFECT (**futur antérieur**) is made up of the future of the AUXILIARY + THE PAST PARTICIPLE of the verb. Ex.: j'**aurai parlé**, je **serai sorti.**

13. When is the future perfect used in French where the English might use the present perfect?

Quand Albert **aura écrit** la lettre, je vous la montrerai.

When *Albert* has written *the letter,* *I'll show it to you.*

The FUTURE PERFECT is used in French with adverbial conjunctions of time such as **quand, lorsque, dès que, aussitôt que,** and **après que** to express an action which will have taken place before another future action. English generally uses the present perfect in such cases.

F. *Traduisez en français.*

1. (*vous*) That family will have already left when you arrive in Tours.
2. (*tu*) When you have finished that, send it to me.   3. (*vous*) When we have bought our new car, come and[1] see it.   4. As soon as they have arrived, we'll go for a walk.   5. Jack will learn to play[2] the violin after his brother has learned to play[2] the piano.   6. When I

---

[1] Translate: *Come to see it.*   [2] Omit *to play* in translation.

have received my check, I'll cash it immediately.   7. (*tu*) Come back as soon as you get out of the meeting.

PATTERN PRACTICE: the future perfect

Pattern 9

> YOU HEAR   Jean écrira la lettre et puis il vous la montrera.
> YOU SAY   Quand Jean aura écrit la lettre, il vous la montrera.

VI. Conditional Sentences

14. What are the most common types of French conditional sentences?

(a) Si nous **travaillons,** nous **gagne-rons** de l'argent.

If we work, *we* will earn *some money.*

(b) Si nous **étions** riches, nous **irions** en France.

If we were *rich, we* would go *to France.*

(c) Si vous **aviez parlé** français, Marie-Claire vous **aurait compris.**

If you had spoken *French, Marie-Claire* would have understood *you.*

The three most common tense sequences in conditional sentences are:

si-(*if*)-CLAUSE	CONCLUSION
present	future
imperfect	conditional
pluperfect	past conditional

G. *Remplacez les infinitifs par la forme convenable du verbe.*

1. Si Philippe partait, il (falloir) lui demander pourquoi.   2. Si vous me (poser) la question, je vous aurais répondu.   3. S'il le faut, nous (se battre).   4. Je (être) très content si mon frère réussissait.   5. Si je (savoir) cela, je n'y serais pas allé.   6. Je (partir) si vous continuez à me regarder comme cela.   7. Si l'auto ne marche pas, nous (prendre) l'autobus.   8. S'il avait fait beau, nous (aller) vous voir.

9. Si Olga (parler) français, vous n'auriez pas besoin d'un interprète.

H. *Traduisez en français.*

1. (*tu*) If you do what I tell you, everything will come out all right.
2. I would be glad if I could retire[1] next year.   3. If I were free,
I'd accept their invitation.   4. If he would speak louder, one could
hear what he is saying.   5. (*vous*) You would have seen our slides if
you had come sooner.   6. If I earned more[2], I'd look for a larger
apartment.   7. If I go to Paris now, I will not come back until[3]
Easter.   8. I would have answered him if I had heard him call.
9. If Margaret had not been sick, she would have attended the
lecture.

---

[1] **prendre ma retraite**   [2] **davantage**   [3] **avant**

PATTERN PRACTICE: conditional sentences

Pattern 10

YOU HEAR   Quand nous aurons assez d'argent, nous irons en Angleterre.

YOU SAY   Si nous avons assez d'argent, nous irons en Angleterre.

Pattern 11

YOU HEAR   Je ne suis pas riche. Je n'achète pas beaucoup de disques.

YOU SAY   Si j'étais riche, j'achèterais beaucoup de disques.

Pattern 12

YOU HEAR   Je n'ai pas appris le français. Je n'ai pas compris Monsieur
Alain.

YOU SAY   Si j'avais appris le français, j'aurais compris Monsieur
Alain.

15. What other tense sequences exist in conditional sentences?

PLUPERFECT + CONDITIONAL

Si vous **aviez fait** votre travail, vous   *If you* had done *your work, you* could
pourriez venir avec nous au-   *come with us today.*
jourd'hui.

PRESENT + PRESENT

S'il **pleut,** je **reste** à la maison.   *If it* rains, *I* stay *home.*

Si nous **avions pris** des précautions, nous n'**aurions** pas ces ennuis maintenant.	*If* we had taken *precautions, we* wouldn't have *this trouble now.*

S'ils **ont pris** l'avion, ils **seront** bientôt ici.	*If* they have taken *the airplane, they* will *soon* be *here.*

Almost any tense sequence which is possible in English conditional sentences is also possible in French conditional sentences. However:

Si vous **faites** votre travail, vous **gagnerez** beaucoup d'argent.	If *you* will do *your work, you* will earn *a lot of money.*
Si elle **écoutait** ses parents, elle ne **sortirait** jamais.	If *she* would obey *her parents, she* would *never* go out.

In French, neither the future nor the conditional can ever be used after **si** when **si** means *if*.

Je ne sais pas **si** Jean **viendra.**	*I don't know* whether *John will come.*

When **si** means *whether*, the French future and conditional may follow it.

I. *Traduisez en français.*

1. (*vous*) If you had left earlier, you would already be in Cannes. 2. If the children have gone to bed, they must be[1] asleep now. 3. If the students spent a lot of money, they always managed to[2] get more. 4. (*vous*) If you listen carefully, you will be able to follow his thought. 5. If he would paint his car, he could keep it another[3] year. 6. (*tu*) If you like football, come and[4] see the game[5] with me. 7. (*vous*) You mustn't hesitate to tell me if you are bored. 8. If he has found[6] that out, he must be furious.

---

[1] *be asleep* = **dormir** [2] **pour en avoir davantage** [3] **encore un an** [4] Not «**et**». [5] **le match** [6] *find out* = **apprendre**

J. *Remplacez l'infinitif par la forme convenable du verbe.*

1. Quand ils ne (être) plus là, je ne sais pas ce que je ferai. 2. Voilà

un mois que vous (avoir) mon livre. Pouvez-vous me le rendre?
3. Quel sale temps! Il (pleuvoir) depuis ce matin.   4. Nous (préparer) un excellent dîner quand les invités ont téléphoné qu'ils ne
pouvaient pas venir.   5. Georges (aller) obtenir son diplôme quand
il est tombé malade.   6. Je garderai cette grammaire quand je
(finir) mon cours.   7. Si tu (épouser) cette jeune fille, tes parents
(être) très heureux.   8. J'ai toujours pensé que cela (finir) mal.
9. Je lirai ce roman quand je (avoir) le temps.   10. Il avait cru
qu'elle (pouvoir) nous aider le lendemain.   11. Dès que je (apprendre) cela, je suis parti.   12. Donnez-moi la main si vous (avoir)
peur.   13. Encore un mot et je (s'en aller).   14. Quand vous lui
(écrire), faites-lui mes amitiés.   15. Si j'avais su, je (agir) tout autrement.   16. Je (s'endormir) déjà[1] quand ses cris m'ont réveillé.
17. Elle s'est trouvée mieux dès qu'elle (prendre) ce remède.
18. Quand ils (partir), je vous montrerai quelque chose d'intéressant.
19. Si vous (écouter) ses conseils, vous n'en seriez pas là.

---

[1] Where will **déjà** come in the compound tense of a verb?

K. *Traduisez en français. Indiquez oralement la raison de chaque temps.*

1. I must hurry; I am leaving this evening.   2. I wrote them that
we would go to see them Sunday.   3. They had already washed the
car when it began to rain.   4. (*vous*) Tell me what she says[1] to you
as soon as you have seen her.   5. (*vous*) If you were willing to see
him, he would be very happy.   6. When I came into the living
room, everyone had already left.   7. He has been studying Russian
for two years, but he does not know it very well.   8. He will be
horrified when he learns what has happened.   9. If she had understood me, things[2] would have been very different.   10. As soon as
she had won the contest, she changed.   11. (*vous*) Did you tell him
that we would not be home tomorrow?   12. I'll speak to him of
that matter as soon as I see him.   13. We had finished our meal
when we heard the newscast.   14. I will travel when I have saved[3]
enough.   15. If the weather[4] is good, I always take a walk. 16. (*tu*)
What are you doing tonight?   17. (*tu*) When you speak to him, be
very polite.   18. When he realized that he was wrong, he changed
his mind.   19. I'll talk to him only if you come with me.

---

[1] Does this verb express something happening now or something that will happen?   [2] Use
the definite article.   [3] *save enough* = **faire assez d'économies**   [4] Use an idiomatic expression with **faire.**

Problem Words

31. little

(a) When to use peu

Jeannot lit **peu**, il préfère s'amuser.   *Johnnie reads* little, *he prefers to have a good time.*

When **peu,** unaccompanied by the indefinite article, modifies a verb, it means *little, only a little, not very much.*

(b) When to use un peu

Si tu as **un peu** d'argent, mets-le de côté.   *If you have* a little *money, save it.*

But **un peu** means *a little* or *some.*

32. live

(a) When to use habiter

Nos amis **habitent** { à Genève. / Genève.   *Our friends* live *in Geneva.*

To indicate where one lives, the French commonly use the verb **habiter,** which may be followed either directly by the place or by the French equivalent of *in + place.* It is somewhat synonymous with the English *inhabit,* but it is much more common.

The verb **demeurer,** formerly very frequently used for *live* in the above sense, has now been almost entirely replaced by **habiter.**

(b) When to use vivre

Monsieur Seydoux **vit** de ses revenus.   *Mr. Seydoux* lives *from his income.*
Il est mort comme il **a vécu.**   *He died as he* lived.
Monsieur Rochebois **vivait** entière- ment pour sa famille.   *Mr. Rochebois* lived *entirely for his family.*

The verb **vivre** means *live* in a larger and more general sense and is sometimes synonymous with *exist.* It is occasionally used in the sense of **habiter,** but the learner should avoid using it in this sense.

33. long

(a) How to say *as long as*

Tant que je serai là, il n'y aura rien à craindre.

As long as I am *there, there will be nothing to fear.*

The time expression *as long as* is rendered in French by **tant que** and is followed by the FUTURE whenever futurity is implied.

(b) How to say *how long*

Combien de temps avez-vous travaillé pour lui?

How long *have you worked for him?*

Pendant combien de temps êtes-vous resté en France?

How long *did you stay in France?*

The English *how long,* meaning *how much time,* may be expressed in French by **combien de temps** or **pendant combien de temps.**

Depuis quand êtes-vous ici?

How long *have you been here?*

Depuis combien de temps attends-tu?

How long *have you been waiting?*

The expressions **depuis quand** and **depuis combien de temps** are often used with the PRESENT where English uses *how long* + PRESENT PERFECT PROGRESSIVE to express the same idea.

(c) How to say *for a long time*

Nous avons parlé **longtemps** de ton avenir.

We spoke about your future for a long time.

Il y a **longtemps** que je connais les Jourdan.

I have known the Jourdans for a long time.

The English *a long time* is expressed in French by the adverb **longtemps.**

(d) How to say *at length*

Nous avons parlé **longuement** de ton avenir.

We spoke at length *of your future.*

The English *at length* is expressed in French by the adverb **longuement,** when *at length = in detail.*

34. make

How to say *make someone* + ADJECTIVE

Vous **me rendez très heureux** en
disant cela.

You make me very happy *in saying
that.*

The French equivalent of *to make someone* + ADJECTIVE is **rendre
quelqu'un** + ADJECTIVE.

CAUTION: Do NOT use the construction «faire quelqu'un» + adjective. French uses **rendre** in such situations.

L. *Remplacez les mots anglais par leur équivalent français.*

1. Je ne conduis pas depuis (*a long time*), mais je suis très prudente.
2. Inutile de se faire trop de soucis; il faut (*live*) au jour le jour.
3. Henriette écrit (*little*), mais elle nous téléphone souvent. 4. Votre
présence (*made*) la soirée très agréable. 5. J'ai (*at length*) réfléchi à
ce que vous m'avez dit. 6. Monsieur et Madame Renaud ont une
belle auto, mais ils (*live*) dans une très vieille maison. 7. Il faut faire
(*a little*) de gymnastique tous les matins. 8. J'observe vos progrès
depuis (*a long time*) sans rien dire.

M. *Traduisez en français. Attention aux mots en italique.*

1. I know your friend Daniel *a little*. 2. I *lived* in a large city for
twenty years. 3. (*vous*) If you remain here too *long*, you will forget
your native language. 4. (*vous*) Don't smoke so much, it[1] will *make*
you sick. 5. (*vous*) You really give me *little* time to[2] do that. 6. People
live a great deal *longer* today than formerly. 7. The mayor spoke
at length concerning the traffic problems. 8. Mr. Mollet no longer
reads the newspaper; it[1] *makes* him nervous. 9. Those young people
went out for[3] *a long time* together before getting married. 10. (*tu*)
Wait *a little*.

---

[1] **ça** [2] **pour** [3] Omit in translation.

Verb Review

Review the verbs **envoyer** and **faire** according to the outline on page 283.

CHAPTER 10

Relatives

A relative pronoun is one which connects a dependent to an independent clause. The relative pronoun is part of the dependent clause, performs a function in that clause and usually begins the dependent clause. The English relative pronouns are *who, whom, whose, which, that,* and *what*. Ex.: The student *who* wrote that essay is a genius.

The relative pronoun normally refers back to some noun in the independent clause. This noun is called the antecedent of the pronoun. In the above example, the antecedent of *who* is "student."

Sometimes, however, the relative pronoun is indefinite. In that case, there is no antecedent in the English sentence. Ex.: My father does not know *what* I am doing.

1. What relative pronoun is used as the subject of its clause?

C'est le professeur **qui** parle.　　　　*It is the teacher* who *is talking.*
C'est une voiture **qui** coûte très cher.　　*It is a car* which *costs a great deal.*

The relative pronoun **qui** is used as the subject of its clause, whether it refers to a person or a thing.

PATTERN PRACTICE: the use of **qui**

Pattern 1

　　YOU HEAR　Voilà une belle jeune fille. Elle va se marier.
　　YOU SAY　Voilà une belle jeune fille qui va se marier.

125

2. What relative pronoun is used as the object of its clause?

Je voudrais voir les malades **que**   *I should like to see the sick persons* whom
vous soignez.   *you are taking care of.*
Montrez-moi la voiture **que** vous   *Show me the car* that *you want.*
voulez.

The relative pronoun **que** is used as the object of its clause, whether it refers to a person or a thing.

The object relative pronoun may be omitted in English but not in French. Ex.: *Is the book you bought interesting?* Est-ce que le livre **que** vous avez acheté est intéressant?

PATTERN PRACTICE: the use of **que**

Pattern 2

    YOU HEAR   Voilà un beau tableau. Je vais l'acheter.
    YOU SAY   Voilà un beau tableau que je vais acheter.

3. Which two relative pronouns are used after prepositions?

Où habitent les amis avec $\begin{cases} \textbf{qui} \\ \textbf{lesquels} \end{cases}$ *Where do the friends with* whom *you*
vous parlez français?   *speak French live?*

Montrez-moi la clé avec **laquelle**   *Show me the key with* which *you opened*
vous avez ouvert ma porte.   *my door.*

After a preposition, either **qui** or a form of **lequel** may be used to refer to persons; a form of **lequel** is used to refer to things.

The forms of **lequel** are: **lequel, laquelle, lesquels, lesquelles.**

PATTERN PRACTICE: preposition + relative

Pattern 3
(In this exercise, the antecedent is always a person, therefore, either **qui** or a form of **lequel** could be used. However, use **qui,** which is simpler and more common.)

    YOU HEAR   Voilà le professeur. Je lui ai donné mon livre ce matin.
    YOU SAY   Voilà le professeur à qui j'ai donné mon livre ce matin.

Pattern 4

YOU HEAR   Voilà ma machine à écrire. J'ai écrit cette lettre avec
           cette machine à écrire.

YOU SAY   Voilà la machine à écrire avec **laquelle** j'ai écrit cette
           lettre.

4. How is the relative pronoun *what* expressed in French? And how is *everything that* **expressed?**

(a) SUBJECT

Ce qui est sur la table est à moi.	*What is on the table is mine.*
Il ne faut pas faire **ce qui** est dé-fendu.	*You mustn't do* what *is forbidden.*
Avez-vous lu **tout ce qui** est dans votre bibliothèque?	*Have you read* everything *that is in your library?*

(b) OBJECT

Ce que vous écrivez est intéressant.	*What you are writing is interesting.*
Savez-vous **ce que** Jean a dit?	*Do you know* what *John said?*
Dites-moi **tout ce que** vous faites.	*Tell me* everything that *you are doing.*

(c) AFTER A PREPOSITION

Ce à quoi je pense est un secret.	*What I am thinking* about *is a secret.*
Je ne comprends pas **de quoi** vous parlez.	*I don't understand* what *you are talking about.*
Maurice a fini ses devoirs, **après quoi** il est sorti.	*Maurice finished his exercises,* after which *he went out.*

The English *what* is expressed in French by
- (a) **ce qui** when it is the subject of its clause;
- (b) **ce que** when it is the object of its clause;
- (c) PREPOSITION + **quoi** or **ce** + PREPOSITION + **quoi** when it is used with a preposition.

In these combinations, **ce** constitutes the antecedent of **qui** and **que.**

The relative **quoi** is sometimes an indefinite which is expressed in English by *which.*

The English *everything that* is expressed in French by
- (a) **tout ce qui** when it is the subject of its clause;
- (b) **tout ce que** when it is the object of its clause.

PATTERN PRACTICE: **ce qui** and **ce que**

Pattern 5

> YOU HEAR   Montrez-moi la lettre qui est sur la table.
> YOU SAY   Montrez-moi ce qui est sur la table.

Pattern 6

> YOU HEAR   J'ai corrigé l'exercice que Jean a écrit.
> YOU SAY   J'ai corrigé ce que Jean a écrit.

5. How can the relative pronouns be presented in graphic tabular form?

FUNCTION	PERSONS	THINGS	*what*
SUBJECT	**qui**	**qui**	**ce qui**
OBJECT	**que**	**que**	**ce que**
after preposition	**qui** **lequel***	**lequel***	**quoi**

A. *Remplacez le mot anglais par le mot français.*

1. (*What*) vous dites est vrai.   2. Les conseils (*that*) vous m'avez donnés sont excellents.   3. Les choses (*which*) semblent compliquées sont souvent bien simples.   4. L'acte dans (*which*) elle était le mieux était le dernier.   5. Il voudrait savoir à (*what*) vous vous intéressez. 6. (*What*) se passe aujourd'hui est terrible!   7. Le professeur (*who*) va parler vient de France.   8. L'ami sur (*whom*) je comptais n'est pas venu.   9. L'homme (*whom*) la police vient d'arrêter est un espion. 10. C'est Jeanne avec (*whom*) je suis sorti dimanche.   11. (*What*) je vais chanter maintenant est très connu.   12. Moi (*who*) vous parle, j'ai passé par là.   13. Les roses (*which*) vous m'avez données sont superbes.

---

* i.e., **lequel, laquelle, lesquels,** or **lesquelles,** according to the gender of the antecedent. Sometimes **ce** + preposition + **quoi** is required.

B. *Traduisez en français.*

1. (*vous*) The dress[1] you are wearing is very pretty.   2. The carpenter to whom I spoke is very nice.   3. (*vous*) My father, who is a businessman, will come to see you.   4. What we are studying is very useful.   5. (*tu*) The friend whom you invited is charming.   6. (*vous*) I do not understand what you are speaking of.   7. The road by which he came is very bad.   8. (*vous*) Show me everything that you have in your drawer.   9. (*tu*) Tell me of[2] what you are thinking.   10. She gave the children some cookies, after which they left.   11. (*vous*) What is on the table is yours, but everything that is on the desk is mine.

---

[1] The relative pronoun is missing in English but must be expressed in French. See page 126, §2.   [2] Not «de».

PATTERN PRACTICE: various relatives

Pattern 7

YOU HEAR   Vous avez écrit un conte qui est intéressant.

YOU SAY   Le conte que vous avez écrit est intéressant.

Pattern 8

(This exercise contains various types of relatives. You are to choose the proper one.)

YOU HEAR   Voilà une belle voiture. J'aimerais l'acheter.

YOU SAY   Voilà une belle voiture que j'aimerais acheter.

6. How is de + relative normally expressed in French?

Le livre **dont** vous parlez est connu.   *The book* of which *you are speaking is well known.*

The form **dont** normally replaces **de** + RELATIVE.

NOTE: When a preposition or a prepositional phrase comes between the antecedent and the relative, then **de** + RELATIVE are used instead of **dont**. The relative **dont** must follow its antecedent immediately and therefore must stand first in its clause. Ex.: C'est un livre au milieu **duquel** il y a de jolies illustrations.

Also, *from which* (meaning *whence*) is usually expressed by **d'où** rather than **dont**. Ex.: Je n'ai jamais visité la ville **d'où** il vient.

PATTERN PRACTICE: the use of **dont**

Pattern 9

YOU HEAR   Marie est une jeune fille. Vous m'avez souvent parlé d'elle.
YOU SAY   Marie est une jeune fille dont vous m'avez souvent parlé.

7. Sentences with the French word *dont* present certain problems of word order. What is a practical way of determining the word order of such sentences?

Voici le docteur Galand   *Here is Dr. Galand*
   dont le fils est mon meilleur ami.   { whose *son is my best friend.*
                                     { of whom *the son is my best friend.*

Note that in French, when **dont** is identified with the subject of its clause, the subject is modified by the definite article.

Montrez-moi le livre   *Show me the book*
   dont vous connaissez l'auteur.   { whose *author you know.*
                                  { of which *you know the author.*

Note that when **dont** is identified with the object of its clause, that object is in quite a different position than it is in the corresponding English clause.

The word order of a French clause introduced by **dont** is:

***

dont + SUBJECT + VERB + rest of sentence

***

In order to arrive at the French word order in **dont**-clauses, instead of using *whose* in the English sentence, substitute *of whom* or *of which*. The rest of the English sentence will then fall into exactly the same word order that the French clause normally has.

PATTERN PRACTICE: **dont** modifying the subject and the object of its clause

Pattern 10

YOU HEAR   Voilà une pauvre femme. Son fils travaille chez nous.
YOU SAY   Voilà une pauvre femme dont le fils travaille chez nous.

Pattern 11

YOU HEAR   Paris est une ville. Nous connaissons ses divers quartiers.
YOU SAY   Paris est une ville dont nous connaissons les divers quartiers.

C. *Traduisez en français.*

1. That is a decision of which he will repent.   2. Jack is a young man whose parents are very strict.   3. *(vous)* We know the lady whose husband you saw in Paris.   4. I finally found the book the title of which I had forgotten.   5. I recommend the doctor whose office[1] is on the first[2] floor.   6. He has trouble[3] with the neighbors whose dogs bark so much.   7. *(vous)* The family whose address you sent me has moved.   8. That actress, whose talent I admire so much, lives in Sweden now.   9. The friend whose children George adopted died ten years ago.

---

[1] Not «bureau».   [2] Not «premier étage».   [3] The plural form of **ennui, histoire** or **difficulté.**

8. How is the relative *when* expressed in French?

Au moment **où** nous sommes arrivés ils étaient tous à table.	*At the time* when *we arrived, they were all at the table.*
Je vous dirai cela le jour **où** vous vous marierez.	*I'll tell you that the day* when *you get married.*

The ordinary French word for *when* is **quand.** But when the English word *when* modifies a preceding noun — usually a time expression —, it is normally expressed by **où** in French.

The relative **où** also means *where* and indicates place, but this **où** constitutes no problem to the English-speaking student. Ex.: J'ai visité la ville **où** ce poète a vécu.

D. *Traduisez en français.*

1. *(vous)* Show me the house where Balzac was born.   2. *(tu)* Do you remember the day when we saw each other for the first time?   3. I'll leave the moment[1] he arrives[2].   4. *(tu)* I did not feel well the evening when you came to see me.   5. *(vous)* Have you forgotten the winter when it was so cold?   6. I prefer the months when there is sun.

---

[1] French uses **au moment** followed by a relative pronoun.   [2] What tense? See page 112, §6.

PATTERN PRACTICE: the relative **où**

Pattern 12

    YOU HEAR   J'ai rencontré Jean cette année-là. Il était à Paris.
    YOU SAY   J'ai rencontré Jean l'année où il était à Paris.

Pattern 13

YOU HEAR   Nous avons parlé des vacances quand nous nous sommes rencontrés dans la rue. (le jour)

YOU SAY   Nous avons parlé des vacances le jour où nous nous sommes rencontrés dans la rue.

EXERCICES D'ENSEMBLE

E. *Remplacez le mot anglais par son équivalent français.*

1. Pouvez-vous me prêter les livres (*which I need*)?   2. Connaissez-vous la femme (*who*) vient de passer?   3. Il est parti; c'est le mois (*when*) il prend ses vacances.   4. Où est la montre (*which*) je vous ai achetée?   5. Racontez-nous seulement (*what*) est important.   6. Je me demande avec (*what*) ils ont pu faire cela.   7. Les élèves (*of which*) vous vous plaignez ne travaillent pas assez.   8. La sonnerie (*that*) vous entendez marque la fin de la classe.   9. Il fait (*everything that*) il veut.   10. Je vous prêterai ma voiture le jour (*when*) vous aurez du travail.   11. Elle vous promettra tout (*that*) vous voulez.   12. L'homme (*who*) doit venir me voir ce matin est russe.   13. C'est un ami pour (*whom*) je ferais n'importe quoi.   14. Puisque vous le pouvez, prenez donc (*what*) est devant vous.   15. Je ne sais pas exactement à (*what*) il pense.   16. Le train dans (*which*) je me trouvais a eu un accident.

F. *Traduisez en français.*

1. (*vous*) The person you are making fun of is one of my friends.   2. I remember the year when we went to Europe.   3. The man for whom I work is very nice.   4. (*vous*) What you say concerning[1] them does not surprise me.   5. (*tu*) You must ask him what he is suffering from.   6. (*tu*) I cannot read what you wrote.   7. The friends who invited us have a sailboat.   8. (*vous*) Tell[2] me about the young man whose aunt is so rich.   9. The chair on which he sat down broke[3].   10. What is happening in those countries is dangerous.   11. (*vous*) I should like to know what you are thinking of[4] now.   12. She left the[5] moment I entered.   13. The dress with which she had[6] so much success came from Paris.   14. I cannot stand the noise the neighbors[7] are making.   15. I like people who are optimistic.   16. (*tu*) Tell me

---

[1] **à leur sujet**   [2] *tell about* = **parler de**   [3] Use the reflexive form of the verb in this case.   [4] Not «de».   [5] The French say the equivalent of the English *at the moment when*.   [6] Use the **passé composé**.   [7] Place this subject after its verb.

what makes[8] you so sad.   17. Where are the books whose titles I mentioned yesterday?

---

[8] Use a form of **rendre.**

Problem Words

35. marry

(**a**) How to say *to get married*

Michelle **s'est mariée** au mois de juin.	*Michelle* got married *in the month of June.*

French expresses *to get married* by **se marier.**

(**b**) How to say *to marry someone*

Robert **s'est marié avec la fille du patron.**	*Robert* married the boss's daughter.
Isabelle devrait **épouser un homme riche.**	*Isabelle should* marry a rich man.

French expresses *to marry someone* by either **se marier avec quelqu'un** or **épouser quelqu'un.**

(**c**) How to say *to marry someone to someone*

Les Moreau **vont marier leur fille à** l'aîné des Duparc.	*The Moreaux* are going to marry their daughter to *the oldest Duparc boy.*

French expresses *to marry someone to someone* by **marier quelqu'un à quelqu'un.**

36. miss

(**a**) When *miss = feel the absence of*

Nous **regrettons** notre ancienne maison.	*We* miss *our former house.*

The verb **regretter** may be used in the sense of *miss;* in that case, the subject of the English and French sentences is the same.

Ma voiture **me manque** beaucoup ici.	I miss *my car a great deal here.*

The verb **manquer** may also be used in the sense of *miss,* but in that case, the object missed becomes the subject of the French sentence.

(b) When *miss = fail to reach*

Gérard **a manqué** l'autobus; il va encore être en retard.	*Gerard* missed *the bus; he is going to be late again.*
Pourquoi **avez**-vous **manqué** la classe?	*Why did you* miss *class?*

French uses the verb **manquer** to express the idea of missing a means of transportation or of missing a gathering of some kind. With this sense, the subject of **manquer** is the person and the object of the sentence is the thing missed. Note that **manquer la classe** means *to cut class.*

37. more

(a) How to say *more and more*

Je m'intéresse **de plus en plus** à la politique.	*I am becoming* more and more *interested in politics.*
Je suis **de plus en plus** étonné.	*I am* more and more *surprised.*

The English *more and more* + ADJECTIVE is expressed by **de plus en plus** modifying an adjective, an adverb or a verb.

NOTE: The formula *more and more* is really an intensive comparative, so that it also includes the English comparatives in *-er:*

Georges devient **de plus en plus** grand.	*George is getting* taller and taller.

(b) How to say *the more . . . the more . . .*

Plus je connais Marianne, **plus** j'apprécie ses qualités.	The more *I know Marianne*, the more *I appreciate her good qualities.*
Plus Georges est riche, **plus** il veut d'argent.	The richer *George is*, the more *money he wants.*

CAUTION: Do NOT express *the more . . . the more* by «le plus . . . le plus». The correct formula is **plus . . ., plus . . . .**

French expresses *the more . . . the more* by **plus** + CLAUSE, followed by **plus** + CLAUSE.

NOTE: The formula *the more . . . the more* is a type of comparative, so that it also includes the English comparatives in *-er*, as in the sentence:

Les gens croient que **plus** on est riche, **plus** on est heureux.	*People think that* the richer *one is*, the happier *one is.*

38. next

(a) When *next* is expressed by **prochain**

Nous irons voir vos amis en France   *We'll go to see your friends in France*
   l'été **prochain**.   *next summer.*
Est-ce que Toulon est le **prochain** *Is Toulon the next stop?*
   arrêt?

The ordinary French word for *next* is **prochain**. In general, it can be used, except when one could substitute *following* for *next* in the English sentence without changing the meaning of the sentence.

(b) When *next* is expressed by **suivant**

J'ai expliqué à Robert pourquoi   *I explained to Robert why we had re-*
   nous étions retournés en Suisse *turned to Switzerland the next (= fol-*
   l'été **suivant**.   *lowing) summer.*
Regardez la page **suivante**.   *Look at the next (= following) page.*

Whenever *next = following* and when *following* can be substituted for *next* without changing the meaning of the sentence, French uses **suivant**.

CAUTION: Do NOT use «prochain» for *next* when, *next = following*. This is a very common error.

(c) How to say *the next day*

Le **lendemain**   ⎫
Le **jour suivant**   ⎬ nos invités sont partis.   *The next day our guests left.*
Le **jour après**   ⎭

The next day may be expressed by **le lendemain, le jour suivant** or **le jour après**.

CAUTION: Do NOT say «le jour prochain» for *the next day*.

(d) How to say *the next morning (afternoon, evening,* etc.)

Le **lendemain matin** ⎫
Le **matin suivant**   ⎬ il a plu sans arrêt.   *The next morning it rained*
Le **matin après**   ⎭   *continually.*

The adverb **lendemain** is used with times of day to express the English *next*.

G. *Remplacez les mots anglais par leur équivalent français.*

1. On ne demande plus beaucoup aujourd'hui l'avis de ses parents pour (*get married*). 2. Allons bon! nous (*missed*) le train de sept heures quarante-cinq. 3. (*The more*) ça change, (*the more*) c'est la même chose. 4. Je serai à New York à minuit, et je m'envolerai pour Paris (*the next night*). 5. On dit que cet acteur va (*marry*) une ancienne camarade d'enfance. 6. Quand je voyage, je (*miss*) le confort de ma maison. 7. Je suis (*more and more*) étonné par ton indifférence. 8. Madame Drouet passera (*next week*) chez nous, et elle ira chez vous (*the next week*). 9. Paul (*got married*) beaucoup trop jeune. 10. J'ai passé mon baccalauréat et (*the next year*) j'ai fait mon service militaire. 11. Suivez mon conseil: (*marry*) une jeune fille de votre condition.

H. *Traduisez en français. Attention aux mots en italique.*

1. (*vous*) Why don't you *marry* Albertine? 2. Robert will spend *next* year in Italy. 3. *The more* I know Paris, *the more* I like it. 4. Do the children *miss* the television set? 5. Mr. Martel would like to *marry* his daughter to a doctor. 6. (*vous*) If you *miss* your bus[1], you will have to wait until tomorrow morning. 7. That child is becoming *more and more* unbearable. 8. Edmond went to bed late and the *next* morning, he didn't hear his alarm clock. 9. (*tu*) I *miss* you a great deal these days. 10. If they arrive at midnight, they will certainly not leave[2] again the *next* day. 11. Michael and Colette met at Nice and will *get married* in Paris. 12. I arrived in London on[3] June 7 and the *next* week I went to Brussels. 13. *The older* one is, *the harder* it is to get around.

---

[1] In French, a city bus is **un autobus,** whereas an interurban bus is **un autocar.**   [2] *leave again* = **repartir**   [3] For how to express French dates, see page 159.

Verb Review

Review the verbs **falloir** and **lire** according to the outline on page 283.

CHAPTER 11

The Subjunctive

In connection with the subjunctive, we must consider four important questions:

(a) What is the basic function of the subjunctive as compared with that of the indicative?

(b) Under what specific circumstances is the subjunctive used in French, and how do those uses fit into the basic concept of the function of the subjunctive?

(c) When is the present subjunctive used and when the past subjunctive, in other words, what is the concept of time in the subjunctive tenses?

(d) When must the infinitive be used instead of the subjunctive, even though the nature of the main clause seems to indicate a subjunctive in the subordinate clause?

1. What is the essential difference between the indicative and the subjunctive mode when they deal with facts?

INDICATIVE	SUBJUNCTIVE
Jean **est** à la maison.	**Nous sommes contents** que Jean **soit** à la maison.
John is *at home.*	We are glad *that John* is *at home.*
Marie ne **sait** pas la leçon.	**Je regrette** que Marie ne **sache** pas la leçon.
Marie does *not* know *the lesson.*	I regret *that Marie* does *not* know *the lesson.*

Les enfants **ont perdu** leur ballon.   **C'est dommage** que les enfants
                                             aient perdu leur ballon.

The children lost *their ball.*   It is too bad *that the children* lost
                                             their ball.

The INDICATIVE states an objective fact. It is concerned with the fact as a fact.

The SUBJUNCTIVE sometimes deals with facts, but in such cases it deals with them not objectively but from the point of view of the speaker of the main clause. It indicates the subjective attitude of the speaker in the main clause toward the action in the subordinate clause.

2. What other type of state or action does the subjunctive deal with? (Compare it with the indicative in this respect.)

INDICATIVE	SUBJUNCTIVE
Vous **faites** votre travail.	**Je voudrais** que vous **fassiez** votre travail.
You do *your work.*	I wish *that you* would do *your work.*
Monsieur Texier **viendra** demain.	**Il est possible** que Monsieur Texier **vienne** demain.
Mr. Texier will come *tomorrow.*	It is possible *that Mr. Texier* will come *tomorrow.*
Nous **sommes arrivés** trop tard.	**Roger avait peur** que nous **soyons arrivés** trop tard.
We arrived *too late.*	Roger was afraid *that we* arrived *too late.*

The INDICATIVE states an objective fact, whether in the present, past or future.

The SUBJUNCTIVE often deals with hypothetical actions, that is, actions which have not occurred and may never occur. It often states the attitude of the subject in the main clause toward such hypothetical actions.

3. Which types of verbs in the main clause are followed by the subjunctive in the subordinate clause, and why?

Il veut que nous l'**aidions.**   He wishes *us* to help *him.*
Nous craignons qu'il **pleuve.**   We fear *that it* will rain.

Monsieur Bertrand **préférerait** que   *Mr. Bertrand* would prefer to have
sa fille <u>fasse</u> sa médecine à Paris.   *his daughter* study *medicine in Paris.*

Verbs of wishing, preferring, suggesting, etc., and verbs and expressions of emotion, such as fearing, being glad, being sorry, etc.,
all of which indicate the attitude of the subject of the main clause
toward either a fact or a hypothetical action, are followed by the
subjunctive in the subordinate clause, that is, in the clause introduced
by **que.**

NOTE 1: In affirmative statements, the verb **espérer** is always followed by
the indicative. Ex.: J'**espère** que nos invités **viendront.** In interrogative
sentences, it is usually followed by the indicative but may be followed by the
subjunctive. In negative statements, it is followed by the subjunctive.

NOTE 2: Verbs of advising, commanding, permitting, preventing, request-
ing, etc. may be followed by a subjunctive clause, but they are usually followed by **de** + INFINITIVE.

USUAL CONSTRUCTION	POSSIBLE CONSTRUCTION
L'avocat **a conseillé** à son client <u>**d'être**</u> moins exigeant.	L'avocat **a conseillé** <u>que son client **soit**</u> moins exigeant.
L'inspecteur <u>vous</u> **permettra de télé-phoner** à votre femme.	L'inspecteur **permettra** <u>que vous **téléphoniez**</u> à votre femme.
Nous <u>les</u> **avons empêchés** <u>**d'aller**</u> plus loin.	Nous **avons empêché** <u>qu'ils **aillent**</u> plus loin.

**4. When is the present subjunctive used in French? When the past subjunctive?
What is the concept of time in the subjunctive?**

Je suis content que Maurice **puisse**   *I am glad that Maurice* can *do it now.*
le faire maintenant.
Je suis content que Maurice **puisse**   *I am glad that Maurice* will be able *to*
le faire demain.   *do it tomorrow.*
Je suis content que Maurice **ait pu**   *I am glad that Maurice* could *do it*
le faire hier.   *yesterday.*

The only two tenses of the subjunctive used in conversational
French are the present and the past. The PRESENT SUBJUNCTIVE is
used if the action of the subordinate clause takes place <u>at the same
time</u> as the action of the main clause or <u>after</u> the action of the main
clause. The PAST SUBJUNCTIVE is used if the action of the subordinate

clause took place <u>before</u> the action of the main clause. In other words, time in the subjunctive is relative to time in the main clause.

The past subjunctive (**passé du subjonctif**) is a compound tense corresponding to the compound past in the indicative. Ex. (COMPOUND PAST OF INDICATIVE): j'**ai vu,** tu **as parlé,** il **est parti,** (PAST SUBJUNCTIVE): . . . que j'**aie vu,** . . . que tu **aies parlé,** . . . qu'il **soit parti,** etc.

5. When must the infinitive be used instead of a *que*-clause with the subjunctive even after constructions which seem to require a subjunctive?

SUBJUNCTIVE	INFINITIVE
Avez-<u>**vous**</u> peur **que** <u>Marcel</u> **fasse cela?**	Avez-**vous** peur **de faire cela?**
Are <u>you</u> *afraid* that <u>Marcel</u> will do it?	*Are* <u>you</u> *afraid* that <u>you</u> will do it?
<u>**Anne-Marie**</u> veut **que** <u>vous</u> le **sachiez.**	**Anne-Marie** veut **le savoir.**
<u>Anne-Marie</u> *wants* <u>you</u> to know it.	<u>Anne-Marie</u> *wishes* that <u>she</u> might know it.
<u>Je</u> suis content **que** <u>vous</u> **ayez gagné.**	**Je** suis content **d'avoir gagné.**
<u>I</u> *am glad* that <u>you</u> won.	<u>I</u> *am glad* that <u>I</u> won.

When the subject of a subordinate clause requiring the subjunctive would be the same as the subject of the main clause, the INFINITIVE is normally required instead of **que** with the SUBJUNCTIVE.

Verbs of wishing are followed directly by the infinitive without a preposition; verbs of emotion require **de** before an infinitive.

A. *Remplacez les infinitifs entre parenthèses par la forme convenable du verbe.*

(These verbs must be either in the present or past subjunctive or in some tense of the indicative. Often the sentence will give some indication in its wording of the tense required.)

1. Je veux que tu me (dire) où tu iras ce soir. 2. Nous craignons qu'il (perdre) tout son argent l'année dernière. 3. Georges dit que vous (pouvoir) partir tout de suite. 4. Je suggère que vous (rentrer)

chez vous immédiatement.   5. Nous espérons qu'il ne (pleuvoir) pas demain.   6. Je remarque que Michel et Colette (aller) bien souvent au cinéma ces jours-ci.   7. Vous devez être heureux que votre belle-fille (être) si gentille.   8. Je vois que vous (se moquer) de nous.   9. Êtes-vous content que vos cousins (arriver) hier soir?   10. Elle a toujours peur que son mari (être) en retard.   11. Je m'étonne que nous ne (avoir) pas de ses nouvelles mardi dernier.   12. Vous savez bien que Pierre (finir) son travail le mois prochain.   13. Nous regrettons que vous ne (pouvoir) pas venir avec nous demain.

B. *Traduisez en français.*

(The verbs in the subordinate clauses of the sentences of this exercise are in the present or past subjunctive or in some tense of the indicative, or, the infinitive must be used instead of a **que**-clause.)

1. (*vous*) I am afraid that you do not understand me.   2. (*tu*) You know that she will not come this morning.   3. The announcer says that it will rain tomorrow.   4. I am sorry that I arrived too late.   5. (*vous*) We are glad that you have a new car.   6. When he is somewhere[1] else, he wishes[2] that he were here.   7. (*tu*) We are sorry that Gilbert is not with you.   8. (*tu*) I am afraid that I do not[3] know what you want.   9. (*vous*) Do you want us to speak German with Irene?   10. (*tu*) Aren't you glad that you will spend next year in Spain?   11. I am surprised that Lucy isn't here.   12. (*vous*) I see that you are wearing a new dress.   13. We are surprised that he spoke Italian so fluently at the meeting.   14. (*vous*) We are glad that we were able to go out with you last[4] night.   15. (*tu*) I hope that you are not sick.   16. They are sorry that they cannot[3] stay longer[5].   17. I am afraid that I've lost my billfold.

---

[1] *somewhere else* = **ailleurs**   [2] Use the conditional of **vouloir** to express *wish*   [3] Both parts of the negative precede a simple infinitive. Ex.: **Il est impossible de ne pas rire.**   [4] *last night* = **hier soir**   [5] **plus longtemps**

PATTERN PRACTICE: various types and tenses of the subjunctive, the use of the infinitive for the subjunctive

Pattern 1

YOU HEAR   Georges apprend le français.
YOU SAY   Je veux que Georges apprenne le français.

Pattern 2

YOU HEAR   Mon fils suit vos conseils. J'en suis heureux.
YOU SAY   Je suis heureux que mon fils suive vos conseils.

Pattern 3

YOU HEAR   Je regrette que tu ne puisses pas venir.
YOU SAY   Je regrette que tu n'aies pas pu venir hier.

Pattern 4

YOU HEAR   Sylvie est heureuse que nous connaissions des artistes.
YOU SAY   Sylvie est heureuse de connaître des artistes.

Pattern 5

YOU HEAR   Je regrette d'avoir tellement à faire.
YOU SAY   Je regrette que vous ayez tellement à faire.

6. When is the indicative and when the subjunctive used after impersonal expressions?

INDICATIVE

Il est certain que Louis **est** *intelligent*.
It is certain *that Louis* is intelligent.

Il est évident que vous **savez** votre leçon.
It is obvious *that you* know *your lesson.*

Il est exact que Monsieur et Madame Minard **vont** en France cet été.
It is true *that Mr. and Mrs. Minard* are going *to France this summer.*

SUBJUNCTIVE

Il est possible que Louis **soit** intelligent.
It is possible *that Louis* is *intelligent.*

Il est important que vous **sachiez** votre leçon.
It is important *that you* know *your lesson.*

Il est naturel que Monsieur et Madame Minard **aillent** en France cet été.
It is natural *that Mr. and Mrs. Minard* should go *to France this summer.*

Impersonal expressions which insist on a fact or on the certainty of a fact are followed by the INDICATIVE.

Impersonal expressions where not the fact but the attitude or opinion of the speaker toward a hypothetical state or action is given are followed by the SUBJUNCTIVE.

Among the impersonal expressions followed by the INDICATIVE are:	Among the impersonal expressions followed by the SUBJUNCTIVE are:	
Il est certain	Il est bien	Il est possible
Il est clair	Il est bon	Il est préférable
Il est évident	Il est douteux	Il est peu probable
Il est exact	Il est étonnant	Il est rare
Il est probable	Il est étrange	Il est temps
Il est sûr	Il est important	Il faut
Il est vrai	Il est impossible	Il importe
	Il est juste	Il se peut
	Il est naturel	Il suffit
	Il est nécessaire	Il vaut mieux

C. *Dans le devoir suivant, mettez les infinitifs indiqués entre parenthèses soit au présent soit au passé du subjonctif ou au temps convenable de l'indicatif. Justifiez oralement votre choix du temps et du mode.*

1. Il est évident que vous (avoir) besoin de leçons. 2. Il est étrange que Jacqueline ne nous (écrire) pas depuis son départ. 3. Docteur, vaut-il mieux que vous lui (dire) la vérité? 4. Il est possible que Monsieur Moreau (acheter) cette maison l'année dernière. 5. Il est certain que l'accusé (être) coupable. 6. —Vous paraissez si jeune, Madame! Il est impossible que vous (être) sa mère. 7. Il est sûr qu'ils ne (revenir) pas la semaine dernière. 8. Il serait bon que vous (se reposer) un peu. 9. Il est possible que vous (connaître) cette affaire mieux que moi. 10. Il est vrai que nous (avoir) peur de lui. 11. —Mon garçon, il est grand temps que tu (prendre) tes responsabilités. 12. Il suffit que son fils (dire) ce qu'il veut pour l'obtenir.

D. *Traduisez en français. Justifiez oralement l'emploi du temps et du mode.*

1. (*vous*) It is rare that your wife comes to see us. 2. (*vous*) It is clear that you are mistaken. 3. (*vous*) It is important for you not to speak of this story[1]. 4. It is probable that the teacher will punish those pupils. 5. (*tu*) It is good that you have already finished your work. 6. It is surprising that he is so hateful[2]. 7. (*tu*) It is necessary for[1] me to think[3] before answering you. 8. It is time that the president

---

[1] Rearrange the wording before translating.   [2] **méchant**   [3] Use a form of **réfléchir.**

act energetically.   9. It is doubtful that they have found the money. 10. (*tu*) It is natural that you should wish to have a good time. 11. It is remarkable that man can go to[4] the moon.   12. It is correct[5] that he has never read a single book.   13. I[6] am surprised, but it is possible that I said that.   14. (*vous*) It is evident that you do not work too much.

---

[4] **dans** or **sur**   [5] Not «**correct**»   [6] **Ça m'étonne**

PATTERN PRACTICE: impersonal expressions followed by a clause

Pattern 6

     YOU HEAR   Il est certain que vous savez son adresse. (Il est possible . . .)

     YOU SAY   Il est possible que vous sachiez son adresse.

Pattern 7

     YOU HEAR   Il est indispensable que vous réussissiez à votre examen. (Il est certain . . .)

     YOU SAY   Il est certain que vous réussirez à votre examen.

7. What mode follows verbs of 'thinking' and 'believing' in French?

AFFIRMATIVE	NEGATIVE AND INTERROGATIVE
Je **crois** que vous **êtes** malade.	Je **ne crois pas** que vous $\begin{cases}\textbf{êtes} \\ \textbf{soyez}\end{cases}$ malade.
Il **pense** que sa femme **partira**.	Il **ne pense pas** que sa femme $\begin{cases}\textbf{partira.} \\ \textbf{parte.}\end{cases}$
Nous **croyons** que Paul **a lu** cela.	**Croyez-vous** que Paul $\begin{cases}\textbf{a lu} \text{ cela?} \\ \textbf{ait lu} \text{ cela?}\end{cases}$
Moi, je **trouve** qu'il **a bien fait**.	**Trouvez-vous** qu'il $\begin{cases}\textbf{a} \text{ bien } \textbf{fait?} \\ \textbf{ait} \text{ bien } \textbf{fait?}\end{cases}$

Affirmative forms of verbs of thinking and believing are ALWAYS followed by the indicative — NEVER by the subjunctive.

Negative and interrogative forms of verbs of thinking and believing may be followed by the subjunctive when there is considerable doubt on the part of the speaker and when the speaker is a person who is grammatically precise in his use of the subjunctive. When the element of doubt is minor and especially when the idea in the subordinate clause is of a future nature, the indicative is normally used.

Forms of the verb **douter** are also normally followed by the subjunctive.

NOTE: It is true that the subjunctive after forms of the verb **douter** and after expressions such as **Je ne crois pas** indicates <u>doubt</u>. However, in the great majority of cases, the subjunctive is used to show attitudes other than those of doubt. For instance, the subjunctive after **Il faut que** . . . or **Je suis content que** . . . indicates not the slightest indication of doubt. Students should not try to justify the use of a given subjunctive by saying that it expresses doubt except where doubt is actually involved.

E. *Mettez les infinitifs à la forme convenable et expliquez oralement le temps et le mode que vous aurez choisis.*

1. Je trouve que cette robe vous (aller) très bien.   2. Nous doutons que votre idée (valoir) grand-chose.   3. Je ne pense pas que nous (pouvoir) nous revoir.   4. Ils croient que leur fils (être) toujours un enfant.   5. Ne croyez-vous pas que vos amis (savoir) cela?   6. Je ne crois pas que Jean (venir) demain.   7. Je trouve qu'il (conduire) bien.   8. Je crois que cet homme (connaître) bien son métier. 9. Nous ne pouvons pas croire que Philippe (venir) hier soir.

F. *Traduisez en français.*

1. He thinks we are foolish.   2. (*vous*) Do you think that he will do that?   3. I do not believe that he can get to the airport in time. 4. He believes that they are going to Paris.   5. (*tu*) Do you believe that they will invite us?   6. (*vous*) I don't think that you understand the problem.

PATTERN PRACTICE: affirmative verbs of 'believing' and 'thinking'

Pattern 8

    YOU HEAR   Vous pouvez partir demain.
    YOU SAY   Je crois que vous pouvez partir demain.

8. What are the subordinate conjunctions which are always followed by the subjunctive in French, and what in the nature of their meaning causes them to be followed by a subjunctive rather than an indicative?

afin que ⎫ *in order that* pour que ⎭	à moins que *unless*
bien que ⎫ *although* quoique ⎭	sans que *without*
	avant que *before*
pourvu que ⎫ *provided that* à condition que ⎭	jusqu'à ce que *until*

Each of these expressions embodies a concept which is concerned either with a hypothetical action or with an attitude toward a real action:

(a) **afin que** and **pour que** indicate purpose, and the intended purpose is hypothetical, not yet real.

(b) **bien que** and **quoique** indicate concession on the part of the speaker toward what is either a reality or something which could be so and is therefore hypothetical.

(c) **pourvu que** and **à condition que** introduce a restrictive condition which is not a reality.

(d) **à moins que** and **sans que** also introduce a restrictive condition which is not a reality.

(e) **avant que** and **jusqu'à ce que** are conjunctions concerned with actions to take place at some time after the action of the main clause and which, in the mind of the speaker, depend on some other action taking place. Thus they are restrictive to a certain extent.

9. Under what conditions are these conjunctions replaced by a corresponding preposition which is followed by an infinitive?

Je lui écrirai **pour qu'il sache** cela.
  I *will write him* so that he may know *that.*

Je lui écrirai **pour savoir** cela.
  I *will write him* so that I may know *that.*

Je conduirai vite **afin que vous arriviez** à l'heure.
  I'*ll drive fast* so that you arrive *on time.*

Je conduirai vite **afin d'arriver** à l'heure. ⎧ in order to arrive *on time.*
  I'*ll drive fast* ⎨ so that I may arrive *on time.*

Je viendrai **à moins que** Marc soit malade.
  I'*ll come* unless Mark is sick.

Je viendrai **à moins d'**être malade.
  I'*ll come* unless I am sick.

Je partirai **avant que** Georges ap-prenne les résultats de l'exa-men.

I'*ll leave* before George learns *the results* of the examination.

Je ferai cette affaire **sans que** vous **perdiez** un sou.

I *will carry this thing out* without your losing *a penny.*

Je partirai **avant d'apprendre** les résultats de l'examen.

I'*ll leave* before learning *the results* of the examination.

Je ferai cette affaire **sans perdre** un sou.

I'*ll carry this thing out* without losing *a penny.*

When the subject of the subordinate clause introduced by con-junctions requiring the subjunctive in French would be the same as the subject of the main clause, French normally uses a preposition with an infinitive if such a construction exists.

NOTE: In a few cases, such as in sentences with **bien que, quoique, pourvu que,** and **jusqu'à ce que,** it is impossible to replace a clause in the subjunc-tive by an infinitive construction even when the subject of the main clause and that of the dependent **que**-clause would be the same, since there is no prepositional construction which corresponds to the subordinate conjunc-tions. In these few special cases only, the subjunctive may be used even when the subject of the main clause and that of the dependent clause are the same. Ex.: Nous viendrons **bien que nous soyons** fatigués. Jean-Paul le fera pourvu **qu'il soit** libre.

However, in the case of **à moins que,** one finds both **à moins que** + the subject of the main clause and **à moins de** + the infinitive.

G. *Traduisez en français les phrases suivantes. Attention au temps et au mode.*

1. (*tu*) I'll go with you although I am very busy. 2. (*vous*) Do some-thing so that they will go away sooner. 3. (*tu*) I'll go[1] to the office before I come to see you. 4. (*vous*) Do what you[2] please, provided that you do not make any[3] noise. 5. Daniel will always be poor unless his uncle should die. 6. She refuses to speak, although she knows the whole story. 7. He left without having done half[4] the work. 8. She truly loves me although she doesn't tell me so[5]. 9. How[6] can we leave without their being angry? 10. I sent this letter today so that I might have an answer tomorrow. 11. (*tu*) Have a good time before it is too late. 12. They did everything so that their children might be happy. 13. I'll work until I understand these rules.

---

[1] *go to the office* = **passer par le bureau** [2] Either **vous voulez** or **vous voudrez** [3] **de** [4] *half the* = **la moitié de** + DEFINITE ARTICLE [5] **le** [6] *How can we leave* = **Comment partir**

PATTERN PRACTICE: adverbial conjunctions followed by the subjunctive

Pattern 9

YOU HEAR Je travaillerai. Vous me téléphonerez. (jusqu'à ce que)
YOU SAY Je travaillerai jusqu'à ce que vous me téléphoniez.

Pattern 10

YOU HEAR Je resterai avec vous pour que vous écriviez cette lettre.
YOU SAY Je resterai avec vous pour écrire cette lettre.

10. Why do the sentences on the left use the indicative in the subordinate clause while those on the right use the subjunctive?

INDICATIVE	SUBJUNCTIVE
	(a) the antecedent is as yet un-attained
J'ai un domestique **qui sait** tout faire.	Je cherche un domestique **qui sache** tout faire.
	(b) doubt is expressed as to the attainability of the antecedent
Vous avez un collègue **qui est** très au courant de ces choses.	Avez-vous un collègue **qui soit** très au courant de ces choses?
	(c) the antecedent is negative
Je connais quelqu'un **qui peut** vous accompagner.	Je ne connais personne **qui puisse** vous accompagner.
Il y a des professeurs **qui vont** en Europe tous les ans.	Il n'y a pas de professeur **qui aille** en Europe tous les ans.

The INDICATIVE is normally used in dependent relative clauses, since relative clauses normally state a fact.

The SUBJUNCTIVE is often used in relative clauses where there is some doubt or denial of the existence or attainability of the antecedent, but certain tenses of the indicative are also found in such clauses.

H. *Remplacez l'infinitif entre parenthèses par le temps convenable de l'indicatif ou du subjonctif, selon le cas.*

1. Avez-vous une amie qui (pouvoir) venir avec nous dimanche? 2. Il y a à la porte un homme qui (vouloir) vous voir. 3. Pouvez-vous m'indiquer un film qui (plaire) à tout le monde? 4. Il cherche

quelqu'un qui (vouloir) bien acheter sa vieille maison. 5. Y a-t-il ici un étudiant qui (savoir) parler chinois? 6. Connaissez-vous une seule personne qui (être) capable de se sacrifier pour cela? 7. Nous cherchons un cadeau qui lui (faire) plaisir. 8. Je vous apporte un livre qui vous (intéresser). 9. Y a-t-il quelque chose que je (pouvoir) faire pour vous?

I. *Traduisez en français.*

1. (*vous*) We do not know anyone who is able to solve your problem. 2. He is looking for someone who can help him. 3. I know a girl who drives very well. 4. (*vous*) Can you tell me the name of a student who knows how to type? 5. Is there a restaurant near here which is not too expensive? 6. (*tu*) Bring me a book which is not too long. 7. We are looking for an apartment which is near a shopping center. 8. I see no one I know. 9. There are many people who know how to speak several languages. 10. There is nothing that can save that child.

PATTERN PRACTICE: clauses with a special antecedent

Pattern 11

YOU HEAR   Nous avons une chambre qui est très fraîche en été.
YOU SAY   Nous cherchons une chambre qui soit très fraîche en été.

Pattern 12

YOU HEAR   Je connais un homme qui sait le russe.
YOU SAY   Je ne connais personne qui sache le russe.

11. When and why is the subjunctive used in the following examples?

C'est **le plus beau musée** que je **connaisse**.
It is the most beautiful museum *that I* know.

Quel est **le plus grand édifice** qu'on **ait** (**a**) construit à Paris?
What is the largest building *that they* have built *in Paris?*

C'est **le seul homme** qui **puisse** (**peut**) faire cela.
He is the only man *who* can *do that.*

C'est **le plus long voyage** que nous **avons** (**ayons**) jamais fait.
It is the longest trip *that we* have *ever* taken.

In clauses whose antecedent is modified by a superlative or by adjectives such as **premier, dernier,** and **seul,** the verb may be in either the indicative or subjunctive. The INDICATIVE is used when the speaker wishes to state an objective fact. When there is an element of doubt or personal opinion or of subjective feeling, the SUBJUNCTIVE may be used.

J. *Traduisez en français.*

1. (*vous*) Who[1] is the most interesting author that you have read? 2. It is the first thing that he must do. 3. Here are the only friends that we were able to find. 4. Is France the only country where one is really free? 5. It's the last book that I am obliged to read for this course. 6. (*tu*) What is the most beautiful opera you ever heard? 7. Here is the only person who saw the accident. 8. (*vous*) Who is the best teacher you have had?

---

[1] **Quel**

12. How does French express the English indefinites whoever, whatever, wherever, however, **etc.? Why is the verb of French clauses introduced by such indefinites in the subjunctive?**

Qui que ce **soit,** il n'a pas le droit de fumer.

Whoever he {*is* / *may be,*} *he does not have the right to smoke.*

Quel que soit son métier, il faut qu'il fasse son service militaire.

Whatever his trade {*is* / *may be,*} *he must do his military service.*

Quoi qu'il en **soit,** vous devez revenir.

However that may be, you must come back.

Où que nous **soyons,** nous n'oublierons pas nos parents.

Wherever we {*are* / *may be,*} *we will not forget our parents.*

Si riches qu'ils **soient,** ils ne sont pas heureux.

However rich they {*are* / *may be,*} *they are not happy.*

Quelles que soient vos objections, il s'en ira.

Whatever your objections {*are* / *may be,*} *he will go away.*

The common French indefinites which correspond to the English indefinites in *-ever* are:

qui que	*whoever*	**quoi que**	*whatever*
quel que	*whoever, whatever*	**si** + ADJECTIVE + **que**	*however* + ADJECTIVE

When a clause introduced by one of the above indefinites indicates concession, that is, admits that something is or may be the case, its verb is in the subjunctive. Clauses of this kind have a certain vagueness which places them in the realm of the hypothetical subjunctive rather than in that of the factual indicative.

NOTE 1: The idea of concession is illustrated in the above examples. For instance, **Quel que soit son métier** concedes that he does or may have a trade. **Si riches qu'ils soient** admits that they are or may be rich.

NOTE 2: The **quel** of the expression **quel que** agrees with the noun it modifies in gender and number. Ex.: **Quelle que** soit <u>votre préférence</u> . . . (Whatever <u>your preference</u> *is/may be* . . .); **Quelles que** soient <u>ses raisons</u> . . . (Whatever <u>his reasons</u> *are/may be* . . .).

NOTE 3: The English *However* + ADJECTIVE is expressed in current spoken French by **Si** + ADJECTIVE. Ex.: **Si** <u>intéressant</u> que soit ce roman . . . (However <u>interesting</u> *this novel is/may be* . . .), **Si** <u>grands</u> que soient ces jeunes gens . . . (However <u>tall</u> *these young men are/may be* . . .).

K. *Traduisez en français.*

1. Whoever[1] he is, tell him to come to see me at once.   2. (*vous*) Whatever[2] your religion may be, you must help your neighbor[3].   3. (*vous*) Whatever[2] your ideas are, keep them to[4] yourself.   4. Whatever he does, he will not be able to change the situation.   5. However[5] lazy they may be, they are obliged to work in order to live.   6. (*vous*) However that may be, you must come to class every day.   7. Wherever he goes, he makes[6] friends easily.   8. Whatever he does, fate is against him.   9. However[5] good[7] they may be, their mother is never satisfied[8].

---

[1] Either **Qui que ce soit** or **Quel qu'il soit**.   [2] In such constructions, the **Quel** must agree with the noun that follows.   [3] **prochain**   [4] *to yourself* = **pour vous**   [5] Use **si** + ADJECTIVE.   [6] Use a form of **se faire**.   [7] **sages**   [8] **contente**

EXERCICES D'ENSEMBLE

L. *Remplacez les infinitifs entre parenthèses par la forme convenable de l'indicatif ou du subjonctif, ou bien gardez l'infinitif où il le faut.*

1. Il est certain que ces gens ne (savoir) pas ce qu'ils font.   2. Nous cherchons une maison qui (être) climatisée et qui (avoir) un grand jardin.   3. Je pense que vous (travailler) mieux la semaine pro-

chaine.　4. Claire craint de (rentrer) seule chez elle la nuit.　5. Monsieur Dutour regrette beaucoup que vous (refuser) son offre hier matin.　6. Je vous prêterai cette somme pourvu que vous me (promettre) de me rembourser dans un an.　7. Où que vous (aller), je vous suivrai.　8. Nous nous étonnons de (voir) que le gouvernement ne fait rien pour ces gens.　9. Demande l'auto à ton père avant qu'il (aller) se coucher.　10. Anne-Lise a peur que son père la (mettre) en pension.　11. Je sais que vous (plaisanter) sur tout, mais ce n'est pas le moment.　12. Réfléchissez donc avant de (répondre) n'importe quoi.　13. C'est le plus grand acteur que nous (avoir) jamais vu.　14. Il est naturel que les étudiants (vouloir) faire connaître leur point de vue.　15. Nos parents sont désolés que vous (décider) de ne plus venir à nos réunions.　16. Qui que vous (être), vous avez les mêmes droits que les autres.　17. Il est possible que vous (avoir) une allergie quelconque.　18. Il faut être bien naïf pour (croire) tout ce qu'il raconte.　19. Il faut que nous (prendre) une décision une fois pour toutes.

M.　*Traduisez en français.*

1. It is true that we are sometimes too demanding toward others[1].　2. (*vous*) Do you know someone who can repair my television right away?　3. (*tu*) Madame Lesage is glad that you promised to come to her evening party.　4. (*vous*) I don't find that you are making a great deal of progress.　5. They questioned the suspect until he confessed his crime.　6. (*tu*) I believe that this new novel will interest you, but I do not believe that you can read it in[2] two hours.　7. The boss wants everyone to be at the office at eight o'clock.　8. (*vous*) However busy you may be, give[3] some[4] time to your family.　9. The children are sorry that they were so nasty this afternoon.　10. His uncle will take him to Paris on the condition that he passes his examination.　11. Is he the only man who can really save the country?　12. (*vous*) It is important for you not to say a word about[5] that affair.　13. Whatever his reasons are, he did not explain them.　14. I'll go to see him next week unless he writes me not[6] to come.　15. I believe that it will soon be necessary to buy a new air-conditioner.　16. (*tu*) I am giving you this ring so that you will remember me.　17. It is probable that we will not come back before Christmas.

---

[1] **les autres**　[2] **en**　[3] Use a form of **consacrer**.　[4] *some time* = **quelques heures**　[5] **sur**
[6] Both parts of the negative precede a simple infinitive.

Problem Words

39. notice

(a) When *to notice* is expressed by **remarquer**

Avez-vous **remarqué** ces deux per-   *Did you* notice *those two people in the*
sonnes au premier rang?   *first row?*
J'**ai remarqué** tout de suite que tu   *I* noticed *right away that you had not*
n'avais pas reconnu Monsieur   *recognized Mr. Lévêque.*
Lévêque.

The verb **remarquer** may be used for *notice* in almost any circumstances.

(b) When *to notice* is expressed by **apercevoir**

J'**ai aperçu** Elizabeth dans un taxi.   *I* noticed *Elizabeth in a taxi.*

The verb **apercevoir** means *notice* in the sense of *catch sight of*.

(c) When *notice* is expressed by **s'apercevoir**

Le conférencier ne **s'aperçoit** pas   *The lecturer doesn't* notice (= realize)
qu'on ne l'écoute plus.   *that people are no longer listening to*
                                           him.
Je **me suis aperçu** de son inquiétude. *I* noticed (= realized) *his uneasiness.*

The verb **s'apercevoir** may be followed by **que** or by **de**. It is synonymous with *realize* or *be aware of*. When **s'apercevoir** is followed by **de,** the object of **de** is something intangible.

40. opportunity

(a) When *opportunity* = **l'occasion**

J'espère que nous aurons souvent   *I hope that we will often have* the oppor-
l'occasion de nous revoir.   tunity *to see each other.*

When *opportunity* means a favorable conjunction of circumstances, it is expressed by **l'occasion.**

(b) When *opportunity* = **la possibilité**

Ces étudiants n'ont pas encore eu **la**   *Those students haven't yet had* the op-
possibilité d'aller en France.   portunity *to go to France.*

The English *opportunity* is expressed by **la possibilité** when *opportunity* means *possibility*.

CAUTION: Do NOT use the word «opportunité» for *opportunity*. The word **opportunité** means *opportuneness* and is relatively uncommon.

41. paper

(**a**) When *paper = a piece of paper*

Jacques dit qu'il ne peut pas finir son devoir parce qu'il n'a plus de **papier.**	*John says that he can't finish his homework because he doesn't have any more paper.*
Votre livre est imprimé sur un beau **papier.**	*Your book is printed on very good paper.*

When *paper* means *material to write on* it is expressed by **le papier.**

(**b**) When *paper = newspaper*

Avez-vous lu **le journal** ce matin?	*Did you read* the paper *this morning?*

When *paper* is used in the sense of *newspaper*, it is **le journal.**
CAUTION: Do NOT use «papier» for *newspaper*.

(**c**) When *paper* is *a classroom exercise*

Remettez vos **copies** à la fin de l'heure.	*Hand in your* papers *at the end of the hour.*

For *papers* to be handed in to the teacher one can say **les copies, les devoirs** or **les exercices.** The classroom expression: *Hand in your papers* is: **Remettez vos copies** or **Donnez-moi vos copies.**

CAUTION: Do NOT use «papier» for *classroom exercise*, and do not say «Passez les papiers» for: *Hand in your papers.* The classroom exercise is **la copie**; say: **Remettez les copies** for: *Hand in your papers.**

(**d**) When *paper* is *a classroom report*

J'ai **un travail** à préparer.	*I have* a paper *to prepare.*

In French, there are various names for *classroom report*, such as **un travail, un compte-rendu, une composition, une dissertation** or **une étude** — but NOT «un papier».

---

* Either the definite article or the possessive adjective may be used in this sentence.

42. people

(**a**) When *people* is expressed by **personnes**

Ses idées ont offensé plusieurs **per-**   *His ideas offended several* people.
sonnes.

   When *people* means *a few persons*, French uses **personnes**.

(**b**) When *people* is expressed by **gens**

Il y a trop de **gens** sur la Côte d'Azur   *There are too many* people *on the French*
   en été.   *Riviera in summer.*
Il y a des **gens** qui n'ont aucun   *There are* people *who have no scruples.*
   scrupule.

   When *people* means *a considerable number of persons*, French often uses
les gens.

(**c**) When *people* is expressed by **monde**

Il y avait beaucoup de **monde** au   *There were many* people *at the concert.*
   concert.

   To state that there were *many people* at some function, French often
uses **monde**. When used in this sense, **monde** cannot be modified by
a relative clause.

(**d**) When *people* is expressed by **peuple**

Les Italiens sont **un peuple** très   *The Italians are* a *very musical* people.
   musicien.

   The English *a people* in the sense of *a nation* is expressed by **le peuple**.

   Note that **le peuple** also sometimes means *the masses*.

   CAUTION: Do NOT use «peuple» to express *people* except when it
means *nation* or *the masses*.

(**e**) When *people* is expressed by **on**

Qu'est-ce qu'**on** dirait si on savait   *What would* people *say if they knew*
   cela?   *that?*

   When *people* has the very indefinite sense of *people in general*, French
uses the indefinite pronoun **on**.

N. *Remplacez les mots anglais par leur équivalent français.*

1. (*vous*) (*Notice*) que nous sommes presque du même avis. 2. (*People*) n'aime pas conduire quand il neige. 3. Venez me voir à la première (*opportunity*). 4. Étienne corrige des (*papers*) pour le professeur Grémillot. 5. Les Hongrois sont un (*people*) très artiste. 6. Nous (*noticed*) un renard au bord de la route cette nuit. 7. Deux (*people*) sont venues pendant que vous étiez absent. 8. Ce (*paper*)-là a des tendances libérales. 9. J'aimerais vivre dans ce pays, mais je n'aurais pas la (*opportunity*) d'y travailler. 10. D'où vient tout ce (*people*)? 11. Ce (*paper*) n'est pas assez bon pour taper une thèse. 12. Tous ces (*people*) attendent[1] la sortie des artistes. 13. Il lui a fallu long-temps pour (*notice*) qu'on le volait. 14. (*People*) aime bien prendre des vacances l'été.

---

[1] are waiting for the artists to come out

O. *Traduisez en français. Attention aux mots en italique.*

1. Anne always writes on purple *paper*. 2. Several *people* came to see me this morning. 3. Irene *noticed* the new painting as soon as she entered the house. 4. A *people* should know its history. 5. I have never had the *opportunity* to visit Sweden. 6. I *noticed* too late that I had left my briefcase in the taxi. 7. One mustn't believe everything one sees in the *paper*. 8. I saw many *people* that I didn't know. 9. I *noticed* Guy at the theater last evening. 10. Would there be an *oppor-tunity* to see the director? 11. Were there many *people* at the recep-tion? 12. (*vous*) Don't forget to hand in your *papers*. 13. The teacher didn't *notice* that I was finishing my exercises in class. 14. (*vous*) Don't believe everything that *people* tell you.

Verb Review

Review the verbs **mettre** and **mourir** according to the outline on page 283.

CHAPTER 12

The Article

1. What are the forms of the definite and indefinite articles?

	DEFINITE		INDEFINITE	
	Singular	*Plural*	*Singular*	*Plural*
MASCULINE	**le**	**les**	**un**	**des**
FEMININE	**la**	**les**	**une**	**des**

Before any singular noun or adjective beginning with a vowel or a mute **h, le** and **la** elide, that is, they become **l'**.

This elision must be made before a noun or adjective beginning with a vowel or mute **h.**

2. What is the commonest use of the definite article in both French and English?

Les pommes sont dans **le** réfrigéra-teur.

The *apples are in* the *refrigerator.*

Le papier et **les** crayons sont sur **la** table.

The *paper and pencils are on* the *table.*

The definite article is used to indicate a particular noun.

When there is more than one noun used with the definite article, the article must be repeated before each noun. English often uses the article before the first noun only.

3. How do English and French differ in their treatment of nouns used in a general sense?

Les pommes sont bonnes pour la santé.	Apples *are good for the health.*
J'aime beaucoup **les pommes.**	I *like* apples *a great deal.*
La justice est une chose bien relative.	Justice *is a very relative thing.*
Le travail éloigne de nous trois grands maux: **l'ennui, le vice** et **le besoin.** (Voltaire)	Work *protects us from three great evils:* boredom, vice, *and* need.

In French the definite article is placed before nouns used in a general sense. This is not the case in English.

A great many nouns used in a general sense are abstract.

PATTERN PRACTICE: nouns used in a general sense

Pattern 1

> YOU HEAR   champagne
> YOU SAY   Le champagne coûte plus cher que l'année dernière.

Pattern 2

> YOU HEAR   peinture
> YOU SAY   J'aime beaucoup la peinture.

Pattern 3

> YOU HEAR   Voulez-vous de la glace?
> YOU SAY   Oui, j'aime beaucoup la glace.

4. In French, how is the definite article used with the days of the week?

Lundi nous aurons un examen.	Monday *we'll have a test.*
Nous avons toujours un examen **le lundi.**	*We always have a test* Mondays.

Days of the week are used without the article when they refer to an occurrence which takes place once on a given day. The definite article is used with the singular form of the day of the week when the occurrence takes place regularly every week on a given day.

PATTERN PRACTICE: the article with days of the week

Pattern 4

> YOU HEAR   J'irai à l'église dimanche.
> YOU SAY   Je vais toujours à l'église le dimanche.

5. How is the article used with dates?

le lundi 30 avril   Monday, *April 30*

When both the day of the week and the date are given, the definite article is normally placed before the day of the week but not before the day of the month. No comma separates the day of the week from the day of the month. Also found is **lundi,** 30 avril. In this case, a comma separates the day of the week from the day of the month.

le 30 avril 1980   *April 30, 1980*

When the date alone is given, the article normally precedes the day of the month. No commas are used.

6. When is the article used with the seasons?

Le printemps est très beau.   Spring *is very beautiful.*
Nous en parlerons **l'été** prochain.   *We'll speak of it next* summer.
Au printemps nous avons beaucoup   In the spring *we have a great deal to*
  à faire.   *do.*
Où irez-vous **en hiver?**   *Where will you go* in winter?

The article is used with names of seasons, except when they are preceded by **en.** Note the expressions **au printemps, en été, en automne, en hiver.**

PATTERN PRACTICE: the article with seasons

Pattern 5

YOU HEAR   Je fais du bateau en été.
YOU SAY   L'été est une bonne saison pour faire du bateau.

7. When is the article used with names of languages?

Le français est une langue facile.   French *is an easy language.*
Comprenez-vous **l'allemand?**   *Do you understand* German?
Je ne parle pas **anglais.**   *I do not speak* English.
Marie parle bien **(le) russe.**   *Marie speaks* Russian *well.*
En italien on prononce toutes les   In Italian *all the letters are pronounced.*
  lettres.

The article is used with names of languages except when the language is preceded by **en** or when it follows a form of the verb **parler.**

When the language does not follow a form of the verb **parler** immediately, sometimes the article is used with the language, sometimes not.

All names of languages are masculine.

PATTERN PRACTICE: the use of the article with languages

Pattern 6

> YOU HEAR   On parle chinois à Hong-kong.
> YOU SAY   Le chinois est une langue très répandue.

Pattern 7

> YOU HEAR   Le portugais est une langue romane.
> YOU SAY   Comment dit-on «bonjour» en portugais?

A. *Traduisez en français.*

(All exercises in this lesson are English-to-French. In each sentence there is some word with which the definite article must be either used or omitted. Identify this word and connect it with one of the rules in the preceding sections. Explain orally why you use or omit the definite article.)

1. Summer is a very beautiful season.   2. It is necessary to be patient with children.   3. For the United States the Second World War began on December 7, 1941.   4. The flowers that I prefer are roses. 5. We celebrate our anniversary Tuesday, March 8.   6. I like to hear my friend Sergio Tonelli speak Italian.   7. He loves animals. 8. In spring all nature awakens.   9. It is difficult to know German well[1].   10. In English they use the word "sorry" a great deal. 11. Men are truly curious.   12. (*vous*) Do you like French coffee? 13. (*tu*) Are you free Saturday afternoon?   14. Many Frenchmen speak Spanish.   15. Sundays I always go to church.   16. There are interesting concerts in winter.   17. French is a beautiful language. 18. We never have any class on Saturday.   19. Undeveloped countries need help.

---

[1] Place this adverb before *know*.

8. When is the article used with nouns in apposition?

Pasteur, **le grand savant français,** mourut en 1895.	*Pasteur*, the great French scientist, *died in 1895.*
Philippe, **le fils de notre voisin,** est parti à l'armée.	*Philip*, our neighbor's son, *has left for the army.*
Pierre Dupont, **étudiant en médecine,** habite à Paris.	*Pierre Dupont*, a medical student, *lives in Paris.*
Yvetot, **petite ville de Normandie,** se trouve entre Le Havre et Rouen.	*Yvetot*, a little Norman town, *lies between Le Havre and Rouen.*

In French, the definite article is normally used with nouns in apposition where it would be in English, to state what the speaker considers a well-known fact.

But in French, the indefinite article is not often used with nouns in apposition. Wherever the noun in apposition furnishes additional and presumably unknown information, the noun in apposition tends to be used without any article.

9. What about the use of the article with a noun following the preposition en?

Jacques est un étudiant **en droit.**	*Jack is a* law *student.*
L'Europe est divisée **en pays.**	*Europe is divided* into countries.

Normally, no article follows the preposition **en.**

L'Arc de Triomphe fut construit **en l'honneur** des armées de Napoléon.	*The Arc de Triomphe was constructed* in honor *of Napoleon's armies.*
L'agent a tiré **en l'air.**	*The policeman fired a shot* into the air.
En l'absence du professeur les élèves ont fait beaucoup de bruit.	In the absence *of the teacher the pupils made a lot of noise.*

In certain set expressions, the commonest of which are **en l'honneur, en l'air** and **en l'absence,** the article is used after **en.**

10. Is the article used with given (first) names?

Marie est partie hier avec **le petit Claude** et son frère Henri.	*Mary left yesterday with* little Claude *and her brother Henry.*

The article is not normally used with first names. But it is used with first names modified by an adjective.

11. When speaking of someone, how is the article used with titles?

Hier, j'ai vu **le docteur Lemaître.**	*Yesterday, I saw* Dr. Lemaître.
Le capitaine Lebeau arrivera demain.	Captain Lebeau *will arrive tomorrow.*
Connaissez-vous **le professeur Dupré?**	*Do you know* Professor Dupré?
Le président Wilson est allé en Europe en 1919.	President Wilson *went to Europe in 1919.*

When speaking of a person, the definite article is used before titles indicating a profession.

Monsieur Lebrun habite 30, rue de Vaugirard.	Mr. Lebrun *lives at 30 Vaugirard Street.*
Où est **Madame Rivière?**	*Where is* Mrs. Rivière?
Jacques sort souvent avec **Mademoiselle Moreau.**	*Jack often goes out with* Miss Moreau.

But no article is used before **monsieur, madame,** or **mademoiselle** when they are followed by the person's name.

CAUTION: When **madame** and **mademoiselle** are used as common nouns, they must not be accompanied by an article. Do not say: "La mademoiselle qui passe là-bas est une avocate." Say: La **demoiselle** qui passe là-bas est une avocate.

monsieur = **M.**   madame = **Mme** or **M**^{me} mademoiselle = **Mlle** or **M**^{lle}

A period is used after the abbreviation for **monsieur** but no period is used after the abbreviations for **madame** and **mademoiselle.**

12. How is the article used with titles when addressing a person?

Docteur, je ne me sens pas bien du tout.	Doctor, *I don't feel well at all.*
J'ai suivi vos conseils, **Dr. Perret.**	*I followed your advice*, Dr. Perret.

In addressing a doctor, no article is used either with or without the name of the doctor.

—Bonjour, **mon capitaine.**	*"Good morning,* captain."
—Je suis à vos ordres, **mon commandant.**	*"I am at your orders,* major."

In the military, when a soldier of lower rank or an officer speaks to an officer of higher rank, the possessive adjective is used before the title.

Bonsoir, **Monsieur.**	*Good evening,* Mr. Jones.
Bonjour, **Madame.**	*Good morning,* Mrs. Leroque.
Mademoiselle, j'espère que nous nous reverrons.	Miss Smith, *I hope that we'll see each other again.*

In French, a person is usually addressed as **Monsieur, Madame** or **Mademoiselle,** and no last name is normally used when addressing a person, although the last name is sometimes heard in familiar speech.

Je n'ai pas encore lu ce livre, **monsieur.**	*I haven't yet read that book,* Professor Lemercier.

In addressing teachers in France, including professors, neither the title nor the name is used, but simply **monsieur, madame,** or **mademoiselle.**

Monsieur le Président, vous avez toujours raison.	Mr. President, *you are always right.*
Monsieur le professeur, voulez-vous nous donner votre opinion?	Professor Bruce, *will you give us your opinion?*

With certain titles, the formula **Monsieur le . . .** is sometimes used in address.

B. *Traduisez en français.*

1. He was speaking of Mr. Leduc, a publisher from Strasbourg.
2. There will be a big dinner in honor of Senator Amieux.   3. (*tu*) Have you invited beautiful Sylvia to the dance?   4. She knows Prince Louis very well[1].   5. General Lacaze will inspect the troops to-morrow morning.   6. Pasteur, the great French scientist[2], was a very generous man.   7. They spent the night in prison.   8. In the absence of the manager, his assistant will make[3] the decisions.   9. Doctor, I don't know what[4] is the matter with me.   10. (*vous*) I'll do what you wish, colonel.   11. Miss Duneau, a mathematics professor at the university, has just written a new book.   12. We'll go to France by[5] plane.   13. She loves Roger and would like to marry him. 14. The best specialist in that field[6] is Dr. Petit.   15. (*vous*) I'll follow you everywhere, lieutenant.

---

[1] Where will these words come in relation to the verb?   [2] Not «scientiste».   [3] Not a form of «faire».   [4] This is an idiom.   [5] **en** or **par**   [6] **domaine**

13. When is the article used before names of countries and continents?

La France est un grand pays.	France *is a large country.*
Je suis allé **en Angleterre.**	*I went* to England.
Il vient **de Grèce.**	*He comes* from Greece.

Nous sommes arrivés **au Portugal.**   *We arrived* in Portugal.
Il vient **du Danemark.**   *He comes* from Denmark.

The article is normally used before names of countries and continents.

But the article is not used after **en** (which expresses *in* or *to* with feminine countries) nor after **de** (meaning *from*) when it precedes a feminine country.

PATTERN PRACTICE: the use of the article with countries

Pattern 8

    YOU HEAR   Mes amis sont en France.
    YOU SAY   Ils visitent la France tous les ans.

14. Is the article used with names of cities?

Il va à **Paris.**   *He is going to* Paris.
Avez-vous vu **Londres?**   *Have you seen* London?
La Nouvelle-Orléans est en Loui-   New Orleans *is in Louisiana*, Le
   siane, **Le Havre** en France.   Havre *in France.*

The article is not usually found with names of cities. However, a few cities, such as **La Haye** (*The Hague*), **La Nouvelle Orléans, Le Havre, La Rochelle,** etc., have the article as part of the name.

15. When is the article used before names of streets and avenues?

Dites-moi où est **la rue Racine.**   *Tell me where* Racine Street *is.*
Le Boulevard Saint-Germain est   Boulevard Saint-Germain *is very pic-*
   très pittoresque.   *turesque.*

Connaissez-vous   **l'avenue   des**   *Do you know* Champs-Elysées Ave-
   Champs-Élysées?   nue?

The article is normally used before names of streets and avenues.

Nous   sommes   arrivés   **Boulevard**   *We arrived at* St. Michel Boulevard.
   Saint-Michel.
On me trouvera **rue Royale.**   *They'll find me on* Royal Street.

When the prepositions *in* or *on* precede the street name in English, the French tend to omit the preposition and article. However, the preposition and the article may be used.

The French say:

dans la rue	*on the street*
dans⎱**l'avenue**	*on the avenue*
sur ⎰	
sur la place	*in the square*
sur le boulevard	*on the boulevard*

16. How is the English word *per* **expressed in French with various types of units of measure?**

(a) speed per hour

Le train roulait à cent soixante kilomètres **à l'heure**.   *The train was going at a hundred miles per hour.*

With expressions of *time indicating speed*, **à** + ARTICLE is used, and this is especially common with **à l'heure**.

(b) money per hour

Marie gagne trois dollars **de l'heure**.   *Mary earns three dollars per hour.*

Money per hour is expressed by **de l'heure**.

(c) something accomplished per unit of time

Dans ce pays on travaille huit heures **par jour** et quarante heures **par semaine**.   *In this country they work eight hours a day and forty hours per week.*

Jacques gagne neuf cent dollars **par mois**.   *Jack earns nine hundred dollars per month.*

In general, French expresses *per* + UNIT OF TIME by **par** + UNIT OF TIME: **par jour, par semaine, par mois, par an**. No article is used after **par**.

(d) expressions of dry measure, weight, etc.

Les pommes de terre coûtent cinq francs **la livre**.   *Potatoes cost five francs per pound.*

Le sucre coûte deux francs **le kilo**.   *Sugar costs two francs per kilogram.*

French expresses *per* with expressions of *dry measure, weight*, and so on, by placing the definite article before the expression.

17. What prepositions are used with expressions of means of locomotion, and when is the article used?

Nous sommes venus **en train** (or **par le train**), **en** voiture, **en** avion (or **par avion**), **à** pied, **à** bicyclette.

We came on the train, in a car, by plane, on foot, on a bicycle.

The prepositions used with means of locomotion must often be learned. In general **dans** or **en** is used if one can enter the vehicle, **à** if one is on the vehicle. However for *on a motorcycle* the French say **en moto.**

18. What about the use of the article in stating the profession, nationality, or religion of the subject of the sentence?

M. Delong est **avocat.**
Sa femme est **américaine.**
Mlle Bajard est **un excellent professeur.**

Mr. Delong is a lawyer.
His wife is (an) American.
Miss Bajard is an excellent teacher.

After forms of the verb **être,** French designates profession, religion, nationality, etc., by an unmodified noun. English uses the noun modified by an indefinite article.

In French, if the name of the profession, nationality, or religion is modified, the indefinite article is used as in English.

C. *Traduisez en français.*

1. Mrs. Dallier is an interior decorator. 2. Did they arrive by train or on[1] a motorcycle? 3. Products imported from Japan are cheap. 4. In the United States people[2] work a great deal. 5. Mr. Perrier is Catholic. 6. First we arrived at Peace Street, where we found some very elegant stores. 7. In summer there are sometimes several storms per day. 8. It is dangerous to go[3] faster than eighty kilometers per hour. 9. *They* left on foot, *we* in a car. 10. His mother is a good doctor. 11. These toys come from Germany. 12. Formerly there was a prison in the Place de la Bastille. 13. There are many lakes in Canada. 14. I caught a fish which I'll sell at a dollar a pound. 15. Our neighbors came back from Poland yesterday. 16. She charges[4] ten dollars an hour, which[5] seems expensive.

---

[1] en   [2] on   [3] Use a form of **rouler à plus de.**   [4] Use a form of **prendre.**   [5] **ce qui**

17. My mother-in-law comes to see us twice a year.   18. I should like to go to Italy.   19. They left[6] for Portugal yesterday.   20. In Paris life has a special charm.   21. He earns $550 a week, but that will not last.

---

[6] Use a form of **partir**.

PATTERN PRACTICE: the article before names of professions, etc.

Pattern 9

YOU HEAR   Monsieur Monod est un excellent pasteur.
YOU SAY   Monsieur Monod est pasteur.

Pattern 10

YOU HEAR   Monsieur Lalou est ingénieur.
YOU SAY   Monsieur Lalou est un ingénieur très connu.

Problem Words

43. piece

(**a**) How to say *piece* in general

Aimez-vous ce **morceau** de musique?   *Do you like this* piece *of music?*

The general word for *piece* is **le morceau.**

(**b**) Ways of saying *a piece of paper*

Donnez-moi **un bout de papier.**
Donnez-moi **un morceau de papier.** } *Give me* a piece of paper.
Donnez-moi **une feuille de papier.**

The word *piece* in *piece of paper* may be expressed by **morceau** or **feuille** (*sheet*) or **bout** (somewhat familiar).
The noun **bout** is also used with **fil** (*thread, wire*) and **ficelle** (*string*) to mean *piece.*

CAUTION: Do NOT use «la pièce» for *piece;* **la pièce** means *play* (to be acted) or *room.*

44. place

(**a**) When *place* is expressed by **endroit**

Le guide nous fera voir les **endroits**   *The guide will show us the most curious*
les plus curieux.   places.

Il y a bien des **endroits** où la vie est plus facile qu'ici. — *There are many places where life is easier than here.*

The common word for *place* is **l'endroit** (*m.*).

(b) When *place* is expressed by **lieu**

Il paraît qu'on revient toujours au **lieu** de son crime. — *It seems that one always returns to the place of his crime.*

The word **le lieu** means *place* in the sense of *spot*. It is literary and not very common, but it is used specifically in certain instances and also in some compound expressions such as **le chef-lieu** (county seat). It is also used in the idiomatic expression **avoir lieu.** It is best to avoid using **lieu** in other cases.

(c) When *place* means *space*

Avez-vous **de la place** pour ma voiture dans votre garage? — *Do you have a place for my car in your garage?*

When *place* means *space*, French uses **la place.**

(d) When *place* means *a seat*

Montez vite dans le train si vous voulez **une place** près de la fenêtre. — *Get on the train right away if you want a place near the window.*

When *place* means *a seat*, often a paid accommodation, *place* is expressed by **la place.**

(e) When *place* means *a job*

Jean-Paul a une bonne ⎰ **situation. / position. / place.** — *Jean-Paul has a good place (= job).*

When the English word *place* means *job*, it may be expressed by **la situation, la position** or **la place.**

CAUTION: Do NOT use «place» to express *place in general*. The ordinary word for *place* is **endroit.**

45. rather

(**a**) How to say *rather than*

Je voudrais une revue **plutôt qu**'un journal.	*I would like a magazine* rather than *a newspaper.*
Allez vous promener **plutôt que de** rester ici par ce beau temps.	*Go and take a walk* rather than *staying here in this nice weather.*

The expression *rather than* is often rendered in French by **plutôt que** and when it precedes an infinitive, it may be rendered by **plutôt que de**.

(**b**) How to say *rather* + ADJECTIVE or ADVERB

Je suis **assez fatigué** ce soir après cette longue journée.	*I am* rather tired *this evening after this long day.*
Après un an d'étude vous parlerez **assez couramment.**	*After a year of study you will speak* rather fluently.

When the adverb *rather* modifies an adjective or another adverb, French uses **assez.**

(**c**) How to say *I would rather . . .*

Nous **aimerions mieux** rester à la maison ce soir.	*We* would rather *stay home this evening.*
Nous **préférerions** rester à la maison ce soir.	
J'**aimerais mieux** jouer au bridge qu'au poker.	*I* would rather *play bridge than poker.*
Je **préférerais** jouer au bridge **plutôt** qu'au poker.	

The English *would rather* + VERB may be expressed in French by the conditional of **aimer mieux** + INFINITIVE or of **préférer** + INFINITIVE. In comparisons, **plutôt** is required to complete the meaning of **préférer.**

46. reason

(**a**) How to say *the reason for*

Quelle est **la raison de** votre refus?	*What is* the reason for *your refusal?*

French expresses *the reason for* by **la raison de.**

(b) How to say *the reason that*

Philippe m'a expliqué **la raison pour laquelle** il n'a pas pu venir.
Philippe m'a expliqué **pour quelle raison** il n'a pas pu venir.
Philippe m'a expliqué **pourquoi** il n'a pas pu venir.

Philip explained to me the reason that *he could not come.*

French expresses *the reason that* (colloquially *the reason why*) by **la raison pour laquelle** or **pour quelle raison** or simply by **pourquoi.**

CAUTION: Do NOT say «la raison pourquoi», which is incorrect even colloquially.

D. *Remplacez les mots anglais par leur équivalent français.*

1. Je ne peux pas être dans deux (*places*) à la fois. 2. Béatrice est (*rather*) découragée par tout ce qui s'est passé. 3. Je voudrais savoir (*the reason*) Monsieur Béraud a changé d'avis. 4. Allez en avant et gardez-nous une (*place*). 5. Il me faut un petit (*piece*) de cette étoffe. 6. Les enfants (*would rather*) passer leurs vacances à la mer qu'à la montagne. 7. Il n'y a pas assez de (*place*) pour deux dans ce bureau. 8. Le beau vase chinois s'est cassé en mille (*pieces*). 9. Juliette a laissé une lettre pour expliquer (*the reason for*) son départ. 10. On ira voir (*the place*) de l'accident. 11. Faisons quelque chose chez nous (*rather than*) d'aller au restaurant ce soir.

E. *Traduisez en français. Attention aux mots en italique.*

1. I know a *place* where we can work in peace. 2. Lucien works *rather* well, but he could do better. 3. (*vous*) Now you know the *reason* I came back. 4. The children don't have enough *place* to play. 5. What are those *pieces* of paper on the floor? 6. (*tu*) Johnnie, give your *place* to that lady. 7. I would *rather* leave this evening than tomorrow morning. 8. What is the *reason* for his absence? 9. (*vous*) Do you take one *piece* of sugar or two? 10. I decided that Jack should do that work *rather* than George.

Verb Review

Review the verbs **ouvrir** and **pouvoir** according to the outline on page 283.

CHAPTER 13

Indefinite Nouns

1. A noun may be definite, general, or indefinite. How is an indefinite noun expressed in English and in French?

Il y a **du papier** sur mon bureau.	*There is* (some) paper *on my desk.*
Vous trouverez **des cartes postales** dans le tiroir.	*You will find* (some) postcards *in the drawer.*
Avez-vous **des enfants?**	*Have you* any children?

In English, a noun is made indefinite either by the use of <u>the noun alone</u> or by the use of *some* or *any* with the noun.

In French, a noun is usually made indefinite by the partitive construction.

NOTE: In both French and English, a noun modified by the indefinite article is also indefinite. Ex.: **un livre** (*a book*), **une pomme** (*an apple*).

2. What are the partitive articles?

	Singular	*Plural*
MASCULINE	**du**	**des**
FEMININE	**de la**	**des**
MASCULINE or FEMININE	**de l'**	**des**

If the word following the partitive singular begins with a vowel or a mute **h,** the form **de l'** must be used.

The partitive construction is, in effect, **de** + DEFINITE ARTICLE, but as a partitive it has lost its original meaning of *of the.*

3. What is the partitive construction?

Vous trouverez **du beurre** et **de la crème** au supermarché.	*You will find* butter *and* cream *in the supermarket.*
Y a-t-il **des chevaux** dans la ferme?	*Are there* any horses *on the farm?*

The partitive construction indicates that an indefinite quantity of a given noun (part of all there is) exists in the sentence at hand.

In French, a noun is made indefinite by the partitive construction except in certain cases, when <u>the noun alone</u> indicates indefiniteness. It is the fact that there are times when <u>the noun alone</u> rather than the partitive is used that complicates the problem.

4. When an indefinite noun is modified by a preceding adjective, how is the partitive construction modified?

(**a**) when the noun is singular

Nous avons entendu **de la belle musique.**	*We heard* some beautiful music.
Avez-vous **du bon vin?**	*Do you have* any good wine?

When an adjective precedes an indefinite singular noun, the partitive construction normally is used.

(**b**) when the noun is plural

Nous avons vu **de jolies fleurs** dans le bois.	*We saw* some pretty flowers *in the woods.*
Il y a **de magnifiques châteaux** dans ce pays.	*There are* some magnificent castles *in that country.*

When a preceding adjective modifies a plural indefinite noun, **de** takes the place of the partitive construction. One normally finds **de** + ADJECTIVE + PLURAL NOUN.

5. When does one find des + <u>adjective</u> + <u>plural noun</u>?

Ils ont vu **des jeunes gens** sur le boulevard.	*They saw* some young men *on the boulevard.*
Y a-t-il **des jeunes filles** dans cette pension?	*Are there* any girls *in that boarding house?*
Voulez-vous **des petits pois?**	*Do you want* any peas?

When ADJECTIVE + NOUN constitute a unit, so that the adjective has lost its identity as an adjective, the construction is treated like a single word, and as a single word it is modified by the partitive article **des** with the plural noun.

A. *Remplacez les tirets par l'article partitif ou par* **de.** *Expliquez oralement votre choix.*

1. Il y a _____ arbres tout le long de la Seine. 2. Les étudiants vont au café passer _____ bons moments avec leurs camarades. 3. Avez-vous entendu _____ belle musique hier soir? 4. Les femmes aiment acheter _____ nouvelles robes. 5. Avez-vous trouvé _____ petits pois dans ce magasin? 6. Il y a _____ excellents romans dans votre bibliothèque. 7. Ce fermier vient nous vendre _____ pommes de terre et _____ maïs. 8. Il n'est pas très intelligent, mais il a _____ bonne volonté.

B. *Traduisez en français. Expliquez oralement chaque article partitif et chaque* **de.**

1. (*vous*) I saw some cats and dogs in your garden. 2. There were some girls in the group who did not know how to speak French. 3. One finds good milk in Denmark. 4. Is there any ice in the refrigerator? 5. We drank some good cider in Normandy. 6. (*tu*) Were there any young men[1] on your boat? 7. There were numerous tourists on the beach. 8. They spent long hours in[2] the library.

---

[1] The plural of **jeune homme** is NOT «jeunes hommes».   [2] **à la**

PATTERN PRACTICE : partitives

Pattern 1

> YOU HEAR   Catherine aime beaucoup les fleurs.
> YOU SAY   Donnez-lui des fleurs.

6. Is an indefinite noun always modified by a partitive article?

J'ai **faim.**	*I'm* hungry. (lit. *I have* hunger.)
Jacques a travaillé avec **soin.**	*Jack worked with* care (*carefully*).
Nous sommes arrivés sans **argent.**	*We arrived without* money.
La maison est pleine de **poussière.**	*The house is full of* dust.

There are several cases in which an indefinite noun is not modified by a partitive but rather in which the noun stands alone.

We shall now examine each of these cases — and their exceptions.

7. When is the noun alone used in idiomatic sentences with avoir?

Marie **a soif.**	*Mary* is thirsty. (lit. *Mary* has thirst.)
J'**ai mal** à la gorge.	*I* have a sore throat. (lit. *I have* hurt *in the throat.*)

Certain set expressions made up of a form of **avoir** + the noun alone came into the language before there was any partitive article. Many of these expressions still exist.

8. When is the preposition avec used with the noun alone?

Pierre a parlé <u>avec</u> **hésitation.**	*Peter spoke <u>with</u> hesitation (i.e., hesitatingly, in a hesitating manner.).*
Sa femme l'a reçu <u>avec</u> **joie.**	*His wife received him <u>with</u> joy (joyfully).*

The preposition **avec** is used with abstract nouns alone when the resulting prepositional phrase indicates manner. Often this phrase can be expressed by an adverb in English.

9. When is the noun alone used with sans and ni . . . ni . . . ?

Paul est parti <u>sans</u> **livres.**	*Paul left <u>without</u> books.*
Nous n'avons <u>ni</u> **crayons** <u>ni</u> **papier.**	*We have <u>neither</u> pencils <u>nor</u> paper.*

The noun alone follows **sans** and **ni . . . ni . . .** when it is an indefinite noun.

PATTERN PRACTICE: the indefinite noun after **sans** and **ni . . . ni . . .**

Pattern 2

YOU HEAR   Michel est venu chez nous avec des disques.
YOU SAY   Michel est venu chez nous sans disques.

Pattern 3

YOU HEAR   Monsieur Simon vend des cigares et des cigarettes.
YOU SAY   Monsieur Simon ne vend ni cigares ni cigarettes.

C. *Traduisez en français. Expliquez oralement chaque omission de l'article partitif devant un nom indéfini.*

1. The poor child is hungry. 2. Without friends life is not pleasant. 3. They fought with courage, but they lost. 4. Was he able to fix the faucet without tools? 5. What are we going to do? There are neither chairs nor tables here. 6. He claims that he has a headache. 7. We left their house without regret. 8. (*vous*) What are you afraid of? 9. (*vous*) If you are right, I must be wrong. 10. (*tu*) We need your dictionary. 11. (*tu*) Did you go out without a hat? 12. (*vous*) Are you sleepy? You are yawning all[1] the time. 13. (*tu*)—Will you help me move? —With pleasure. 14. They are ashamed of their mistakes. 15. He is a lawyer; he speaks with ease. 16. I am cold, and I have a sore throat.

---

[1] Use **sans** with the noun **arrêt** (m.).

10. How is an indefinite noun expressed when it is immediately preceded by the preposition de?

J'ai beaucoup **de travail.**	*I have a lot* of work.
Jacques n'a pas **de chance.**	*Jack doesn't have* any luck.
Ne me privez pas **de cigarettes.**	*Don't deprive me* of cigarettes.
Elle porte une robe **de soie.**	*She is wearing a* silk dress.

Whenever the preposition **de** precedes an indefinite noun for any reason whatever, the noun follows **de** immediately, without any partitive article.

We will now examine the cases in which **de** most often precedes an indefinite noun.

11. What construction follows adverbs of quantity?

Nous avons **beaucoup de livres.**	*We have* many books.
Avez-vous **assez d'argent?**	*Have you* enough money?
Il y a **trop de voitures** dans la rue.	*There are* too many cars *in the street.*

Adverbs of quantity are followed by **de** because of the nature of their meaning (*much of, enough of, too much of, more of,* etc.). The noun alone follows **de.**

NOTE 1: However, the adverb of quantity **bien** (meaning *many*) is followed by the partitive **des** before a plural indefinite noun. Ex.: Il a **bien des** ennuis. (He has *many* troubles.) **Bien des** fois nous restons à la maison. (*Many* times we stay home.)

The adverb **bien** is simply an intensifier; it does not affect the partitive article of the construction which follows it.

NOTE 2: **La plupart des** (*the majority of*) is followed by a definite noun and the plural form of the verb. Ex.: **La plupart des** romans sont intéressants. Here, **des** = **de** + **les** means *of the* and is not a partitive.

The only singular construction with **la plupart** is **la plupart du temps**. Otherwise, say: **la plus grande partie**. Ex.: **la plus grande partie de l'été**, etc.

12. By what construction is the negative *pas* followed when it indicates negative quantity?

Je n'ai **pas de** <u>temps</u> à perdre.   *I don't have* any <u>time</u> *to lose.*
Nous ne voyons **pas de** <u>bateaux</u>.   *We see* no <u>boats</u>.

When **pas** indicates negative quantity, it is followed by **de** as are other adverbs of quantity. Then **pas** is translated into English as *not . . . any* or *no*.

NOTE: By analogy, **de** also follows other negatives used quantitatively Ex.: Il **n'a jamais d'argent**. (*He* never *has* any *money*.)

13. What construction follows *pas* when it indicates a type?

Ce n'est **pas <u>du beurre</u>.**   *That isn't* butter.
Ce ne sont **pas <u>des soldats</u>.**   *Those aren't* soldiers.

When **pas** is used as an absolute negative and indicates type or quality, **pas** is followed by <u>the partitive article before the noun</u>, and in that case it is translated into English as *not*. This construction is most often found in sentences such as: **Ce n'est pas . . .** and **Ce ne sont pas . . . .**

14. How is the indefinite noun expressed after verbs and adjectives regularly followed by *de*?

Les enfants seront **privés de <u>dessert</u>.**   *The children will be* deprived of dessert.

La maison est **entourée d'<u>agents</u>.**	*The house is* surrounded by policemen.
Il y a encore trop de gens qui **manquent de <u>pain</u>.**	*There are still too many people who* lack bread.
Le pays **manque de <u>ressources</u>.**	*The country* lacks resources.
Il **a rempli** le sac **de <u>billets</u>** de mille francs.	*He* filled *the bag* with *thousand franc* bank notes.
J'ai besoin de <u>timbres</u>.	*I* need stamps.

Whenever a verb, adjective, or special construction is followed by **de,** <u>the</u> indefinite <u>noun alone</u> follows **de.**

15. How are English adjectives or phrases indicating material expressed in French?

une maison **de <u>bois</u>**	*a* wooden *house*
un chapeau **de <u>paille</u>**	*a* straw *hat*

Where English uses an adjective or a phrase of 'material', French uses an adjectival phrase consisting of **de** + NOUN.

NOTE: Sometimes **en** is used to indicate material. One can say: **une maison de pierre** or **une maison en pierre.** But distinguish between **un sac d'argent** (*a bag of money*, or, *a bag of silver*) and **un sac en argent** (*a silver bag*, i.e., a bag made of silver).

D. *Remplacez les tirets par l'article partitif ou par* **de.** *Expliquez oralement votre choix.*

1. J'aimerais avoir un bon pull-over ＿＿ laine. 2. Ces arbres ne sont pas ＿＿ orangers, ce sont des pommiers. 3. Bien ＿＿ étrangers viennent visiter l'Amérique. 4. Ses parents lui laissent trop ＿＿ liberté pour son âge. 5. Donnez-moi une tasse ＿＿ thé avec ＿＿ citron, s'il vous plaît. 6. Ils ont plus ＿＿ ressources que vous. 7. Nous ne mangeons pas ＿＿ viande le soir. 8 Nous avons tous besoin ＿＿ affection pour vivre. 9. Il y a bien ＿＿ gens qui seraient heureux d'aller en France avec vous. 10. Cet arbre est plein ＿＿ oiseaux tous les soirs. 11. Ce sont des taudis, ce ne sont pas ＿＿ maisons. 12. Je me passerai ＿＿ café, parce qu'il m'empêche de dormir.

E. *Traduisez en français. Expliquez oralement chaque emploi de l'article partitif ou du* **de.**

1. We'll give them a silver tray for their wedding. 2. These men aren't spies. 3. Many[1] times I regretted my indifference. 4. They are students, and they have few distractions. 5. The room was full of people. 6. He bought a new silk shirt to go to Florida. 7. Those aren't mountains; they are hills. 8. That house is very quiet; one doesn't hear any noise there. 9. Today they use[2] machines for all sorts of things. 10. They always look at television and do not read any books. 11. He has good[3] qualities, but he lacks initiative. 12. We know few people in our building[4]. 13. They sent him a package[5] filled with toys. 14. The majority of people like to travel.

---

[1] Use **bien.** [2] Use a form of **se servir de.** [3] *good qualities* = **qualités** [4] Use **immeuble.** [5] Use **colis.**

PATTERN PRACTICE: the use of the noun alone after **de**

Pattern 4

YOU HEAR   Avez-vous du travail? (trop)
YOU SAY   J'ai trop de travail.

Pattern 5

YOU HEAR   Je vois des taxis dans la rue.
YOU SAY   Je ne vois pas de taxis dans la rue.

Pattern 6

YOU HEAR   Nous avons un appartement.
YOU SAY   Nous n'avons pas d'appartement.

Pattern 7

YOU HEAR   Est-ce que c'est du café italien?
YOU SAY   Non, ce n'est pas du café italien.

Pattern 8

YOU HEAR   Ce n'est pas du café italien.
YOU SAY   Nous n'avons pas de café italien.

Pattern 9

YOU HEAR   Jacques a besoin des timbres que vous avez achetés.
YOU SAY   Nous avons aussi besoin de timbres.

F. *Traduisez en français. Expliquez oralement chaque emploi de l'article partitif ou du* **de.**

1. One sees a lot of students without hats. 2. (*vous*) Invite some entertaining people for[1] dinner. 3. In that house there are some very valuable pictures. 4. They aren't Japanese; they are Chinese. 5. It is necessary to learn as soon as possible to get along without money. 6. (*vous*) If you want to please[2] your wife, buy her a fur coat. 7. (*vous*) You have courage to[3] speak so frankly. 8. (*vous*) I learned with regret that you will no longer be with us next year. 9. In[4] the university they do not want professors without a doctorate. 10. There are elegant[5] hotels in all the large cities. 11. (*tu*) If you need cigarettes, you have only to tell me. 12. The majority of the pilots are strong men. 13. There are many[6] people who would like to have his position[7]. 14. There are still some poor areas which have no schools. 15. We spent long hours in[4] Notre-Dame. 16. (*vous*) If you have neither pencil nor paper, you can return home. 17. These aren't amateurs; they are true artists. 18. There are many interesting things to see when one travels. 19. We lack soap. 20. There is enough room in the car for everyone. 21. I know some young men who are really remarkable. 22. Certain authors write with ease, but I write with difficulty. 23. (*vous*) Don't go to[8] that café; they serve bad wine there. 24. I have just bought a beautiful leather suitcase for my trip.

---

[1] **à dîner** [2] Use a form of **faire plaisir à.** [3] **pour** [4] **à** [5] First write this sentence with **élégant** following its noun, then write it with **élégant** preceding its noun. [6] Use **bien.** [7] **place** [8] **dans**

Problem Words

47. return

(**a**) When *return = give back*

Guy ne m'a pas encore **rendu** mon magnétophone.	Guy has *not yet* returned *my tape recorder to me.*

The verb **rendre** means *to return* in the sense of *give back.*

(b) When *return = come back*

Revenez le plus tôt possible.   Return   }
                                        Come back *as soon as possible.*

The verb **revenir** means *return* in the sense of *come back.*

(c) When *return = go back*

Je ne **retournerai** pas tout de suite   *I will not* { return / go back *to Paris at once.*
à Paris.

The verb **retourner** means *return* in the sense of *go back.*

CAUTION: Do NOT use «retourner» when you mean *return* in the sense of *come back* or *give back.* The verb **retourner** does not have the all-inclusive meaning of the English *return.*

(d) When *return = return home*

Tu devrais parler à Georges; il **est**   *You should speak to George; he*
rentré à trois heures du matin.   *returned / came back home* } *at three in the morning.*

The verb **rentrer** means *return* in the sense of *return home.*

48. room

(a) How to express *room* without indicating the type of room

Combien de **pièces** y a-t-il dans ce   *How many rooms are there in that castle?*
château?

The general word for *room* is **la pièce.**

(b) When *room = bedroom*

Est-ce que Madame Renaud loue   *Does Mrs. Renaud rent rooms?*
des **chambres**?

The word **chambre** indicates a *bedroom.*

(c) When a *room* is used for meetings

Nous avons besoin d'une grande salle pour notre prochaine réunion. | *We need a large* room *for our next meeting.*

The word **salle** indicates a room used for meetings.

(d) When *room* = *space*

Il n'y a pas beaucoup de **place** dans ta voiture. | *There isn't much* room *in your car.*

When *room* = *space*, the French use **place**.
Note that **le salon** is the formal living room, but the room where the family lives is **la salle de séjour,** also called **le séjour.**

49. save

(a) When *save* means *to save from destruction*

Marius m'a **sauvé** la vie. | *Marius saved my life.*
L'inondation a tout emporté; on n'a rien pu **sauver.** | *The flood took everything; we couldn't save anything.*

The verb **sauver** indicates *saving a person or a thing from destruction*. It is most often used to refer to saving persons.

(b) When *save* means *to keep*

Nous **avons gardé** quelques fruits pour vos amis. | *We* saved *some fruit for your friends.*

The verb **garder** means *save* in the sense of *to keep*.

(c) How to say *save money*

Jean **a fait des économies** pour s'acheter une moto. | *John* has been saving up *in order to buy himself a motorcycle.*
J'ai donné une tirelire aux enfants pour les encourager à **économiser.** | *I gave a piggy bank to the children to encourage them* to save.
Économisez votre argent au lieu de le dépenser inutilement. | Save *your money instead of spending it uselessly.*

The expression **faire des économies** is often used to mean *to save money* in the sense of *to save up;* the verb **économiser** is used with or without an object to mean *to save money.*

(d) When *save* is expressed by **mettre de côté**

Je **mettrai** mes notes **de côté,** elles pourront vous être utiles plus tard.	*I will* save *my notes; they can be useful to you later.*
Les Berger **ont mis** assez **de côté** pour se faire construire une belle maison.	*The Bergers* saved *enough to have a nice house constructed for themselves.*

The expression **mettre de côté** means *save* in the sense of *put aside* something for later use, whether it be money or something else.

50. sit

(a) How to say that *someone is sitting = seated*

La dame **assise** devant moi avait une coiffure si haute que je ne pouvais rien voir.	*The lady* {sitting / seated} *in front of me had such a high hair-do that I couldn't see anything.*

When **assis** is used as a pure adjective, it means *sitting* or *seated*.

Tout le monde **est assis**; on peut commencer.	*Everyone is* {sitting down / seated}*; we can begin.*

When **assis** follows the verb **être,** it is also an adjective. When *is sitting* (or its equivalent in other tenses) expresses a state rather than an action, it must be expressed by a form of **être assis.**

CAUTION: Do NOT express *is sitting* by the verb «s'asseoir»; rather, use a form of **être assis.**

(b) How to say that *someone is sitting down*

Après avoir chanté l'hymne national, tout le monde **s'est assis.**	*After singing the national anthem, everyone* sat down.

When *sit down* indicates an action rather than a state, a form of the verb **s'asseoir** must be used.

Note the difference between:

Elle **est assise.**	*She* is sitting (= is seated).
Elle **s'est assise.**	*She* sat down.

G. *Remplacez les mots anglais par leur équivalent français.*

1. Est-ce que le voisin nous (*returned*) notre scie? 2. Les enfants sont trop grands; il leur faut une (*room*) à chacun. 3. Il y a bien des façons de (*save*). 4. Ouf! Quelle journée! Je suis content de (*sit down*). 5. Cela vaut toujours la peine de (*save*). 6. Le maire devrait faire construire une plus grande (*room*) pour les fêtes. 7. Attendez-moi; je (*will return*) dans un instant. 8. On a pu (*save*) tous les papiers importants de l'incendie. 9. On est content de se remettre au travail en (*returning*) de vacances. 10. Inutile d'acheter ce buffet; il n'y aurait pas de (*room*) dans la salle à manger. 11. Même dans les moments les plus durs, je (*saved*) de l'argent. 12. Les Arnoux ont acheté une maison de dix (*rooms*) dans la banlieue. 13. Marguerite (*will not return*) à l'Hôtel Terminus, parce qu'il est devenu trop cher. 14. Lucie a fait un grand nettoyage; elle ne (*saved*) que quelques objets. 15. L'étudiant qui (*is sitting*) au cinquième rang s'endort toujours pendant le cours.

H. *Traduisez en français. Attention aux mots en italique.*

1. (*tu*) If you didn't smoke, you would *save* a great deal of money. 2. How can that family live in those two *rooms?* 3. Guy will *return* to Japan next year. 4. Marie-Claire bought some pretty green curtains for her *room*. 5. I *save* all the stamps I receive from abroad for Regis. 6. Juliette *sat down* on the sofa and listened to the music. 7. (*vous*) *Save up* for your old age. 8. In what *room* will the tournament be held? 9. (*tu*) *Return* home early this evening, since we are going out. 10. I like houses with a lot of *room*. 11. My old grandmother *was sitting* in her armchair near the window. 12. Their dog *saved* a child's life. 13. (*vous*) I am willing to lend you that book if you promise to *return* it to me. 14. When Roland receives his check, he always *saves* ten percent of it. 15. (*vous*) I didn't know that you had already *returned*.

Verb Review

Review the verbs **prendre** and **rire** according to the outline on page 283.

CHAPTER 14

The Passive Voice and the Causative Construction

I. The Passive Voice

When the subject of the sentence acts, we say that the sentence is in the ACTIVE VOICE. When the subject of the sentence is acted upon, we say that the sentence is in the PASSIVE VOICE.

ACTIVE VOICE	PASSIVE VOICE
John found *the money*.	*The money* was found *by John*.
The teacher will correct *that examination*.	*That examination* will be corrected *by the teacher*.

In the two above examples, note:

(a) The subject of the sentence in the active voice, (*John, teacher*) becomes the object of the preposition *by* and is called the 'agent' of the sentence in the passive voice.

(b) The object of the sentence in the active voice, (*money, examination*) becomes the subject of the sentence in the passive voice.

(c) The verb of the sentence in the passive voice is in the same tense as the verb of the sentence in the active voice.

(d) The verb of the sentence in the passive voice is made up of a form of the auxiliary *to be* + THE PAST PARTICIPLE of the verb in the active voice.

1. How is the passive voice formed in French?

Cet escroc **sera mis** en prison.	*This swindler* will be put *in prison.*
Les enfants **étaient** toujours **récompensés** pour leurs bonnes notes.	*The children* were *always* rewarded *for their good marks.*
La maison **a été vendue** hier.	*The house* was sold *yesterday.*

In French, the passive voice is made up of

> a form of the auxiliary verb **être** + PAST PARTICIPLE

2. How and with what does the past participle of a verb in the passive voice agree?

(See examples in §1.)

The past participle of a verb in the passive voice agrees in gender and number with the subject of the sentence.

3. By what preposition is the agent usually introduced in French?

Cet article sera certainement lu **par tout le monde.**	*That article will certainly be read* <u>by</u> everyone.
Ce roman a été écrit **par un Russe.**	*That novel was written* <u>by</u> a Russian.
Cette maison a été détruite **par l'incendie.**	*This house was destroyed* <u>by</u> the fire.

In French, **par** usually introduces the phrases indicating the agent.
The agent is the person or the thing by which the action of a sentence in the passive voice is caused or performed.

4. When is *de* used to introduce the phrase indicating the agent?

Elle était aimée **de tous.**	*She was loved* <u>by</u> all.
Le Président était suivi **de plusieurs ministres.**	*The President was followed* <u>by</u> several ministers.
Il sera accompagné **de deux secrétaires.**	*He will be accompanied* <u>by</u> two secretaries.
La maison était entourée **d'un jardin.**	*The house was surrounded* <u>by</u> a garden.

The preposition **de** is less strong than **par.** It usually follows verbs which indicate a state, a mental action, or an habitual action, where the role of the agent is less dynamic.

Also, certain verbs are normally followed by **de,** as, for example, **entourer de, couvrir de, remplir de,** etc.

5. If a verb can be followed by both *par* and *de,* what determines whether *par* or *de* should introduce the phrase indicating the agent?

Les verres ont été de nouveau remplis **par** le garçon.	Les verres étaient remplis **de** vin.
L'enfant qui allait tomber a été saisi **par** son frère.	L'enfant était saisi **de** terreur.
Irène était très aimée **par** son fiancé.	Irène était aimée **de** ses amis.

One can almost always use **par** to introduce a phrase indicating the agent unless the past participle is habitually followed by **de.**

The preposition **par** is dynamic, the preposition **de** is weaker. When the role of the agent is forceful, **par** is likely to be used, when the role of the agent is less active, **de** is often found. The preposition **par** is likely to indicate an action that took place at one time; both **par** and **de** may indicate habitual actions.

A. *Mettez les verbes des phrases suivantes à la voix passive en employant le temps indiqué.*

1. (PASSÉ COMPOSÉ) Cette chambre (réserver) par Monsieur et Madame Arnaud, mais ils ne peuvent pas venir. 2. (PRÉSENT DE L'INDICATIF) Les fleurs (récolter) pour en faire des parfums. 3. (PRÉSENT DU SUBJONCTIF) J'aimerais que Charlotte (inviter) à votre soirée. 4. (FUTUR) Les manifestations (interdire) à l'Université. 5. (IMPARFAIT) Ce restaurant (tenir) par les parents de Pierre. 6. (FUTUR) Si le coup réussit, ce peuple (gouverner) par des gens capables de tout. 7. (PASSÉ DU SUBJONCTIF) Je ne crois pas que ce poème (écrire) par Georges. 8. (IMPARFAIT) Les hommes les plus influents (inviter) chez le maire. 9. (PASSÉ COMPOSÉ) Le petit garçon du voisin (mordre) par son chien. 10. (FUTUR) Dépêchez-vous, sinon toutes les cerises (cueillir).

B. *Traduisez en français.*

1. I wonder why Mr. Lenoir is being watched by the police. 2. Considerable sums are being spent each year by the state. 3. The criminal was being defended by Maître Olivier. 4. Everything they

had was lost in this fire.   5. The new ambassador was received by the President.

PATTERN PRACTICE: using the passive

Pattern 1

YOU HEAR   Son livre sera publié demain.
YOU SAY   Son livre a été publié hier.

Pattern 2

YOU HEAR   On a réparé ma voiture.
YOU SAY   Ma voiture a été réparée.

6. How does French often avoid an English passive when there is no agent expressed in the English sentence?

On a donné le prix au meilleur élève.
The prize was given *to the best pupil.*

On verra l'éclipse demain soir.
The eclipse will be seen *tomorrow evening.*

Although the passive is by no means uncommon in French, it is not used as frequently as in English. There are certain verbs with which it is never used, other verbs with which it is not used in certain tenses, still others where it could be used but sounds somewhat unnatural. Long experience in speaking French is necessary to develop a precise feeling for when a French sentence sounds natural in the passive and when it does not. But French has various other ways of expressing certain sentences which English puts into the passive.

To express an English passive in a sentence where there is no agent, French often uses the indefinite pronoun **on** + VERB IN ACTIVE VOICE.

C. *Traduisez en français en évitant la voix passive.*

1. Why was I awakened at six o'clock?   2. How is this sentence translated?   3. That was said at the beginning of the hour.   4. The prizes will be distributed to the winners Saturday morning.   5. The door was opened to allow[1] a little more air to come in.   6. Bridge will be played after the reception.   7. Christmas carols are always

---

[1] *allow to come in* = **laisser entrer**

sung in the month of December.   8. That evening[2] the doors were
locked at 8:30.   9. French is spoken in that store.   10. His name
was[3] taken out of the telephone book.

---

[2] In time expressions referring to the past, how is *that* expressed?   [3] *take out* = **enlever**

PATTERN PRACTICE: avoiding the passive voice

Pattern 3

YOU HEAR   Cette maison sera vendue la semaine prochaine.
YOU SAY   On vendra cette maison la semaine prochaine.

7. How does French often avoid an English passive when an agent is expressed in the English sentence?

Un célèbre humoriste **a dit** cela.   *That* was said *by a famous humorist.*
Ceux qui l'ont vu n'**oublieront** pas   *That incident* will not be forgotten *by*
   cet incident.   *those who saw it.*

French often uses the active voice to express an idea which English
might express with a sentence in the passive voice. Some French
verbs are not normally used in the passive voice.

D. *Traduisez en français en évitant la voix passive.*

1. That explosion was heard by several persons.   2. The boss would
be liked by everyone if he were more patient.   3. All the money for
the family was earned by the oldest brother.   4. This doctor had
been criticized by several of his colleagues.   5. The problem was
explained to the students by the teacher.   6. That talk will be given[1]
by a well-known specialist.   7. The car was driven by a sixteen-
year-old boy[2].   8. By whom was that man seen?

---

[1] Use a form of **faire**.   [2] The French say: *a boy of sixteen years*.

8. How does French express an English passive sentence whose subject would be the indirect object in the active sentence?

Le notaire montrera le testament   The heirs will be shown *the will* by
   aux héritiers jeudi.   the notary *Thursday.*
On a permis à Suzanne de passer   Suzanne was allowed *to spend the*
   le week-end chez les Grillet.   *weekend at the Grillets.*

Consider the passive and active forms of the following English sentence:

Passive: *I was given* the book by a friend.
Active: A friend *gave* the book *to me*.

The subject of the passive sentence is *I*. This *I* would become *to me* in the active sentence. Thus, the subject of the passive sentence is the indirect object of the active sentence. As you can see from the examples above, this is not the case in French.

The indirect object of the active form of a French sentence CAN- NOT become the subject of the passive form of that sentence. In- stead, French expresses the sentence <u>in the active voice only</u>.

E. *Traduisez en français.*

1. We were forbidden to enter that room.   2. The workmen were promised a raise in[1] pay.   3. (*vous*) You will be given the necessary information by my secretary.   4. We were served coffee and sand- wiches in the plane.   5. The delegates were told to come back the next day.   6. The defendant was asked by the lawyer where he had been that evening.   7. (*vous*) You will be sent some samples by the salesman[2] of that company[3].   8. We were shown some snapshots at the Arnauds'[4].   9. The children were allowed to go to the movies yesterday evening.

---

[1] de   [2] représentant   [3] maison   [4] In French, proper names do not take an -*s* in the plural. The plural is indicated by the plural form of the definite article.

9. When is the English passive expressed by a French reflexive?

Ce produit **se vend** partout.   *That product* is sold *all over.*
Ça ne **se fait** pas ici.   *That* isn't done *here.*

The reflexive form of a French verb is often used to express an English passive when the sentence describes a general rather than a specific action.

Compare the following three sentences, each of which has a differ- ent meaning, although English uses approximately the same con- struction in each.

a. Ce livre **se vend** partout.   *That book is sold everywhere.*

Here, French uses the reflexive form of the verb to describe a general action.

b. Ce livre **est vendu.**   *That book is sold.*

Here, a form of **être** + PAST PARTICIPLE describes a state, so that **vendu** is an adjective, and the sentence is not in the passive voice at all.

c. Ce livre **a été vendu** hier.   *That book was sold yesterday.*

Here, **a été vendu** is a real passive which describes one specific action.

10. In what other way is the reflexive form of a French verb used to express an English passive?

Mon ami **s'appelle** Jean Colin.   *My friend is called Jean Colin.*
Orléans **se trouve** au sud de Paris.   *Orleans is located to the south of Paris.*

The reflexive forms of certain French verbs are used idiomatically where English uses the passive voice. Each verb of this type must be learned individually with its meaning.

F. *Traduisez en français.*

1. Everything is done automatically in that factory.   2. The Pyrenees are¹ situated between France and Spain.   3. That telephone is used² only in case of an³ emergency.   4. Green⁴ was worn a great deal last year.   5. That is said, but it⁵ isn't written.   6. Hundreds⁶ of novels are published each year.

---

¹ Use a form of **trouver.**   ² Use a form of **employer.**   ³ Omit in French.   ⁴ Supply the definite article.   ⁵ **ça**   ⁶ Here *hundreds* is a noun.

II. The Causative Construction

11. What is the causative construction? With what verb does French express it?

Le professeur **fera lire** les élèves.   *The teacher will have the pupils read.*
Notre voisin **a fait peindre** la maison.   *Our neighbor had the house painted.*

The causative construction expresses the idea of 'having something done' or of 'having someone do something' — of causing something to be done or of causing someone to do something.

NOTE: When the English infinitive follows a form of *have*, it is used without *to*. For example, in the sentence "The teacher will have the pupils read," *read* is an infinitive without *to*.

In English, this idea is expressed by *have* + INFINITIVE or *have* + PAST PARTICIPLE.

NOTE: When the infinitive follows a form of *have*, it is used without *to*.

In French, the causative is expressed by **faire** + INFINITIVE.
The causative always has at least one object and often it has two objects.

NOTE: Consider the sentence: **Le professeur fera lire les élèves.** In this sentence, **les élèves** is the object of the verb **fera,** and the subject of the infinitive **lire.**

Now consider the sentence: **Notre voisin a fait peindre la maison.** Here, **la maison** is the object of the verb **peindre.**

In a sentence with a causative construction, the object is sometimes governed by a form of **faire,** sometimes by the INFINITIVE following **faire.**

12. When the causative has only one object, what kind of object is it?

Nous **ferons écrire les enfants.**	*We*'ll have the children write.
Ils **faisaient écrire des lettres.**	*They* used to have letters written.

When a causative has only one object, it is always a direct object whether a person or a thing.

G. *Traduisez en français.*

1. The teacher doesn't have Roger[1] work, because he was sick.
2. Our neighbors are having a garage[1] built.   3. (*vous*) Why did you have your father-in-law[1] intervene?   4. (*tu*) When will you have the television[1] repaired?   5. We'll have those records[1] played later.

---

[1] In the causative construction in French, the noun object follows the infinitive directly.

PATTERN PRACTICE: the causative with one noun object

Pattern 4

    YOU HEAR Je lave ma voiture tous les samedis.
    YOU SAY   Je fais laver ma voiture tous les samedis.

13. When a causative construction has two objects—usually a person and a thing—what kind of objects are they?

Nous avons fait étudier **sa leçon à Lucie.**	*We had* <u>Lucy</u> *study her lesson.*
Je ferai ranger **ses affaires à Jean.**	*I'll have* <u>John</u> *put* his things *in order.*

When a causative construction has two objects, the thing is the direct object and the person the indirect object.

NOTE: Occasionally, a causative construction has two personal objects. In such cases, the person receiving the action is the direct object of the infinitive, and the person performing the action is the agent and is introduced by **par.**

Le président fera présenter **le conférencier par son collègue.**	*The president will have* <u>his colleague</u> *introduce* the speaker.

14. Sometimes the use of the indirect object for the person causes ambiguity. How may this ambiguity be avoided?

J'ai fait écrire une lettre **par mon frère.**	*I had* my brother *write a letter.*
Il fait lire ce roman **par tous ses amis.**	*He has* all his friends *read that novel.*

In cases where the use of **à** + PERSONAL OBJECT could result in ambiguity, it is not incorrect to use that construction for the causative, but such a sentence is often made clearer by using instead **par** + PERSONAL OBJECT.

NOTE: Equally correct is: **J'ai fait écrire une lettre à mon frère.** But this could mean either: "I had a letter written to my brother," or, "I had my brother write a letter." Likewise equally correct is: **Il fait lire ce roman à tous ses amis.** But this could mean either: "He has all his friends read that novel," or, "He has that novel read to all his friends."

H. *Traduisez en français.*

1. We had his parents correct his mistakes. 2. Mr. Géré had his wife pack[1] his suitcase. 3. Businessmen have their secretaries[2] write their letters. 4. I will have the cleaning woman wash the windows. 5. That teacher has all his students copy the same poem.

---

[1] *pack a suitcase* = **faire une valise** [2] Use the singular in French.

15. When the causative construction governs a pronoun object, what is the position of the pronoun object?

Jacques **fera lire** le testament de son oncle.	Jacques **le fera lire**.
Nous **ferons réparer** notre voiture demain.	Nous **la ferons réparer** demain.
La ville **a fait abattre** cette vieille maison au propriétaire.	La ville **la lui a fait** abattre.
Mon père **m'a fait recommencer** mes devoirs.	Mon père **me les a fait** recommencer.

The pronoun objects of a causative construction normally precede the form of the verb **faire**. Pronouns come in their usual order.

NOTE: When the causative construction is in the affirmative imperative, pronoun objects follow the form of **faire**. Ex.: **Faites-le lire.**

16. When the verb *faire* is used in a compound tense, what about the agreement of its past participle with a preceding direct object?

Je **les ai fait** vendre.	*I had them sold.*
Où sont **les lettres que** nous **avons fait** copier?	*Where are the letters that we had copied?*

When the past participle of the verb **faire** is followed by an infinitive, the past participle of **faire** is always invariable. In other words, when it is used as part of the causative construction, the past participle of **faire** does not agree with its preceding direct object.

I. Copiez les phrases françaises et traduisez en français les phrases anglaises. Attention à la position et à l'ordre des pronoms compléments.

(Use the French sentence of the exercise as a model in translating the following English sentence. Watch the position and order of pronoun objects and the agreement of the past participle.)

1. Avez-vous fait construire le garage cette année? (*Yes, I had it constructed this year.*) 2. Ferez-vous envoyer ce paquet par avion? (*Yes, I'll have it sent by plane.*) 3. Faisiez-vous travailler vos élèves pendant les week-ends? (*Yes, I used to have them work during the weekends.*) 4. M. Duchamp a-t-il fait couper ces beaux arbres? (*No, he didn't have them cut down.*) 5. Le médecin vous a-t-il fait prendre un nouveau remède? (*No, he didn't have me take any.*) 6. Claude vous a-t-il fait conduire sa voiture? (*Yes, he had me drive it.*) 7. Leur mère a-t-elle fait ranger leurs jouets aux enfants? (*Yes, she had them put them away.*)

PATTERN PRACTICE: the position of pronoun objects governed by a causative

Pattern 5

YOU HEAR   Nous avons fait venir le médecin.
YOU SAY   Nous l'avons fait venir.

Problem Words

51. soon

(a) When *soon* is expressed by **bientôt**

Ma fille aura **bientôt** vingt ans.   *My daughter will* soon *be twenty years old.*

The common word for *soon* is **bientôt**. But **bientôt** is not usually modified.

(b) When *soon* is expressed by **tôt**

Ne venez pas si **tôt**.   *Don't come so soon.*
Vous avez parlé trop **tôt**.   *You spoke too soon.*
Il aurait fallu faire cela **plus tôt**.   *You should have done that sooner.*

To express *soon* modified by an adverb, use **tôt**. Also, **tôt** is used in the expression **tôt ou tard,** which means *sooner or later.*

(c) Expressions embodying *soon*

dès que (common)
aussitôt que (mainly literary)   *as soon as*

dès que possible
aussitôt que possible
le plus tôt possible   *as soon as possible*
au plus tôt

52. spend

(a) When it is a question of *spending money*

Vous **dépensez** beaucoup trop d'**ar-**   *You* spend *much too much* <u>money</u> *for*
gent pour des choses superflues.   *superfluous things.*

The verb **dépenser** is used when it is a question of *spending money.*

(b) When it is a question of *spending time*

Nous **avons passé** <u>**deux semaines**</u>   *We* spent <u>two weeks</u> *in Portugal.*
au Portugal.
J'ai passé <u>**une heure**</u> à écrire cette   *I* spent <u>an hour</u> *writing that letter.*
lettre.

The verb **passer** is used when it is a question of *spending time.*

CAUTION: The verb **passer** must NOT be followed by the present participle to express the idea of spending a given amount of time doing something. French expresses this construction by **à** + INFINITIVE.

53. stop

(a) When *stop* may be expressed by **cesser**

Le bruit **a cessé.**   *The noise* stopped.
Tiens! Il **a cessé** <u>**de neiger.**</u>   *Look! It* has stopped <u>snowing.</u>
Quand est-ce que les gens du dessus   *When will the people upstairs* stop
cesseront <u>**de faire**</u> tout ce bruit?   <u>making</u> *all that noise?*

The verb **cesser** never takes a direct object. It is most often used with **de** + INFINITIVE, although it may be used as in the first example when a thing is the subject of the verb.

(b) When *stop* may be expressed by **arrêter**

Arrêtez donc **la voiture** un peu plus   Stop the car *a little more gently*.
   doucement.
Arrête donc **de prendre** tous ces   Stop <u>taking</u> *all that medicine!*
   médicaments!

The verb **arrêter** is usually followed by a direct object. It is sometimes followed by **de** + INFINITIVE.

(c) When *stop* may be expressed by **s'arrêter**

Nous **nous sommes arrêtés** pour   *We* stopped *to admire the view.*
   admirer la vue.
Je ne peux pas **m'arrêter** si près du   *I can't* stop *so near the crossing.*
   carrefour.
Il **s'est arrêté de parler**.   *He* stopped <u>talking</u>.

The reflexive form **s'arrêter** is used when no object follows. It is sometimes followed by **de** + INFINITIVE.

54. such

(a) How to say *such a* + NOUN

Avez-vous jamais entendu **une his-**
   toire <u>pareille</u>?
Avez-vous jamais entendu **une his-**
   toire <u>comme ça</u>?   } *Have you ever heard* <u>such</u> *a story?*
Avez-vous jamais entendu **une <u>telle</u>**
   histoire?

The English *such* + NOUN may be expressed by **un tel** + NOUN, **un** + NOUN + **pareil,** and by **un** + NOUN + **comme ça.**

(b) How to say *such a* + ADJECTIVE

Je n'ai jamais entendu une histoire
   aussi (tellement) drôle.   } *I never heard* such a funny *story.*
Je n'ai jamais entendu une histoire
   aussi drôle que ça.

The English *such a* + ADJECTIVE may be expressed by **aussi** (or **tellement**) + ADJECTIVE or **aussi** + ADJECTIVE + **que ça.**

J. *Remplacez les mots anglais par leur équivalent français.*

1. Pourquoi Nicolas est-il rentré (*sooner*) que toi?   2. (*tu*) Où (*will you spend*) les trois mois d'été?   3. Voulez-vous (*stop*) votre taxi au coin de la rue?   4. Si Marcel ne revient pas (*soon*), je m'en vais.   5. J'ai dû (*stop*) plusieurs fois en route pour me reposer.   6. Personne ne peut (*spend*) tant d'argent sans se ruiner.   7. (*As soon as*) vous recevrez sa lettre, prévenez-moi.   8. Je ne peux rien entendre; (*stop*) l'aspirateur, s'il te plaît.   9. Quand Thomas (*stops*) de travailler, c'est pour dormir.

K. *Traduisez en français. Attention aux mots en italique.*

1. (*vous*) You'll come to see me *soon*, won't you?   2. Ah, that Micheline! She never *stops* talking!   3. I never saw *such* a hard exercise!   4. *Stop* making that noise!   5. (*vous*) If you *spend* your money like that, you won't go[1] far.   6. (*vous*) Come *soon* enough to have[2] dinner with us.   7. (*tu*) If you need information, *stop* someone on[3] the street.   8. *Such* a man should be the mayor of the city.   9. I *stopped* to have[4] lunch at the Hôtel de la Poste.   10. We are invited to *spend* the evening at Dr.[5] Beaugendre's.   11. (*vous*) Come[6] and see me *as soon as possible*.   12. Won't it ever *stop* raining?   13. I have rarely heard *such* a boring lecture.   14. (*tu*) Have you ever seen *such* a monster?

---

[1] Use a form of **aller loin**.   [2] *have dinner* = **dîner**   [3] **dans**   [4] *have lunch* = **déjeuner**   [5] Use the article before such titles.   [6] French uses **venir** + INFINITIVE.

Verb Review

Review the verbs **savoir** and **suivre** according to the outline on page 283.

CHAPTER 15

The verb *devoir*

The verb **devoir** constitutes a difficulty to an English-speaking person, because no one English verb corresponds exactly to the French verb **devoir.** Each tense of **devoir** has its own translation, and in some tenses **devoir** may have several meanings, according to the context.

1. What meanings may *devoir* have in the present tense?

M. Guillot **doit** arriver demain.	*Mr. Guillot* is to *arrive tomorrow.*
Vous **devez** partir tout de suite.	*You* must (have to) *leave at once.*
Anne **doit** beaucoup aimer la musique.	*Anne* must *like* (probably *likes*) *music a great deal.*
Votre fils **doit** lire beaucoup.	*Your son* must *read* { (has *to read*) (probably *reads*) } *a great deal.*

In the present tense, **devoir** means either *is to* (*am to, are to*) or *must.*

But *must* itself has two possible meanings: *has to* and *probably does.*
In the second example above, *must* clearly means *have to.* The *must* of the third example clearly means *probably does.* But in the fourth example, there are two possibilities. "*Your son must read a great deal*", may mean: *Your son* <u>has to</u> *read a great deal,* or: *Your son* <u>probably</u> *reads a great deal.* When the two possible interpretations exist, the context decides.

198

A. *Traduisez en anglais les phrases suivantes. Attention au verbe* **devoir.** *Si vous traduisez ce verbe par* must, *indiquez le sens de* must.

1. Mon collègue *doit* me rendre mon livre demain, et je vous le passerai. 2. Si vous *devez* leur écrire, faites-le tout de suite. 3. Il *doit* y avoir des ours dans cette forêt. 4. On *doit* toujours faire de son mieux. 5. Le professeur *doit* nous expliquer ces règles cette semaine.

PATTERN PRACTICE: the use of the present of **devoir**

Pattern 1

YOU HEAR   Il faut que je parte demain.
YOU SAY   Je dois partir demain.

Pattern 2

YOU HEAR   Vous parlez probablement plusieurs langues.
YOU SAY   Vous devez parler plusieurs langues.

2. What meanings may *devoir* have in the imperfect?

M. Guillot **devait** arriver ce matin.	*Mr. Guillot was to arrive this morning.*
Gilbert **devait** travailler plus dur pour se rattraper.	*Gilbert had to work harder to catch up.*
Ces gens-là **devaient** être très riches.	*Those people must have been (probably were) very rich.*
Votre fils **devait** lire beaucoup.	*Your son* {*used to have to read* / *probably used to read*} *a great deal.*

In the imperfect **devoir** sometimes means *was to* (*were to*), sometimes *had to*, and sometimes *must have*. (Occasionally, the imperfect of **devoir** has other less common meanings.)

3. When does the imperfect of *devoir* mean *had to* and when *must have*?

Claude **devait** finir son travail avant de s'occuper de nous.	*Claude had to finish his work before turning his attention to us.*
Cet homme **devait** savoir plusieurs langues.	*That man must have known (probably knew) several languages.*

When the imperfect of **devoir** represents the past of the English *must = have to*, it is often translated by *had to*.

When the imperfect of **devoir** is the past of the English *must =
probably does*, it is usually translated by *must have = probably did*.

When the imperfect of **devoir** is expressed by the English *must have*,
it normally represents an habitual state or action. Even though *must
have* looks like an English present perfect, it corresponds to the French
imperfect of **devoir**. The best way to determine the proper translation is to rephrase the sentence, using the word *probably* + THE MAIN
VERB.

B. *Traduisez en anglais les phrases suivantes. Attention au verbe* **devoir**.

1. Nous *devions* partir demain, mais c'est impossible.   2. Avant de
sortir le soir, nous *devions* montrer à nos parents ce que nous avions
fait.   3. Votre voisin *devait* être bien embarrassé chaque fois que
vous lui racontiez cette histoire.   4. Quand Florence habitait chez
nous, elle *devait* passer l'après-midi à garder les enfants.   4. Les
Lemire *devaient* faire le tour du monde cet été, mais ils n'ont pas pu.

PATTERN PRACTICE: the use of the imperfect of **devoir**

Pattern 3

YOU HEAR   Il fallait toujours que nous arrivions à l'heure.
YOU SAY   Nous devions toujours arriver à l'heure.

Pattern 4

YOU HEAR   Votre collègue comprenait probablement l'espagnol.
YOU SAY   Votre collègue devait comprendre l'espagnol.

4. What two meanings may *devoir* have in the compound past?

J'**ai dû** travailler toute la nuit pour faire mes devoirs.	*I had to work the whole night to do my exercises.*
Guy **a dû** se faire mal en tombant.	*Guy must have hurt himself (probably hurt himself) when he fell.*
Leurs portes étaient fermées à clé; les voisins **ont dû** entrer par la fenêtre.	*Their doors were locked; the neighbors must have* ⎫ *probably* ⎭ *entered through the window.*

In the compound past, the verb **devoir** sometimes means *had to*,
which is the past of *must = has to*. This is clearly the case in the first
example above. It sometimes means *must have = probably did*, which

is the past of *must* = *probably does*. This is clearly the case in the second example above. But in the third example, either possibility is present, and the context must decide.

When the imperfect of **devoir** means *must have*, it describes a customary state or action, whereas when the compound past of **devoir** means *must have*, it indicates a past action at one definite past time.

C. *Traduisez en anglais les phrases suivantes. Attention au verbe* **devoir**.

1. Si vous étiez chez les Lagarde, vous *avez dû* voir Pierre.   2. Personne ne parlait anglais ici; Agnès *a dû* aller en Angleterre pour l'apprendre.   3. Comme il n'y avait pas assez de place dans la voiture, nous *avons dû* laisser les enfants à la maison.   5. Juliette n'est pas encore là; elle *a dû* se tromper de route.

PATTERN PRACTICE: the use of the compound past of **devoir**

Pattern 5

YOU HEAR   Il a fallu que je finisse mon travail avant de sortir.
YOU SAY   J'ai dû finir mon travail avant de sortir.

Pattern 6

YOU HEAR   Il est probable que Félix est parti ce matin.
YOU SAY   Félix a dû partir ce matin.

5. What does *devoir* mean in the conditional?

On annonce le froid; vous **devriez** mettre un manteau.	*They say it will be cold; you* should *put on an overcoat.*
Les Lepic **devraient** être plus patients avec leurs enfants.	*The Lepics* ought to *be more patient with their children.*

In the conditional, **devoir** means *should, ought to.*

6. What does *devoir* mean in the past conditional?

Les Aubry n'**auraient** pas **dû** acheter cette voiture.	*The Aubrys* should *not* have *bought that car.*
Vous **auriez dû** nous dire que vos parents seraient là.	*You* ought to have *told us that your parents would be there.*

In the past conditional, **devoir** means *should have, ought to have.*

D. *Traduisez en anglais. Attention au verbe* **devoir.**

1. Les Bréger *auraient dû* prendre l'avion pour venir ici. 2. Nous *devrions* leur dire de quoi il s'agit. 3. Georges, tu *devrais* aider ton frère à finir sa leçon. 4. Robert *aurait dû* faire cela quand je le lui ai demandé. 5. Ce film est très drôle; vos amis *devraient* aller le voir.

PATTERN PRACTICE: the conditional and past conditional of **devoir**

Pattern 7

YOU HEAR   J'irai chez les Minard demain.

YOU SAY   Je devrais aller chez les Minard demain.

Pattern 8

YOU HEAR   Robert n'est pas parti avant onze heures.

YOU SAY   Robert aurait dû partir avant onze heures.

7. In what other ways does French express the idea of *must = has to***?**

Il faut que vous vous couchiez plus tôt.	You must *go to bed earlier.*
Nous étions obligés de surveiller cet enfant tout le temps.	We used to have to *watch that child all the time.*

Note the following equivalents:

Je dois + INFINITIVE	**Il faut que je** + SUBJUNCTIVE	**Je suis obligé de** + INFINITIVE
Je devais + INFINITIVE	**Il fallait que je** + SUBJUNCTIVE	**J'étais obligé de** + INFINITIVE
J'ai dû + INFINITIVE	**Il a fallu que je** + SUBJUNCTIVE	**J'ai été obligé de** + INFINITIVE
Je devrai + INFINITIVE	**Il faudra que je** + SUBJUNCTIVE	**Je serai obligé de** + INFINITIVE

In the present, imperfect, compound past, and future, the INFINITIVE appropriate tenses of *must = have to* may also be expressed by forms of **il faut que** + SUBJUNCTIVE and by forms of **être obligé de** + INFINITIVE.

The **il faut que** construction is somewhat stronger than **devoir.** When *must* is expressed by forms of **être obligé de,** it is about the equivalent of *to be obliged to.* Sometimes, but not always, any of the three forms may be used to express the same idea.

E. *Traduisez en français chaque phrase de trois façons différentes.*

1. We used to have to work every day except Sunday. 2. Yesterday I had to leave at five o'clock. 3. Our friends have to stay in Bordeaux this evening. 4. The Leclercs[1] will have to move next week.

---

[1] In French, the plural form of proper names does not take an -*s*.

EXERCICES D'ENSEMBLE

F. *Remplacez par la forme convenable de* **devoir** *les mots anglais entre parenthèses.*

1. Nous (*had to*) prendre l'autocar pour aller à Paris hier. 2. Même si cela vous ennuie, vous (*must*) faire cette visite. 3. Les acteurs (*must have been*) furieux chaque fois qu'ils lisaient les critiques de M. Lafont. 4. Georges (*has to*) finir cette affaire avant de partir. 5. Maurice est seul; nous (*should have*) l'inviter pour dimanche. 6. Je (*am to*) passer mon examen aujourd'hui. 7. Madame Gervaise est toute pâle, elle (*must*) être malade. 8. François (*must have*) perdre sa montre, il n'en porte plus. 9. Les Gaspard (*were to*) arriver ce matin; je me demande pourquoi ils ne sont pas là. 10. Vous (*should*) acheter une nouvelle voiture. 11. Le gardien (*had to*) nous ouvrir la porte chaque fois que nous arrivions tard dans la nuit.

G. *Traduisez en français les phrases suivantes, en employant dans chaque phrase une forme du verbe* **devoir.**

1. (*vous*) You *should* always *knock* before entering a room[1]. 2. Mrs. Henriot was always very elegant; her husband *must have spent* a lot of money on[2] her. 3. The visitors *must* not *touch* the paintings. 5. We *had to hand in* our papers[3] yesterday morning. 4. Hubert *was to write* me every day, but I have received only one letter from him. 6. George doesn't have any money; he *must have spent* it last week. 7. Our neighbors have a new boat; they *must be* rich. 8. My friends are late; they *should have taken* a taxi. 9. We *are to eat* at grandmother's today. 10. When I was young, I *used to have to get up* at six in[4] the morning.

---

[1] **pièce** [2] **pour** [3] Not «papiers». [4] **du**

Problem Words

55. take

(a) When *take* is expressed by **prendre**

Qui **a pris** la voiture?   *Who took the car?*

The verb **prendre** is the commonest way to express *take*. But it cannot be used indiscriminately to express *take*.

(b) When *take* is expressed by **porter**

Le chauffeur **a porté** nos valises au   *The driver took our suitcases to the taxi.*
taxi.

When *take* is the equivalent of *carry to*, it is usually expressed by **porter.**

(c) When *take* is expressed by **emporter**

N'**emporte** pas <u>la télévision</u> dans ta   *Don't take <u>the television</u> into your room.*
chambre.

When *take* means *to carry something away*, it may be expressed by **emporter.**

(d) When *take* is expressed by **mener**

Nous **avons mené** <u>nos invités</u> au   *We took our <u>guests</u> to the restaurant.*
restaurant.

French has several ways of expressing *to take a person* (*somewhere*). When the verb **mener** is used, the destination must be indicated.

(e) When *take* is expressed by **emmener**

J'**emmène** <u>Françoise</u> ce soir.   *I am taking <u>Frances</u> (with me) this evening.*

J'**emmène** <u>Françoise</u> **au cinéma** ce   *I am taking <u>Frances</u> to the movies this evening.*
soir.

The verb **emmener** means *to take someone away*. It may be used either with or without the destination.

NOTE: In certain cases, forms of the verb **amener** may also be used to express the idea of taking *a person* or *thing away*, but **amener** also has the meaning of *bringing a person* or *a thing*.

(f) How to say *to take time to* . . .

Le menuisier **a mis** cinq jours $\begin{cases} à \\ pour \end{cases}$ *The carpenter* took *five days* to do *that work.*

faire ce travail.

The idiomatic **mettre** + period of time + **à** (or **pour**) + INFINITIVE expresses *to take so much time to do something*.

(g) How to say *to take an examination*

Nous **passons notre examen** à deux heures.   *We* take our test *at two o'clock.*

The expression **passer un examen** means *to take an examination.*

NOTE: In present-day French, **passer un examen** is also often used to mean *to pass an examination.*

(h) How to say *to take a course*

Suivez-vous **des cours** intéressants?   Are *you* taking *interesting* courses?

The expression **suivre un cours** means *to take a course.* It is becoming more and more common to say **prendre un cours,** but it is best for the learner to avoid this expression.

(i) How to say *to take a magazine*

Je vais **m'abonner à** plusieurs revues.   *I am going* to take *several magazines.*
Je **suis abonné** au journal du matin.   *I* take *the morning paper.*

When *take = subscribe to,* French uses **s'abonner à** to indicate the action of subscribing or the state of being a subscriber, and **être abonné à** to indicate the state of being a subscriber.

(j) How to say *to take (away) from*

Ce jouet est dangereux. **Enlevez**-le à cet enfant.   *That toy is dangerous.* Take *it* away from *that child.*
A qui **as**-tu **pris** cet argent?   *Who(m) did you* take *that money* from?

When *to take from* has the clear implication of *to take away from*, **enlever** is usually found with an indirect object. Otherwise, **prendre** may be often used with an indirect object.

(**k**) How *take* is expressed by **faire** in some expressions

There are many idiomatic expressions with **faire** which English expresses with *to take*, such as

faire une promenade	*take a walk*
faire un tour	*take a stroll*
faire un voyage	*take a trip*

56. teach

(**a**) When *teach* is expressed by **enseigner**

Qui **a enseigné votre classe** pendant votre absence?	*Who* taught your class *during your absence?*
Mademoiselle Bouillet **enseigne les mathématiques** au lycée.	*Miss Bouillet* teaches mathematics *in high school.*

The verb **enseigner** is used with a direct object to mean *teach*. The direct object may be the subject taught, but not normally the person taught. For instance, to express in French: *Mr. Duparc teaches John,* one would have to say something like: **Monsieur Duparc est le professeur de Jean.**

Qui **enseignera** le latin **à Philippe?**	*Who will* teach *Latin* to Philip?

The verb **enseigner** may also be used with a direct object indicating who is taught and an indirect object indicating who is taught.

(**b**) When *teach* may be expressed by **apprendre**

C'est un ami brésilien qui **nous a appris le portugais.**	*It is a Brazilian friend who* taught us Portuguese.
C'est un ami brésilien qui **a appris le portugais à Brigitte.**	*It is a Brazilian friend who* taught Brigitte Portuguese.

The basic meaning of **apprendre** is *learn*. But it means *teach* when it is followed by a direct object denoting the thing taught and an indirect object indicating the person taught.

Ma mère **a appris à ma sœur à**   *My mother* taught my sister to play
  jouer du piano.   *the piano.*

The verb **apprendre** means *teach* when followed by a *personal indirect object* + **à** + INFINITIVE.

57. time

(**a**) When *time* is expressed by **le temps**

Je n'ai pas **le temps** de réparer la   *I don't have* the time *to repair the radio.*
  radio.
Combien de **temps** faut-il pour faire   *How much* time *is needed to do that?*
  cela?

The general word for *time* is **le temps.**

The following expressions are used with **temps**:

à temps	*in time (for)*
en même temps	*at the same time*
de temps en temps	*from time to time*

In certain contexts **le temps** means *weather.*

(**b**) When *time* is expressed by **la fois**

Robert a dû répéter son explication   *Robert had to repeat his explanation*
  trois **fois.**   *three* times.
Chaque **fois** que tu viens il pleut.   *It rains each* time *you come.*

The word **fois** is somewhat synonymous with *occasion*. It is used with numerals as well as with other words which indicate quantity.

(**c**) When *time* is expressed by **heure**

Quelle **heure** est-il?   *What* time *is it?*
C'est **l'heure** du thé.   *It is tea* time.

The word **heure** is used to ask *what time it is* and sometimes to indicate the *time* of a given function. When it tells time in sentences such as: **Il est cinq heures,** it is expressed by *o'clock* in English.

(d) When *time* is expressed by **le moment**

En ce moment nous apprenons le latin. — At this time *we are learning Latin.*

A ce moment-là j'étais en France. — At that time *I was in France.*

The word **moment** indicates *a point in time;* **en ce moment** means *now* or *at this time,* **à ce moment-là** means *then* or *at that time.*

(e) When *time* is expressed by **l'époque**

A cette époque-là nous n'avions pas le téléphone. — At that time *we didn't have a telephone.*

The word **époque** indicates a longer period of time than does **moment** and usually refers to a time which is farther in the past.

(f) How to express *have a good time*

Passez une bonne soirée. — Have a good time this evening.

Nous **avons fait un excellent séjour** en France cet été. — *We* had a very good time *in France this summer.*

Les enfants **se sont bien amusés** au cirque. — *The children* had a very good time *at the circus.*

The French have no word-for-word translation of the English expression *to have a good time.* The verb **s'amuser** is often used to express this idea, especially when referring to younger people, but, depending on the occasion, other expressions such as those found in the above examples are also used.

H. *Remplacez les mots anglais par leur équivalent français.*

1. Il faut (*take*) Pierrot à sa leçon de danse tous les jeudis. 2. Nous parlions justement de vous (*at the time*) où vous êtes entré. 3. Lucienne voudrait (*take*) une revue de mode de Paris. 4. Il ne faut jamais regretter le (*time*) passé. 5. Cette lettre est importante; je la (*will take*) moi-même à la poste. 6. Il faut réussir à ce concours pour (*teach*) dans un lycée. 7. Ce film est excellent; je l'ai vu trois (*times*). 8. En juin la plus grande partie des élèves (*take*) des examens. 9. Je crois que nous (*will have a good time*) chez les Barois. 10. Si tu veux

me faire plaisir, (*take*) les enfants au jardin zoologique. 11. C'est Florence qui me (*taught*) à nager quand j'avais quatre ans. 12. Nous n'avons plus besoin de ces affaires; vous pouvez les (*take*) chez vous. 13. (*At the time*) où j'habitais Londres, les choses n'étaient pas faciles. 14. Il faut (*take*) les choses un peu plus au sérieux, mon ami. 15. C'est toi qui a permis à Pierre de (*take*) l'auto? 16. A quelle (*time*) est le dernier métro? 17. Jeannot (*takes*) un journal de sport. 18. Depuis son mariage, Lucie n'a plus le temps de (*take*) des cours.

I. *Traduisez en français. Attention aux mots en italique.*

1. Someone *has taken* the silverware. 2. (*vous*) If you don't have *time* to write, telephone me Sunday. 3. (*vous*) Will you *take* Mr. Galant to the laboratory? 4. (*vous*) At what *time* do you want to see me? 5. I wonder who *taught* Rose to cook. 6. I think I am going to *take* another magazine. 7. (*tu*) Did you have a good *time* last night? 8. (*tu*) Don't forget to *take* your suit to the cleaner's. 9. Louise *teaches* art, and her sister *teaches* history. 10. Susan *is taking* some Spanish courses[1]. 11. Claude can't *take* us; his car broke down. 12. Felix arrived just at the *time* when I was leaving. 13. Did Peter pass the examination he *took* last week? 14. Every *time* he comes, Paul brings us something. 15. (*tu*) When are you going to *take* your vacation? 16. At the *time* of my grandparents there wasn't any television[2]. 17. I *took* an hour to read that novel.

---

[1] **cours d'espagnol**   [2] Use the definite article.

Verb Review

Review the verbs **tenir** and **valoir** according to the outline on page 283.

CHAPTER 16

Constructions with Prepositions

I. Prepositions of Place

TO, IN, AT

In French, *in*, *at* and *to* are all expressed by the same preposition before proper nouns used as place names. The preposition used depends on whether the place name is a city, a masculine country, or a feminine country or continent.

1. What preposition of place is used to express *in*, *at*, and *to* with cities?

Nous sommes **à** Paris.   *We are* in (at) *Paris.*
Gérard va **à** Tours.   *Gerard is going* to *Tours.*

The preposition **à** is used before cities to express the English prepositions *in*, *at* or *to*.

2. How can one determine the gender of countries in French?

la France • **la** Grèce • **la** Belgique • **la** Suisse • **la** Bolivie • **la** Chine

All countries ending in **-e** are feminine except **le Mexique.**

le Canada • **le** Japon • **le** Portugal • **le** Danemark • **le** Pérou

All countries not ending in **-e** are masculine.

NOTE: These rules hold usually with the well-known and well-established countries, but they do not always seem to apply to the so-called "emerging countries," where uniform usage has not yet been well determined. Likewise, **en** is used to express *in* or *to* with certain masculine countries beginning with a vowel, as, for instance, **en Iran.**

210

3. What preposition of place is used to express *in* **or** *to* **before feminine countries and continents?**

Michel est **en** France.	*Michael is in France.*
Louise va **en** France.	*Louise is going to France.*
Maurice a passé deux ans **en** Afrique.	*Maurice spent two years in Africa.*

French uses **en** to express both *in* and *to* before feminine countries and continents.

4. What preposition of place is used to express *in* **or** *to* **before masculine countries?**

Charlotte est **au** Danemark.	*Charlotte is in Denmark.*
Gilbert va **au** Danemark.	*Gilbert is going to Denmark.*
Restez-vous longtemps **aux** États-Unis?	*Are you staying in the United States for a long time?*
Nous allons **aux** États-Unis l'année prochaine.	*We are going to the United States next year.*

French uses **à** + DEFINITE ARTICLE to express *in* or *to* before masculine countries.

NOTE 1: Although the same preposition **à** and **en** is used to express both *in* and *to* with French place names, this does not ordinarily lead to ambiguity. **Je suis allé en France** clearly means *I went to France*, **Je suis allé au Canada** clearly means *I went to Canada*. **J'ai passé un an en France** clearly means *I spent a year in France*, **J'ai passé un an au Canada** clearly means *I spent a year in Canada*.

NOTE 2: In sentences with the verb **voyager,** however, a problem does exist. **J'ai voyagé en France cet été** means *I traveled in France this summer*, and not "I traveled to France this summer." To avoid ambiguity in expressing the idea of traveling *to a place*, it is best to use the verb **aller.** Ex.: **Je suis allé en France cet été.**

NOTE 3: However, *in* or *to Cuba* is expressed by **à** alone. Ex.: Nous sommes allés **à Cuba** avant la révolution. Le sucre est une industrie très importante **à Cuba.**

NOTE 4: French make certain states of the United States feminine by ending them in **-e.** Ex.: **la Californie, la Géorgie, la Floride.** With such states, *in* and *to* are therefore expressed by **en.** With other states, which are considered masculine, **dans le** is most often used, although one sometimes finds **au.** Ex.: <u>dans l'Ohio</u>, <u>dans le</u> **Texas,** <u>dans le</u> **Michigan.**

5. What preposition of place is used before modified countries, cities, and continents?

(a) if the modifying phrase or adjective is an integral part of the place name

Il habite **à** la Nouvelle Orléans.	*He lives* in *New Orleans.*
Nous allons **en** Amérique du Sud.	*We are going* to *South America.*
Le Maroc, l'Algérie et la Tunisie sont **en** Afrique de Nord.	*Morocco, Algeria and Tunisia are* in *North Africa.*

If the modifying phrase or adjective is an integral part of the place name, the same preposition would be used as if the place were not modified.

(b) if the modifying phrase or adjective is not an integral part of the place name

Quelle université est située **dans la** Belgique flamande?	*What university is located* in the *Flemish part of Belgium?*
Nous avons passé des journées **dans le** vieux Paris.	*We spent days* in *old Paris.*

When a place name is modified by an adjective or phrase which is not an integral part of the name, **dans** + DEFINITE ARTICLE is used to express *in* or *to*. But this construction is rather rare.

A. *Remplacez les tirets par la préposition convenable.*

1. Beaucoup de catholiques vont _____ Rome pour voir le Vatican.
2. Quand vous serez _____ Naples, allez donc voir les ruines de Pompéi. 3. Quand j'étais _____ Angleterre, j'aimais prendre le thé à quatre heures. 4. Puisque vous aimez les sports d'hiver, allez passer l'hiver _____ Colorado. 5. Nous avons renoncé à aller _____ Chine, c'est un trop long voyage. 6. Ces jeunes Français passeront un mois _____ États-Unis pour étudier la chimie. 7. Quand vous serez _____ Danemark, vous verrez que presque tout le monde parle anglais.

B. *Traduisez en français.*

1. They want to spend their vacation in Madrid, but they do not know Spanish. 2. (*vous*) If you want to go to Canada, I advise you to take the train at eight in[1] the evening. 3. Many Americans go

---
[1] **du**

to Florida to spend the winter.   4. Our friends were² to come back, but they want to stay in Portugal in April.   5. A large number of American engineers work³ in Mexico.   6. I took some very beautiful photographs on arriving in Japan and some others⁴ while I was in China.   7. We did not stay in Russia long⁵ enough to learn Russian. 8. This old man would now like to go back to Italy to see his relatives.

---

² Use a form of **devoir**.   ³ This verb is in the plural.   ⁴ **d'autres**   ⁵ **assez long temps pour**

PATTERN PRACTICE: *in, at,* and *to* with place names

Pattern 1

YOU HEAR   France
YOU SAY   Cet été je vais en France.

FROM

6. How is *from* expressed with cities?

Je suis parti **de** Paris hier pour voir les environs.

I left Paris yesterday to see the surrounding country.

With cities, *from* is expressed by **de**.

7. How is *from* expressed with feminine countries and continents?

Nous sommes revenus **de** France la semaine dernière.

We returned from France last week.

Philippe partira-t-il **d'**Angleterre la semaine prochaine?

Will Philip leave England next week?

Before feminine countries and continents, *from* is expressed by **de**.

8. How is *from* expressed with masculine countries?

Nos cousins sont partis **du** Canada hier.

Our cousins left Canada yesterday.

Quand reviendrez-vous **du** Portugal?

When will you come back from Portugal?

Before masculine countries, *from* is expressed by **de** + DEFINITE ARTICLE (**du, de l', des**).

C. *Remplacez les tirets par l'équivalent français de* from.

1. Il part _____ Japon la semaine prochaine à cause de la situation politique. 2. A votre accent, je devine que vous venez _____ Belgique. 3. Des avions partent tous les jours _____ Canada pour l'Europe. 4. Ces messieurs viennent _____ Lyon pour montrer leurs étoffes de soie. 5. Beaucoup de gens qui reviennent _____ Mexique sont contents de retrouver la cuisine américaine. 6. Les Russes ne peuvent pas toujours sortir librement _____ Russie. 7. Si vous allez _____ France en Angleterre, prenez donc l'avion.

D. *Traduisez en français.*

1. I like to take the boat when I go from Japan to the United States. 2. It is sometimes difficult to say whether someone comes from the United States or from England. 3. We are coming back from Greece delighted[1] by the beauty of that country. 4. He is coming back from Spain, where he spent the whole month of July. 5. (*tu*) When you come back[2] from Portugal, we'll go to Wisconsin.

---

[1] **enchantés par**   [2] Not the present tense.

PATTERN PRACTICE: *from* with place names

Pattern 2

YOU HEAR   France
YOU SAY   Jean est revenu de France lundi.

II. Verb + Preposition + Infinitive

9. What words does French use to join a verb to a following infinitive?

Je **voudrais aller** en France.	*I* should like <u>to</u> go *to France.*
Nous **avons commencé à lire.**	*We* began <u>to</u> read.
Les ouvriers **ont refusé de travailler.**	*The workmen* refused <u>to</u> work.

Some verbs are followed directly by an infinitive, some verbs require **à** before an infinitive, some require **de** before an infinitive, a few require still other prepositions.

10. How can one determine which construction to use before an infinitive?

Ils **viendront voir** leur nouveau petit-fils la semaine prochaine.	*They* will come <u>to</u> see *their new grandson next week.*
Nous **voulons régler** cette affaire le plus tôt possible.	*We* want <u>to</u> take care *of this matter as soon as possible.*

Verbs of motion (**aller, venir**) and the common verbs of wishing (**vouloir, désirer**) are followed directly by the infinitive.

Le mari de Janine lui **a demandé de faire des économies.**	*Janine's husband* asked *her* <u>to</u> be saving.
Nous **avons regretté d'apprendre** son départ si précipité.	*We* were sorry <u>to</u> learn *of his very hasty departure.*

Verbs of telling, asking, ordering, advising, etc. (someone to do something) and most verbs of emotion (**craindre, avoir peur, regretter, s'étonner,** etc.) are followed by **de** before an infinitive.

But except for these, the preposition to be used after each verb before an infinitive must be learned.

11. Which verbs require no preposition before an infinitive?

The following are the commonest verbs which are followed directly by the infinitive:

aimer	*like*	falloir	*be necessary*
aimer mieux	*prefer*	laisser	*leave, allow, let*
aller	*go, be going*	oser	*dare*
compter	*intend*	pouvoir	*can, be able*
croire	*believe*	préférer	*prefer*
désirer	*desire, wish*	savoir	*know, know how*
devoir	*am to, must, should*	sembler	*seem*
entendre	*hear*	venir	*come*
espérer	*hope*	voir	*see*
faire	*do, make, have*	vouloir	*want, wish*

12. Which verbs require de before an infinitive?

The following are the commonest verbs which require **de** before an infinitive:

avoir peur de	*be afraid*	finir de	*finish*
cesser de	*cease*	ordonner de	*order*
craindre de	*fear*	oublier de	*forget*
décider de	*decide*	permettre de	*permit*
défendre de	*forbid*	prier de	*beg, ask, pray*
demander de	*ask*	promettre de	*promise*
se dépêcher de	*hurry*	refuser de	*refuse*
dire de	*tell*	regretter de	*regret*
écrire de	*write*	remercier de	*thank*
empêcher de	*prevent*	tâcher de	*try*
essayer de	*try*		

13. Which verbs require à before an infinitive?

The following are the commonest verbs which require **à** before an infinitive:

aider à	*help*	demander à*	*ask*
s'amuser à	*amuse oneself*	enseigner à	*teach*
apprendre à	*learn, teach*	s'habituer à	*accustom oneself*
arriver à	*succeed*	hésiter à	*hesitate*
avoir à	*have*	inviter à	*invite*
commencer à	*begin*	recommencer à	*begin again*
consentir à	*consent*	réussir à	*succeed*
continuer à	*continue*	songer à	*think, dream*
se décider à	*decide*	tarder à	*delay in*

E. *Remplacez les tirets par une préposition s'il[1] y a lieu.*

1. —Allô chérie, j'ai invité le patron ____ dîner chez nous ce soir.
2. J'avais un oiseau en cage, mais je l'ai laissé ____ partir. 3. Dépêche-toi ____ finir ton travail pour qu'on puisse sortir. 4. Je n'aime pas qu'il s'amuse ____ faire des expériences de chimie dans la maison. 5. Dépêche-toi, ils peuvent ____ arriver d'un moment à l'autre. 6. Cessez ____ bavarder avec votre voisin, ou prenez la porte. 7. Il faut ____ vivre mieux que ça; je vais ____ essayer ____ gagner un peu plus d'argent. 8. Il vient d'avoir cinquante ans et il a décidé ____ se remarier. 9. Commencez ____ économiser de l'argent dès que possible. 10. J'aime mieux ____ sortir quand il pleut, l'air est plus pur. 11. Oseriez-vous ____ répéter ce que vous

---

[1] *if one is necessary*

* The verb **demander** + AN INDIRECT OBJECT meaning *to ask to* requires **de** before an infinitive. Compare: Il demande **à** venir. Il demande à son ami **de** venir.

venez de dire? 12. Beaucoup de réfugiés refusent absolument ____ retourner dans leurs pays.

F. *Remplacez les tirets par une préposition s'il y a lieu.*

1. Il est malade, mais il continue ____ faire ses classes. 2. J'ai été un peu brusque, je crains ____ l'avoir vexé. 3. Faites un petit effort pour apprendre ____ parler correctement. 4. A partir de demain, je veux ____ travailler dix heures tous les jours. 5. Je regrette ____ ne pas être plus riche. 6. Il est bon de savoir ____ faire plusieurs métiers. 7. Bien des Américains espèrent ____ aller un jour en Europe. 8. J'ai cru qu'ils ne se décideraient jamais ____ partir. 9. Il faut s'habituer ____ vivre dans l'incertitude. 10. Si vous voulez un chat, nous cherchons ____ placer les nôtres. 11. S'il tarde ____ rentrer, sa femme imagine qu'il a eu un accident. 12. On doit ____ réfléchir avant de parler.

G. *Traduisez en français. Attention aux prépositions.*

1. His wife prevents him from playing poker with his friends. 2. I completely forgot to telephone him[1] today, and it's[2] too late now. 3. Several friends will help me paint my house. 4. (*vous*) Don't hesitate to interrupt me if you have a question. 5. As soon as one speaks of France, Anne begins[3] to dream. 6. He is stubborn; I didn't succeed in changing his opinion. 7. Few people like to write long letters. 8. (*tu*) If you want to see him, come quickly, because he is going to leave. 9. (*vous*) Look at that man; he seems to want to speak to us.

---

[1] Which type of object is this? [2] Either **il est** or **c'est,** but with a slight difference in meaning. [3] Use a form of **se mettre.**

PATTERN PRACTICE: the use of prepositions before an infinitive

Pattern 3

YOU HEAR	Cet élève a peur
YOU SAY	Cet élève a peur de parler français.

Pattern 4

YOU HEAR	Vous allez
YOU SAY	Vous allez sortir ce soir.

III. The *à* + *de* Verbs

14. How does French express the idea 'to tell someone to do something'?

J'ai dit **à** mon frère **de** partir tout de suite.	I told my brother to *leave immediately.*
Michel **a promis à ses enfants de** leur apporter des jouets.	*Michael* promised his children to *bring them some toys.*

Certain verbs require **à** before a noun object and **de** before a following infinitive in French but not necessarily in English. These may be called the **à** + **de** verbs. Among these are:

conseiller à quelqu'un de	*advise someone to*	Je **conseille à Paul de** partir.
défendre à quelqu'un de	*forbid someone to*	Il **défend à Marie de** sortir.
demander à quelqu'un de	*ask someone to*	Elle **demande à sa mère de** venir.
dire à quelqu'un de	*tell someone to*	Je **dis à mon frère de** se taire.
écrire à quelqu'un de	*write someone to*	Nous **écrivons à Guy de** rester.
ordonner à quelqu'un de	*order someone to*	Il **ordonne au soldat de** tirer.
permettre à quelqu'un de	*permit someone to*	Je **permets à Jean d'**entrer.
promettre à quelqu'un de	*promise someone to*	Elle **promet à Henri de** lui écrire.
téléphoner à quelqu'un de	*telephone someone to*	Il **téléphone à Claude de** revenir.

H. *Traduisez en français.*

1. (*vous*) Telephone your father to send you some money. 2. After that trouble[1], I advised Gerard to leave town[2]. 3. (*vous*) If you want to marry my daughter, promise me to come to work here every day. 4. There are always people who want to forbid others[2] to do what they wish. 5. (*tu*) Ask your uncle to buy you a car, since he is rich. 6. (*vous*) If he comes, tell Mr. Fondeville to leave his address and

---

[1] **histoire**   [2] Use the definite article.

I'll write him.   7. (*vous*) You are wrong to[3] permit your children to do everything[4] they wish.   8. (*vous*) I'll write my friends to come to get[5] you at the airport.

---

[3] de   [4] tout ce que   [5] chercher

PATTERN PRACTICE: the **à** + **de** verbs

Pattern 5

YOU HEAR   dire

YOU SAY   J'ai dit à Pierre de rester à Paris.

IV. Verb (+ Preposition) + Noun

15. How do the <u>verb</u> + <u>noun</u> constructions in French compare with those in English?

Nous **attendons** le train.	*We* are waiting for *the train.*
Je **suis entré dans** la maison.	*I* entered *the house.*
Il **pense à** ses examens.	*He* is thinking of *his examinations.*

While many VERB + NOUN constructions are the same in French and English, some verbs require a preposition before a noun in French but not in English, and others require a preposition before a noun in English but not in French. Still other verbs require one preposition in English, another in French.

16. What are some common verbs which require a direct object in French but a preposition before the object in English?

attendre	*wait for*	Paul **attend** son ami.
chercher	*look for*	Marie **cherche** son livre.
demander	*ask for*	Pierre **demande** cinq cents francs.
écouter	*listen to*	Nous **écoutons** la musique.
payer	*pay for*	Il **a payé** cet objet mille francs.
regarder	*look at*	Je **regarde** le plan de Paris.

The verbs listed above require a direct object in French.

17. What are some common verbs which require a preposition before the object in French but a direct object in English?

s'approcher de	*approach*	Nous nous **approchons de** la rivière.
assister à	*attend*	Il **assiste à** la réunion.
changer de	*change*	Elle **a changé de** robe.
entrer dans	*enter*	Qui **entre dans** la salle?
échapper à	*escape*	Le soldat **a échappé à** la mort.
s'échapper de	*escape*	Le voleur **s'est échappé de** prison.
jouer à	*play*	Je **joue au** football, lui **aux** échecs.
jouer de	*play*	Elle **joue du** piano et **du** violon.
manquer de	*lack*	Je **manque de** renseignements.
se marier avec	*marry*	Denise **se marie avec** Jean-Pierre.
obéir à	*obey*	Paul **obéit à** son père.
plaire à	*please*	Yvonne **plaît à** tout le monde.
répondre à	*answer*	Je **réponds à** la lettre.
résister à	*resist*	Il **résiste à** la tentation.
ressembler à	*resemble*	Maurice **ressemble à** son frère.
se servir de	*use*	Ils **se servent de** la machine à écrire.
se souvenir de	*remember*	Je **me souviens de** la guerre.

The verbs listed above require a preposition before the object in French.

NOTE: The verb **échapper à** means *to escape getting into something*, **s'échapper de** means *to escape from something one has gotten into*.

The construction **jouer à** means *to play a game*, the construction **jouer de** means *to play a musical instrument*.

18. What are some common verbs which require one preposition in French and another in English?

s'intéresser à	*be interested in*	Il **s'intéresse à** la musique.
s'occuper de	*busy oneself with*	Je **m'occupe de** la maison.
penser à	*think of*	Il **pense à** son travail.
penser de	*think of*	Que **pensez-vous de** cet homme?
remercier de	*thank for*	Il **a remercié** sa mère **de** son cadeau.
~ire de	*laugh at*	Nous **rions de** ce clown.
~nger à	*think of*	Il **songe à** son voyage en France.

The verbs listed above require one preposition in French and another in English.

NOTE: The construction **penser à** means *to think of someone or something*, the construction **penser de** is most often used in questions *to ask one's opinion of someone or something*.

The verb **remercier** may also be followed by **pour** before a noun. Ex.: Il
a remercié sa mère **pour** son cadeau.

I. *Remplacez les expressions anglaises entre parenthèses par les équivalents
français.*

(Each sentence has a verb which entails the use or non-use of a preposition.
In certain sentences, it may be necessary to combine a preposition with the
definite article.)

1. Je (*am looking for*) une bonne réponse à sa lettre, mais c'est difficile.
2. Certains élèves peuvent travailler en (*listening to*) la radio.
3. (*Look at*) bien le ciel et vous verrez peut-être des satellites.
4. Avec cette foule il sera impossible de (*approach*) la scène. 5. Sauve
qui peut! Un ours (*has escaped from*) sa cage. 6. Il faut de longues
années d'étude pour (*play*) le violon en virtuose. 7. Trop de familles
(*lack*) argent. 8. Chacun rêve de (*marry*[1]) la personne idéale. 9. Il
y a des gens qui croient pouvoir (*escape*) la maladie. 10. Tout
évolue et il est impossible de (*resist*) longtemps les changements.
11. (*Concern yourself with*[2]) vos affaires. 12. Il faut le (*thank for*) les
fleurs qu'il m'a envoyées. 13. Ce n'est pas gentil de (*laugh at*) une
personne qui tombe. 14. Il (*is waiting for*) son amie, mais je sais
qu'elle ne viendra pas.

[1] Use a form of **se marier**.   [2] Use a form of **s'occuper**.

J. *Traduisez en français. Attention aux prépositions.*

1. (*vous*) Live in the present; do not think too much of the past.
2. I attended a fine concert last evening. 3. They change cars every
other year. 4. I have lost my key, and I can't get into the house.
5. It is amusing to[1] play chess. 6. Teen-agers often refuse to obey
their parents. 7. He is spending a fortune to please that woman.
8. (*vous*) Do not wait to[2] answer those letters. 9. He does not
resemble his father at all[3]. 10. Today one uses[4] knives and forks[5] to[2]
eat. 11. She doesn't like sports; she is interested in poetry. 12. (*tu*)
What do you think of the work of that painter?

[1] **de**   [2] **pour**   [3] Place directly after **pas**.   [4] Use a form of **se servir**.   [5] Repeat the preposition before the second noun.

V. The *It is* + Adjective + Infinitive Constructions

19. What construction follows the impersonal *Il est* + adjective?

Il est impossible **de** partir aujour-   It is *impossible* <u>to</u> *leave today.*
d'hui.

Il serait difficile **de** lui donner cet   It would be *hard* <u>to</u> *give him that money.*
argent.

The construction used with the impersonal **il est** + ADJECTIVE is:

> (impersonal) **il est** + ADJECTIVE + **de** + INFINITIVE (+ idea)

NOTE: In conversational French, this impersonal **il** may always be replaced by **ce,** and the following construction is exactly the same as though the impersonal **il** were used.

20. What construction follows idea + *C'est* + adjective?

Est-ce que cet écrivain écrit vrai-   *Does that author really write well? It's*
ment bien? **C'est** difficile **à** dire.   *hard* <u>to</u> *say.*

Votre frère est-il bon élève? Non, et   *Is your brother a good student? No, and*
c'est impossible **à** comprendre.   *it's impossible* <u>to</u> *understand.*

When **c'est** + adjective refers to a preceding idea without gender or number, the following construction is used:

> IDEA in preceding sentence + **c'est** + ADJECTIVE + **à** + INFINITIVE

K. *Remplacez les tirets par* **à** *ou* **de,** *selon le cas.*

1. —Les planètes sont-elles habitées? —Peut-être, mais c'est impossible _____ prouver. 2. Il est maintenant possible _____ aller dans la lune. 3. Il est agréable _____ prendre un petit cognac après un bon repas. 4. —Comment avez-vous fait pour apprendre à jouer si bien? —C'est difficile _____ expliquer. 5. Les candidats ont discuté pendant une heure. C'était interessant _____ écouter. 6. Il n'est pas toujours facile _____ dire ce qui est bien et ce qui est mal. 7. Vous l'avez vraiment vu voler cette montre? C'est difficile _____ croire.

L. *Traduisez en français.*

1. It is interesting to see a football[1] game between two good teams.
2. Man is master of his destiny. It's easy to say. 3. It is necessary to write a great many letters, even if it is sometimes boring to do. 4. It is difficult to understand certain scientific theories. 5. It is amusing to observe people in the street. 6. Maurice wants to buy an airplane. It's impossible to believe. 7. I'm going to paint my house. It's easy to do. 8. It is restful to interrupt one's[2] work from time to time. 9. Mark is so stubborn that it is useless to try to convince him. 10. Jack says that he is capable of writing a novel. It is hard to imagine. 11. Mr. Laroque does not believe that his son was at my house last night, but it's easy to prove. 12. It is impossible to get[3] to the top of that mountain.

---

[1] *football game* = **match de football**   [2] Use a form of **son.**   [3] Use a form of **arriver à.**

PATTERN PRACTICE : *It is* + adjective constructions

Pattern 6

YOU HEAR   Parler français est facile.
YOU SAY   Il est facile de parler français.

VI. Verbal Constructions after Prepositions; Constructions with *pour*

Most English prepositions are followed by the present participle. One says *on arriving, in coming, by working, without leaving,* etc. But this is not usually the case in French.

21. What verbal construction usually follows a French preposition?

Ne partez pas **sans laisser** votre   *Don't go away* without leaving *your*
adresse.   *address.*

All French prepositions except **en** are followed by the infinitive.

When we use the term infinitive, we mean SIMPLE INFINITIVE, for it is by far the most common infinitive to be used. But there is also a COMPOUND INFINITIVE which is made up of the infinitive of **avoir** or **être** and the past participle of the main verb. The compound infinitive is also known as the PAST INFINITIVE.

Simple infinitive	*Compound infinitive*
parler	avoir parlé
finir	avoir fini
venir	être venu(e)(s)
se laver	s'être lavé(e)(s)

22. By what verbal construction is the preposition *en* followed?

En entrant dans le café, nous avons vu Robert et Marie.

On entering *the café, we saw Robert and Marie.*

The preposition **en** is followed by the present participle. (For a complete treatment of **en** + PRESENT PARTICIPLE, see pages 62–63.)

23. When is a French preposition followed by the compound infinitive?

Les voisins ont puni leur fils **pour avoir cassé** nos vitres.

The neighbors punished their son for breaking *our windowpanes.*

When the verbal action after a preposition clearly takes place before the action of the main verb of the sentence, the compound infinitive is used in order to preserve the time distinction.

24. What French construction is used to express the English *before* + **verb** + *-ing*?

Regardez à droite et à gauche **avant de traverser** la rue.

Look left and right before crossing *the street.*

French uses **avant de** + INFINITIVE for the English *before* + VERB + *-ing*.

25. What French construction is used to express the English *after* + **verb** + *-ing*?

Après avoir lu le journal, je me suis mis au travail.

After reading the newspaper, I got down to work.

French uses **après** + COMPOUND INFINITIVE to express the English *after* + VERB + *-ing*.

26. How does French express purpose?

Notre voisin a acheté ce terrain **pour planter** des arbres fruitiers.	*Our neighbor bought this land* to plant *some fruit trees.*

To express purpose, English uses $\begin{cases} to \\ in\ order\ to \end{cases}$ + VERB. French uses the preposition **pour** + THE INFINITIVE to indicate purpose.

27. When may the preposition *pour* be omitted before the infinitive in purpose phrases?

Jean **est venu** (pour) **travailler** avec Daniel aujourd'hui.	*John* came (in order) to work *with Daniel today.*
Nous **sommes allés** à la ferme (pour) **chercher** du lait.	*We* went *to the farm* (in order) to get *some milk.*

In purpose phrases, the preposition **pour** is usually omitted after forms of **aller** and **venir** and sometimes after other verbs of motion. When **pour** is used after forms of **aller** and **venir,** it emphasizes the idea of purpose much as *in order to* does in English. The preposition **pour** is also often used when several words separate the main verb and the infinitive.

28. How does French express the idea of *enough . . . to* and *too much . . . to* or *too . . . to?*

Louise chante **assez** bien **pour** faire partie du chœur.	*Louise sings well* enough to *be in the choir.*
Nous avons **trop** à faire **pour** partir maintenant.	*We have* too much to *do to leave now.*
Jacques est **trop** jeune **pour** rester dehors après neuf heures du soir.	*Jack is* too *young* to *stay out after nine o'clock at night.*

French expresses the idea of *enough . . . to* by **assez . . . pour** and of *too much . . . to* and *too . . . to* by **trop . . . pour.**

M. *Remplacez l'infinitif entre parenthèses par la forme convenable du verbe, s'il y a lieu.*

1. Pourquoi êtes-vous venu ici sans (téléphoner) d'avance?   2. Il faut aller au Maroc pour (acheter) un beau tapis.   3. Après (monter)

dans ma chambre, j'ai réfléchi à ce qui venait de se passer. 4. En (parler) à mon voisin, j'ai appris ce qui s'était passé. 5. Faites peser mes lettres avant de les (mettre) à la poste. 6. Nous avons commencé par (ouvrir) toutes les fenêtres. 7. Michel a répondu après (réfléchir) un moment. 8. Au lieu de (se[1] plaindre), vendez donc votre voiture. 9. Je me suis intéressé à la science en (lire) la biographie de Pasteur. 10. Jean est encore parti sans (fermer) la porte. 11. On apprend mieux quelque chose en l'(expliquer) à d'autres.

---

[1] Even in the infinitive form, the reflexive object must agree in person with the subject of the sentence. In what person is the subject of an imperative sentence?

N. *Traduisez en français.*

1. Paul is too proud to admit his error. 2. Someone came to ask for some information[1] concerning[2] Jack. 3. We left after hearing the results of the election. 4. Robert is old[3] enough to have a motorcycle. 5. (*vous*) Did you come to our house only to talk business? 6. The children went to play at the neighbor's. 7. (*vous*) Before leaving for Paris, reserve a room in a good hotel. 8. (*tu*) You are intelligent enough to understand those things. 9. Paul went to get[4] some books at the library. 10. I am too tired to go out this evening. 11. (*vous*) Correct your mistakes before erasing the sentences. 12. (*tu*) At what time will you come to get[4] me?

---

[1] Use the plural.   [2] **sur**   [3] **âgé**   [4] **chercher**

PATTERN PRACTICE: **avant de** + infinitive

Pattern 7

YOU HEAR   J'ai eu des doutes en prenant cette décision.
YOU SAY   J'ai eu des doutes avant de prendre cette décision.

PATTERN PRACTICE: **après** + compound infinitive

Pattern 8

YOU HEAR   J'ai eu des doutes en prenant cette décision.
YOU SAY   J'ai eu des doutes après avoir pris cette décision.

Problem Words

58. very much

Ways of expressing *very much* and *very many*

J'ai **énormément** à faire. ⎫

J'ai {**un tas** / **des tas**} **de choses** à faire. ⎬ *I have* very much *to do.*

J'ai **une quantité de choses** à faire. ⎭

Ces étudiants ont **énormément de** livres à lire. ⎫

Ces étudiants ont **des tas** de livres à lire. ⎬ *Those students have* very many *books to read.*

Ces étudiants ont **une quantité de** livres à lire. ⎭

Depending on the exact sentence, *very much* and *very many* may be expressed by **énormément de, une quantité de, un tas de, des tas de**[1], and other like expressions. In familiar speech, the French sometimes say **beaucoup** twice, so that one might hear: **J'ai beaucoup beaucoup à faire,** and: **Ces étudiants ont beaucoup beaucoup de livres à lire.** This latter construction should be avoided in writing.

French often expresses *not very much* by **pas grand-chose.** This is somewhat colloquial. Ex.: Je n'ai **pas** fait **grand-chose** ce matin.

CAUTION: In French, **très** cannot modify **beaucoup.** Therefore, *very much* and *very many* can<u>not</u> be expressed by «très beaucoup».

---

[1] The expressions **un tas de** and **des tas de** are colloquial.

59. visit

(**a**) How to say *to visit a person*

Hier je **suis allé voir Monsieur Moreau.**   *Yesterday I* visited *Mr. Moreau.*

The commonest way of saying *to visit a person* is **aller voir quelqu'un.**

Il faudra **faire une visite aux**   *We must* visit the neighbors.
voisins.

Another way of saying *to visit a person* is **faire une visite à quel-qu'un.**

Nous **avons rendu visite à Madame**   *We* visited (paid a visit to) Mrs. de
de Rosemont.   Rosemont.

More formal and therefore less common is **rendre visite à quel-qu'un.**

CAUTION: Do NOT use the verb «visiter» to express the idea of *visiting a person*. The commonest way of saying *to visit a person* is **aller voir une personne.**

(b) How to say *to visit a place*

Avez-vous **visité le Louvre?**   *Did you* visit the Louvre?
Quand nous étions en Italie, nous   *When we were in Italy, we* visited
  avons visité Naples.   Naples.
Ne manquez pas de **visiter les vieux**   *Don't fail* to visit the old sections *of*
  quartiers de Paris.   *Paris.*

The verb **visiter** is used to express the idea of *visiting a place*.

60. while

(a) When to express *while* by **pendant que**

Attendez-moi dans la voiture **pen-**   *Wait for me in the car* while *I go and get*
  dant que je vais chercher les   *the children.*
  enfants.

When *while* means *during the time that*, it is expressed by **pendant que.**

(b) When to express *while* by **tandis que**

Marc travaille bien, **tandis que**   *Mark works well* while *Joseph doesn't*
  Joseph ne fait pas grand-chose.   *do much of anything.*

When *while* means *whereas*, it is expressed by **tandis que.** (Pronounced either [tãdikə] or [tãdiskə]).

Sometimes **tandis que** is also used in the sense of *during the time that*, but it is best for the learner to reserve **tandis que** for *while = whereas*.

61. wish

(**a**) How to *wish someone something*

Je vous **souhaite** un bon voyage.   *I wish you a good trip.*

The verb **souhaiter** is used to *wish someone something*.

(**b**) How **désirer** expresses *wish*

Pauline **désire** toujours avoir ce   *Pauline always* wishes *to have what*
qu'ont les autres.   *others have.*

The verb **désirer** means *wish* or *desire*. It may be used in the spoken language but is much less common than the verb **vouloir.**

(**c**) How to express *wish* by the conditional of **vouloir** and **aimer**

François{**voudrait** / **aimerait**} être très riche.   *Francis wishes that he were very rich.*

The conditional of **aimer** and **vouloir** is used with the INFINITIVE to express wish when the subject of the main and subordinate clauses are the same in the English sentence.

Nous{**voudrions** / **aimerions**} que Roger vienne avec nous.   *We wish (that) Roger would come with us.*

The conditional of **aimer** and **vouloir** + **que** + SUBJUNCTIVE is used to express wish when the subject of the main and subordinate clauses are different in both the English and French sentences.

O. *Remplacez les mots anglais par leur équivalent français.*

1. Vincent est marié, mais il (*visits*) sa mère tous les jours. 2. Vous avez accepté sa proposition tout de suite (*while*) vous auriez dû discuter. 3. Le directeur (*wishes*) vous parler. 4. Il peut bien être fatigué, il a (*very much*) travaillé. 5. Nous (*visited*) plusieurs musées à Rome. 6. Je travaillerai au bureau (*while*) tu seras chez Martine. 7. Les Marcellin sont revenus de la mer; nous devrions (*visit them*). 8. Je (*wish*) que tu m'apprennes à jouer de la guitare. 9. Il fait bon chez vous (*while*) il fait toujours froid chez nous. 10. Si vous n'avez pas le temps de (*visit*) la ville, montez au moins sur la colline. 11. Jean a un examen aujourd'hui; (*wish*)-lui bonne chance.

P. *Traduisez en français. Attention aux mots en italique.*

1. (*vous*) If I have time, I will *visit* you Friday afternoon.   2. (*tu*) I *wish* you a¹ Happy New Year.   3. Louis learned Arabic *while* he was in Africa.   4. This morning I *visited* my former teacher.   5. I have always *wished* to travel.   6. I speak only one language, *while* Alexander speaks several.   7. (*vous*) Have you ever *visited* Athens?   8. I *wish* I could go to Portugal this year.   9. I would be glad to see Madeleine again; I like her *very much*.

---

¹ **une bonne année**

Verb Review

Review the verbs **venir** and **vivre** according to the outline on page 283.

CHAPTER 17

Problem Prepositions

I. English Words which are both Prepositions and Conjunctions

Certain English words, such as *after, as, before,* and *since* are sometimes used as prepositions, to introduce a prepositional phrase, and sometimes as conjunctions, to introduce a dependent clause, which has its own subject and verb. It is important to know when such English words are used as a preposition and when as a conjunction, for French often uses one word to express the English preposition and another to express the English conjunction.

Among the most common English words used both as a preposition and a conjunction are:

PREPOSITION	CONJUNCTION

1. after

après*	après que
Nous sommes partis **après** l'annonce des résultats.	Nous sommes partis **après que** Jean a annoncé les résultats.
We left after *the announcement of the results.*	*We left* after *John announced the results.*

Après is used to express English *after* when a preposition a, and **après que** when conjunction.

---

* For **après** + VERBAL CONSTRUCTION, see page 224, §25.

2. as

comme	comme
Comme mécanicien, il est excellent.	**Comme** j'ai du travail à finir, je ne peux pas aller chez vous.
As a *mechanic, he is excellent.*	As *I have work to finish, I cannot go to your house.*

Sometimes **comme** is used to express the English *as* both when a preposition and a conjunction.

The preposition **comme,** meaning *as,* is normally followed by the noun alone, without **un, une** or **des** and is used in a phrase which has a general sense.

On the other hand, when **comme** is followed by **un, une** or **des** plus a noun, it means *like* and is used in a phrase implying a comparison. Ex.: Il parle **comme** un professeur. (*He talks* like *a teacher.*) Il conduit **comme** un fou. (*He drives* like *a madman.*)

As a conjunction, **comme** means *as* = *because.*

en	à mesure que
Il s'est conduit **en** véritable ami.	**A mesure** qu'il vieillissait, il devenait moins sévère.
He behaved as *a true friend.*	As *he got older, he became less strict.*

The preposition **en** followed by the noun unmodified by **un, une** or **des,** means *as* in the sense of *in the character of.*

The conjunction **à mesure que** means *as* = *in proportion as.*

3. before

avant	avant que
Nous sommes partis **avant** l'annonce des résultats.	Nous sommes partis **avant que** Jean annonce les résultats.
We left before *the announcement of the results.*	*We left* before *John announced the results.*

The conjunction **avant que** is always followed by the subjunctive, and both the present and past subjunctive are found with it. Thus: «Nous sommes partis **avant que** Jean **ait annoncé** les résultats» is also correct.

4. because

| à cause de | parce que |

Je suis resté à la maison **à cause de** la pluie.

Je suis resté à la maison **parce qu'**il pleuvait.

I stayed home because *of the rain.*

I stayed home because *it was raining.*

The English preposition *because of* is expressed in French by **à cause de** and is followed by a noun or pronoun, whereas the English conjunction *because* is expressed in French by **parce que** and is followed by a clause.

5. but

| sauf | mais |

Tout le monde est parti **sauf** Suzanne.

Georges est parti, **mais** où est-il allé?

Everyone left but *Suzanne.*

George left, but *where did he go?*

The word *but* is usually a conjunction. However, it is occasionally used as a preposition, and then it is equivalent to the English *except*. The preposition *but* may be expressed in several ways*, the most common of which is probably **sauf.**

6. for

| pour | car |

Nous avons fait cela **pour** vous.

Nous avons fait cela, **car** vous n'étiez pas ici.

We did that for *you.*

We did that, for *you were not here.*

The commonest way of expressing *for* as a preposition is **pour.****

The conjunction *for* is always expressed by **car,** and its meaning is somewhat similar to that of *because.*

7. since

| depuis | depuis que |

Philippe est chez nous **depuis** jeudi.

Philippe est chez nous **depuis que** ses parents sont partis pour la Suisse.

---

* For other ways, see page 240, §18.   ** For other ways, see page 240, §19.

Philip has been with us since *Thursday.*	*Philip has been with us* since *his parents left for Switzerland.*

When *since* indicates time, it is expressed by **depuis** as a preposition and by **depuis que** as a conjunction.

Note that the preposition **depuis** and its equivalents are usually followed by the present in French where English uses the present perfect.

puisque

Puisque vous partez pour la Suisse, Philippe peut venir chez nous.

Since *you are leaving for Switzerland, Philip can come to our house.*

When *since = because*, it is a conjunction and is expressed in French by **puisque.**

8. until

jusqu'à	jusqu'à ce que
Nous resterons ici **jusqu'à** dimanche.	Nous resterons ici **jusqu'à ce que** vous reveniez.
We'll stay here until *Sunday.*	*We'll stay here* until *you come back.*

In affirmative sentences, the English *until* is expressed by **jusqu'à** when used as a preposition; as a conjunction, French expresses *until* by **jusqu'à ce que,** and the verb of dependent clause is always in the subjunctive.

pas avant	pas avant que
Nous n'irons <u>pas</u> à Paris **avant** dimanche.	Nous n'irons <u>pas</u> à Paris **avant que** vous soyez rétabli.
We will <u>not</u> go to Paris until Sunday.	*We will <u>not</u> go to Paris* until *you are better.*

In negative sentences, the English *not until* (= *not before*) is expressed by **pas avant;** as a conjunction, French expresses *not until* (=*not before*) by **pas avant que,** and the verb of the dependent clause is always in the subjunctive.

A. *Remplacez les mots anglais indiqués entre parenthèses par l'équivalent français.*

1. Nous vous traiterons tout à fait (*as a*) camarade.   2. Marie a retrouvé toutes ses clés (*but*) celle de sa voiture.   3. Roland regrette de ne pas avoir connu Françoise (*before*) elle se marie.   4. Vous viendrez me voir (*after*) la classe.   5. Je m'ennuyais (*before*) votre arrivée.   6. Il ne faut pas renoncer à un projet (*because*) on a des difficultés.   7. (*Since*) nous sommes ici, il pleut tous les jours.   8. Cherchez (*until*) vous trouviez la solution de ce problème.   9. Ma colère montait (*as*) son avocat parlait.

B. *Remplacez les mots anglais indiqués entre parenthèses par l'équivalent français.*

1. Il ne faut pas négliger votre famille (*because of*) vos affaires.   2. Je vous dirai mon opinion (*after*) vous aurez vu ce dossier.   3. (*Since*) votre séjour en Égypte, vous n'êtes plus le même.   4. Je voulais vous voir, (*but*) je n'ai pas pu.   5. (*Before*) son accident, il faisait toutes sortes de sports.   6. (*Since*) vous êtes debout, voulez-vous m'apporter le dictionnaire?   7. Cet argent leur permettra de vivre (*until*) la fin du mois.   8. Tu ne peux pas trouver mieux (*as a*) ami.   10. Ne partez pas (*until*) je revienne.

C. *Traduisez en français.*

1. The children will come[1] home immediately after the movies.
2. I visited every country in Europe but Spain.   3. Juliette was becoming[2] more and more worried as time went by.   4. (*vous*) Mr. Forestier will give you a good job after you have done[3] your military service.   5. We'll not go out this evening because of the snow.
6. Since my operation, I am[4] much better.   7. Almost everyone left before Mr. Ponsard's lecture.   8. Mark and Irene danced until six o'clock in[5] the morning.   9. As a minister, Mr. Boyer was remarkable.   10. Anne cannot come until five o'clock.   11. Victor has many shortcomings, but he is very nice.   12. (*tu*) All that hap-

---

[1] *come home* = **rentrer**   [2] *become worried* = **s'inquiéter**   [3] What tense does French use here?
[4] *be much better* = **aller beaucoup mieux**   [5] **du**

pened because you were careless. 13. As we have little time, we'll take an[6] airplane. 14. (*vous*) Since you like the theater, why don't you go there more often? 15. (*vous*) The director would like to speak to you before you hand[7] in your resignation. 16. The astronaut was received in his native city as a hero.

---

[6] Use the definite article. [7] *hand in* = **donner**

II. Other English Prepositions which Pose Problems in French

Certain English prepositions pose problems in French (1) because they may also be used as another part of speech, in which case they are expressed by two different words according to their function; (2) because some English prepositions have several connotations, each of which is expressed in a special way in French.

The words presented in this section are all used as prepositions some of the time. Sometimes it seems sufficient just to give the French equivalent, at times examples best show the differences, other times an explanation of usage appears clearest.

9. about

(a) *concerning* = **de, sur, au sujet de, à propos de**

Nous parlions **de** votre nouvelle maison de campagne.	*We were speaking* about *your new country house.*
Paul nous a écrit plusieurs lettres **sur** son voyage.	*Paul wrote us several letters* about *his trip.*
Qu'est-ce que vous avez à dire **au sujet de** votre conduite?	*What do you have to say* about *your behavior?*
Personne n'a rien dit **à propos de** mon absence.	*No one said anything* about *my absence.*

When *about* means *concerning*, it is a preposition and is sometimes expressed by **de** (especially after forms of **parler**), sometimes by **sur**, sometimes by **au sujet de** or **à propos de.** At times, but not always, several of these words could express *about* in the same sentence.

(b) *approximately* = **environ, vers, à peu près, -aine** (appended to a cardinal numeral)

J'ai vu **environ** dix appartements.	*I saw* about *ten apartments.*
Michel est arrivé **vers** six heures.	*Michael came at* about *six o'clock.*
Il est **environ** dix heures.	*It is* about *ten o'clock.*
C'est **à peu près** ce que j'ai dit.	*That's* about *what I said.*
Il s'est passé une **vingtaine** d'années.	About *twenty years went by.*

The word **environ** modifies a numeral. The preposition **vers** is usually found in sentences with the time of day except when the verb of such sentences is a form of **être**. In that case, *about* is expressed by **environ**. When the suffix **-aine** is appended to a cardinal numeral, it indicates an approximation. The expression **à peu près** may be used for **environ**, but it may also modify words other than numerals.

(c) *be about to* = **être sur le point de**

Nous étions **sur le point de** partir.	*We were* about *to leave.*

10. above

En général les avions volent **au-dessus des** nuages.	*Airplanes generally fly* above *the clouds.*

The preposition *above* meaning *over, in* or *to a higher place* is expressed in French by **au-dessus de**.

11. according to

Selon ⎫ **Suivant** ⎬ Voltaire, il faut cultiver **D'après** ⎭ son jardin.	*According to Voltaire, one must culti-* *vate one's garden.*

The English preposition *according to* is expressed by **selon, suivant,** and **d'après,*** which are normally interchangeable.

12. across

Marc a couru après son chien **à travers** les champs.	*Mark ran after his dog* across *the fields.*
Je l'ai vu **traverser** la place **en courant.**	*I saw him run* across *the square.*

---

* See §13 below for another use of **d'après.**

Je l'aurais salué, mais il était **de l'autre côté** de la rue.	*I would have greeted him, but he was across the street.*
Nous **avons traversé** le pont.	*We went across the bridge.*

The preposition *across* is often expressed by **à travers.** But when *across* means *on the other side of*, the French say **de l'autre côté de,** and to *run across* is **traverser en courant.** The idea of *to go across* is often expressed by using the verb **traverser.**

13. after

On **l'a appelé** Victor **d'après** son parrain.	*They named him Victor after his godfather.*

The preposition *after* is usually **après,** but *to name after* is **appeler d'après.**

14. along

Il est agréable de se promener **le long de** la Seine.	*It is pleasant to walk along the Seine.*
Il y a des voitures stationnées tout **le long de** la rue.	*There are cars parked all along the street.*
Il **a suivi le chemin** jusqu'au pont.	*He went along the road up to the bridge.*

The preposition *along* is usually expressed by **le long de.** But *to go along the road* is **suivre le chemin** (**la route**) and *to go along the street* is **suivre la rue.**

D. *Remplacez le mot anglais indiqué entre parenthèses par l'équivalent français.*

1. George fume (*about*) vingt-cinq cigarettes par jour. 2. Claude et Sophie se promènent (*along*) la rivière. 3. Avez-vous vu ce qui se passe (*across*) la frontière? 4. Hier, j'ai entendu parler (*about*) votre voyage. 5. C'est (*about*) la même chose. 6. (*According to*) le traité, il n'y aura plus de douane entre ces pays. 7. Il y avait des fleurs tout (*along*) le sentier. 8. J'ai entendu une conférence (*about*) l'énergie atomique. 9. Ils se sont revus (*at about*) six heures et demie. 10. (*After*) qui avez-vous appelé votre fils Christian? 11. (*According to*) les experts, on ne peut pas construire un pont à cet endroit. 12. Donnez-moi (*about twenty*) francs. 13. Qu'est-ce que c'est que

ce fil (*above*) le pont?   14. Il ne faut pas vous inquiéter (*about*) vos enfants.   15. (*According to*) les journaux, on trouvera bientôt le coupable.   16. Je n'aime pas avoir des gens bruyants dans l'appartement (*above*) me.   17. Je voudrais vous demander des renseignements (*about*) les hôtels à Paris.   18. Il est (*about*) trois heures du matin.

E. *Traduisez en français.*

1. According to his father, Francis doesn't work enough.   2. It is about five o'clock now, but Mr. Dupont locked the door at about four thirty.   3. We went along the road up to the white house. 4. After the lecture, we went home.   5. Have you heard about George's accident?   6. Our friends traveled across the whole country on a motorcycle.   7. There were about two hundred people before the library.   8. We had some good discussions about modern music. 9. We called my daughter Rose after her grandmother.   10. The little boy ran across the street.   11. Louise spoke before the class about her trip to Mexico.   12. According to Mr. Parain, they are going to build a new city hall.   13. Our friends were about to telephone us when we arrived.   14. My friend lives across the street. 15. The sun was directly above us.   16. There are about thirty girls in the dormitory.   17. It's about all I have to do.   18. Professor Martin wrote me about my examination.

15. at

With nouns, *at* is usually expressed by **à** or **dans**.

The preposition *at* with place names is taken up on page 210.

With the connotation of *at the home of* or *at the place of business of* or *in the country of*, *at* is often expressed by **chez**. Note the uses of **chez** in the following sentences.

Nous irons passer la soirée **chez les Moreau.**

We'll go to spend the evening at the Moreaus.

Chez nous on dîne à six heures du soir.

In our country* we eat at six in the evening.

N'oublie pas de passer **chez le boulanger** à ton retour.

Don't forget to go to the bakery on your return.

On retrouve cette même idée **chez tous les grands écrivains.**

One finds this same idea in the works of all the great writers.

---

* In this sentence, **chez nous** may also mean *at our house*.

16. before

Il y a un tableau **devant** la classe.   *There is a blackboard* before *the class.*

Venez **avant** huit heures.   *Come* before *eight o'clock.*

Nous avons **déjà** fait ça.
Nous avons fait ça **avant.**   }   *We did that* before.

The preposition *before* is expressed by **devant** when it indicates place and means *in front of* and by **avant** when it indicates *time*. As an adverb, *before* may be expressed by **déjà, avant,** and **auparavant.**

17. down

Ils **sont* descendus** tout de suite.   *They* came down *at once.*

Nous **avons* descendu** la rue.   *We* went down *the street.*

The English *down* is often part of the French verb **descendre,** which may mean *to come down* or *to go down*. The English *to go down the street* is expressed in French by **descendre la rue.**

18. except

Tout le monde m'a félicité   *Everyone congratulated me* except *Mr.*
sauf   *Gervais.*
à part   } M. Gervais.
excepté

The English *except* may be expressed by **sauf, à part,** and **excepté.**

19. for (time)

Nos amis sont chez nous **depuis**   *Our friends have been with us* for *two* quinze jours.   *weeks.*

When an action begins in the past and is still going on in the present, French uses **depuis** with the present to express *for*.**

Nos amis sont restés chez nous   *Our friends stayed at our house* (for) (**pendant**) quinze jours.   *two weeks.*

---

* Intransitive verbs of motion are usually conjugated with **être,** but when a verb of motion governs a direct object, it becomes transitive and is then conjugated with **avoir.**
** For other ways of expressing this idea, see page 111.

A completed action describing a certain duration of time uses **pendant** with the compound past, where English uses *for*. This **pendant** may be omitted, just as *for* may be omitted in the English sentence.

Ces jeunes gens voyageront en Afrique **pendant** quinze jours.	*These young men will travel in Africa for two weeks.*

In the future *for* is usually expressed by **pendant**.

J'irai à Paris **pour** quinze jours.	*I'll go to Paris for two weeks.*
Pour combien de temps partirez-vous?	*For how long will you be gone?*

However, with verbs of motion and the verb **être** the future is often used with **pour** to express duration of time.

20. in

(**a**) The preposition *in* with place names is taken up on pages 210–212.

(**b**) *in* + A COMMON NOUN

Nos amis sont **au** restaurant.	*Our friends are in the restaurant.*
Jacques est **dans** sa chambre.	*Jack is in his room.*

The usual word for *in* is **dans,** but **à** + DEFINITE ARTICLE is often used to express *in the*.

(**c**) *in* + **matin, après-midi, soir**

Ne faites pas de bruit **le soir** après dix heures.	*Don't make any noise in the evening after ten o'clock.*

For *in the morning, in the afternoon,* and *in the evening* French says **le matin, l'après-midi,** and **le soir** without the preposition **dans.**

(**d**) *in* to express time required to do something

Monsieur Goulet travaille très vite; il pourrait réparer votre télévision **en une heure.**	*Mr. Goulet works very fast; he could fix your television set in an hour.*

To indicate the length of time required to do something, French uses **en** to express the English *in*.

(e) *in* to express time at which an action can begin

Je n'ai pas le temps maintenant, *I don't have time now, but I could fix*
mais je pourrais réparer votre *your television set* in (meaning
télévision **dans trois jours.** 'after') three days.

To indicate the moment at which an action can begin, French uses **dans** to express the English *in.*

(f) *in* used to introduce a phrase of manner

Madame Renard parle **d'une voix** *Mrs. Renard speaks* in a very soft
très douce. voice.

Phrases of manner are often introduced by the preposition **de.**

(g) — *o'clock in the* —

Je me suis réveillé **à deux heures** *I woke up* at two o'clock in the morn-
du matin. ing.

In expressions such as **deux heures du matin, trois heures de l'après-midi,** and **huit heures du soir,** the English *in the* is expressed in French by **de** + DEFINITE ARTICLE.

F. *Remplacez les mots anglais indiqués entre parenthèses par leur équivalent français.*

1. Paul fait tout bien (*except*) ses leçons de musique. 2. Vous êtes fou de dépenser votre argent (*in*) une façon aussi extravagante. 3. Couchez-vous de bonne heure (*in the evening*). 4. Jean a passé le week-end (*at*) les Biéville. 5. (*For*) dix jours on ne savait pas où ils étaient. 6. Je viens de parler à Nicole; elle était (*in*) mauvaise humeur. 7. Le petit a dormi jusqu'à quatre heures (*in the afternoon*). 8. Nous partirons (*for*) huit jours. 9. (*In*) Molière il y a toujours des choses amusantes. 10. Marc a fait ses devoirs (*in*) vingt minutes. 11. Nous regardons la télévision (*for*) deux heures. 12. Dépêchez-vous, le train part (*in*) une demi-heure. 13. Cela ne se passe pas comme ça (*at*) les Italiens. 14. Son mari lui a répondu (*in*) un ton ferme. 15. (*For*) combien de temps partirez-vous à Londres?

G. *Traduisez en français.*

1. Those boys have been playing here for an hour. 2. My alarm clock rang at six o'clock in the morning. 3. I will go to Portugal for

three days. 4. (*vous*) Your little boy went down the street a little while ago. 5. (*vous*) Do you want to see me at your home or in your office? 6. I saw Mr. Lebrun at the barber's. 7. I'll begin that work in a half hour. 8. We get up early in the morning. 9. I slept a great deal during my illness. 10. Everyone came except Michael. 11. In Balzac one finds extraordinary characters[1]. 12. I can finish that book in an hour. 13. One is always well received at their home. 14. We read that before.

---

[1] Not «caractères». See page 38.

21. in spite of

Malgré le mauvais temps, je vais sortir ce soir.　　In spite of *the bad weather, I'm going out this evening.*

The English *in spite of* is expressed in French by **malgré.**

22. instead of

Au lieu d'un cadeau, j'ai donné de l'argent à Jacques.　　Instead of *a gift, I gave Jack some money.*

The English *instead of* is expressed in French by **au lieu de,** which may be followed by a noun, a pronoun, or an infinitive.

23. out of

(**a**) *out of* = **hors de**

Votre ami est **hors de** danger maintenant.　　*Your friend is* out of *danger now.*

The commonest equivalent of *out of* is **hors de.**

(**b**) *out of* = *without*

Vous êtes toujours **sans** argent.　　*You are always* out of *money.*

When *out of* means *without*, it is expressed by **sans.**

(**c**) *out of* between numerals (one *out of* three)

Un étudiant **sur** cinq a déjà été en France.　　*One student* out of *five has already been in France.*

When *out of* is used idiomatically between numerals in phrases such as *two out of three*, French expresses *out of* by **sur**.

(**d**) *go out of, come out of, fall out of*

Louis **est sorti de** la maison avec son chien.

Louis came out of *the house with his dog.*

Votre carte d'identité **est tombée de** votre portefeuille.

Your identification card has fallen out of *your billfold.*

The verbs *come out of* and *go out of* are expressed by **sortir de,** and *fall out of* is expressed by **tomber de.**

24. toward

Tout le monde s'est précipité **vers** la porte.

Everyone rushed toward *the door.*

Vers la fin de la journée, je me sens fatigué.

Toward the end of the day I feel tired.

The word *toward* is usually expressed by **vers,** whether it indicates motion or means *about* with an expression of time.

Il faut être loyal **envers** ses amis.

One must be loyal toward *one's friends.*

Quelle est son attitude **envers** ses parents?

What is his attitude toward *his parents?*

Used figuratively in referring to a person, *toward* is expressed by **envers.**

25. under

Le métro passe **sous** la Seine.

The subway goes under *the Seine.*

The commonest way of expressing *under* is **sous.**

Les Delorme habitent **au-dessous de** nous.

The Delormes live under *us.*

Raymond a quinze employés **au-dessous de** lui.

Raymond has fifteen employees under *him.*

However, *under* and *underneath* are expressed by **au-dessous de** when used figuratively and when *under* does not mean *immediately under.*

26. up

Je **monte** cet escalier cinq fois par jour.

I go up that stairway five times a day.

En sortant de son bureau, Monsieur   *On leaving his office, Mr. Clement* went
  Clément **a remonté la rue.**   up the street.

The English *up* is often part of the French verb. Two of the common expressions which express *up* are **monter,** meaning *to go up*, and **remonter la rue,** which means *to go up the street.*

27. with

(a) *with* = **avec**

Je vous ai vu **avec** une dame hier   *I saw you* with *a lady yesterday evening.*
  soir.

The common way of expressing *with* is **avec.**

(b) *with* = **de** after verb or adjective

Son bureau est toujours **couvert de**   *His desk is always* covered <u>with</u> *dust.*
  poussière.
Es-tu **content de** ta voiture?   *Are you* satisfied <u>with</u> *your car?*

Certain verbs and adjectives are regularly followed by **de** in French and their English equivalents are followed by *with.*

(c) *with* = **chez**

Louise habite **chez** sa tante.   *Louise lives* with *her aunt.*
Chez Verlaine, la qualité musicale   *With Verlaine, the musical quality of the*
  des mots est très importante.   *words is very important.*

When *with* means *at the house of* or *in the case of* + A PERSON, French generally uses **chez.**

(d) *with* in phrases of manner = **de**

Françoise regardait sa montre **d'un**   *Frances was looking at her watch* with
  air anxieux.   *an anxious air.*

French phrases of manner are introduced by **de.** Sometimes this **de** is expressed in English by *with*, sometimes by *in.*

(e) *with* in phrases of characteristic = **à** + ARTICLE

Cette brune **aux yeux bleus** a beau-   *That brunette* with *blue eyes has a*
  coup de charme.   *great deal of charm.*

French uses **à** + DEFINITE ARTICLE to indicate a characteristic of a person. English uses the preposition *with* in the same way.

(f) *with* to express attitude or manner of a part of the body = DEFINITE ARTICLE

Louis dort toujours **les bras sous les**   *Louis always sleeps* with his arms un-
couvertures.   der the blankets.

English uses *with* to express attitude or manner of a part of the body, whereas French uses the DEFINITE ARTICLE without a preposition.

H. *Remplacez par l'équivalent français les mots anglais entre parenthèses.*

1. Restez à la maison (*instead of*) vous fatiguer.   2. Je suis allé en classe (*in spite of*) la neige.   3. Connaissez-vous ce jeune homme (*with*) cheveux roux?   4. Les enfants (*under*) sept ans paient demi-place.   5. Cet homme est toujours (*out of*) travail.   6. Nous nous sommes dirigés (*toward*) le centre de la place.   7. Nous sommes très satisfaits (*with*) vos progrès. 8. Êtes-vous toujours indulgents (*toward*) vos amis?   9. Comment trouvez-vous la famille qui habite (*under*) vous?   10. Nous habitons (*at*) mes beaux-parents.   11. Dans ce pays, deux personnes (*out of*) sept savent une langue étrangère. 12. La terre était couverte (*with*) neige.   13. Aidez-moi à porter ce bureau (*toward*) la fenêtre.   14. Achetez une voiture (*instead of*) une moto.

I. *Traduisez en français.*

1. He looked at me with his mouth open.   2. Read instead of looking at television.   3. Who is that girl with bare feet?   4. (*vous*) What is your attitude toward foreigners?   5. (*vous*) Are you satisfied[1] with your new job?   6. (*tu*) What fell out of your pocket?   7. My son lives at his grandmother's.   8. Toward the end of the play, everybody was laughing.   9. (*tu*) What do you have under your coat? 10. The room was filled with smoke.   11. (*vous*) Don't forget to go to the dentist's before going to the movies.   12. Our friends came to see us in spite of the bad weather.   13. One girl out of three gets married before the age of twenty[2].   14. Who just came out of the office?   15. (*vous*) I hope that your brother is out of danger.   16. My

---

[1] **content**   [2] Supply **ans.**

brother-in-law has been out of work for a month. 17. When Mr.
Saunier came out of the hotel, he went up the street.

Problem Words

62. would

(a) When *would* is used to express a condition

Je **partirais** tout de suite si j'avais   *I would leave immediately if I had*
   le temps.   *time.*

The word *would* is often a part of the conclusion of an English conditional sentence. In this case, French puts the verb in the CONDI-
TIONAL.

Que **ferais**-tu à ma place?   *What* would *you* do *in my place?*

Sometimes *would* is the auxiliary of the verb of an implied condition, that is, one in which the *if*-clause is missing but is implied. The
above sentence, for instance, means: *What would you do if you were I?*
In an implied condition French uses the CONDITIONAL of the verb of
the sentence to express the English *would*.

(b) When *would* means *used to*

Je **partais** de bonne heure tous les   *I would* (= used to) *leave early every*
   matins.   *morning.*

When *would* = *used to*, it indicates a customary past action, and in
such cases the IMPERFECT of the verb must be used.

CAUTION: Whenever you find *would* in an English sentence which
you wish to express in French, determine whether *would* is part of a
condition or whether it is used to describe a customary action and is
the equivalent of *used to*. If *would* is the equivalent of *used to*, use the
imperfect rather than the conditional.

63. year

(a) When *year* is expressed by **année**

En quelle **année** êtes-vous né?   *In what* year *were you born?*

Cette **année**-là il a beaucoup neigé.   *That* year *it snowed a great deal.*

J'ai passé beaucoup d'**années** en   *I spent many* years *in France.*
   France.

Ma troisième **année** à l'université a été très amusante.	*My third* year *at the university was very entertaining*.

The most common word for *year* is **année**. It should be used except in the cases stated in (**b**).

(**b**) When *year* is expressed by **an**

Nous avons passé **trois ans** en France.	*We spent* three years *in France*.
Nous y retournons **tous les ans.**	*We go back there* every year.
Sans indiscrétion, combien gagnez-vous **par an?**	*If it isn't indiscreet to ask, how much do you earn* a year?

The word **an** is used for *year* when it is modified by a cardinal numeral, in the expressions **tous les ans** (*every year*) and **par an** (*per year*), and occasionally in other circumstances.

64. yes

(**a**) When *yes* is expressed by **oui**

—Êtes-vous arrivé hier?	*"Did you arrive yesterday?"*
—**Oui,** je suis arrivé hier.	"Yes, *I arrived yesterday.*"

The usual word for *yes* is **oui;** it indicates the speaker's agreement with the previous statement or question.

(**b**) When *yes* is expressed by **si**

—**N'êtes**-vous **pas** arrivé hier?	"Didn't *you arrive yesterday?"*
—**Si,** je suis arrivé hier.	"Yes, *I arrived yesterday.*"
—Guy **ne** comprend **pas** bien l'anglais.	*"Guy* doesn't *understand English well."*
—**Si,** il le comprend bien.	"Yes, *he does understand it well."*

After a negative statement or question, **si** is used for *yes*. It contradicts the preceding statement or question.

65. young men

How to express the plural of **jeune homme**

Il y avait **des jeunes gens** et des jeunes filles à cette réception.	*There were some young men and some young ladies at that reception.*
Lucile voudrait connaître **des jeunes gens** avec qui elle puisse sortir.	*Lucille would like to get acquainted with some young men with whom she could go out.*

The plural of **jeune homme** is **jeunes gens**. A frequent meaning of **jeunes gens** is therefore *young men*. The expression **les jeunes hommes** seldom occurs, and you should avoid using it.

Les **jeunes gens** s'amusent beaucoup pendant la traversée en bateau.	Young people *have a very good time during a boat trip.*

The term **jeunes gens** also means *young people*. The context must decide where **jeunes gens** means *young men* and where *young people*.

J. *Remplacez les mots anglais par leur équivalent français.*

1. Dans quelques (*years*) j'espère savoir plusieurs langues.   2. Ces (*young men*) avec leurs cheveux longs ressemblent à des filles.   3. Nos amis mexicains ne sont pas retournés dans leur pays depuis dix (*years*).   4. —Pourquoi ne prenez-vous pas le train de cinq heures? —Parce que je (*would arrive*) au milieu de la nuit.   5. —Je ne parle pas bien le français. —(*Yes*), vous le parlez fort bien.   6. Agnès ne veut sortir qu'avec des (*young men*) de son âge.   7. Le patron change de voiture (*every year*).   8. Quand je préparais mes examens, je (*would get up*) à six heures du matin.   9. —Voulez-vous m'accompagner chez les Bridoux? —(*Yes*), volontiers.

K. *Traduisez en français. Attention aux mots en italique.*

1. I think I could go to France in¹ two *years*.   2. (*vous*) *Would* you lend me your car this weekend?   3. Our cousins from Pontigny come to see us twice a *year*.   4. (*tu*) "Do you like that music?" "*Yes*, very much."   5. Robert and Roger are very serious *young men*.   6. (*vous*) In² what *year* did you come to the United States?   7. When we were young, we *would* go to church every Sunday.   8. I found the first *year* of medicine the most difficult.   9. (*tu*) "Haven't you seen Alain?" "*Yes*, he's coming."

---

¹ **dans**   ² **en**

Verb Review

Review the verbs **voir** and **vouloir** according to the outline on page 283.

The Texts

To the Student

There follow eight texts from twentieth century French authors. Each of these selections presents an image or an experience which reveals some aspect of life and which gives the passage an interest in itself as well as constituting a part of a complete work.

Each text is interesting in content and could be studied uniquely for subject matter. Each has its peculiar style and might be examined from the point of view of the author's literary technique.

In addition to having esthetic and intellectual qualities, each selection contains examples of various syntactical constructions common in present-day French. To facilitate your study of these texts from a grammatical point of view, we have edited them with questions and comments on the language.

Since no French author writes in order to illustrate only certain syntactical points, these texts naturally contain many different kinds of constructions. From each, we have chosen certain significant grammatical topics on which to focus your attention.

*　　*　　*

These texts may be assigned to you for study at any time during your course.

If the earlier texts are assigned toward the beginning of the course, you will find in them questions based on grammatical constructions which you will not as yet have studied in the course. But that does not matter. It is stimulating to be confronted with a construction for the first time in an author, to study its usage there without any previous knowledge of it, and then later to delve into the same subject in a more organized and formal fashion. The fact that you have already examined a topic in a text will help you to understand it better when you take it up in detail.

If the texts are assigned toward the end of the course, you will probably be able to answer many of the questions from what you have already learned in the course. But if you cannot answer the questions from what you have observed in the example of the selection and from what you already know about French grammar, look in the index to find the topic under discussion and read the references to it which you find there.

In making questions on the grammar of the texts, we have tried to avoid repeating questions on the same types of grammar in succeeding texts except where it seemed wise to do so in order to emphasize the importance of knowing certain difficult aspects of the language. But your instructor may ask you questions on these points of grammar in every text in order to review them.

Your instructor may direct you to analyze a text grammatically for home preparation, and then, when you come to class, spend some time discussing all aspects of the texts. To this end, you should read the passage carefully, think of it from all points of view, and be able to answer the various types of questions your instructor may ask.

Texte N° 1

JEAN COCTEAU

Homme extraordinaire, universel, romancier, dramaturge, essayiste, mais poète avant tout, mêlé à tous les mouvements d'avant-garde dans l'art et la littérature, Jean Cocteau a «étonné» son époque. Nul n'est resté jeune plus longtemps que ce magicien et ne s'est plus intéressé à la jeunesse.

A la sortie d'un lycée, une fin d'après-midi à Paris, une bataille a lieu à coups de boules de neige entre deux groupes de garçons d'une douzaine d'années. Le chef d'un des camps est Dargelos, le héros de son école. Il vient de lancer brutalement une boule de neige sur un jeune camarade qui l'admire. Celui-ci, blessé, tombe évanoui; on le transporte dans la loge du concierge, et le censeur vient voir ce qui se passe.

Dargelos était[1] debout dans la porte. Derrière la porte se pressaient[1] des têtes curieuses. Gérard pleurait[1] et tenait[1] la main de son ami.

—Racontez, Dargelos, dit[2] le censeur.

5 —Il n'y a rien à raconter, m'sieur. On lançait[3] des boules de[4] neige. Je lui en ai jeté[5] une. Elle devait[6] être très dure. Il l'a reçue[7] en pleine poitrine, il a fait «ho!» et il est tombé comme ça. J'ai d'abord cru[8] qu'il saignait du nez à cause d'une autre boule de neige.

—Une boule de neige ne défonce pas la poitrine.

10 —Monsieur, monsieur, dit alors l'élève qui répondait au nom de Gérard, il avait entouré[9] une pierre avec de la neige.

—Est-ce[10] exact? questionna le censeur.

Dargelos haussa les[11] épaules.

—Vous ne répondez pas?

15 —C'est[10] inutile. Tenez, il ouvre les[11] yeux, demandez-lui . . .

253

Le malade se ranimait. Il appuyait la tête contre la manche de son camarade.

—Comment vous sentez-vous?

—Pardonnez-moi . . .

—Ne vous excusez pas, vous êtes malade, vous vous êtes évanoui.   20

—Je me rappelle.

—Pouvez-vous me dire à la suite de quoi vous vous êtes évanoui?

—J'avais reçu une boule de neige dans la poitrine.

—On ne se trouve pas mal en recevant une boule de neige!

—Je n'ai rien[12] reçu d'autre.   25

—Votre camarade prétend que cette boule de neige cachait une pierre.

Le malade vit que Dargelos haussait les épaules.

—Gérard est fou, dit-il. Tu es fou. Cette boule de neige était une boule de neige. Je courais, j'ai dû avoir une congestion.   30

Le censeur respira[13].

Dargelos allait sortir. Il se ravisa[14] et on pensa[14] qu'il marchait vers le malade. Arrivé en face du comptoir où les concierges vendent des porte-plume, de l'encre, des sucreries, il hésita, tira des sous de sa poche, les posa sur le rebord et prit en échange un de ces rouleaux de   35 réglisse qui[15] ressemblent à des lacets de bottine et que[15] sucent les collégiens. Ensuite, il traversa la loge, porta la main à sa tempe dans une sorte de salut militaire et disparut.

Les Enfants terribles
(Extrait)

© *Éditions Gallimard*

NOTES AND QUESTIONS

1. You notice that the selection starts with four verbs in the imperfect tense. What do these verbs do for the selection? Why did the author put them in the imperfect rather than in the simple past?

2. What sort of word order does **dit le censeur** exemplify? Whenever a like phrase follows part of a conversation, it is always in inverted word order.

3. Why is this form of the verb **lancer** written with a **ç** (**c cédille**)?

4. Analyze the expression **de neige.** Of what two parts of speech does it consist? How would **boule de neige** be expressed in English? What then is the function of **de neige?** Can you make a generalization concerning this sort of case? Your generalization should read something like this: "English often uses a noun as an adjective. In like cases, French uses **de** + NOUN and places them after the word they modify."

5. The verb **lancer** in the previous sentence was in the imperfect. Why does Dargelos now switch to the compound past?

6. How would you express **devait être** in English? If you are not sure, look up the imperfect of **devoir** on page 199, §§2, 3.

7. With what does **reçue** agree? What is the rule for the agreement of a past participle of a verb conjugated with the auxiliary **avoir?**

8. This is a verb of mental action, yet it is in the compound past rather than the imperfect. Why?

9. What tense is **avait entouré?** Why would such a tense be used here rather than the compound past?

10. What type of **ce** is this? To what does it refer? If you are not sure, see page 103, which discusses this in reference to demonstrative pronouns.

11. How would you say in English: **Dargelos haussa les épaules? Il ouvre les yeux?** What rule for the use of the French definite article applies in this case? If you are not sure, consult page 73 in the chapter on possessives. Find another example of this same construction in the following sentences.

12. In this sentence, notice the position of **rien** in a compound tense. What generalization can you make concerning the position of **rien** in a compound tense? Also, notice the **d'** in the expression **rien d'autre** (*nothing else*). In French, an indefinite is always separated from a following adjective by **de.**

13. The verb **respirer** often means *breathe,* but breathing is a continuous operation. Here the simple past is used, and therefore, what would the meaning of **respirer** as used here be?

14. The verbs **se ravisa** and **pensa** constitute mental actions. Why are they put in the simple past here?

15. Note the relative pronouns **qui** and **que.** Both refer to **ces rouleaux de réglisse.** Why is **qui** used in one instance and then **que?**

Texte N° 2

COLETTE

Colette est célèbre pour sa finesse, son esprit enjoué, le charme de son style. Par sa peinture sensible de l'amour et son observation originale de la nature, elle donne vie à tout un monde de tendresse et de fraîcheur. Dans *La Maison de Claudine* elle raconte des souvenirs d'enfance.

La petite fille de treize ans passe ses vacances dans la maison familiale avec son grand frère et Maurice, un camarade d'études de celui-ci. Elle est d'abord secrètement amoureuse de lui, mais elle se raisonne et ils deviennent de bons amis. Quand elle apprend qu'il va se marier, elle joue subtilement de sa coquetterie et, avec un plaisir mêlé de tristesse, elle réussit pour la première fois à troubler un homme.

C'est en écoutant[1] causer les deux jeunes gens que j'appris le mariage, encore assez lointain, de Maurice. Un jour que[2] nous étions seuls au[3] jardin, je m'enhardis[4] jusqu'à lui demander le portrait de sa fiancée. Il me le tendit: une jeune fille souriante, jolie, extrêmement coiffée, enguirlandée de mille ruches de dentelle.   5

—Oh! dis-je maladroitement, la[a] belle robe!

Il rit si franchement que je ne m'excusai pas.

—Et qu'allez-vous faire, quand vous serez[5] marié?

Il cessa de rire et me regarda.

—Comment, ce que je vais faire? Mais je suis déjà presque avocat[6], 10 tu[7] sais!

—Je sais. Et elle, votre fiancée, que fera-t-elle, pendant que vous serez avocat?

—Que[8] tu es drôle! Elle sera ma femme, voyons.

—Elle mettra d'autres[9] robes avec beaucoup de petites ruches?   15

—Elle s'occupera de notre maison, elle recevra . . . Tu te moques de moi? Tu sais très bien comment on vit quand on est marié.

---

[a] *What a beautiful dress!* The definite article is sometimes used to modify a noun in an exclamation.

—Non, pas très bien. Mais je sais comment nous vivons[10] depuis un mois et demi.

20 —Qui donc, «nous»?

—Vous, mon frère et moi[11]. Vous êtes bien[12], ici? Étiez-vous heureux? Vous nous aimez?

Il leva ses[13] yeux noirs vers le toit d'ardoises brodé de jaune, vers la glycine en sa seconde floraison, les arrêta un moment sur moi et 25 répondit comme à lui-même:

—Mais oui . . .

—Après, quand vous serez marié, vous ne pourrez plus, sans doute, revenir ici, passer les vacances? Vous ne pourrez plus jamais vous promener à côté de mon frère, en tenant mes deux nattes par 30 le bout, comme des rênes?

Je tremblais de tout mon corps, mais je ne le quittais pas des yeux. Quelque chose changea[14] dans son visage. Il regarda autour de lui, puis il parut mesurer, de la tête aux pieds, la fillette qui s'appuyait à un arbre et qui levait la tête en lui parlant, parce qu'elle n'avait pas 35 encore assez grandi. Je me souviens qu'il ébaucha une sorte de sourire contraint, puis il haussa les épaules, répondit assez sottement:

—Dame, non, ça va de soi[15] . . .

Il s'éloigna vers la maison sans ajouter[16] un mot et je mêlai pour la première fois, au grand regret enfantin que j'avais de perdre bien- 40 tôt Maurice, un petit chagrin victorieux de femme.

La Maison de Claudine
(Extrait)

© *Libraire Hachette*

NOTES AND QUESTIONS

1. Here, the present participle is used with **en.** When the present participle is used with **en,** to what word in the sentence does it refer? If you are not sure, see pages 64–65. Find another example of the present participle with **en** in this selection.

2. The expression **un jour que** means *a day when.* You learned on page 131 that *when*, relative, is normally **où.** However, when the antecedent indicating a period of time is modified by **un** or **une,** it is fairly common to find *when* expressed by **que,** although it may also be expressed by **où.**

3. The expression **au jardin** means *in the garden*. Notice that French often uses **au** instead of **dans le** for the English *in the*. There is no general rule to determine which is used, and sometimes either is used.

4. The expression **je m'enhardis** means *I became bold*. Comment on the use of the reflexive verb and especially of the compound past and the simple past of the reflexive verb to express the English *become* + ADJECTIVE. If you are not sure of this usage, see page 24, §5(c) and page 69, §19(e).

5. English would use the present tense here. Under what conditions does French use the future in constructions in which English uses the present? Find another similar example several lines down.

6. English would say: *I am already almost a lawyer*. When does French omit the indefinite article where English would use it?

7. The little girl has been using the **vous** form when speaking to Maurice. Why does he use the **tu** form when answering her? Notice the use of **vous** and **tu** throughout this text.

8. Note that here **que** is used as an exclamation. English would say: *How funny you are!* French also uses **comme** in such cases, so that **Comme tu es drôle!** is equally possible.

9. Why is **d'** used instead of **des?** If you are not sure, consult page 172, §4.

10. How does English express . . . **nous vivons depuis un mois et demi?** Give the general rule for the use of the present tense in such constructions.

11. What kind of pronoun is **moi?** Why is it used here?

12. Here, **bien,** which is more often an adverb, is used as an adjective with a special meaning. What does **bien** mean here? Note that **bien** may be used as an adjective when it is in the predicate after a form of **être.** It is much less frequently used thus to modify a noun directly.

13. You have learned that when the subject of the sentence acts with a part of the body, French normally uses the article where English uses a possessive adjective. Yet here, French uses a possessive adjective — because the part of the body is modified. When a part of the body is modified, French tends to use the possessive adjective just as does English.

14. Why is an **e** inserted between the stem and ending of this form of the verb **changer?**

15. The disjunctive form of the reflexive pronoun **se,** which is **soi,** is used in what circumstances? If you are not sure, see page 48.

16. The French **sans ajouter un mot** would be expressed in English by *without adding a word*. Thus, after a preposition English uses a present participle where French uses an infinitive.

Texte N° 3

MARGUERITE DURAS

Des nombreuses femmes écrivains d'aujourd'hui, Marguerite Duras est parmi les plus connues dans la littérature et dans le cinéma. Elle fait partie de l'école du «nouveau roman», surtout par sa technique de stricte observation, qui donne à ses œuvres un air neutre, détaché. Mais ce qu'elle écrit est toujours évocateur et souvent poignant.

Cette scène à trois voix est l'ouverture du drame passionnel qui va bientôt se dérouler. Un professeur de piano questionne en vain le petit garçon à qui l'on impose des leçons de musique alors qu'il rêve d'autres choses.

—Veux-tu lire ce[a] qu'il y a d'écrit au-dessus de ta partition? demanda la dame.

—Moderato cantabile, dit l'enfant.

La dame ponctua cette réponse d'un[1] coup de crayon sur le clavier.
5 L'enfant resta[2] immobile, la[3] tête tournée vers sa partition.

—Et qu'est-ce que ça veut dire, moderato cantabile?

—Je[b] sais pas.

Une femme, assise à trois mètres de là, soupira.

—Tu es sûr de ne pas[4] savoir ce que ça veut dire, moderato canta-
10 bile? reprit la dame.

L'enfant ne répondit pas. La dame poussa un cri d'impuissance étouffé, tout[5] en frappant de nouveau le clavier de son crayon. Pas[6] un cil dē l'enfant ne bougea. La dame se retourna.

—Madame Desbaresdes[c] quelle[d] tête vous avez là, dit-elle.

15 Anne Desbaresdes soupira une nouvelle fois.

—A[e] qui le dites-vous, dit-elle.

---

[a] *what is written.* The **d'** in this expression is the **de** which separates a modifying adjective from an indefinite pronoun in expressions such as **rien de difficile, quelque chose de beau,** etc.
[b] In familiar spoken French, the **ne** of the negative **ne . . . pas** is often slurred over or entirely omitted.
[c] Desbaresdes is pronounced [debarɛd].
[d] *what a stubborn child* [e] *You're telling me!*

L'enfant, immobile, les yeux baissés, fut seul à se souvenir que le
soir venait d'éclater. Il en[7] frémit.

—Je te l'ai dit la dernière fois, je te l'ai dit l'avant-dernière fois, je
te l'ai dit cent fois, tu es sûr de ne pas le savoir?   20

L'enfant ne jugea pas bon de répondre. La dame reconsidéra une
nouvelle fois l'objet qui était devant elle. Sa fureur augmenta.

—Ça recommence, dit tout bas Anne Desbaresdes.

—Ce qu'il y a, continua la dame, ce qu'il y a, c'est que tu ne veux
pas le dire.   25

Anne Desbaresdes aussi reconsidéra cet enfant de ses pieds jusqu'à
sa tête mais d'une[8] autre façon que la dame.

—Tu vas le dire tout de suite, hurla la dame.

L'enfant ne témoigna aucune surprise. Il ne répondit toujours[9]
pas. Alors la dame frappa une troisième fois sur le clavier, mais si   30
fort que le crayon se cassa[10]. Tout à côté des mains de l'enfant.
Celles-ci[11] étaient à peine écloses, rondes, laiteuses encore. Fermées
sur elles-mêmes, elles ne bougèrent pas.

—C'est un enfant difficile, osa dire Anne Desbaresdes, non sans
une[12] certaine timidité.   35

L'enfant tourna la tête vers cette voix, vers elle, vite, le[f] temps de
s'assurer de son existence, puis il reprit sa pose d'objet, face à la
partition. Ses mains restèrent fermées.

—Je ne veux pas savoir s'il est difficile ou non, Madame Desbaresdes, dit la dame. Difficile ou pas, il faut qu'il obéisse, ou[g] bien.   40

Dans le temps qui suivit ce propos, le bruit de la mer entra par la
fenêtre ouverte. Et avec lui, celui, atténué, de la ville au cœur de
l'après-midi de ce printemps. . . .

—Une dernière fois. Tu es sûr de ne pas le savoir? . . .

L'enfant ouvrit sa[13] main, la déplaça et se[13] gratta légèrement le   45
mollet. Son geste fut désinvolte et peut-être la dame convint-elle de
son innocence?

—Je sais pas, dit-il, après s'être[14] gratté.

Les couleurs du couchant devinrent tout à coup si glorieuses que
la blondeur de cet enfant s'en trouva modifiée.   50

—C'est facile, dit la dame un peu plus calmement.

Elle se moucha longuement.

---

[f] **le temps de** = *long enough to*   [g] *or else*

—Quel enfant j'ai là, dit Anne Desbaresdes joyeusement, tout de même, mais quel enfant j'ai fait là, et comment se fait-il qu'il me
55 soit[15] venu avec cet entêtement-là . . .

La dame ne crut pas bon de relever tant d'orgueil.

—Ça veut dire, dit-elle à l'enfant — écrasée — pour la centième fois, ça veut dire modéré et chantant.

—Modéré et chantant, dit l'enfant totalement en[h] allé où?

60 La dame se retourna.

—Ah, je[i] vous jure.

Moderato cantabile
(Extrait)

© *Les Éditions de Minuit*

---

[h] **en allé où** = *blankly* (lit. *gone off . . . where?*)   [i] (In a tone of exasperation) *honestly!*

NOTES AND QUESTIONS

1. What is the meaning of **d'un coup de crayon?** What is the function of **de** in such a phrase? If you are not sure, see page 245, §27(**d**).

2. Notice that although **resta** seems to indicate a state, it is in the simple past because it constitutes a new phase of the action and by so doing forwards the action of the narrative.

3. How would we express **la tête tournée** in English? How does French use the article with parts of the body in such cases? Find another example of the same use of the article in the text. This case is discussed on page 77, §10 of the grammar.

4. Here we find both parts of the negation without an intervening verb. When a negative modifies a simple infinitive, the two parts of the negation precede this infinitive.

5. How would you express **tout en frappant** in English? How does **tout** affect the meaning of **en frappant?**

6. Here, **pas** precedes **ne,** which is unusual. Make a generalization as to the positions of **ne** and **pas** in a French sentence.

7. How would you express this **en** in English? Remember that **en** usually takes the place of **de** + NOUN.

8. How would you express **d'une autre façon** in English? What is the function of **de** in such a phrase? If you are not sure, see page 242, §20(**f**).

9. Here, **toujours** does not mean *always*. What does it mean?

10. In English, we would say: *The pencil broke*. No reflexive pronoun would be used. But in French many verbs require a reflexive object to complete their meaning.

11. What is the meaning of **celles-ci** in this sentence? To what word does it refer?

12. The preposition **sans** normally is followed directly by an indefinite noun without an article. But here, note that **une certaine timidité** has, as a matter of fact, an element of definiteness, hence the use of the article.

13. Note first of all the use of the possessive adjective with an unmodified part of the body. Perhaps more frequent is **L'enfant ouvrit la main.** In the second part of the sentence, we find **se gratta légèrement le mollet.** When is the REFLEXIVE OBJECT + THE ARTICLE used in French where English would use only a possessive adjective?

14. What verbal construction is used after the preposition **après?** And why is this verb conjugated with the auxiliary **être?**

15. What is the basic reason for the use of the subjunctive here? If you are in doubt, see page 142. And why would the past rather than the present subjunctive be required?

Texte N° 4

ALAIN ROBBE-GRILLET

D'abord ingénieur, Alain Robbe-Grillet est devenu le maître du «nouveau roman», de l'école dite du regard. Il rejette l'appareil psychologique traditionnel et semble ne faire qu'enregistrer avec minutie ce qui frappe la vue et l'imagination d'une personne. Il donne aux objets une grande importance: ils ont chez lui une substance, une épaisseur qui révèle mieux le monde des hommes.

Sa vision s'applique particulièrement bien à un paysage comme cette plage où marchent trois enfants qui se rendent à l'école; le temps qui s'écoule est marqué par le soleil, la mer, le sable, les empreintes des pas, la falaise et la troupe d'oiseaux qui arpente le rivage. Les enfants avancent fragiles dans la nature; le plus petit détail, la moindre description contribuent à donner une dimension nouvelle à la scène et une vie intense aux personnages que le lecteur accompagne pas à pas et dont il partage les sensations.

Trois[1] enfants marchent[2] le long d'une grève. Ils s'avancent[3], côte à côte, se tenant par la main. Ils ont sensiblement la même taille, et sans doute aussi le même âge: une douzaine[4] d'années. Celui[5] du milieu, cependant, est un peu plus petit que les deux autres.

5 Hormis ces[1] trois enfants, toute la longue[6] plage est déserte. C'est[7] une bande de sable assez large, uniforme, dépourvue de[8] roches isolées[9] comme de trous d'eau, à peine inclinée entre la falaise abrupte[9], qui paraît sans issue, et la mer.

Il fait très beau. Le soleil éclaire le sable jaune d'une lumière 10 violente, verticale. Il n'y a pas un[10] nuage dans le ciel. Il n'y a pas, non plus, de[10] vent. L'eau est bleue, calme, sans la moindre ondulation venant du large, bien que la plage soit[11] ouverte sur la mer libre, jusqu'à l'horizon.

Mais à intervalles réguliers, une vague soudaine, toujours la même, 15 née à quelques mètres du bord, s'enfle brusquement et déferle aussitôt, toujours sur la même ligne. On n'a pas alors l'impression que l'eau avance[3], puis se retire; c'est, au contraire, comme si tout ce mouvement s'exécutait[12] sur place. Le gonflement de l'eau produit d'abord une légère[13] dépression, du côté de la grève, et la vague 20 prend un peu de recul, dans un bruissement de graviers roulés; puis elle éclate et se répand, laiteuse, sur la pente, mais pour regagner seulement le terrain perdu. C'est à peine si une montée plus forte, çà et là, vient mouiller un instant quelques décimètres supplémentaires.

25 Et tout reste de nouveau immobile, la mer, plate et bleue, exactement arrêtée à la même hauteur sur le sable jaune de la plage, où[14] marchent côte à côte les trois enfants.

Ils sont blonds, presque de la même couleur que le sable: la peau un peu plus foncée, les cheveux un peu plus clairs. Ils sont habillés 30 tous les trois de la même façon, culotte courte et chemisette, l'une et l'autre en grosse toile d'un bleu délavé. Ils marchent côte à côte, se tenant par la main, en ligne droite, parallèlement à la mer et parallèlement à la falaise, presque à égale distance des deux, un peu plus près de l'eau pourtant. Le soleil, au zénith, ne laisse pas d'ombre à 35 leur pied.

Devant eux le sable est tout à fait vierge, jaune et lisse depuis le rocher jusqu'à l'eau. Les enfants s'avancent en ligne droite, à une vitesse régulière, sans faire le plus petit[6] crochet, calmes et se tenant par la main. Derrière eux le sable, à peine humide, est marqué des trois lignes d'empreintes laissées par leurs[1] pieds nus, trois successions 40 régulières d'empreintes semblables et pareillement espacées, bien creuses, sans bavures.

Les enfants regardent droit devant eux. Ils n'ont pas un coup d'œil vers la haute[6] falaise, sur leur gauche, ni vers la mer dont les petites vagues éclatent périodiquement, sur l'autre côté. A plus forte 45 raison ne se retournent-ils pas, pour contempler derrière eux la distance parcourue. Ils poursuivent leur chemin, d'un pas égal et rapide.

Devant eux, une troupe d'oiseaux de mer arpente le rivage, juste à la limite des vagues. Ils progressent parallèlement à la marche des 50 enfants, dans le même sens que ceux-ci[15], à une centaine[4] de mètres environ. Mais, comme les oiseaux vont beaucoup moins vite, les enfants se rapprochent d'eux. Et tandis que la mer efface au fur et à mesure les traces des pattes étoilées, les pas des enfants demeurent inscrits avec netteté dans le sable à peine humide, où les trois lignes 55 d'empreintes continuent de s'allonger.

Instantanés
(Extrait)

© *Les Éditions de Minuit*

NOTES AND QUESTIONS

1. Numerals, demonstrative adjectives and possessive adjectives are known as limiting adjectives, for they limit the meaning of the noun they modify rather than describing it. Where are limiting adjectives placed in relation to the noun they modify?

2. The verb **marchent** and all the other verbs in the selection are in the present tense. What effect does the use of the present tense throughout the selection give?

3. In this passage we find both the reflexive form **s'avancer** and the non-

reflexive form **avancer.** It is difficult to explain exactly when one and when the other is used, but it may be noted that **avancer** is used with both persons and things, whereas **s'avancer** seems to be limited in use to persons.

4. The suffix **-aine** is used on both **douzaine** and **centaine.** What effect does the addition of **-aine** to a cardinal number have on that number?

5. What kind of pronoun is **celui?** This sort of pronoun must be followed by what types of words? Can they be followed by two types of words at the same time?

6. What position in respect to their noun do certain short adjectives such as **long, petit** and **haut** have? Notice that they do not have the more usual position of descriptive adjectives, possibly because they are short and common.

7. This is the introductory **ce.** Under what conditions can this **ce** be used?

8. The noun **roche** is indefinite rather than definite. Why is it preceded by **de** rather than **des?**

9. In the expressions **roches isolées** and **falaise abrupte,** each adjective is descriptive and therefore follows its noun. Notice that when an adjective follows its noun, it is in a more emphatic position than when it precedes its noun, and that it then indicates how this noun is different from all other nouns of the same category — that is, **roches isolées** are different from all other **roches.**

10. Here we find **pas un nuage** but **pas de vent.** Normally, the negative **pas** is followed by **de.** When **un** follows **pas,** as in **pas un nuage,** the emphasis is on **un** — *not a single cloud.*

11. What in the nature of the meaning of the relative adverb **bien que** would require that it be followed by the subjunctive?

12. How would you express **s'exécutait** in English? Certain French reflexives are regularly expressed in English by a passive. It is difficult to explain this construction, but in such cases the subject of the sentence acts upon itself by means of the reflexive object.

13. The descriptive adjective **léger** usually follows its noun. What is its meaning here? Why does it precede its noun here?

14. Note the word order of **où marchent côte à côte les trois enfants.** The French could also use our English word order and say **où les trois enfants marchent côte à côte,** but is is more natural in a situation like this to put the subject at the end of the sentence for reasons of rhythm and emphasis.

15. Here we find a demonstrative pronoun followed by **-ci** but with no corresponding **ceux-là.** What is the meaning of **ceux-ci** in this case? To what noun does it refer?

Texte N° 5

Antoine de Saint-Exupéry

Homme d'action, pilote de ligne à l'époque héroïque de l'aviation, puis pilote de guerre, Saint-Exupéry était en même temps un grand écrivain. L'avion lui a donné une nouvelle vision du monde qu'il a exprimée dans ses œuvres. Il n'est pas possible de voler toujours dans les étoiles; aussi Saint-Exupéry a-t-il cherché à établir une civilisation plus humaine, fondée sur le courage, le devoir et la solidarité.

Dans ce passage, l'auteur raconte son calvaire physique et moral dans le désert où son avion est tombé. Épuisé par une marche de trois jours, par la faim, par la soif, par les hallucinations, il va succomber avec son camarade Prévot quand un Bédouin se profile sur une dune.

Un autre Arabe apparaît[1,2] de profil sur la dune. Nous hurlons, mais tout bas[a]. Alors, nous agitons les[3] bras et nous avons l'impression de remplir le ciel de signaux[4] immenses. Mais ce Bédouin regarde toujours[5] vers la droite . . .

Et voici que, sans hâte[6], il a amorcé un quart de tour. A la seconde même[7] où il se présentera de face, tout sera accompli. A la seconde même où il regardera vers nous, il aura déjà effacé[8] en nous la soif, la mort et les mirages. Il a amorcé un quart de tour qui, déjà, change le monde. Par un mouvement de son seul[9] buste, par[b] la promenade de son seul regard, il crée la vie, et il me paraît[2] semblable à un dieu . . .

C'est[10] un miracle . . . Il marche vers nous sur le sable, comme un dieu sur la mer . . .

L'Arabe nous a simplement regardés[11]. Il a pressé, des[12] mains, sur nos[13] épaules, et nous lui avons obéi. Nous nous sommes étendus[14]. Il n'y a plus ici ni races[15], ni langages, ni divisions . . . Il y a ce nomade pauvre qui a posé sur nos épaules des mains d'archange[16].

Nous avons attendu, le[17] front dans le sable. Et maintenant, nous buvons à plat ventre, la[17] tête dans la bassine, comme des veaux. Le

5

10

15

---

[a] They yell in a whisper because of their exhaustion.   [b] *by simply looking toward us*

Bédouin s'en[c] effraye et nous oblige, à chaque instant, à nous inter-
20 rompre. Mais dès qu'il nous lâche, nous replongeons tout notre visage
dans l'eau.

L'eau!

Eau, tu n'as ni goût, ni couleur, ni arome, on ne peut pas te définir,
on te goûte, sans te connaître. Tu n'es pas nécessaire à la vie: tu es la
25 vie. Tu nous pénètres d'un plaisir qui ne s'explique[18] point par les
sens. Avec toi rentrent en nous tous les pouvoirs auxquels nous avions
renoncé. Par ta grâce, s'ouvrent en nous toutes les sources taries de
notre cœur.

Tu es la plus grande richesse qui soit[19] au monde, et tu es aussi la
30 plus délicate, toi si pure au ventre de la terre. On peut mourir sur une
source d'eau magnésienne. On peut mourir à deux pas d'un lac d'eau
salée. On peut mourir malgré deux litres de rosée qui retiennent en
suspens quelques sels. Tu n'acceptes point de mélange, tu ne supportes
point d'altération, tu es une ombrageuse divinité . . .
35 Mais tu répands en nous un bonheur infiniment simple.

Quant à toi qui nous sauves[20], Bédouin de Lybie, tu t'effaceras
cependant à jamais de ma mémoire. Je ne me souviendrai jamais de
ton visage. Tu es l'Homme et tu m'apparais avec le visage de tous
les hommes à la fois. Tu ne nous as jamais dévisagés et déjà tu nous as
40 reconnus. Tu es le frère bien-aimé. Et, à mon tour, je te reconnaîtrai
dans tous les hommes.

Tu m'apparais[2] baigné de noblesse et de bienveillance, grand
Seigneur qui a le pouvoir de donner à boire. Tous mes amis, tous mes
ennemis en toi marchent vers moi, et je n'ai plus un seul[d] ennemi au
45 monde.

Terre des hommes
(Extrait)

© *Éditions Gallimard*

---

[c] becomes (i.e. became) frightened because of it   [d] *single*

NOTES AND QUESTIONS

1. Note that throughout this passage the present tense is used to relate what
   happened in the past. The use of the present tense for the simple past in
   a narrative is extremely common in French. It makes the events stand
   out more vividly than would the simple past.

2. French has two verbs to express the English *appear:* **paraître,** meaning *look* or *seem,* and **apparaître,** meaning *to come into view.*

3. English would use the possessive adjective to modify *arms.* Why does the French use the definite article to modify **bras?** If you are not sure, see page 74, §6.

4. What is the singular form of **signaux?**

5. The basic meaning of **toujours** is *always.* But in this sentence its meaning is linked with its verb, so that . . . **regarde toujours** . . . means *kept on looking* or *continued to look.*

6. Why is **hâte** used here without any partitive article?

7. The basic meaning of the adjective **même** is *same* when it precedes its adjective. Here it follows its adjective. What does it mean?

8. What tense is **aura effacé?** How would this be expressed in English?

9. Although **seul** does precede its adjective here, it does not mean "same." What does it mean?

10. Under what conditions is **C'est** rather than **Il est** used to express *It is?* If you are not sure, see page 103, §10.

11. With what does **regardés** agree? Under what conditions does such an agreement take place?

12. What is the meaning of **des** in this phrase?

13. French generally uses the article with parts of the body where English would use a possessive adjective. Why does French use **nos** here instead of **les?** If you are not sure, try translating the sentence with **sur les épaules,** and reread page 74, §5 (a).

14. With what does **étendus** agree? Under what conditions does the past participle of a reflexive verb agree?

15. Why are races, languages and divisions used without a partitive article?

16. This phrase would be expressed in English by *who put the hands of an archangel on our shoulders.* Because of the fact that **mains** is modified by **des, archange** is not modified by **un.** However, one might find **les mains d'un archange.**

17. How would you express **le front dans le sable** and **la tête dans la bassine** in English? What is the difference between the French and English way of expressing such phrases? If you are not sure, consult page 77, §10.

18. How would English express **qui ne s'explique point par les sens?** What type of use of the reflexive is this? It is mentioned on page 190, §11.

19. This sentence means *You are the greatest richness that exists in the world.* Why is the subjunctive used in the **qui** clause?

20. With what does **sauves** agree? In French, if **qui** refers to a first or second person pronoun, the verb of the **qui**-clause agrees in person and number with that word.

Texte Nᵒ 6

ANDRÉ PIEYRE DE MANDIARGUES

Auteur de poèmes, de récits, de romans, André Pieyre de Mandiargues est un des écrivains les plus intéressants d'aujourd'hui. Malgré son aspect ésotérique, son œuvre a connu un grand succès. C'est qu'il exprime dans des visions où se mêlent le lyrisme et un humour subtil, le fantastique et un érotisme brutal, les obsessions révélées par la psychologie et la psychanalyse modernes. Son style, recherché, précieux dans le meilleur sens du mot, est celui qui convient au monde onirique où l'auteur nous mène.

Le récit s'ouvre sur cette scène inaccoutumée entre le bijoutier et sa fille.

Le Diamant

> *. . . Comme une gelée vivante*
> *où la lumière se[a] fût faite*
> *chair par l'opération d'un*
> *sortilège inconcevable.*
> (JULIEN GRACQ)

—Les nouveaux diamants sont arrivés, dit à Sarah son père. Prends la clé du coffre. Tu les examineras demain matin.

Il avait parlé sans lever[1] les yeux du tapis, qui faisait un soyeux fond rouge et brun autour de ses pieds menus, chaussés d'un cuir si souple
5 que cela semblait travail plutôt de gantier que de bottier. Posées sur des accoudoirs de velours, ses[2] mains étaient petites aussi, avec des ongles pointus. Sa[2] tête, en revanche, était grosse exagérément[3], et elle se trouvait grossie par l'effet d'une barbe en collier fauve qui rejoignait une chevelure abondamment bouclée, dressée en éventail
10 sur le dossier du fauteuil. Monsieur Mose (Césarion-David) était lapidaire, tout[b] de même que l'avaient[4] été ses parents et ancêtres[5] depuis plusieurs siècles. Outre son commerce et la clientèle, il tenait d'eux une maison ancienne dont[6] on admirait les belles ferrures dorées, dans le haut de la rue des Lions. C'est[7] là qu'il avait son
15 magasin, au rez-de-chaussée, et il habitait le premier étage avec sa fille, laquelle[8] un jour lui[9] succéderait, sans doute, puisqu'il n'avait

---

[a] *would have become flesh*   [b] *just as*

269

pas d'autre héritier.

—Nous les attendions[10] depuis longtemps, dit la jeune fille. Je suis curieuse de voir cette grande pierre bleutée que[11] tu vas payer très cher[12], et qui devrait avoir l'éclat de la planète Vénus, si le vieux Benaïm ne nous a pas trompés dans sa description. 20

—Le vieux Benaïm ne m'a jamais trompé, dit le lapidaire. Je suis certain que la pierre est admirable, mais je ne veux la voir qu'après toi. Il appartient d'abord à une vierge de juger de la froideur et du feu d'un diamant. 25

La jeune fille leva la tête dans un mouvement de fierté. Elle avait de[13] grands yeux sombres, striés de gris et de vert, dans un visage ovale, un peu brun et très lisse; elle avait des cheveux noirs, tressés en deux nattes qui posaient à[c] l'endroit de ses petits seins, sur la robe d'une absurde étoffe où des poissons inversés jouaient parmi des 30 fleurs d'eau; son[2] cou et ses[2] mains étaient longs (plus longs encore de ne porter aucun bijou), ses jambes étaient très longues.

Monsieur Mose la regarda.

—Tu as l'air d'une couleuvre au soleil, dit-il. La plupart des[14] femmes sont fascinées par les pierres brillantes comme les souris par 35 les yeux des serpents. D'autres restent indemnes, mais elles n'ont que de l'indifférence[15]. Tandis que toi, peut-être, à cause de cette nature bizarrement serpentine, tu es en accord spontané avec les pierres. Tu sais les voir et les peser, tu leur parles, tu les caresses; on dirait que tu[d] vas au fond, car tu m'as signalé des défauts qui avaient échappé aux 40 plus roués trafiquants anversois. Tu feras bien de ne pas[16] te marier, si tu veux garder l'amitié des pierres vraiment nobles, le diamant et l'émeraude. En tout cas, tu ne ressembles pas à ta mère.

—Je ne pense pas à[17] me marier, et je suis contente de ne pas[16] ressembler à ma mère[9], dit Sarah Mose. 45

Feu de braise
(Extrait)

© *Éditions Bernard Grasset*

---

[c] *on the right side of*   [d] *you go deep down inside*

NOTES AND QUESTIONS

1. English would say *without raising his eyes*. French generally uses the definite article with parts of the body where English uses the possessive

adjective. Sometimes French also uses a reflexive indirect object with such a construction. Why is no reflexive indirect object used here? If you are not sure, consult page 74, §6.

2. Here, French must use the possessive adjective with the part of the body. Why? If you do not know, see page 74, §5(c).

3. How are many French adverbs formed from adjectives?

4. The **l'** in **l'avaient été** is an example of the "neuter" **le**, that is, the invariable **le** which is sometimes used to refer to a previously mentioned noun or adjective and which is used with a form of the verb **être**. French requires this **le** to complete the meaning of the sentence: "Mr. Mose was a lapidary, just as his parents and ancestors had been *it* for several centuries." English does not use this construction; therefore, the "it" in the above sentence seems superfluous to us.

5. Usually the possessive adjective is repeated before each noun, but when two nouns connected by **et** are closely related in meaning, often the possessive adjective is found before only the first noun.

6. To what word in the . . . **dont on admirait les belles ferrures dorées** . . . does **dont** refer? What is the function of **ferrures** in its clause? When **dont** modifies the object of its clause, how does French word order differ from English word order in the same type of construction? This question is taken up on page 130.

7. Notice that the English *That is where* . . . is expressed in French by **C'est là que** . . . .

8. Normally the relative pronoun **qui** is used as the subject of its clause. In literary style, a form of **lequel** may be used. It is more precise but rather rare.

9. In French, certain verbs, such as **obéir, succéder** and **ressembler** are followed by an indirect rather than a direct object. This means that their noun object will be preceded by **à**, and a third person pronoun object will be **lui** if it is singular, **leur** if it is plural.

10. In French, the imperfect is used with **depuis** where the English normally uses the pluperfect progressive. Technically, then, this should be rendered by *We had been waiting for them for a long time*, indicating that the waiting had taken place in the past, since the diamonds have now arrived.

11. Most often, French expresses the equivalent of *to pay for something* by **payer quelque chose**. However, sometimes **payer pour quelque chose** is also used.

12. What part of speech is **cher** in **que tu vas payer très cher**? The explanation of **cher** used in this type of construction is found in the note on page 30.

13. Under what conditions is **de** used rather than the partitive article when a noun is modified by a preceding adjective? See page 172, §4(b).

14. The expression **la plupart des femmes** means *the majority of the women.* Therefore, **des** is **de** + **les** (definite article) and not a partitive article. Because it means *the majority (of the)*, **la plupart** is normally followed by **des.**

15. Although **ne . . . que** gives the appearance of being a negative because of the **ne,** it is actually not a negative. Therefore, the indefinite noun that follows it is modified by the partitive article, not by **de** alone.

16. Under what circumstances do the two parts of a negative — in this case **ne pas** — precede their verb? If you do not remember, see page 261, note 4.

17. One can say **Je ne pense pas me marier,** meaning *I don't think I'll get married*, and **Je ne pense pas à me marier,** meaning *I'm not thinking of getting married.*

Texte Nº 7

Simone de Beauvoir

 Elevée strictement dans une famille bourgeoise, Simone de Beauvoir fait sa philosophie à Paris où elle se lie avec Jean-Paul Sartre, dont elle partage les idées existentialistes. Comme lui, elle les met en œuvre dans des romans, des pièces, des essais qui la mettent au premier rang des femmes écrivains de notre époque. Elle se fait en outre la championne de la cause féministe, et elle écrit des *Mémoires* où se reflète la conscience d'une génération extrêmement brillante.

 Ici la jeune fille—elle a vingt-trois ans alors—, libérée à tous les égards, voyage avec ses amis dans une Espagne encore peu fréquentée par les touristes. Là comme ailleurs, elle se mêle tout entière au pays et à ses habitants pour découvrir leur âme secrète.

 Voyager: ç'avait toujours été un de mes désirs les plus brûlants. Avec quelle nostalgie, jadis, j'avais écouté Zaza[a] quand elle était revenue d'Italie[1]! Parmi les cinq sens, il y en avait un que je plaçais, de loin, au-dessus de tous les autres: la vue. Malgré mon goût pour la conversation, j'étais stupéfaite quand j'entendais dire que les sourds 5 sont plus tristes que les aveugles; et s'il m'avait fallu choisir, j'aurais

---

[a] a childhood girlfriend of Simone de Beauvoir

sans hésiter[2] renoncé à avoir un visage pour garder les yeux. A l'idée
de passer six semaines à[3] me promener et à[3] regarder, j'exultais.
Cependant, j'étais raisonnable; l'Italie, l'Espagne, la Grèce, j'irais[4]
10 sûrement, mais plus tard; cet été-là[5], j'envisageais avec Sartre de
visiter la Bretagne. Je n'en crus pas mes oreilles quand Fernand[b]
nous suggéra de venir à Madrid; nous habiterions[4] chez lui, et le
cours de la peseta était si bas que nos déplacements ne nous coûte-
raient presque rien. Ni l'un ni l'autre nous n'avions jamais franchi la
15 frontière et quand nous aperçûmes[6] à Port Bou les bicornes vernis des
carabiniers, nous nous sentîmes jetés en plein exotisme. Je n'oublierai
jamais notre première soirée à Figueras; nous avions retenu une
chambre et dîné dans une petite *posada*[c]; nous marchions autour de la
ville, la nuit descendait sur la plaine et nous nous[7] disions: «C'est
20 l'Espagne».

Nous avions acheté des *kilometricos*[d] de première classe, sinon nous
n'aurions pu monter que dans les trains omnibus; il nous resta à peine
de quoi joindre les deux bouts, en vivant chichement; peu m'importait: le luxe n'existait pas pour moi, même en imagination; pour
25 rouler à travers la Catalogne, je préférais les autobus[e] de campagne
aux pullmans[f] touristiques. Sartre me laissait le soin de consulter les
horaires, de combiner nos itinéraires; j'organisais le temps et l'espace
à ma guise: je profitai avec ardeur de cette nouvelle espèce de liberté.
Je me rappelais mon enfance: quelle histoire, pour aller de Paris à
30 Uzerche[g]! On s'épuisait à[3] faire les bagages, les transporter, les
enregistrer, les surveiller; ma mère s'emportait contre les employés
de la gare, mon père insultait les voyageurs qui partageaient notre
compartiment, et tous deux se querellaient; il y avait toujours de
longues attentes affolées, beaucoup de bruit et beaucoup d'ennui. Ah!
35 je m'étais bien[8] promis, que ma vie serait différente! Nos valises ne
pesaient pas lourd[9], nous les remplissions, nous les vidions en un

---

[b] a friend of Sartre and of Simone de Beauvoir who was living in Madrid at that time

[c] The Spanish word for *inn*

[d] A **kilometrico** is a little book containing coupons for trips up to a given number of
kilometers. It must be used within a stated length of time and in a certain class of the train.
For those who travel a great deal it represents a considerable saving.
[e] The **autobus de campagne** is a bus which goes between towns. The French usually
confine the meaning of **autobus** to a city bus, whereas interurban buses are called **auto-
cars.**
[f] The **pullman** is a luxury bus often used to transport tourist groups.
[g] Uzerche is a French town in the Massif Central where Simone de Beauvoir used to spend
her vacations while a child.

tournemain; que[10] c'était amusant d'arriver dans une ville inconnue, d'y choisir un hôtel! J'avais définitivement balayé tout ennui, tout souci.

Tout de même, j'abordai Barcelone avec un peu d'anxiété. La ville 40 grouillait autour de nous, elle nous ignorait, nous ne comprenions pas son langage: quel moyen inventer[11] pour la faire entrer dans nos vies? C'était une gageure dont tout de suite la difficulté m'exalta. Nous descendîmes près de la cathédrale, dans une[h] pension des plus médiocres, mais notre chambre me plut; l'après-midi[12], pendant la 45 sieste le soleil dardait des feux rouges à travers les rideaux d'andrinople[i], et c'était l'Espagne qui brûlait ma peau. Avec quel zèle nous la pourchassions! Comme la plupart des touristes de notre époque, nous imaginions que chaque lieu, chaque ville avait un secret, une âme, une essence éternelle et que la tâche du voyageur était de les dévoiler; 50 cependant, nous nous sentions beaucoup plus modernes que Barrès[j] parce que les[k] clés de Tolède ou de Venise, nous savions qu'il ne fallait pas les chercher seulement dans leurs musées, leurs monuments, leur passé, mais au présent, à travers leurs ombres et leurs lumières, leurs foules, leurs odeurs, leurs nourritures... Nous nous mêlions aux 55 promeneurs des Ramblas[l], je respirais soigneusement l'odeur moite des rues où nous nous égarions. Convaincus d'après nos lectures que la vérité d'une ville se dépose dans ses bas-fonds, nous passions toutes nos soirées au "Barrio Chino"[m].... Cependant, je tenais aussi à remplir les tâches classiques du touriste. Nous montâmes au Tibidabo[n] 60 et pour la première fois, je vis scintiller à mes pieds, pareille à un grand morceau de quartz fracassé, une cité méditerranéenne.

La Force de l'âge
(Extrait)

© *Editions Gallimard*

---

[h] in a very mediocre "pension"
[i] *bright red*
[j] Maurice Barrès (1862–1923), a well-known novelist and exponent of "le culte du moi" and author of attractive descriptions of lands in which he travelled.
[k] *we knew that we must not look for the keys of Toledo or Venice just in their museums* ... In order to emphasize the object of the sentence, the author places it first in its clause, then summarizes it by placing the redundant **les** immediately before **chercher.**
[l] a picturesque boulevard lined with trees which goes through the original part of Old Barcelona from the Plaza de Cataluña to the harbor; it is characterized by its flower merchants and by the throngs of people that walk up and down the middle of the street.
[m] Formerly a section of the old part of Barcelona which represented the underworld of the city.
[n] a high hill which overlooks all Barcelona on which a sanctuary is located.

NOTES AND QUESTIONS

1. Under what circumstances is *from* expressed by **de** when followed by the name of a country? If you are not sure, consult page 213, §7.
2. In English **sans hésiter** is expressed by *without hesitating*. What principle governs the verbal construction used after French prepositions? If you are not sure, see pages 223–224, §§21–22.
3. How does English express **à me promener, à regarder** and **à faire les bagages?** What is the nature of the **à** that introduces these infinitive phrases? Generalize on their use. This question is taken up briefly on page 195 under the CAUTION at the end of **52. spend.** In general, French expresses manner of spending time by **à** + INFINITIVE where English uses the present participle.
4. Why does the author say **j'irais** rather than **j'irai** and **nous habiterions** rather than **nous habiterons?** The conditional is sometimes used to express a future possibility which is much more vague and less certain than one expressed by a future.
5. Usually one finds **-là** after a noun only when there is another noun in the sentence followed by **-ci.** What exception to this practice is illustrated by **cet été-là?** If you do not know, read page 97, §2, the last paragraph.
6. Notice that **apercevoir** means *to notice* in the sense of *to catch sight of* physically, whereas **s'apercevoir** means *to notice* in the sense of *to realize* or *to be aware of.*
7. How is this **nous** expressed in English? What type of pronoun is it? When **nous** means *ourselves* or *to ourselves,* it is a reflexive pronoun. When it means *each other* or *to each other,* it is known as a reciprocal pronoun.
8. Note that here **bien** simply strengthens and intensifies the meaning of **je m'étais promis.** It could be expressed by the English *really.* In French it is common to use **bien** to emphasize the verb it modifies.
9. Here is an example of the adjective **lourd** used as an adverb. This use of the adjective as an adverb is explained on page 30, §3, note.
10. French often begins an exclamation with **que.** English expresses this idea with a different word order. We would say: *How amusing it was to arrive . . . !*
11. French often uses the infinitive in a general sense where English would use a personal pronoun as a subject. We might say: *What means could we find to make it a part of our life?*
12. How would **l'après-midi** as used here be expressed in English? Can you generalize on the use in French of a definite article with periods of the day such as **le matin** and **l'après-midi?** If not, see page 241, §20(c).

Texte N° 8

JEAN TARDIEU

Longtemps producteur à la Radio-Télévision française, Jean Tardieu est avant tout un grand poète. Il est aussi l'auteur de pièces de théâtre, courtes comédies riches de sens «au carrefour du burlesque et du lyrique», dit-il, et d'essais sur les arts. Lucide et tendre, il crée un univers un peu surnaturel, plein de symboles familiers, et favorable à l'homme ouvert à son merveilleux.

Le Professeur Frœppel est une création humoristique de Jean Tardieu. Personnage un peu pompeux, philologue de profession, il prend facilement «un mot pour un autre». Une longue maladie, non guérie, l'a rendu étranger au monde; il va le redécouvrir, lui redonner un sens, non plus ici par le langage mais par le comportement des êtres et des choses.

Lorsque le Professeur Frœppel, après six mois de séjour, sortit de la clinique (les médecins, ne comprenant rien à[1] son cas, avaient renoncé à le soigner), descendit pour la première fois dans la rue, il fut[2] frappé du[3] comportement bizarre des passants. Tous avaient l'air de gens poursuivis par une menace invisible. La plupart d'entre eux 5 marchaient[4] vite, d'un pas saccadé, et si quelques-uns, rompant le rythme général, s'arrêtaient devant les vitrines des magasins, ce n'était pas sans avoir, au préalable, jeté à droite, à gauche, des regards inquiets et furtifs qui rappelaient la mimique de certains animaux: lézards, écureuils ou gibbons, par exemple. 10

Intrigué, le Professeur, après avoir été un peu étourdi par tout ce mouvement, décida de s'attacher aux pas d'un ou plusieurs spécimens caractéristiques. Il choisit un jeune couple très alerte et tout d'abord parcourut à sa suite plusieurs rues, sans rien avoir à noter de[5] particulier. Tout à coup les deux jeunes gens stoppèrent. Le Professeur, à 15 quelques mètres en arrière, s'arrêta instantanément et attendit. Il aperçut alors, sur l'autre trottoir, un jeune homme de mine joviale qui s'avançait rapidement vers eux en donnant tous les signes de la satisfaction. Lorsqu'il ne fut plus qu'à un mètre de distance, le jeune homme, de sa main gauche, souleva rapidement son chapeau, tandis 20

qu'il avançait la main droite en direction de l'autre jeune homme. Celui-ci[6], sans hésiter, accomplit presque au même instant le même mouvement, de sorte que les deux mains, bien qu'en sens opposé, se rencontrèrent et se refermèrent l'une sur l'autre. Pendant une fraction
25 de seconde, elles restèrent dans cette position, puis les deux hommes secouèrent ensemble leur bras droit, ce qui[7] eut pour résultat de faire remonter et redescendre trois ou quatre fois de suite les mains encore accrochées l'une à l'autre. Finalement, elles se séparèrent, mais pour rentrer à nouveau en mouvement aussitôt après: en effet, la jeune
30 femme, à son tour, tendit sa main droite au nouvel arrivant, tandis que son ami, libéré de l'étreinte de celui-ci[6], reprenait affectueusement son bras.

Cette scène n'avait duré qu'un court instant, mais elle avait suffi à plonger le Professeur dans une profonde méditation, accompagnée
35 d'un certain malaise. Sans songer à recueillir d'autres renseignements, du moins pour cette fois-ci, il rentra chez lui, afin de prendre note de ce qu'il avait vu.

*   *   *

Après quelques jours d'expériences semblables—toutes soigneusement notées, comparées et cataloguées,—le Professeur Fræppel en
40 vint à conclure qu'il y avait parmi les hommes, sous le langage «parlé», un langage muet, fait de signes et de symboles, de gestes convenus et stéréotypés dont les manifestations, certes, n'avaient plus de secret pour lui, mais dont le sens lui échappait.

Que signifiaient par exemple, dans un compartiment du métro, ces
45 petits gestes à peine esquissés que semblaient «s'adresser» les uns aux autres les voyageurs assis en vis-à-vis sur les banquettes: si l'un touchait le rebord de son chapeau, aussitôt un autre détournait les yeux; une femme faisait-elle battre ses paupières trois ou quatre fois de suite, voici qu'un vieillard reniflait ou qu'une autre jeune femme
50 soupirait ou bien qu'un militaire rectifiait nerveusement sa tenue...

Devant l'étrangeté manifeste de ce comportement, le Professeur n'en finissait pas de se poser à lui-même[8] les questions les plus angoissantes. N'y avait-il pas au fond de tout cela une sorte de code secret, un «chiffre», un sous-entendu permanent, pourquoi ne pas dire le
55 mot?—une véritable «conspiration»?

Cette hypothèse le bouleversait tellement que, lorsqu'il se trouvait dans un lieu public, il n'osait presque plus faire un geste de peur d'entrer malgré lui[8] dans ce vaste et mystérieux complot auquel tous les hommes semblaient participer.

Mais ce soupçon de la signification cachée, cette peur d'être exclu, 60
et en même temps, cette crainte de l'expression révélatrice involontaire, n'étaient encore que des tourments bien[9] supportables auprès
des inquiétudes plus profondes et véritablement cosmiques dont il
allait être bientôt la proie.

Il s'aperçut un jour, en effet, que cette entente secrète ne régnait 65
pas seulement entre les êtres humains, mais s'étendait à la nature
entière.

Les signes, les avertissements, les mots de passe étaient partout:
dans l'agitation des feuilles, dans la forme et les couleurs des nuages,
dans une tache de soleil sur un mur, dans l'aboiement d'un chien, le 70
claquement d'une porte, un pas qui s'éloigne, un cri d'enfant, une
girouette qui grince, un train qui siffle, un caillou qui dégringole, un
ruisseau qui bouillonne, une fleur qui tremble, la buée d'une haleine
sur une vitre . . .

Cette découverte remplit l'âme du Professeur Frœppel d'une in- 75
commensurable[10] fierté . . .

Ce jour-là, il entreprit de composer son plus important ouvrage: le
« Dictionnaire de la Signification universelle », celui-là même qui devait[11]
rendre[12] son nom immortel.

Un Mot pour un autre
(Extrait)

© *Editions Gallimard*

NOTES AND QUESTIONS

1. English would render **ne comprenant rien à son cas** by *not understanding
   anything about his case.* When a negative form of **comprendre** is followed
   by **à** + THING, it takes on the meaning of *understand about.*
2. What voice is **fut frappé**? Of what two parts is it made up? Why is
   the simple past used here?
3. Why is **frappé** followed by **de** instead of **par?** This problem is discussed on page 185, §4.
4. Notice that **la plupart,** meaning *the majority,* is always followed by a
   third person plural verb form in French. This avoids the hair-splitting
   problems which arise in English as to whether one should say, for
   instance, "the majority eats" or "the majority eat."
5. Notice that an indefinite pronoun is always separated from a following
   modifying adjective by the preposition **de.** This is true even when the
   adjective does not follow the indefinite immediately. In cases like **sans**

rien avoir à noter de particulier, rien usually comes before the infinitive.

6. What does **celui-ci** mean in these sentences? How do French and English differ in the word order of *the former* and *the latter?*

7. To what does **ce qui** refer? Why is **ce qui** rather than **qui** the appropriate relative pronoun to use here? Notice that in this context **ce qui** means *which*. In all the cases given on page 127, §4, it means *what*. But this is a special case in which **ce qui** refers to an entire clause.

8. In each of the cases given **(à lui-même, malgré lui)**, the disjunctive pronoun refers to the subject and is rendered in English by *himself*. Note that **soi** and **soi-même** normally are used only if the subject is indefinite — if it is **on, chacun** or if the sentence begins with an impersonal expression. Otherwise, *-self* in combinations such as *himself*, *herself*, *themselves*, is expressed by **lui, elle,** or **eux** or **lui-même, elle-même,** or **eux-mêmes.**

9. Here **bien** modifies the adjective **supportables.** What does **bien** mean when it modifies an adjective? It serves to intensify the meaning of the adjective.

10. What effect is produced by placing a descriptive adjective before its noun? Consult page 21, §21 if you are not sure.

11. What is the meaning of **devait** in this sentence?

12. Here **rendre** is used with a noun object and an adjective. Notice that when **rendre** is used in this way it is expressed by the English *make*.

Verbs

The Organization of the French Verb

To be able to use the French verb adequately, you must know the forms of the present, imperfect, future and compound past of the indicative, the conditional, and the present and past subjunctive of each type of regular verb and of the common irregular verbs. To have a complete picture of the verb, you should also know the other compound tenses, the simple past, and the imperfect subjunctive of these verbs.

Regular verbs may be classified as follows:

1. **-er** verbs
2. **-ir** verbs which insert **-iss-** in the plural of the present, throughout the imperfect, and in the present subjunctive
3. **-ir** verbs which do not insert **-iss-** anywhere
4. **-re** verbs

In addition to these, you should know the forms of verbs in **-cevoir,** such as **recevoir,** verbs in **-aindre** and **-eindre,** such as **craindre** and **peindre,** verbs with past participles in **-ert,** such as **ouvrir,** and the following frequently used irregular verbs:

aller	être	rire
avoir	faire	savoir
boire	falloir	suivre
courir	lire	tenir
croire	mettre	valoir
devoir	mourir	venir
dire	pouvoir	vivre
écrire	prendre	voir
envoyer		vouloir

Once you know the forms of an irregular verb such as **prendre,** you can also handle its compounds, such as **apprendre** and **comprendre.**

Regular verbs are formed on the verb stem which is found by taking the infinitive ending from the infinitive:

INFINITIVE	STEM
1. **donn**-er	**donn-**
2. fin-ir	**fin-**
3. **dorm**-ir	**dorm-**
4. **perd**-re	**perd-**

Both types of **-ir** verbs have peculiarities.

Verbs of the type of **finir** insert an **-iss-** between the stem and the ending in the present participle, the plural forms of the present indicative, throughout the imperfect indicative, and in the present subjunctive.

Verbs of the type of **dormir** drop the last consonant of the stem before adding the endings in the singular of the present indicative.

Irregular verbs are formed on several stems.

In order to get a complete picture of the verb and thus facilitate learning it, it is helpful to know the five principal parts of the verb and also to know which tenses are formed from each of these principal parts.

Below are the five principal parts of the regular verbs and of some of the irregular verbs. The stems are in boldface type.

INFINITIVE	PRESENT PARTICIPLE	PAST PARTICIPLE	PRESENT (*singular*)	SIMPLE PAST (*singular*)
donner	**donn**ant	donné	je **donne**	je **donn**ai
finir	**finiss**ant	fini	je **fini**s	je **fini**s
dormir	**dorm**ant	dormi	je **dors**	je **dorm**is
perdre	**perd**ant	perdu	je **perds**	je **perd**is
recevoir	**recev**ant	reçu	je **reçois**	je **reçus**
craindre	**craign**ant	craint	je **crains**	je **craign**is
ouvrir	**ouvr**ant	ouvert	j'**ouvre**	j'**ouvr**is
boire	**buv**ant	bu	je **bois**	je **bus**
écrire	**écriv**ant	écrit	j'**écris**	j'**écriv**is
faire	**fais**ant	fait	je **fais**	je **fis**
venir	**ven**ant	venu	je **viens**	je **vins**

There follows a list of the five principal parts of the verb along with the tenses derived from each principal part:

INFINITIVE	PRESENT PARTICIPLE	PAST PARTICIPLE	PRESENT	SIMPLE PAST
future	plural of	compound past	singular of	simple past
conditional	present	pluperfect	present	imperfect
	imperfect	indicative		subjunctive
	indicative	future perfect		
	present	past conditional		
	subjunctive	past anterior		
		«passé		
		surcomposé»		
		past subjunctive		
		pluperfect		
		subjunctive		

Here is the conjugation of the verb **boire** with the tenses arranged under the principal part from which each is derived.

INFINITIVE	PRESENT PARTICIPLE	PAST PARTICIPLE	PRESENT INDICATIVE	SIMPLE PAST
boire	**buvant**	**bu**	je **bois**	je **bus**
			tu bois	tu bus
	PLURAL OF PRESENT	COMPOUND PAST	il boit	il but
	INDICATIVE	INDICATIVE		nous bûmes
FUTURE	nous buvons	j'ai bu, etc.		vous bûtes
je boirai	vous buvez			ils burent
tu boiras	ils boivent			
il boira		PLUPERFECT		
nous boirons		INDICATIVE		IMPERFECT
vous boirez		j'avais bu, etc.		SUBJUNCTIVE
ils boiront	IMPERFECT			que je busse
	INDICATIVE			que tu busses
CONDITIONAL	je buvais	FUTURE PERFECT		qu'il bût
je boirais	tu buvais	j'aurai bu, etc.		que nous bussions
tu boirais	il buvait			que vous bussiez
il boirait	nous buvions	PAST CONDITIONAL		qu'ils bussent
nous boirions	vous buviez	j'aurais bu, etc.		
vous boiriez	ils buvaient			
ils boiraient		PAST ANTERIOR		
	PRESENT	j'eus bu, etc.		
	SUBJUNCTIVE			
	que je boive	PASSÉ SURCOMPOSÉ		
	que tu boives	j'ai eu bu, etc.		
	qu'il boive			
	que nous buvions	PAST SUBJUNCTIVE		
	que vous buviez	que j'aie bu, etc.		
	qu'ils boivent			
		PLUPERFECT		
		SUBJUNCTIVE		
		que j'eusse bu, etc.		

The regular and the common irregular verbs are conjugated by tenses on pages 284–301. This is practical for easy reference, but the verbs will be easier to learn if you rearrange them by stems as shown in the above conjugation of the verb **boire.**

At the end of each lesson are two verbs to be reviewed. If your instructor directs you to do so, learn to write each tense under the proper principal part as above. To find the forms you do not know, consult pages 284–301.

The conjugation of the verb

INFINITIVE AND PARTICIPLES	INDICATIVE			
	PRESENT	IMPERFECT	SIMPLE PAST	FUTURE
1. -er *verbs*	parle	parlais	parlai	parlerai
parler	parles	parlais	parlas	parleras
(*speak*)	parle	parlait	parla	parlera
parlant	parlons	parlions	parlâmes	parlerons
parlé	parlez	parliez	parlâtes	parlerez
	parlent	parlaient	parlèrent	parleront
	COMPOUND PAST	PLUPERFECT	PAST ANTERIOR	FUTURE PERFECT
	ai parlé	avais parlé	eus parlé	aurai parlé
	as parlé	avais parlé	eus parlé	auras parlé
	a parlé	avait parlé	eut parlé	aura parlé
	avons parlé	avions parlé	eûmes parlé	aurons parlé
	avez parlé	aviez parlé	eûtes parlé	aurez parlé
	ont parlé	avaient parlé	eurent parlé	auront parlé
	PRESENT	IMPERFECT	SIMPLE PAST	FUTURE
2. -ir *verbs*	finis	finissais	finis	finirai
finir	finis	finissais	finis	finiras
(*finish*)	finit	finissait	finit	finira
finissant	finissons	finissions	finîmes	finirons
fini	finissez	finissiez	finîtes	finirez
	finissent	finissaient	finirent	finiront
	COMPOUND PAST	PLUPERFECT	PAST ANTERIOR	FUTURE PERFECT
	ai fini	avais fini	eus fini	aurai fini
	as fini	avais fini	eus fini	auras fini
	a fini	avait fini	eut fini	aura fini
	avons fini	avions fini	eûmes fini	aurons fini
	avez fini	aviez fini	eûtes fini	aurez fini
	ont fini	avaient fini	eurent fini	auront fini
	PRESENT	IMPERFECT	SIMPLE PAST	FUTURE
3. -re *verbs*	perds	perdais	perdis	perdrai
perdre	perds	perdais	perdis	perdras
(*lose*)	perd	perdait	perdit	perdra
perdant	perdons	perdions	perdîmes	perdrons
perdu	perdez	perdiez	perdîtes	perdrez
	perdent	perdaient	perdirent	perdront
	COMPOUND PAST	PLUPERFECT	PAST ANTERIOR	FUTURE PERFECT
	ai perdu	avais perdu	eus perdu	aurai perdu
	as perdu	avais perdu	eus perdu	auras perdu
	a perdu	avait perdu	eut perdu	aura perdu
	avons perdu	avions perdu	eûmes perdu	aurons perdu
	avez perdu	aviez perdu	eûtes perdu	aurez perdu
	ont perdu	avaient perdu	eurent perdu	auront perdu

La conjugaison du verbe

CONDITIONAL	IMPERATIVE	SUBJUNCTIVE	

PRESENT CONDITIONAL
parlerais
parlerais
parlerait
parlerions
parleriez
parleraient

IMPERATIVE:
parle
parlons
parlez

PRESENT
parle
parles
parle
parlions
parliez
parlent

IMPERFECT
parlasse
parlasses
parlât
parlassions
parlassiez
parlassent

PAST CONDITIONAL
aurais parlé
aurais parlé
aurait parlé
aurions parlé
auriez parlé
auraient parlé

PAST
aie parlé
aies parlé
ait parlé
ayons parlé
ayez parlé
aient parlé

PLUPERFECT
eusse parlé
eusses parlé
eût parlé
eussions parlé
eussiez parlé
eussent parlé

PRESENT CONDITIONAL
finirais
finirais
finirait
finirions
finiriez
finiraient

IMPERATIVE:
finis
finissons
finissez

PRESENT
finisse
finisses
finisse
finissions
finissiez
finissent

IMPERFECT
finisse
finisses
finît
finissions
finissiez
finissent

PAST CONDITIONAL
aurais fini
aurais fini
aurait fini
aurions fini
auriez fini
auraient fini

PAST
aie fini
aies fini
ait fini
ayons fini
ayez fini
aient fini

PLUPERFECT
eusse fini
eusses fini
eût fini
eussions fini
eussiez fini
eussent fini

PRESENT CONDITIONAL
perdrais
perdrais
perdrait
perdrions
perdriez
perdraient

IMPERATIVE:
perds
perdons
perdez

PRESENT
perde
perdes
perde
perdions
perdiez
perdent

IMPERFECT
perdisse
perdisses
perdît
perdissions
perdissiez
perdissent

PAST CONDITIONAL
aurais perdu
aurais perdu
aurait perdu
aurions perdu
auriez perdu
auraient perdu

PAST
aie perdu
aies perdu
ait perdu
ayons perdu
ayez perdu
aient perdu

PLUPERFECT
eusse perdu
eusses perdu
eût perdu
eussions perdu
eussiez perdu
eussent perdu

The conjugation of the verb

INFINITIVE AND PARTICIPLES	INDICATIVE			
	PRESENT	IMPERFECT	SIMPLE PAST	FUTURE
4. 2d *class* **-ir** *verbs* **dormir** (*sleep*) dormant dormi	dors dors dort dormons dormez dorment	dormais dormais dormait dormions dormiez dormaient	dormis dormis dormit dormîmes dormîtes dormirent	dormirai dormiras dormira dormirons dormirez dormiront
	COMPOUND PAST	PLUPERFECT	PAST ANTERIOR	FUTURE PERFECT
	ai dormi as dormi a dormi avons dormi avez dormi ont dormi	avais dormi avais dormi avait dormi avions dormi aviez dormi avaient dormi	eus dormi eus dormi eut dormi eûmes dormi eûtes dormi eurent dormi	aurai dormi auras dormi aura dormi aurons dormi aurez dormi auront dormi
	PRESENT	IMPERFECT	SIMPLE PAST	FUTURE
5. -oir *verbs* **recevoir** (*receive*) recevant reçu	reçois reçois reçoit recevons recevez reçoivent	recevais recevais recevait recevions receviez recevaient	reçus reçus reçut reçûmes reçûtes reçurent	recevrai recevras recevra recevrons recevrez recevront
	COMPOUND PAST	PLUPERFECT	PAST ANTERIOR	FUTURE PERFECT
	ai reçu as reçu a reçu avons reçu avez reçu ont reçu	avais reçu avais reçu avait reçu avions reçu aviez reçu avaient reçu	eus reçu eus reçu eut reçu eûmes reçu eûtes reçu eurent reçu	aurai reçu auras reçu aura reçu aurons reçu aurez reçu auront reçu
	PRESENT	IMPERFECT	SIMPLE PAST	FUTURE
6. *Intransitive verb of motion* **entrer** (*enter*) entrant entré	entre entres entre entrons entrez entrent	entrais entrais entrait entrions entriez entraient	entrai entras entra entrâmes entrâtes entrèrent	entrerai entreras entrera entrerons entrerez entreront
	COMPOUND PAST	PLUPERFECT	PAST ANTERIOR	FUTURE PERFECT
	suis entré(e) es entré(e) est entré(e) sommes entré(e)s êtes entré(e)(s) sont entré(e)s	étais entré(e) étais entré(e) était entré(e) étions entré(e)s étiez entré(e)(s) étaient entré(e)s	fus entré(e) fus entré(e) fut entré(e) fûmes entré(e)s fûtes entré(e)(s) furent entré(e)s	serai entré(e) seras entré(e) sera entré(e) serons entré(e)s serez entré(e)(s) seront entré(e)s

La conjugaison du verbe

CONDITIONAL	IMPERATIVE	SUBJUNCTIVE	

PRESENT CONDITIONAL		PRESENT	IMPERFECT
dormirais		dorme	dormisse
dormirais	dors	dormes	dormisses
dormirait		dorme	dormît
dormirions	dormons	dormions	dormissions
dormiriez	dormez	dormiez	dormissiez
dormiraient		dorment	dormissent

PAST CONDITIONAL		PAST	PLUPERFECT
aurais dormi		aie dormi	eusse dormi
aurais dormi		aies dormi	eusses dormi
aurait dormi		ait dormi	eût dormi
aurions dormi		ayons dormi	eussions dormi
auriez dormi		ayez dormi	eussiez dormi
auraient dormi		aient dormi	eussent dormi

PRESENT CONDITIONAL		PRESENT	IMPERFECT
recevrais		reçoive	reçusse
recevrais	reçois	reçoives	reçusses
recevrait		reçoive	reçût
recevrions	recevons	recevions	reçussions
recevriez	recevez	receviez	reçussiez
recevraient		reçoivent	reçussent

PAST CONDITIONAL		PAST	PLUPERFECT
aurais reçu		aie reçu	eusse reçu
aurais reçu		aies reçu	eusses reçu
aurait reçu		ait reçu	eût reçu
aurions reçu		ayons reçu	eussions reçu
auriez reçu		ayez reçu	eussiez reçu
auraient reçu		aient reçu	eussent reçu

PRESENT CONDITIONAL		PRESENT	IMPERFECT
entrerais		entre	entrasse
entrerais	entre	entres	entrasses
entrerait		entre	entrât
entrerions	entrons	entrions	entrassions
entreriez	entrez	entriez	entrassiez
entreraient		entrent	entrassent

PAST CONDITIONAL		PAST	PLUPERFECT
serais entré(e)		sois entré(e)	fusse entré(e)
serais entré(e)		sois entré(e)	fusses entré(e)
serait entré(e)		soit entré(e)	fût entré(e)
serions entré(e)s		soyons entré(e)s	fussions entré(e)s
seriez entré(e)(s)		soyez entré(e)(s)	fussiez entré(e)(s)
seraient entré(e)s		soient entré(e)s	fussent entré(e)s

The conjugation of the verb

INFINITIVE AND PARTICIPLES	INDICATIVE			

7. Reflexive verb

se laver (*wash oneself*)
se lavant
lavé

PRESENT	IMPERFECT	SIMPLE PAST	FUTURE
me lave	me lavais	me lavai	me laverai
te laves	te lavais	te lavas	te laveras
se lave	se lavait	se lava	se lavera
nous lavons	nous lavions	nous lavâmes	nous laverons
vous lavez	vous laviez	vous lavâtes	vous laverez
se lavent	se lavaient	se lavèrent	se laveront

COMPOUND PAST	PLUPERFECT	PAST ANTERIOR	FUTURE PERFECT
me suis lavé(e)	m'étais lavé(e)	me fus lavé(e)	me serai lavé(e)
t'es lavé(e)	t'étais lavé(e)	te fus lavé(e)	te seras lavé(e)
s'est lavé(e)	s'était lavé(e)	se fut lavé(e)	se sera lavé(e)
nous sommes lavé(e)s	nous étions lavé(e)s	nous fûmes lavé(e)s	nous serons lavé(e)s
vous êtes lavé(e)(s)	vous étiez lavé(e)(s)	vous fûtes lavé(e)(s)	vous serez lavé(e)(s)
se sont lavé(e)s	s'étaient lavé(e)s	se furent lavé(e)s	se seront lavé(e)s

8. Auxiliary verb

avoir (*have*)
ayant
eu

PRESENT	IMPERFECT	SIMPLE PAST	FUTURE
ai	avais	eus	aurai
as	avais	eus	auras
a	avait	eut	aura
avons	avions	eûmes	aurons
avez	aviez	eûtes	aurez
ont	avaient	eurent	auront

COMPOUND PAST	PLUPERFECT	PAST ANTERIOR	FUTURE PERFECT
ai eu	avais eu	eus eu	aurai eu
as eu	avais eu	eus eu	auras eu
a eu	avait eu	eut eu	aura eu
avons eu	avions eu	eûmes eu	aurons eu
avez eu	aviez eu	eûtes eu	aurez eu
ont eu	avaient eu	eurent eu	auront eu

9. Auxiliary verb

être (*be*)
étant
été

PRESENT	IMPERFECT	SIMPLE PAST	FUTURE
suis	étais	fus	serai
es	étais	fus	seras
est	était	fut	sera
sommes	étions	fûmes	serons
êtes	étiez	fûtes	serez
sont	étaient	furent	seront

COMPOUND PAST	PLUPERFECT	PAST ANTERIOR	FUTURE PERFECT
ai été	avais été	eus été	aurai été
as été	avais été	eus été	auras été
a été	avait été	eut été	aura été
avons été	avions été	eûmes été	aurons été
avez été	aviez été	eûtes été	aurez été
ont été	avaient été	eurent été	auront été

La conjugaison du verbe

CONDITIONAL	IMPERATIVE	SUBJUNCTIVE	

PRESENT CONDITIONAL		PRESENT	IMPERFECT
me laverais		me lave	me lavasse
te laverais	lave-toi	te laves	te lavasses
se laverait		se lave	se lavât
nous laverions	lavons-nous	nous lavions	nous lavassions
vous laveriez	lavez-vous	vous laviez	vous lavassiez
se laveraient		se lavent	se lavassent

PAST CONDITIONAL		PAST	PLUPERFECT
me serais lavé(e)		me sois lavé(e)	me fusse lavé(e)
te serais lavé(e)		te sois lavé(e)	te fusses lavé(e)
se serait lavé(e)		se soit lavé(e)	se fût lavé(e)
nous		nous	nous
serions lavé(e)s		soyons lavé(e)s	fussions lavé(e)s
vous seriez lavé(e)(s)		vous soyez lavé(e)(s)	vous fussiez lavé(e)(s)
se seraient lavé(e)s		se soient lavé(e)s	se fussent lavé(e)s

PRESENT CONDITIONAL		PRESENT	IMPERFECT
aurais		aie	eusse
aurais	aie	aies	eusses
aurait		ait	eût
aurions	ayons	ayons	eussions
auriez	ayez	ayez	eussiez
auraient		aient	eussent

PAST CONDITIONAL		PAST	PLUPERFECT
aurais eu		aie eu	eusse eu
aurais eu		aies eu	eusses eu
aurait eu		ait eu	eût eu
aurions eu		· ayons eu	eussions eu
auriez eu		ayez eu	eussiez eu
auraient eu		aient eu	eussent eu

PRESENT CONDITIONAL		PRESENT	IMPERFECT
serais		sois	fusse
serais	sois	sois	fusses
serait		soit	fût
serions	soyons	soyons	fussions
seriez	soyez	soyez	fussiez
seraient		soient	fussent

PAST CONDITIONAL		PAST	PLUPERFECT
aurais été		aie été	eusse été
aurais été		aies été	eusses été
aurait été		ait été	eût été
aurions été		ayons été	eussions été
auriez été		ayez été	eussiez été
auraient été		aient été	eussent été

The conjugation of the verb

INFINITIVE AND PARTICIPLES	INDICATIVE			
	PRESENT	IMPERFECT	SIMPLE PAST	COMPOUND PAST
10. **acquérir** (*acquire*) acquérant acquis	acquiers acquiers acquiert acquérons acquérez acquièrent	acquérais acquérais acquérait acquérions acquériez acquéraient	acquis acquis acquit acquîmes acquîtes acquirent	ai acquis as acquis a acquis avons acquis avez acquis ont acquis
11. **aller** (*go*) allant allé	vais vas va allons allez vont	allais allais allait allions alliez allaient	allai allas alla allâmes allâtes allèrent	suis allé(e) es allé(e) est allé(e) sommes allé(e)s êtes allé(e)(s) sont allé(e)s
12. **asseoir*** (*seat*) asseyant assis	assieds assieds assied asseyons asseyez asseyent	asseyais asseyais asseyait asseyions asseyiez asseyaient	assis assis assit assîmes assîtes assirent	me suis assis(e)* t'es assis(e) s'est assis(e) nous sommes assis(es) vous êtes assis(e)(s) se sont assis(es)
assoyant	assois assois assoit assoyons assoyez assoient	assoyais assoyais assoyait assoyions assoyiez assoyaient		
13. **battre** (*beat*) battant battu	bats bats bat battons battez battent	battais battais battait battions battiez battaient	battis battis battit battîmes battîtes battirent	ai battu as battu a battu avons battu avez battu ont battu
14. **boire** (*drink*) buvant bu	bois bois boit buvons buvez boivent	buvais buvais buvait buvions buviez buvaient	bus bus but bûmes bûtes burent	ai bu as bu a bu avons bu avez bu ont bu

* This verb is usually used in its reflexive form **s'asseoir** (*to sit*). For this reason, the reflexive forms of the compound past and imperative are given.

Certain tenses of this verb have two forms.

La conjugaison du verbe

	CONDITIONAL	IMPERATIVE	SUBJUNCTIVE	
FUTURE			PRESENT	IMPERFECT
acquerrai	acquerrais		acquière	acquisse
acquerras	acquerrais	acquiers	acquières	acquisses
acquerra	acquerrait		acquière	acquît
acquerrons	acquerrions	acquérons	acquérions	acquissions
acquerrez	acquerriez	acquérez	acquériez	acquissiez
acquerront	acquerraient		acquièrent	acquissent
irai	irais		aille	allasse
iras	irais	va	ailles	allasses
ira	irait		aille	allât
irons	irions	allons	allions	allassions
irez	iriez	allez	alliez	allassiez
iront	iraient		aillent	allassent
assiérai	assiérais		asseye	assisse
assiéras	assiérais	assieds-toi*	asseyes	assisses
assiéra	assiérait		asseye	assît
assiérons	assiérions	asseyons-nous	asseyions	assissions
assiérez	assiériez	asseyez-vous	asseyiez	assissiez
assiéront	assiéraient		asseyent	assissent
assoirai	assoirais		assoie	
assoiras	assoirais	assois-toi	assoies	
assoira	assoirait		assoie	
assoirons	assoirions	assoyons-nous	assoyions	
assoirez	assoiriez	assoyez-vous	assoyiez	
assoiront	assoiraient		assoient	
battrai	battrais		batte	battisse
battras	battrais	bats	battes	battisses
battra	battrait		batte	battît
battrons	battrions	battons	battions	battissions
battrez	battriez	battez	battiez	battissiez
battront	battraient		battent	battissent
boirai	boirais		boive	busse
boiras	boirais	bois	boives	busses
boira	boirait		boive	bût
boirons	boirions	buvons	buvions	bussions
boirez	boiriez	buvez	buviez	bussiez
boiront	boiraient		boivent	bussent

* This verb is usually used in its reflexive form **s'asseoir** (*to sit*). For this reason, the reflexive forms of the compound past and imperative are given.

The conjugation of the verb

INFINITIVE AND PARTICIPLES	INDICATIVE			
	PRESENT	IMPERFECT	SIMPLE PAST	COMPOUND PAST
15. conduire (*lead*) conduisant conduit	conduis conduis conduit conduisons conduisez conduisent	conduisais conduisais conduisait conduisions conduisiez conduisaient	conduisis conduisis conduisit conduisîmes conduisîtes conduisirent	ai conduit as conduit a conduit avons conduit avez conduit ont conduit
16. connaître (*be acquainted*) connaissant connu	connais connais connaît connaissons connaissez connaissent	connaissais connaissais connaissait connaissions connaissiez connaissaient	connus connus connut connûmes connûtes connurent	ai connu as connu a connu avons connu avez connu ont connu
17. courir (*run*) courant couru	cours cours court courons courez courent	courais courais courait courions couriez couraient	courus courus courut courûmes courûtes coururent	ai couru as couru a couru avons couru avez couru ont couru
18. craindre (*fear*) craignant craint	crains crains craint craignons craignez craignent	craignais craignais craignait craignions craigniez craignaient	craignis craignis craignit craignîmes craignîtes craignirent	ai craint as craint a craint avons craint avez craint ont craint
19. croire (*believe*) croyant cru	crois crois croit croyons croyez croient	croyais croyais croyait croyions croyiez croyaient	crus crus crut crûmes crûtes crurent	ai cru as cru a cru avons cru avez cru ont cru
20. devoir (*owe, have to*) devant dû, due*	dois dois doit devons devez doivent	devais devais devait devions deviez devaient	dus dus dut dûmes dûtes durent	ai dû as dû a dû avons dû avez dû ont dû

* The masculine singular form of the past participle is written with the circumflex accent to distinguish it from the word **du.** All other forms are written without the accent (**dû, due, dus, dues**).

La conjugaison du verbe

| FUTURE | CONDITIONAL | IMPERATIVE | SUBJUNCTIVE | |
			PRESENT	IMPERFECT
conduirai	conduirais		conduise	conduisisse
conduiras	conduirais	conduis	conduises	conduisisses
conduira	conduirait		conduise	conduisît
conduirons	conduirions	conduisons	conduisions	conduisissions
conduirez	conduiriez	conduisez	conduisiez	conduisissiez
conduiront	conduiraient		conduisent	conduisissent
connaîtrai	connaîtrais		connaisse	connusse
connaîtras	connaîtrais	connais	connaisses	connusses
connaîtra	connaîtrait		connaisse	connût
connaîtrons	connaîtrions	connaissons	connaissions	connussions
connaîtrez	connaîtriez	connaissez	connaissiez	connussiez
connaîtront	connaîtraient		connaissent	connussent
courrai	courrais		coure	courusse
courras	courrais	cours	coures	courusses
courra	courrait		coure	courût
courrons	courrions	courons	courions	courussions
courrez	courriez	courez	couriez	courussiez
courront	courraient		courent	courussent
craindrai	craindrais		craigne	craignisse
craindras	craindrais	crains	craignes	craignisses
craindra	craindrait		craigne	craignît
craindrons	craindrions	craignons	craignions	craignissions
craindrez	craindriez	craignez	craigniez	craignissiez
craindront	craindraient		craignent	craignissent
croirai	croirais		croie	crusse
croiras	croirais	crois	croies	crusses
croira	croirait		croie	crût
croirons	croirions	croyons	croyions	crussions
croirez	croiriez	croyez	croyiez	crussiez
croiront	croiraient		croient	crussent
devrai	devrais		doive	dusse
devras	devrais	dois	doives	dusses
devra	devrait		doive	dût
devrons	devrions	devons	devions	dussions
devrez	devriez	devez	deviez	dussiez
devront	devraient		doivent	dussent

The conjugation of the verb

INFINITIVE AND PARTICIPLES	INDICATIVE			
	PRESENT	IMPERFECT	SIMPLE PAST	COMPOUND PAST
21. **dire**	dis	disais	dis	ai dit
(*say, tell*)	dis	disais	dis	as dit
disant	dit	disait	dit	a dit
dit	disons	disions	dîmes	avons dit
	dites	disiez	dîtes	avez dit
	disent	disaient	dirent	ont dit
22. **écrire**	écris	écrivais	écrivis	ai écrit
(*write*)	écris	écrivais	écrivis	as écrit
écrivant	écrit	écrivait	écrivit	a écrit
écrit	écrivons	écrivions	écrivîmes	avons écrit
	écrivez	écriviez	écrivîtes	avez écrit
	écrivent	écrivaient	écrivirent	ont écrit
23. **envoyer**	envoie	envoyais	envoyai	ai envoyé
(*send*)	envoies	envoyais	envoyas	as envoyé
envoyant	envoie	envoyait	envoya	a envoyé
envoyé	envoyons	envoyions	envoyâmes	avons envoyé
	envoyez	envoyiez	envoyâtes	avez envoyé
	envoient	envoyaient	envoyèrent	ont envoyé
24. **faire**	fais	faisais*	fis	ai fait
(*do, make*)	fais	faisais	fis	as fait
faisant*	fait	faisait	fit	a fait
fait	faisons	faisions	fîmes	avons fait
	faites	faisiez	fîtes	avez fait
	font	faisaient	firent	ont fait
25. **falloir****	il faut	il fallait	il fallut	il a fallu
(*be necessary*)				
fallu				
26. **fuir**	fuis	fuyais	fuis	ai fui
(*flee*)	fuis	fuyais	fuis	as fui
fuyant	fuit	fuyait	fuit	a fui
fui	fuyons	fuyions	fuîmes	avons fui
	fuyez	fuyiez	fuîtes	avez fui
	fuient	fuyaient	fuirent	ont fui
27. **lire**	lis	lisais	lus	ai lu
(*read*)	lis	lisais	lus	as lu
lisant	lit	lisait	lut	a lu
lu	lisons	lisions	lûmes	avons lu
	lisez	lisiez	lûtes	avez lu
	lisent	lisaient	lurent	ont lu

* The **ai** of the stem of these forms is pronounced like mute **e** [ə].
** Used in third person singular only.

La conjugaison du verbe

	CONDITIONAL	IMPERATIVE	SUBJUNCTIVE	
FUTURE			PRESENT	IMPERFECT
dirai	dirais		dise	disse
diras	dirais	dis	dises	disses
dira	dirait		dise	dît
dirons	dirions	disons	disions	dissions
direz	diriez	dites	disiez	dissiez
diront	diraient		disent	dissent
écrirai	écrirais		écrive	écrivisse
écriras	écrirais	écris	écrives	écrivisses
écrira	écrirait		écrive	écrivît
écrirons	écririons	écrivons	écrivions	écrivissions
écrirez	écririez	écrivez	écriviez	écrivissiez
écriront	écriraient		écrivent	écrivissent
enverrai	enverrais		envoie	envoyasse
enverras	enverrais	envoie	envoies	envoyasses
enverra	enverrait		envoie	envoyât
enverrons	enverrions	envoyons	envoyions	envoyassions
enverrez	enverriez	envoyez	envoyiez	envoyassiez
enverront	enverraient		envoient	envoyassent
ferai	ferais		fasse	fisse
feras	ferais	fais	fasses	fisses
fera	ferait		fasse	fît
ferons	ferions	faisons	fassions	fissions
ferez	feriez	faites	fassiez	fissiez
feront	feraient		fassent	fissent
il faudra	il faudrait		il faille	il fallût
fuirai	fuirais		fuie	fuisse
fuiras	fuirais	fuis	fuies	fuisses
fuira	fuirait		fuie	fuît
fuirons	fuirions	fuyons	fuyions	fuissions
fuirez	fuiriez	fuyez	fuyiez	fuissiez
fuiront	fuiraient		fuient	fuissent
lirai	lirais		lise	lusse
liras	lirais	lis	lises	lusses
lira	lirait		lise	lût
lirons	lirions	lisons	lisions	lussions
lirez	liriez	lisez	lisiez	lussiez
liront	liraient		lisent	lussent

The conjugation of the verb

INFINITIVE AND PARTICIPLES	INDICATIVE			
	PRESENT	IMPERFECT	SIMPLE PAST	COMPOUND PAST
28. **mettre** (*put*) mettant mis	mets mets met mettons mettez mettent	mettais mettais mettait mettions mettiez mettaient	mis mis mit mîmes mîtes mirent	ai mis as mis a mis avons mis avez mis ont mis
29. **mourir** (*die*) mourant mort	meurs meurs meurt mourons mourez meurent	mourais mourais mourait mourions mouriez mouraient	mourus mourus mourut mourûmes mourûtes moururent	suis mort(e) es mort(e) est mort(e) sommes mort(e)s êtes mort(e)(s) sont mort(e)s
30. **naître** (*be born*) naissant né	nais nais naît naissons naissez naissent	naissais naissais naissait naissions naissiez naissaient	naquis naquis naquit naquîmes naquîtes naquirent	suis né(e) es né(e) est né(e) sommes né(e)s êtes né(e)(s) sont né(e)s
31. **ouvrir** (*open*) ouvrant ouvert	ouvre ouvres ouvre ouvrons ouvrez ouvrent	ouvrais ouvrais ouvrait ouvrions ouvriez ouvraient	ouvris ouvris ouvrit ouvrîmes ouvrîtes ouvrirent	ai ouvert as ouvert a ouvert avons ouvert avez ouvert ont ouvert
32. **peindre** (*paint*) peignant peint	peins peins peint peignons peignez peignent	peignais peignais peignait peignions peigniez peignaient	peignis peignis peignit peignîmes peignîtes peignirent	ai peint as peint a peint avons peint avez peint ont peint
33. **plaire** (*please*) plaisant plu	plais plais plaît plaisons plaisez plaisent	plaisais plaisais plaisait plaisions plaisiez plaisaient	plus plus plut plûmes plûtes plurent	ai plu as plu a plu avons plu avez plu ont plu
34. **pleuvoir*** (*rain*) pleuvant plu	il pleut	il pleuvait	il plut	il a plu

* Used only in third person singular.

La conjugaison du verbe

	CONDITIONAL	IMPERATIVE	SUBJUNCTIVE	
FUTURE			PRESENT	IMPERFECT
mettrai	mettrais		mette	misse
mettras	mettrais	mets	mettes	misses
mettra	mettrait		mette	mît
mettrons	mettrions	mettons	mettions	missions
mettrez	mettriez	mettez	mettiez	missiez
mettront	mettraient		mettent	missent
mourrai	mourrais		meure	mourusse
mourras	mourrais	meurs	meures	mourusses
mourra	mourrait		meure	mourût
mourrons	mourrions	mourons	mourions	mourussions
mourrez	mourriez	mourez	mouriez	mourussiez
mourront	mourraient		meurent	mourussent
naîtrai	naîtrais		naisse	naquisse
naîtras	naîtrais	nais	naisses	naquisses
naîtra	naîtrait		naisse	naquît
naîtrons	naîtrions	naissons	naissions	naquissions
naîtrez	naîtriez	naissez	naissiez	naquissiez
naîtront	naîtraient		naissent	naquissent
ouvrirai	ouvrirais		ouvre	ouvrisse
ouvriras	ouvrirais	ouvre	ouvres	ouvrisses
ouvrira	ouvrirait		ouvre	ouvrît
ouvrirons	ouvririons	ouvrons	ouvrions	ouvrissions
ouvrirez	ouvririez	ouvrez	ouvriez	ouvrissiez
ouvriront	ouvriraient		ouvrent	ouvrissent
peindrai	peindrais		peigne	peignisse
peindras	peindrais	peins	peignes	peignisses
peindra	peindrait		peigne	peignît
peindrons	peindrions	peignons	peignions	peignissions
peindrez	peindriez	peignez	peigniez	peignissiez
peindront	peindraient		peignent	peignissent
plairai	plairais		plaise	plusse
plairas	plairais	plais	plaises	plusses
plaira	plairait		plaise	plût
plairons	plairions	plaisons	plaisions	plussions
plairez	plairiez	plaisez	plaisiez	plussiez
plairont	plairaient		plaisent	plussent
il pleuvra	il pleuvrait		il pleuve	il plût

The conjugation of the verb

INFINITIVE AND PARTICIPLES	INDICATIVE			
	PRESENT	IMPERFECT	SIMPLE PAST	COMPOUND PAST
35. **pouvoir** (*be able*) pouvant pu	peux, puis peux peut pouvons pouvez peuvent	pouvais pouvais pouvait pouvions pouviez pouvaient	pus pus put pûmes pûtes purent	ai pu as pu a pu avons pu avez pu ont pu
36. **prendre** (*take*) prenant pris	prends prends prend prenons prenez prennent	prenais prenais prenait prenions preniez prenaient	pris pris prit prîmes prîtes prirent	ai pris as pris a pris avons pris avez pris ont pris
37. **rire** (*laugh*) riant ri	ris ris rit rions riez rient	riais riais riait riions riiez riaient	ris ris rit rîmes rîtes rirent	ai ri as ri a ri avons ri avez ri ont ri
38. **savoir** (*know*) sachant su	sais sais sait savons savez savent	savais savais savait savions saviez savaient	sus sus sut sûmes sûtes surent	ai su as su a su avons su avez su ont su
39. **suivre** (*follow*) suivant suivi	suis suis suit suivons suivez suivent	suivais suivais suivait suivions suiviez suivaient	suivis suivis suivit suivîmes suivîtes suivirent	ai suivi as suivi a suivi avons suivi avez suivi ont suivi
40. **tenir** (*hold, keep*) tenant tenu	tiens tiens tient tenons tenez tiennent	tenais tenais tenait tenions teniez tenaient	tins tins tint tînmes tîntes tinrent	ai tenu as tenu a tenu avons tenu avez tenu ont tenu

La conjugaison du verbe

| FUTURE | CONDITIONAL | IMPERATIVE | SUBJUNCTIVE | |
			PRESENT	IMPERFECT
pourrai	pourrais		puisse	pusse
pourras	pourrais		puisses	pusses
pourra	pourrait		puisse	pût
pourrons	pourrions		puissions	pussions
pourrez	pourriez		puissiez	pussiez
pourront	pourraient		puissent	pussent
prendrai	prendrais		prenne	prisse
prendras	prendrais	prends	prennes	prisses
prendra	prendrait		prenne	prît
prendrons	prendrions	prenons	prenions	prissions
prendrez	prendriez	prenez	preniez	prissiez
prendront	prendraient		prennent	prissent
rirai	rirais		rie	risse
riras	rirais	ris	ries	risses
rira	rirait		rie	rît
rirons	ririons	rions	riions	rissions
rirez	ririez	riez	riiez	rissiez
riront	riraient		rient	rissent
saurai	saurais		sache	susse
sauras	saurais	sache	saches	susses
saura	saurait		sache	sût
saurons	saurions	sachons	sachions	sussions
saurez	sauriez	sachez	sachiez	sussiez
sauront	sauraient		sachent	sussent
suivrai	suivrais		suive	suivisse
suivras	suivrais	suis	suives	suivisses
suivra	suivrait		suive	suivît
suivrons	suivrions	suivons	suivions	suivissions
suivrez	suivriez	suivez	suiviez	suivissiez
suivront	suivraient		suivent	suivissent
tiendrai	tiendrais		tienne	tinsse
tiendras	tiendrais	tiens	tiennes	tinsses
tiendra	tiendrait		tienne	tînt
tiendrons	tiendrions	tenons	tenions	tinssions
tiendrez	tiendriez	tenez	teniez	tinssiez
tiendront	tiendraient		tiennent	tinssent

The conjugation of the verb

INFINITIVE AND PARTICIPLES	INDICATIVE			
	PRESENT	IMPERFECT	SIMPLE PAST	COMPOUND PAST
41. **vaincre** (*conquer*) vainquant vaincu	vaincs vaincs vainc vainquons vainquez vainquent	vainquais vainquais vainquait vainquions vainquiez vainquaient	vainquis vainquis vainquit vainquîmes vainquîtes vainquirent	ai vanicu as vaincu a vaincu avons vaincu avez vaincu ont vaincu
42. **valoir** (*be worth*) valant valu	vaux vaux vaut valons valez valent	valais valais valait valions valiez valaient	valus valus valut valûmes valûtes valurent	ai valu as valu a valu avons valu avez valu ont valu
43. **venir** (*come*) venant venu	viens viens vient venons venez viennent	venais venais venait venions veniez venaient	vins vins vint vînmes vîntes vinrent	suis venu(e) es venu(e) est venu(e) sommes venu(e)s êtes venu(e)(s) sont venu(e)s
44. **vivre** (*live*) vivant vécu	vis vis vit vivons vivez vivent	vivais vivais vivait vivions viviez vivaient	vécus vécus vécut vécûmes vécûtes vécurent	ai vécu as vécu a vécu avons vécu avez vécu ont vécu
45. **voir** (*see*) voyant vu	vois vois voit voyons voyez voient	voyais voyais voyait voyions voyiez voyaient	vis vis vit vîmes vîtes virent	ai vu as vu a vu avons vu avez vu ont vu
46. **vouloir** (*wish, want*) voulant voulu	veux veux veut voulons voulez veulent	voulais voulais voulait voulions vouliez voulaient	voulus voulus voulut voulûmes voulûtes voulurent	ai voulu as voulu a voulu avons voulu avez voulu ont voulu

La conjugaison du verbe

	CONDITIONAL	IMPERATIVE	SUBJUNCTIVE	
FUTURE			PRESENT	IMPERFECT
vaincrai	vaincrais		vainque	vainquisse
vaincras	vaincrais	vaincs	vainques	vainquisses
vaincra	vaincrait		vainque	vainquît
vaincrons	vaincrions	vainquons	vainquions	vainquissions
vaincrez	vaincriez	vainquez	vainquiez	vainquissiez
vaincront	vaincraient		vainquent	vainquissent
vaudrai	vaudrais		vaille	valusse
vaudras	vaudrais	vaux	vailles	valusses
vaudra	vaudrait		vaille	valût
vaudrons	vaudrions	valons	valions	valussions
vaudrez	vaudriez	valez	valiez	valussiez
vaudront	vaudraient		vaillent	valussent
viendrai	viendrais		vienne	vinsse
viendras	viendrais	viens	viennes	vinsses
viendra	viendrait		vienne	vînt
viendrons	viendrions	venons	venions	vinssions
viendrez	viendriez	venez	veniez	vinssiez
viendront	viendraient		viennent	vinssent
vivrai	vivrais		vive	vécusse
vivras	vivrais	vis	vives	vécusses
vivra	vivrait		vive	vécût
vivrons	vivrions	vivons	vivions	vécussions
vivrez	vivriez	vivez	viviez	vécussiez
vivront	vivraient		vivent	vécussent
verrai	verrais		voie	visse
verras	verrais	vois	voies	visses
verra	verrait		voie	vît
verrons	verrions	voyons	voyions	vissions
verrez	verriez	voyez	voyiez	vissiez
verront	verraient		voient	vissent
voudrai	voudrais		veuille	voulusse
voudras	voudrais	veuille	veuilles	voulusses
voudra	voudrait		veuille	voulût
voudrons	voudrions		voulions	voulussions
voudrez	voudriez	veuillez	vouliez	voulussiez
voudront	voudraient		veuillent	voulussent

Verbs with Spelling Changes

A. Verbs in **-cer**

Since **c** is pronounced like **s** only before **e** and **i** and like **k** before **a, o,** and **u,** verbs whose infinitives end in **-cer** change **c** to **ç** when the **c** is followed by **a, o,** or **u,** in order to preserve the *s* sound of the **c.** Changes are made then in the tenses below and in the imperfect subjunctive.

EXAMPLE: **effacer.**

PRESENT PARTICIPLE	PRESENT INDICATIVE	IMPERFECT INDICATIVE	SIMPLE PAST
effaçant	j'efface	j'effaçais	j'effaçai
	tu effaces	tu effaçais	tu effaças
	il efface	il effaçait	il effaça
	nous effaçons	nous effacions	nous effaçâmes
	vous effacez	vous effaciez	vous effaçâtes
	ils effacent	ils effaçaient	ils effacèrent

B. Verbs in **-ger**

Since **g** is pronounced like *g* in *get* before **a, o,** and **u,** and like *s* in *pleasure* before **e** and **i,** verbs whose infinitives end in **-ger** insert **e** between **g** and the next vowel whenever that vowel is not **e** or **i.** Changes are made then, in the tenses below and in the imperfect subjunctive.

EXAMPLE: **changer.**

PRESENT PARTICIPLE	PRESENT INDICATIVE	IMPERFECT INDICATIVE	SIMPLE PAST
changeant	je change	je changeais	je changeai
	tu changes	tu changeais	tu changeas
	il change	il changeait	il changea
	nous changeons	nous changions	nous changeâmes
	vous changez	vous changiez	vous changeâtes
	ils changent	ils changeaient	ils changèrent

C. Verbs in -yer

Verbs in **-yer** (**-ayer, -oyer, -uyer**) change **y** to **i** before a mute **e** in the following syllable. This change occurs throughout the present except for the **nous** and **vous** forms and throughout the entire future and conditional.

EXAMPLE: **nettoyer.**

PRESENT INDICATIVE	PRESENT SUBJUNCTIVE	FUTURE	CONDITIONAL
je nettoie	que je nettoie	je nettoierai	je nettoierais
tu nettoies	que tu nettoies	tu nettoieras	tu nettoierais
il nettoie	qu'il nettoie	il nettoiera	il nettoierait
nous nettoyons	que nous nettoyions	nous nettoierons	nous nettoierions
vous nettoyez	que vous nettoyiez	vous nettoierez	vous nettoieriez
ils nettoient	qu'ils nettoient	ils nettoieront	ils nettoieraient

D. Verbs in -e- + { a single consonant } + -er

Many verbs, such as **mener, lever,** and **acheter,** whose stems end in unaccented **e** plus a single consonant, place a grave accent (`) over this **e** whenever the following syllable also has a mute **e**. This indicates that the pronunciation of the **e** [ə] of the stem becomes **è** [ɛ]. The grave accent is found throughout the singular and in the third person plural of the present indicative and subjunctive and throughout the entire future and conditional of all these verbs.

EXAMPLE: **mener.**

PRESENT INDICATIVE	PRESENT SUBJUNCTIVE	FUTURE	CONDITIONAL
je mène	que je mène	je mènerai	je mènerais
tu mènes	que tu mènes	tu mèneras	tu mènerais
il mène	qu'il mène	il mènera	il mènerait
nous menons	que nous menions	nous mènerons	nous mènerions
vous menez	que vous meniez	vous mènerez	vous mèneriez
ils mènent	qu'ils mènent	ils mèneront	ils mèneraient

E. Verbs in **-é-** + $\begin{cases} \text{a single} \\ \text{consonant} \end{cases}$ + **-er**

Verbs whose stems end in **é** followed by a single consonant change this **é** to **è** throughout the singular and in the third person plural of the present indicative and present subjunctive, that is, in those forms in which the following syllable has a mute **e.** In the future and conditional the **é** is retained in writing, but this **é** is usually pronounced **è** because a vowel tends to open in a closed syllable.[1]

EXAMPLE: **espérer**

PRESENT INDICATIVE	PRESENT SUBJUNCTIVE	FUTURE	CONDITIONAL
j'espère	que j'espère	j'espérerai	j'espérerais
tu espères	que tu espères	tu espéreras	tu espérerais
il espère	qu'il espère	il espérera	il espérerait
nous espérons	que nous espérions	nous espérerons	nous espérerions
vous espérez	que vous espériez	vous espérerez	vous espéreriez
ils espèrent	qu'ils espèrent	ils espéreront	ils espéreraient

F. Verbs in **-eler** and some in **-eter**

Verbs in **-eler** and a few verbs in **-eter** double the **l** or **t** when the next syllable contains a mute **e.** This change takes place in the singular and third person plural of the present indicative and of the present subjunctive and throughout the future and conditional.

EXAMPLE: **appeler.**

PRESENT INDICATIVE	PRESENT SUBJUNCTIVE	FUTURE	CONDITIONAL
j'appelle	que j'appelle	j'appellerai	j'appellerais
tu appelles	que tu appelles	tu appelleras	tu appellerais
il appelle	qu'il appelle	il appellera	il appellerait
nous appelons	que nous appelions	nous appellerons	nous appellerions
vous appelez	que vous appeliez	vous appellerez	vous appelleriez
ils appellent	qu'ils appellent	ils appelleront	ils appelleraient

---

[1] The fact that the mute **e** of the infinitive drops out in pronunciation closes the preceding syllable, thus tending to open the **e**; e.g., j'espérerai [ʒɛspɛrre]; il espérerait [ilɛspɛrɛ]; tu céderas [tysɛdra].

French-English Vocabulary

adj.	adjective	*irr. sp.*	irregular spelling	*pers.*	person
adv.	adverb	*m.*	masculine	*prep.*	preposition
cond.	conditional	*n.*	noun	*pres.*	present
conj.	conjugated	*obj.*	object	*pron.*	pronoun
conjunc.	conjunction	*p.*	page	*rel.*	relative
f.	feminine	*part.*	participle	*sing.*	singular
fut.	future	*pl.*	plural	*sp*	simple past
inf.	infinitive	*pp*	past participle	*subjunc.*	subjunctive
interrog.	interrogative			*v.*	verb

* aspirate *h*   (2) **-ir** verbs which do not insert **-iss-;** all other **-ir** verbs insert **-iss-.**

Verbs whose principal parts are given are irregular, and their conjugations may be found on pp. 284–301. The use of the principal parts is explained on page 283. Verbs followed by (*conj. like* . . .) are irregular and follow the pattern of the verb indicated.

Verbs followed by (*irr. sp.* **A** to **F**) undergo a spelling change in certain forms. The letter refers to the appropriate type of change explained on pp. 302–304.

This vocabulary contains all words used in the text and in the *Pattern Practice Manual* except words which have the same form in English and French and certain words of which the French spelling is so near to the English that they are easily recognizable.

A

à at; with; in; by; **à votre accent** by your accent; **c'est à lui** it is up to him

a (*pres. of* **avoir**) has; **il y a** there is, there are; **il y a un an** a year ago

abandonner abandon; **s'abandonner** give way (to)

abattre (*conj. like* **battre**) tear down

aboiement *m.* barking

abondamment abundantly

abord: d'abord at first; **tout d'abord** first of all

aborder approach

aboyer (*irr. sp.* **C**) bark

abrupt steep

absence *f.* absence

absolu absolute

absolument absolutely

absurde absurd; living in the absurd; alienated

accent *m.* accent; **à votre accent** from (by) your accent

accablé overwhelmed; weary

accepter accept

accompagner accompany

accomplir accomplish; **accomplir un mouvement** make a movement

accord *m.* agreement

accoudoir *m.* elbow rest

accroché intertwined; hung up

accueillir receive; welcome

acheter (*irr. sp.* **D**) buy

acte *m.* act

acteur *m.* actor

actif (*f.* **active**) active

actrice *f.* actress

actuel (*f.* **actuelle**) present day

addition *f.* check (in a restaurant)

adieu *m.* goodbye; **faire ses adieux** say goodbye

admirer admire

adresse *f.* address

adresser (**s'**)(**à**+*n.*) go to; ask at; apply

adverbe *m.* adverb

affaire *f.* affair; thing; deal; business; **les affaires** business; one's things

affectif (*f.* **affective**) emotional

affectueusement affectionately

affiche *f.* poster; bulletin

afin de in order to; **afin que** in order that

affolé frantic, panic-stricken

Afrique *f.* Africa; **Afrique du Nord** North Africa

âge *m.* age

âgé old

agent *m.* policeman

agir act; **s'agir de** to be a question of, be about

agitation *f.* movement

agréable pleasant, agreeable

aider (+ *person* + **à** + *inf.*) help

aille (*pres. subjunc. of* **aller**) go

ailleurs elsewhere

aimer (+ *inf.*) like; love

air *m.* air; appearance; **avoir l'air** (+ *adj.*) look; seem; **avoir l'air de** (+ *inf.*) seem to

aise *f.* ease; **être à l'aise** be comfortable

ait (*pres. subjunc. of* **avoir**) has; have

ajouter add

alcool *m.* alcohol

alerte alert

algèbre *m.* algebra

Alger Algiers, a city on the seacoast of North Africa, capital of Algeria

Algérie *f.* Algeria

Allemagne *f.* Germany

allemand German

aller (**allant, allé, je vais, j'allai**) (+ *inf.*) go; **aller voir** go and see, visit; **ça va de soi** that goes without saying; **cette robe vous va bien** this dress fits you well, this dress looks very becoming on you; **s'en aller** go away, leave; start on one's way

allergie *f.* allergy

allié *m.* ally

allô hello

allonger (**s'**)(*irr. sp.* **B**) stretch out

allons bon there now

allumer light; turn on the lights

alors then; **alors que** when; whereas

Alpes *f. pl.* Alps

âme *f.* soul

Verbs with spelling changes are explained on pp. 302–304.

amer (*f.* **amère**) bitter
américain American
Amérique *f.* America; **Amérique du Sud** *f.* South America
ami *m.* friend
amie *f.* friend; **bonne amie** girl friend
amitié *f.* friendship; **faites-lui mes amitiés** give him my best regards
amollir (**s'**) soften
amorcer (*irr. sp.* **A**) start
amour (*m. in sing., f. in pl.*) love
amoureusement lovingly
amoureux *m. pl. or s.* people in love
amoureux (*f.* **amoureuse**) in love
amusant entertaining; amusing
amuser entertain; **s'amuser** (**à** + *inf.*) have fun; have a good time; amuse oneself
an *m.* year
analogue similar
ancêtre *m. or f.* ancestor
ancien (*f.* **ancienne**) old; former
anglais English
Angleterre *f.* England
anglican Anglican
angoissant anguished, distressed
animal *m.* (*pl.* **animaux**) animal
année *f.* year
annonce *f.* announcement
annoncer (*irr. sp.* **A**) announce; say; herald
anthropologie *f.* anthropology
anversois from Antwerp, Belgium, a center for diamond dealers
anxiété *f.* anxiety, worry
anxieux (*f.* **anxieuse**) anxious; worried
apercevoir (*conj. like* **recevoir**) (+ *n.*) notice; catch sight of; **s'apercevoir** (**de** + *n.;* **que** + *clause*) notice, realize
apparaître (*conj. like* **connaître**) appear (physically)
appareil *m.* apparatus; machine
appartement *m.* apartment
appartenir (*conj. like* **tenir**) belong; **il appartient à une vierge de juger** it is for a virgin to judge
appeler (*irr. sp.* **F**) call; **s'appeler** be called, be named
applaudir applaud
appliquer (**s'**) apply oneself; work hard at

apporter bring
apprécier appreciate
appréhender seize
apprendre (*conj. like* **prendre**) (*thing* + **à** + *person;* **à** + *inf.*) learn; teach; **apprendre par cœur** memorize, learn by heart
approcher (**de** + *n.*) approach; **s'approcher** (**de** + *n.*) approach
approuver approve
appuyer (*irr. sp.* **C**) lean; **s'appuyer** lean
après after; afterwards; **d'après** according to; after
après-midi *m. or f.* afternoon
arbre *m.* tree; **arbre fruitier** fruit tree
Arc de Triomphe *m.* Arch of Triumph
archange *m.* archangel
ardemment ardently
ardeur *f.* enthusiasm, ardor
ardoise *f.* slate
argent *m.* money
Argentine *f.* Argentina
armé armed
armée *f.* army
armoire *f.* cupboard; a large piece of furniture used as a wardrobe
arome *m.* aroma, odor
arpenter walk along; stride along; strut along
arrangé set
arranger (*irr. sp.* **B**) fix; arrange; **s'arranger** come out all right, manage
arrêt *m.* stop; **sans arrêt** without stopping, ceaselessly
arrêter (**de** + *inf.*) stop; arrest; fix; **s'arrêter** (**de** + *inf.*) stop
arrière: en arrière behind
arrivant: le nouvel arrivant *m.* the newcomer
arrivée *f.* arrival
arriver arrive, reach; happen
art *m.* art; **beaux-arts** fine arts
artiste *m. or f.* artist
asile *m.* home (for the aged)
aspirateur *m.* vacuum cleaner
asseoir (**asseyant, assis, j'assieds, j'assis**) sit; seat; **s'asseoir** sit down
assez enough; rather
assiette *f.* plate
assis (*pp and sp of* **asseoir**) seated; sitting

Irregular verbs are conjugated on pp. 284–301.

assister (**à** + *n.*) attend, be present at
assurer (**s'**) make sure, assure oneself
astronomie *f.* astronomy
Atlantique *m.* Atlantic
atomique atomic, nuclear
attacher (**s'**) attach; **s'attacher aux pas** follow closely
attaquer attack
attendre (+ *n.*) wait; wait for; expect **s'attendre** (**à** + *n.*) expect
attente *f.* wait
attentif (*f.* **attentive**) attentive
attention *f.* attention; **faire attention à** watch out for; pay attention to; **faire bien attention** pay special attention to; be very careful about; **faites attention** look out
attentivement attentively
atténué attenuated, subdued
atterrir land
attraper catch
au to the; **au revoir** goodbye
aucun any; **ne ... aucun** no; none
audacieux (*f.* **audacieuse**) audacious; bold
au-dessus above
augmentation *f.* raise
augmenter increase; raise
aumônier *m.* chaplain
auprès near; **auprès de** at the side of, near; compared with
aurai, aurais (*fut. and cond. of* **avoir**) will have; would have
aussi also; so, therefore
aussitôt at once, immediately; **aussitôt que** as soon as
auteur *m.* author
auto *f.* car, auto
autobus *m.* (city) bus
autocar *m.* (interurban) bus
automatique automatic
automne *m.* autumn, fall
automobile *f.* car
autour around
autre other
autrement differently; otherwise
Autriche *f.* Austria
auxiliaire auxiliary
avance: d'avance in advance
avancer (*irr. sp.* **A**) advance, move forward; **s'avancer** advance; approach

avant before; ahead; formerly; **avant-dernier** next to the last; **avant-hier** the day before yesterday; **avant tout** above all
avant-garde *f.* avant-garde; pioneer
avec with
avenir *m.* future
aventure *f.* adventure
aventurer (**s'**) venture
avertir warn; inform
avertissement *m.* notice, indication
aveugle (*adj.*) blind; (*n.*) blind person
avez (**avoir**) have
aviateur *m.* flier
avion *m.* airplane
avis *m.* opinion; **changer d'avis** change one's mind
avocat *m.* lawyer
avoir (**ayant, eu, j'ai, j'eus**) (**à** + *inf.*) have; **avoir de la chance** be lucky; **ce qu'il y a** the trouble is; **il y a** there is, there are; ago
avouer confess; admit
ayant (*pres. part. of* **avoir**) having
azur blue; **Côte d'Azur** French Riviera

B

baccalauréat *m.* baccalaureate (state examination given secondary school students)
bagage *m.* baggage; **faire les bagages** pack
bague *f.* ring
baigné de bathed with; suffused with
bain *m.* bath
baissé lowered
baisser lower
bal *m.* dance
balayer (*irr. sp.* **C**) sweep away, push away
ballon *m.* ball
Balzac, Honoré de (1799–1850) French realistic novelist of the nineteenth century
bande *f.* strip; tape (for tape recorder)
banlieue *f.* suburbs
banque *f.* bank; **billet de banque** *m.* banknote
banquette *f.* seat (in a train compartment)

Verbs with spelling changes are explained on pp. 302–304.

banquier *m.* banker

barbe *f.* beard; **barbe en collier** narrow oval-shaped beard

bas (*f.* **basse**) low; **en bas** downstairs; **tout bas** in a whisper

bas-fond *m.* slum, lower quarters, poorer section (of a city)

base *f.* base; airport

bassine *f.* pan

Bastille *f.* square in Paris, formerly the site of the state prison taken and destroyed by the people on July 14, 1789

bataille *f.* battle

bateau *m.* boat; **faire du bateau** take a boatride; go boating; **traversée en bateau** boat trip

bâtiment *m.* building

battre (**battant, battu, je bats, je battis**) beat; **battre les paupières** blink; **se battre** fight; **se battre à coups de boules de neige** have a snowball fight

bavarder talk; chat

bavure smudge; **sans bavure** perfect, unblemished

beau (before vowel sound **bel**; *f.* **belle**) beautiful; handsome; **il fait beau** the weather is good

beaucoup much, many, a great deal, a great many, a lot

Beauvoir, Simone de (1908–) French author

beaux-parents *m. pl.* parents-in-law

bébé *m.* baby

Bédouin a nomadic Arab

Belge *m. or f.* Belgian

Belgique *f.* Belgium

belle (*f. of* **beau**) beautiful; **la belle saison** the summer months

belle-fille *f.* daughter-in-law

berger *m.* shepherd; **l'étoile du Berger** Venus

besoin *m.* need; **avoir besoin** (**de** + *n.*; **de** + *inf.*) need

bête *f.* beast; animal

beurre *m.* butter

bibliothèque *f.* library

bicorne *m.* two-cornered hat worn by the Spanish officers of the *Guardia civil*

bicyclette *f.* bicycle

bien well; well-off; comfortable; good; indeed; very; very much; right; **bien que** although; **ou bien** or else; **qu'on est bien** how comfortable we are; **vouloir bien** be willing; **vous comprenez bien** you must understand

bien-aimé beloved

bientôt soon

bienveillance *f.* kindness, benevolence

bière *f.* beer

bifteck *m.* steak

bijou *m.* jewel

bijoutier *m.* jeweler

billet *m.* ticket; **billet de banque** banknote

biographie *f.* biography

biologie *f.* biology

bistrot *m.* a small café or restaurant (patronized principally by the working class)

bizarre odd, strange; outlandish; **bizarrement** strangely

blanc (*f.* **blanche**) white

blessé *m.* the wounded man

blesser wound

bleu blue

bleuté bluish

blondeur *f.* blondness

boire (**buvant, bu, je bois, je bus**) drink

bois *m.* wood

boîte *f.* box

Bolivie *f.* Bolivia

bon (*f.* **bonne**) good; fit; **allons bon** there now; **bon marché** cheap; **il fait bon** it is cozy, it is comfortably warm

bonbon *m.* candy

bonheur *m.* happiness

bonjour good morning, hello

bonne *f.* maid

bonnet *m.* cap

bord *m.* edge

bottier *m.* bootmaker, shoemaker

bottine *f.* shoe; boot; **lacet de bottine** boot lace

bouche *f.* mouth

bouclé curled

boudin *m.* black pudding

bouger (*irr. sp.* **B**) move

bougie *f.* candle

Irregular verbs are conjugated on pp. 284–301.

bouillonner bubble
boulanger *m.* baker; **chez le boulanger** at the bakery
boule *f.* ball; **se battre à coups de boules de neige** have a snowball fight
bouleverser upset
bourgeois middle-class
bout *m.* end; tip; **joindre les deux bouts** make ends meet
bouteille *f.* bottle
boxe *f.* boxing
braise *f.* glowing embers
bras *m.* arm
Brésil *m.* Brazil
brésilien (*f.* **brésilienne**) Brazilian
breuvage *m.* drink
brièveté *f.* brevity
brillant brilliant; bright
broder embroider
brosser brush
bruissement *m.* slight sound, rustling
bruit *m.* noise; rumor
brûlant burning; passionate
brûler burn
brun brown; dusky
brune *f.* brunette
brusque blunt; brusk
brusquement suddenly; bruskly
brutalement brutally
bruyant noisy
bu, bus (*pp and sp of* **boire**) drunk; drank
buée *f.* steam, vapor; mist or film formed when one breathes on a mirror
Buenos-Ayres Buenos-Aires, capital of Argentina
buffet *m.* buffet, sideboard
bureau *m.* desk; office; **bureau de tabac** tobacco shop; **chef de bureau** head clerk
buste *m.* bust
but *m.* aim
buvant (*pres. part. of* **boire**) drinking

C

ça that; it; **çà et là** here and there
cacher hide
cacheter (*irr. sp.* **F**) seal
cadeau *m.* gift; **faire un cadeau** give a present

café *m.* coffee; café, coffee house
cahier *m.* notebook
caillou *m.* stone, pebble
calculer calculate; estimate
calme *m.* peace; calm; (*adj.*) calm
calmement calmly
calvaire *m.* intense mental suffering or agony
camarade *m. or f.* friend; pal; **camarade d'études** school friend
camp *m.* camp; team
campagne *f.* country; countryside, landscape; **maison de campagne** country home
Canada *m.* Canada
candidat *m.* candidate
cantabile [kantabile] (Italian) melodious; **moderato cantabile** musical term meaning that the piece is to be melodious and moderately paced
capable capable, able; **capable de tout** capable of anything
capitaine *m.* captain
capitale *f.* capital
capitalisme *m.* capitalism
car (*conjunc.*) for
carabinier *m.* member of the Spanish *Guardia civil*
caractère *m.* character (attributes or features which distinguish a person)
carré square
carrefour *m.* crossing; crossroad
caresser caress, fondle
carte *f.* card; map; **carte d'identité** identification card; **carte postale** postcard; **carte de visite** visiting card
cas *m.* case
casser break; **se casser** break
Catalogne Catalonia, region of northeastern Spain of which Barcelona is the capital
cataloguer catalog, classify
cathédrale *f.* cathedral
catholique *m. or f.* Catholic
cause *f.* cause; **à cause de** because of
causer talk; chat; cause
caviar *m.* caviar
ce (*adj.*) this; that; (*pron.*) this; that; it; he; she; they
célèbre famous

Verbs with spelling changes are explained on pp. 302–304.

célibataire *m.* bachelor

celui (*f.* **celle**) this one, that one; the one; **celui-ci** this one, that one; the latter

censeur *m.* vice-principal in charge of attendance and discipline in a **lycée**

cent hundred

centaine *f.* about a hundred

cependant however

cercueil *m.* coffin

cerise *f.* cherry

certain some; certain

certainement certainly

certes certainly

cesse: sans cesse constantly, ceaselessly

cesser (**de** + *inf.*) stop, cease

cet this; that

cette (*f. of* **ce**) this, that

chagrin *m.* sorrow; chagrin

chair *f.* flesh

chaise *f.* chair

chaleur *f.* heat

chambre *f.* bedroom

champagne *m.* champagne

championne *f.* woman champion

Champs-Elysées avenue in Paris leading from the Place de la Concorde to the Place Charles de Gaulle

chance *f.* luck; **avoir de la chance** be lucky

changement *m.* change

changer (*irr. sp.* **B**) change; **changer d'avis** change one's mind

chanson *f.* song

chantant melodious

chanter sing

chanteuse *f.* singer

chapeau *m.* hat

chaque each

chargé loaded; overloaded; **chargé de** filled with

charger (**se**) (**de** + *inf.*) take care

charmant charming

charme *m.* charm

chasse *f.* hunt, hunting; **aller à la chasse** go hunting

chasser hunt, throw out, chase away

chat *m.* cat

château *m.* castle

chaud hot; warm; **j'ai chaud** I am warm; **il fait chaud** it is warm; it is hot

chauffeur *m.* driver; chauffeur

chaussé shod, wearing shoes

chaussure *f.* shoe; *pl.* footwear; shoes

chauve bald

chef *m.* head, leader; chief; **chef de bureau** head clerk

chemin *m.* road; path; way

cheminée *f.* fireplace

chemisette *f.* short-sleeved shirt

chèque *m.* check

cher (*f.* **chère**) dear; expensive

chercher (+ *n.*) look for; meet; go and get; pick up (**à** + *inf.*) try to, seek to; **envoyer chercher** send for

chérie *f.* dear

cheval *m.* (*pl.* **chevaux**) horse

chevelure *f.* head of hair

cheveux *m. pl.* hair

chez at; with; in; at the house of; in the case of; **allez chez vous** go home; **chez le directeur** to the director's office; **chez nous** at our house; in our country; **chez qui** at whose home

chichement frugally, parsimoniously, penuriously

chien *m.* dog

chiffre *m.* cipher; figure

chimie *f.* chemistry

Chine *f.* China

chinois Chinese

chocolat *m.* chocolate; candy

chœur *m.* choir

choisir choose

chose *f.* thing; **pas grand-chose** not much, not very much

chouette *f.* owl

Cid *m.*: **Le Cid** a well-known play by Corneille (1636)

ciel *m.* sky

cigare *m.* cigar

cil *m.* eyelash

cinéma *m.* movie; movies

cinq five

cinquante fifty

cinquième fifth

cirer wax; shine; **toile cirée** oilcloth

cirque *m.* circus

cité *f.* city

citron *m.* lemon

clair clear, light; obvious; **clair de lune** *m.* moonlight

Irregular verbs are conjugated on pp. 284–301.

claquement *m.* slamming
classe *f.* class; classroom; **faire une classe** teach
classique classical
clavier *m.* keyboard
clé *f.* key; **fermer à clé** lock
client *m.* client; customer; patron
clientèle *f.* customers, clientele
climatiser air-condition
clinique *f.* hospital (private)
cloche *f.* bell
clou *m.* nail
clown *m.* clown
Cocteau, Jean (1889–1963) French writer of the twentieth century
cœur *m.* heart; **apprendre par cœur** memorize; **au cœur de** in the middle of; **avoir mal au cœur** be nauseated
coffre *m.* safe
cognac *m.* brandy
coiffée *f.* with one's hair dressed; **extrêmement coiffée** with a high style hairdo
coiffeur *m.* hairdresser; barber
coiffure *f.* hairdo
coin *m.* corner
colère *f.* anger; **en colère** angry; **se mettre en colère** get angry
Colette, Sidonie Gabriel (1873–1954) French woman novelist
colis *m.* package
colle *f.* glue
collectionner collect
collégien *m.* secondary school student
collègue *m.* or *f.* colleague
coller (+*person*) (*colloquial*) fail (someone in a test or course)
collier *m.* necklace; **barbe en collier** narrow oval-shaped beard
colline *f.* hill
combien how much; how many; **tous les combien** how often
combiner plan; draw up; figure out
comédie *f.* comedy; play
comédien *m.* actor; comedian
commander order (a meal)
comme as; like; as well as; since; **comme si** as if; **comme d'habitude** as usual; **comme il faut** properly
commencement *m.* beginning
commencer (*irr. sp.* **A**) begin

comment how; what; What! What do you mean; **comment trouvez-vous** what do you think of
commerce *m.* business
commissaire *m.* police commissioner
commission *f.* errand; **faire des commissions** go shopping
commode convenient
Commodoro a city in Argentina
communisme *m.* communism
communiste *m.* or *f.* communist
compagnie *f.* company; firm
compartiment *m.* train compartment
complètement completely
compliqué complicated
complot *m.* plot; conspiracy
comportement *m.* behavior
comporter require; include; comprise; behave
composé compound; **passé composé** compound past
composition *f.* composition; theme
comprendre (*conj. like* **prendre**) understand; comprise; **ne comprenant rien à son cas** not understanding anything about his case
comprenez (**comprendre**) understand; **vous comprenez bien** you must understand
compte *m.* account; **se rendre compte** (**de** + *n.*) realize
compter count; (+ *inf.*) expect; intend
comptoir *m.* counter
concierge *m.* or *f.* house-porter; janitor; caretaker
conclure (*irr. v.*) conclude; **l'affaire sera conclue** the deal will be closed
concours *m.* competitive examination
condamner condemn
condition *f.* condition; social level; **à condition que** provided that
conduire (**conduisant, conduit, je conduis, je conduisis**) drive; take; **se conduire**
conduite *f.* behavior
conférence *f.* lecture; **en conférence** in conference, at a meeting
conférencier *m.* speaker; lecturer
conflit *m.* conflict
confort *m.* comfort
confortable comfortable

Verbs with spelling changes are explained on pp. 302–304.

connaissance *f.* acquaintance; knowledge; **faire connaissance avec** get
acquainted with, meet; **faire la connaissance de** get acquainted with,
meet
**connaître (connaissant, connu, je con-
nais, je connus)** know, be acquainted
with
connu well known, famous
consciencieux (*f.* consciencieuse) conscientious
conseil *m.* piece of advice; *pl.* advice
conseiller (à + *person* + de + *inf.*)
advise
consolant consoling
consommer consummate; accomplish;
consume
conspiration *f.* conspiracy
construire (*conj. like* conduire) build
contempler view
contenir (*conj. like* tenir) contain
contenter satisfy
contingent accidental
continuellement continually; incessantly
continuer (à + *inf.*) continue; keep on
contraint forced
contraire *m.* contrary; **au contraire** on
the contrary
contribuer contribute
convaincu (*pp of* convaincre) convinced
convenable proper
convenir (*conj. like* venir) agree; be
proper, be suiting; **convenir de** accept; **quelque chose convient** something is proper, something is suitable
convenu agreed; OK; agreed upon
convertir convert
convive *m. or f.* guest
copain *m.* pal, chum, close friend
copie *f.* paper (to hand in); (school)
exercise
copier copy
coquetterie *f.* coquetry; desire to please
a man; flirtatious attitude
coquille *f.* shell
corne *f.* horn
corps *m.* body
correctement correctly
correspondant *m.* correspondent
corriger (*irr. sp.* B) correct
cosmique cosmic, vast

costume *m.* suit
côte *f.* coast; **côte à côte** side by side;
Côte d'Azur French Riviera
côté *m.* side; **à côté de** near, beside,
alongside of; in addition to; **à côté de**
in the direction of; on the side of;
mettre de côté save; **tout à côté** right
near
cou *m.* neck
couchant *m.* sunset
coucher put to bed; spend the night;
se coucher go to bed; *(n.) m.* bedtime
couchette *f.* cot
couleur *f.* color
couleuvre *f.* snake
couloir *m.* corridor
coup *m.* blow; "coup"; **coup d'œil**
glance; **se battre à coups de boules
de neige** have a snowball fight; **coup
de tonnerre** thunderclap; **d'un coup
de crayon** with the tap of a pencil;
tout à coup all of a sudden; **tout
d'un coup** all of a sudden
coupable guilty; *(n.) m. or f.* the guilty
one
couper cut; cut down
cour *f.* yard; court yard; court; **faire
la cour** make love
courageux (*f.* courageuse) brave
courant running; **au courant** informed
**courir (courant, couru, je cours, je
courus)** run
courrier *m.* mail
cours *m.* course; **cours de vacances**
summer courses
course *f.* errand; race
court short
couteau *m.* knife
coûter cost; **coûter cher** be expensive
coûteux (*f.* coûteuse) expensive
couvert (*pp of* couvrir) covered; *(n.)*
m. cover; knives, forks, and spoon
used for eating; **enlever le couvert**
clear the table; *(adj.)* covered
couverture *f.* blanket
craie *f.* chalk
craignais (*imperfect of* craindre) feared
**craindre (craignant, craint, je crains,
je craignis)** fear
crainte *f.* fear
cravate *f.* tie

Irregular verbs are conjugated on pp. 284–301.

crayon *m.* pencil; **d'un coup de crayon** with the tap of a pencil
créer create
crème *f.* cream
créneau *m.* battlement
crêpe *m.* crepe; mourning band
creux (*f.* **creuse**) hollow
cri *m.* cry; screaming; **pousser un cri** utter a cry
crier yell; cry out
criminel *m.* criminal
critique *f.* criticism; review
critiquer criticize
crochet hook; **faire un crochet** swerve
croire (**croyant, cru, je crois, je crus**) believe; **croire bon** deem fit
croisade *f.* crusade
croisé crossed; **mots croisés** crossword puzzle
croiser cross
cru, crus (*pp and sp of* **croire**) believed
cruel (*f.* **cruelle**) cruel
cueillir pick
cuillerée *f.* spoonful
cuir *m.* leather
cuisine *f.* kitchen; cooking
cuisinière *f.* cook
culotte *f.* kneepants
cultiver cultivate
curieux (*f.* **curieuse**) curious; odd; strange; inquisitive; eager
cyclone *m.* hurricane

D

d'abord at first; **tout d'abord** first of all
dame *f.* lady; **dame!** (*interjection*) why, of course
Danemark *m.* Denmark
dangereux (*f.* **dangereuse**) dangerous
dans in, on
danse *f.* dancing; **leçon de danse** dancing lesson
danser dance
danseuse *f.* dancer
darder hurl, send forth
dater date
d'avance in advance
de of; from; by; in; out of; with
déborder overflow

debout standing; **puisque vous êtes debout** since you are up
début *m.* beginning
décapotable *f.* convertible (car)
déchirer tear up
décider (**de** + *inf.*) decide; **se décider** (**à** + *inf.*) make up one's mind
décimètre *m.* decimeter: a unit of the metric system equivalent to about 4 inches
décisif (*f.* **décisive**) decisive
décision *f.* decision; **prendre une décision** make a decision, make up one's mind
décoller (speaking of airplanes) take off
découper cut; cut out
décourager (*irr. sp.* **B**) discourage
découverte *f.* discovery
découvrir (*conj. like* **ouvrir**) discover
défaut *m.* defect; shortcoming
défendre defend; (**à** + *person* + **de** + *inf.*) forbid
défendu forbidden
déferler break
définir define
définitivement definitely
défoncer (*irr. sp.* **A**) smash
dégringoler fall down, tumble down
dehors outside
déjà already
déjeuner have the noon meal; have breakfast; (*n.*) *m.* noon meal (main meal in France)
délacer (*irr. sp.* **A**) free
délavé faded
délicieux (*f.* **délicieuse**) delightful
demain tomorrow; **à partir de demain** from tomorrow on
demander ask; (**à** + *person* + **de** + *inf.*) ask someone to; (**à** + *inf.*) ask to
déménager (*irr. sp.* **B**) move
demeurer remain
demi half; **demi-heure** half an hour; **demi-place** half price (for a seat)
démission *f.* resignation
démonstratif *m.* demonstrative
dent *f.* tooth
dentelle *f.* lace
d'entre of
départ *m.* departure
dépasser go beyond; go around

Verbs with spelling changes are explained on pp. 302–304.

dépêcher (se) (de + *inf.*) hurry
déplacement *m.* travelling
déplacer (*irr. sp.* **A**) shift
déposer (se) be found; settle
dépourvu without
dépression *f.* hollow, fall
depuis since; from; for
déranger (*irr. sp.* **B**) disturb, bother
dernier (*f.* **dernière**) last
dérouler (se) unfold; develop; take place
derrière behind; **la porte de derrière** the back door
dès que as soon as; **dès que possible** as soon as possible
désaccordé out of tune
désappointé disappointed
désastre *m.* disaster
descendre come down; go down; descend
désert deserted
désinvolte natural
désirer (+*inf.*) wish, desire
désolé sorry
dessin *m.* drawing
dessus upstairs; on it
détaché detached
détourner turn away from; **détourner les yeux** look away; turn one's eyes away
détruire (*conj. like* **conduire**) destroy
dette *f.* debt
deuil *m.* mourning; **prendre le deuil** go into mourning
deux two; **tous deux** both; **vous deux** both of you
devant before
devenir (*conj. like* **venir**) become
deviner guess
dévisager look carefully (at someone)
dévoiler uncover; discover
devoir (pp. 198–202) (**devant, dû, je dois, je dus**) have to, must, ought to; should probably + *verb;* (*n.*) *m.* duty; exercise; **devoir connaître** be able to know
diable *m.* devil
diamant *m.* diamond
diapositive *f.* (photographic) slide
dictionnaire *m.* dictionary
Dieu *m.* God

difficile difficult
dimanche *m.* Sunday
diminuer diminish
dîner dine, have dinner
diplomatique diplomatic
diplôme *m.* diploma
dire (disant, dit, je dis, je dis) (**à +** *person* **+ de +** *inf.*) say; tell; **à qui le dites-vous** you're telling me! **c'est-à-dire** that is to say; **on dirait** one would say; it seems; **vouloir dire** mean
directeur *m.* director; manager
diriger (*irr. sp.* **B**) direct; **se diriger** go
disant (*pres. participle of* **dire**) saying
discours *m.* speech
discret (*f.* **discrète**) discreet
discuter discuss; argue about; talk something over
disparaître (*conj. like* **connaître**) disappear
disque *m.* (phonograph) record
distingué distinguished
distribuer distribute
dit (*pres. and pp of* **dire**) say; said; so called; **si le cœur vous en dit** if you so desire
divers various, different
dix ten
docteur *m.* doctor
dodu plump, filled out; puffy
doigt *m.* finger
doit (*pres. of* **devoir**) must; has to; is to; probably does
domestique *m. or f.* servant
donc then; thus; therefore; now; **allez donc voir** be sure and see; **entrez donc** do come in; **pensez donc** think of it; **qui donc** who is that; whom do you mean?
donner give; **donner sur** look out upon
doré gilded
dormir (2) sleep
dos *m.* back
dossier *m.* file
douane *f.* customs
doucement gently
douleur *f.* pain; suffering; sorrow
doute *m.* doubt; **sans doute** probably
douteux (*f.* **douteuse**) doubtful
doux (*f.* **douce**) mild; soft

Irregular verbs are conjugated on pp. 284–301.

douzaine *f.* dozen
dramaturge *m.* dramatist
drame *m.* drama; **drame passionnel** drama of passion
drapeau *m.* flag
dresser raise
droit *m.* study of law; justice; law; (*adj.*) right; straight; **tout droit** erect; straight ahead
droite *f.* right
drôle funny; odd
du of the
dû, due (*pp of* **devoir**) had to, etc.; due to
dur hard
Duras, Marguerite (1914–) contemporary French writer
durer last

E

eau *f.* water
ébaucher begin; start to display
écarter pull aside
échange *m.* exchange
échanger (*irr. sp.* **B**) exchange
échapper (**à** + *n.*) escape, avoid; **s'échapper** (**de** + *n.*) escape
écharpe *f.* scarf
éclaircissement *m.* elucidation; enlightenment
éclairé lighted
éclairer light
éclat *m.* gleam; brightness
éclater burst; break out; flash; **le soir venait d'éclater** evening had just come (upon them)
éclos open; grown; **à peine éclos** not yet fully shaped
école *f.* school
économies *f. pl.* savings; **faire des économies** save
économiser save
écouler (**s'**) elapse, pass
écouter (+ *n.*) listen; listen to
écouteur *m.* receiver
écrasé crushed; overwhelmed
écrire (**écrivant, écrit, j'écris, j'écrivis**) write; **machine à écrire** *f.* typewriter
écrivain *m.* writer
écureuil *m.* squirrel

édifice *m.* building; framework, structure
effacer (*irr. sp.* **A**) erase; obliterate
effet *m.* effect; **en effet** in fact; **par l'effet** because of
effort *m.* effort; **faire un petit effort** try
effrayer (*irr. sp.* **C**) scare, frighten; **s'effrayer** (**de**) become frightened (at)
effroyable frightful
égal equal; **cela m'était égal** it did not make any difference to me
égard: à tous les égards in all respects
égarer (**s'**) wander; lose one's way
église *f.* church
égratignure *f.* scratch
élancer (**s'**) (*irr. sp.* **A**) dart forth
électricité *f.* electricity; **panne d'électricité** power failure
élève *m. or f.* pupil
élevé high; brought up; **bien élevé** well-mannered; **mal élevé** ill-mannered, ill bred
élire (*conj. like* **lire**) elect
éloigner keep away; **s'éloigner** go off, go away
élu (*pp of* **élire**) elected
embarrassé embarrassed
embouteillage *m.* traffic jam
émeraude *f.* emerald
émigrer emigrate
emmener (*irr. sp.* **D**) take away; take along
emparer (**s'**) (**de** + *n.*) sieze
empêcher (*n.* + **de** + *inf.*) hinder, prevent
empereur *m.* emperor
emploi *m.* use
employé *m.* clerk; employee; **petit employé** minor office clerk
employer (*irr. sp.* **C**) use
empoigner seize
emporter take away (a thing); **s'emporter** get angry
empreinte *f.* imprint
emprunter borrow
ému moved
en in; to; as; while; by
en vis-à-vis opposite each other
enchanté delighted
encore again; still; yet; **encore un mot** one more word
encourageant encouraging

Verbs with spelling changes are explained on pp. 302–304.

encre *f.* ink
encrier *m.* inkwell
endormi asleep; sleeping
endormir (s') (2) fall asleep
endroit *m.* place
endurci hardened; confirmed
énergie *f.* energy; power
enfance *f.* childhood
enfant *m. or f.* child
enfantin childish
enfin finally, at last; in short, anyway; well
enfler (s') swell; rise
engagé engaged, involved
engager (*irr. sp.* **B**) hire
enguirlandé decorated, festooned
enhardir (s') pick up enough courage, become bold enough
enjoué sprightly
enlaidir become ugly; make ugly
enlever (*irr. sp.* **D**) take away; take off; enlever le couvert clear the table
ennui *m.* boredom; trouble
ennuyer (*irr. sp.* **C**) bore; bother; s'ennuyer get bored; be lonesome; be bored
ennuyeux (*f.* ennuyeuse) annoying; boring
énorme enormous
énormément very much; considerably
enregistrer record; register; check (baggage)
enseigner (*thing* + à + *person; person* + à + *inf.*) teach
ensemble together; exercices d'ensemble summing-up exercises
ensoleillé sunny
ensuite then
entendre hear; entendre dire que hear that; s'entendre be heard; get along
entendu agreed
entente *f.* understanding; agreement; harmony
enterrement *m.* burial
entêtement *m.* stubbornness
enthousiasme *m.* enthusiasm
entier (*f.* entière) entire; whole; tout entier completely
entouré surrounded
entourer (de + *n.*) surround; cover over
entre between; d'entre of

entrée *f.* entrance; beginning
entreprendre (*conj. like* prendre) undertake
entrer (dans + *n.*) enter; penetrate
envahir invade; come over
enveloppe *f.* envelope
envelopper wrap; wrap up
envers toward
envie *f.* wish, desire; avoir envie de feel like
envier envy
environ about, approximately
environs *m. pl.* surroundings; surrounding territory
envisager consider
envoler (s') take off (in an airplane flight)
envoyer (envoyant, envoyé, j'envoie, j'envoyai) send; envoyer chercher send for
épais (*f.* épaisse) thick
épaisseur *f.* depth
épaule *f.* shoulder; hausser les épaules shrug one's shoulders
épidémie *f.* epidemic
éponger (s') (*irr. sp.* **B**) wipe the sweat from one's forehead
époque *f.* time; period
épouser (+ *person*) marry
éprouver feel; experience
épuisé exhausted
épuiser (s') wear oneself out
érotisme *m.* eroticism, sexual excitement
erreur *f.* mistake
escalier *m.* stairway
escargot *m.* snail
escroc *m.* swindler
ésotérique esoteric; designed for or addressing itself only to a chosen few; incomprehensible to all outside of an especially initiated group
espace *m.* space
espacé spaced
Espagne *f.* Spain
espagnol Spanish
espèce *f.* kind
espérer (*irr. sp.* **E**) (+ *inf.*) hope; expect
espion *m.* spy
espoir *m.* hope
esprit *m.* spirit; wit; mind
esquissé perceptible

Irregular verbs are conjugated on pp. 284–301.

essai *m.* essay
essayer (*irr. sp.* **C**) (**de** + *inf.*) try
essayiste *m.* essayist
essence *f.* essence; gasoline
essuyer (*irr. sp.* **C**) wipe
établir establish
étage *m.* floor; **le premier étage** the second floor
étaler display
étant (*pres. part. of* **être**) being
état *m.* state; shape
Etats-Unis *m. pl.* United States
été (*v.*) (*pp of* **être**) been; (*n.*) *m.* summer
éteindre (*conj. like* **peindre**) turn off; **s'éteindre** come to an end
étendre (**s'**) stretch out; lie down
éternel (*f.* **éternelle**) eternal
étoffe *f.* fabric; material; cloth
étoile *f.* star; **avec des étoiles sur le visage** stars were shining in my face; **l'étoile du Berger** Venus
étoilé star-shaped
étonnant astonishing; remarkable; surprising
étonné surprised
étonner astonish; surprise; **s'étonner** be surprised
étouffé stifled
étourdi stunned, bewildered
étranger *m.* foreigner; estranged man; stranger; **à l'étranger** abroad; (*adj.*) (*f.* **étrangère**) foreign; estranged, alienated; **rendre étranger** alienate
étrangeté *f.* strangeness
être (**étant, été, je suis, je fus**) be; **être à l'aise** be comfortable; **ne pas être en reste** be equal to the situation; **vous n'en seriez pas là** you wouldn't be in such a fix; (*n.*) *m.* being
étreinte *f.* grip; grasp; embrace
étroit narrow; close
étude *f.* study; **camarade d'étude** school friend
étudiant *m.* (college) student
eu, eus (*pp and sp of* **avoir**) had
eux *m.* them
évader (**s'**) escape
évanoui unconscious; fainted
évanouir (**s'**) faint
éveiller awaken; arouse
événement *m.* event

éventail *m.* fan
évidemment obviously
évident obvious
éviter (**de** + *inf.*) avoid
évocateur suggestive; meaningful, inspiring
évoluer develop; evolve; change
exact true; correct
exactement exactly
exagérément in an exaggerated manner; unusually
examen *m.* examination; **passer un examen** take an examination
examiner examine
excepté except
exclure (*irr. v.*) exclude
excuser (**s'**) apologize
exécuter (**s'**) take place
exercice *m.* exercise; **exercices d'ensemble** summing-up exercises
exigeant demanding
existence *f.* existence; life
existentialiste existentialist; referring to the philosophy of existentialism
exister exist
exotisme *m.* exoticism; being from another and strange land; **en plein exotisme** in the middle of an exotic land
expérience *f.* experience; experiment
expliquer explain
exporter export
exposer exhibit
exposition *f.* fair
exprimer express
extraordinaire extraordinary
extrêmement extremely; **extrêmement coiffé** with a high style hairdo
exulter exult, rejoice, be joyful

F

fabriquer make; manufacture
face *f.* face; **d'en face** on the opposite side (of the street); **face à** facing; **faire face à** face up to; accept
fâché angry; sorry
fâcher (**se**) (**contre** + *person*) get angry
facilement easily

Verbs with spelling changes are explained on pp. 302–304.

façon *f.* manner; way; **de la même façon** in the same way
facteur *m.* mailman
faculté *f.* college or school of a university, including buildings and teaching staff
faible weak
faim *f.* hunger; **avoir faim** be hungry
faire (**faisant, fait, je fais, je fis**) (+ *inf.*) do; make; carry out; have (done); **faire l'accord** make the agreement; **faire ses adieux** say goodbye; **faire attention** look out; pay attention; **faire les bagages** pack; **faire du bateau** go boating; **faire un cadeau** give a present; **faire du cheval** go horseback riding; **faire ses classes** teach one's classes; **faire la connaissance de** get acquainted with; meet; **faire un petit effort** try a little; **faire face à** face up to; accept; **faire des farces** play tricks; play jokes; **faire froid** be cold; **faire de la gymnastique** exercise; **faire une lettre** write a letter; **faire mal** hurt; **faire sa médecine** study medicine; **faire de son mieux** do one's best; **faire de la musique** play music; **faire partie de** belong to, be part of; **faire une période militaire** do a short tour of military duty; **faire plaisir à** please, give pleasure to; **faire une promenade** take a walk; **faire du ski** go skiing; **faire des sports** participate in sports; **faire une valise** pack a suitcase; **faire venir** send for; **il a fait «ho»** he exclaimed "ho"; **il fait bon** it's cozy; it is comfortably warm; **se faire mal** hurt oneself; **se faire du souci** worry
falaise *f.* cliff
falloir (—, **fallu, il faut, il fallut**) (+ *inf.*) must, be necessary; **comme il faut** properly; **il faut** it takes; one must; **il me faut** I need
familial (*adj.*) family
familier (*f.* **familière**) familiar; intimate
famille *f.* family; **famille nombreuse** large family
fantaisiste whimsical; fanciful
fantastique *m.* the fantastic, the fanciful; the fantastic quality

farce *f.* farce; **faire des farces** play tricks; play jokes
farine *f.* flour
fasciner fascinate
fasse (*pres. subjunc. of* **faire**) make; do
fatigant tiring; tiresome
fatiguer tire
faut (*pres. of* **falloir**) must, has to; **il faut** one must; it takes; **comme il faut** properly; **il me faut** I need
faute *f.* mistake; **sans faute** without fail
fauteuil *m.* armchair
fauve tawny
faux (*f.* **fausse**) false
favori (*f.* **favorite**) favorite
femme *f.* woman; wife; **femme de ménage** cleaning woman; **Les Femmes savantes** *The Learned Women*, a play by Molière (1672)
fenêtre *f.* window
ferai, ferais (*fut. and cond. of* **faire**) will make, will do; would make, would do
ferme *f.* farm; *adj.* firm; **tenir ferme** hold fast
fermer close; **fermer à clé** lock
fermier *m.* farmer
féroce ferocious
ferrure *f.* iron-work
fête *f.* holiday; festivity; celebration; birthday
feu *m.* fire; **feu rouge** red light; traffic light
feuille *f.* leaf; sheet
ficelle *f.* string; piece of string
fier (**se**) trust; have confidence in
fierté *f.* pride
Figueras a small Spanish town in Catalonia not far from the French border
fil *m.* wire
fille *f.* daughter; girl; **jeune fille** *f.* girl
fillette *f.* young girl; little girl
film *m.* film; movie
fils *m.* son
fin *f.* end
finalement finally
finesse *f.* subtlety; fineness; finesse
finir finish; **finir mal** end up badly; **finir par** end up by; **il n'en finit pas** he never stops
flamand Flemish
flambé bright colored

Irregular verbs are conjugated on pp. 284–301.

fleur *f.* flower; **fleur d'eau** water flower
floraison *f.* blooming
foie *m.* liver
fois *f.* time; **à la fois** at the same time; **une fois pour toutes** once and for all
folle (*f. of* **fou**) crazy; reckless
foncé dark
fond *m.* bottom; background; **au fond** deep down inside
fonder found
fontaine *f.* fountain
football *m.* football; ball
force *f.* strength; force; **la force de l'âge** the prime of life
forêt *f.* forest
forme *f.* form
formidable marvelous
fort (*adj.*) loud; strong; (intellectually) good; *adv.* hard; very
fou (*before vowel sound* **fol,** *f.* **folle**) crazy; reckless
foule *f.* crowd
fourberie *f.* trickery; deceit
fourchette *f.* fork
fourrure *f.* fur
fracassé shattered, broken into pieces
fraîcheur *f.* freshness
frais (*f.* **fraîche**) fresh; cool
fraise *f.* strawberry
franc (*f.* **franche**) frank
Français *m.* Frenchman
français French
franchement frankly
franchir cross
frapper strike; knock
fraternel (*f.* **fraternelle**) fraternal
fraternité *f.* fraternity; brotherhood
frémir quiver, shudder; **il en frémit** it made him shudder
fréquemment frequently
fréquenté visited; **peu fréquenté** not very often visited
fréquenter frequent, go to regularly
frère *m.* brother
frigidaire *m.* refrigerator
froid *m.* cold; **avoir froid** be cold; **il fait froid** it is cold
froidement coldly; coolly
froideur *f.* coldness
front *m.* forehead
fumer smoke

fur: au fur et à mesure gradually
fureur *f.* rage
furieux (*f.* **furieuse**) furious
furtif (*f.* **furtive**) furtive, stealthy
fus, fut (*sp of* **être**) was
fusil *m.* gun; rifle

G

gageure *f.* challenge
gagner win; gain; earn
gant *m.* glove
gantier *m.* glovemaker
garçon *m.* boy; waiter
garde *m.* watchman; guard
garder keep; watch
gardien *m.* watchman
gare *f.* station; railroad station
gare à lui! he'd better look out
Garonne *f.* river in southern France
gâteau *m.* cake
gâter spoil
gauche *f.* left
gazon *m.* lawn
gelée *f.* jelly
gêner disturb; bother; embarrass
gens *m. pl.* people; **jeunes gens** young men; young people
gentil (*f.* **gentille**) nice
géologie *f.* geology
geste *m.* gesture
gibbon *m.* (a sort of) monkey
girouette *f.* weathervane
glissement *m.* sliding; sliding noise; swishing
glisser slip
glorieux (*f.* **glorieuse**) glorious
glycine *f.* glycine (kind of plant), wisteria
gonflement *m.* swelling
gorge *f.* throat
gorgée *f.* spoonful (*lit.* throatful)
goût *m.* taste
goûter taste; **goûter à quelque chose** take a snack, take a little of something
gouvernement *m.* government
gouverner govern
gracieux (*f.* **gracieuse**) graceful; gracious
Gracq, Julien (1909–) French writer of the surrealist school

Verbs with spelling changes are explained on pp. 302–304.

grammaire *f.* grammar
grand great; large; **il est grand temps** it is high time
grand-chose much; **votre idée ne vaut pas grand-chose** your idea isn't worth much
grand-père *m.* grandfather
grandir grow
gratter scratch; **se gratter** scratch
gravier *m.* gravel
Grèce *f.* Greece
grève *f.* beach
grillé toasted
grincer (*irr. sp.* **A**) squeak
gris gray
griser intoxicate
gronder scold; grumble, rumble
gros (*f.* **grosse**) big; fat
grouiller swarm
guère scarcely, hardly
guéri cured; healed
guéridon *m.* small, round table
guerre *f.* war; **pilote de guerre** military pilot
guise: à ma guise to my liking
guitare *f.* guitar
gymnastique *f.* exercise; **faire de la gymnastique** exercise

H

* indicates an aspirate *h*

habiller dress; **s'habiller** dress
habiter (*place;* **à** + *place*) live; inhabit
habitude *f.* habit; **comme d'habitude** as usual
habituer (**s'**) (**à** + *inf.*) get used to
***haine** *f.* hate
haleine *f.* breath
***haletant** breathless, panting
***harmonieux** (*f.* **harmonieuse**) harmonious
***hasard** *m.* hazard; chance; **au hasard** at random
***hausser** raise; **hausser les épaules** shrug one's shoulders
***haut** high; **à haute voix** aloud; **dans le haut de la rue** in the upper part of the street; up-street; up the street
***hauteur** *f.* height; level

***Haye, La** *f.* The Hague, capital of the Netherlands
***hélas** alas
héritier *m.* heir
***héros** *m.* hero
hésitation *f.* hesitation
hésiter hesitate
heure *f.* hour; o'clock; time; **à l'heure** on time; **de bonne heure** early; **tout à l'heure** in a little while; a little while ago
heureux (*f.* **heureuse**) happy
***heurter** (**se**) (**à** + *n.*) run up against
hier yesterday; **avant-hier** the day before yesterday
histoire *f.* story; history; trouble; **quelle histoire!** what a fuss!
hiver *m.* winter
ho: faire «ho» exclaim "ho" (exclamation of pain or surprise)
***hocher** nod; **hocher la tête** nod one's head
homme *m.* man
***Hongrois** *m.* Hungarian
horaire *m.* time table
hormis except for; outside of
***hors** outside; **hors de lui** beside himself
hôte *m.* guest; host
hôtel *m.* hotel; **hôtel de ville** city hall
humain human
humble *m.* humble person, meek person
humeur *f.* humor; mood; **de mauvaise humeur** in a bad mood
humide humid
humoriste *m.* humorist
humoristique humoristic; humorous
humour *m.* humor; comic element
***hurler** yell, howl
hymne *m.* hymn
hypocrite (*adj.*) hypocritical
hypothèse *f.* hypothesis

I

ici here
idée *f.* idea
identité *f.* identification; **carte d'identité** identification card
ignorer not to know; be unaware of
illusoire illusory
image *f.* picture

Irregular verbs are conjugated on pp. 284–301.

imaginer imagine
imbécile *m. or f.* fool
immédiatement immediately
immense immense, vast
immobile motionless
immortel (*f.* **immortelle**) immortal
imparfait *m.* imperfect (tense)
impatienter (**s'**) become impatient
importer matter; be important; **peu m'importait** it mattered little to me
imposer impose
impossible impossible
impression *f.* impression
imprévu unforeseen
imprimer print
inaccoutumé unusual; unaccustomed
incendie *m.* fire
incertitude *f.* uncertainty
incliné sloping
incommensurable incommensurable; lacking in a basis of comprehension
inconnu unknown
incroyable unbelievable
inculpé *m.* accused one
indemne untouched, unharmed
indien (*f.* **indienne**) Indian
indifférence *f.* indifference
indifférent indifferent
indiquer indicate; show
individu *m.* man; individual (often with unfavorable connotation)
inertie *f.* inertia
inestimable priceless
inexplicable unexplainable
infiniment infinitely
infirmière *f.* nurse
influent influential
influer influence
informer (**s'**) (**sur** + *n.*) inquire for information; get information about
ingénieur *m.* engineer
ingrat *m.* ungrateful man
inoffensif (*f.* **inoffensive**) harmless
inondation *f.* flood
inquiet (*f.* **inquiète**) uneasy, worried
inquiéter (**s'**) (*irr. sp.* **E**) worry
inquiétude uneasiness; worry
inscrire (*conj. like* **écrire**) inscribe
insister (**sur** + *thing;* **pour** + *inf.;* **pour que** + *subjunc.*) insist
inspecter inspect

inspecteur *m.* detective
instant *m.* instant; moment; **à l'instant même où** at the very moment when
instantanément suddenly; instantly
insuffisant insufficient
insupportable unbearable
intention *f.* intention; **avoir l'intention de** intend to
interdire (*conj. like* **dire**) forbid
intéresser interest; **s'intéresser** (**à** + *n.*) be interested in
intérêt *m.* interest
interprète *m.* interpreter
interpréter (*irr. sp.* **E**) interpret
interrogatif (*f.* **interrogative**) interrogative
interroger (*irr. sp.* **B**) (*person* + **sur** + *n.*) question; quiz
interrompre interrupt
intervalle *m.* interval
intrigué intrigued
introduire (*conj. like* **conduire**) introduce (something into); insert
inutile useless
inventer invent
inversé inverted; upside down
invité *m.* guest
inviter (**à** + *inf.*) invite; entice
involontaire involuntary
irai, irais (*fut. and cond. of* **aller**) will go; would go
isolé isolated
isoler isolate
issue *f.* exit; **sans issue** impassable
Italie *f.* Italy
italien (*f.* **italienne**) Italian
italique *m.* italics
itinéraire *m.* itinerary

J

jadis [ʒɑdis] formerly
jamais ever; never; **à jamais** forever; **ne ... jamais** never
jambe *f.* leg
Japon *m.* Japan
japonais Japanese
jardin *m.* garden; park; **jardin zoologique** zoo
jardinier *m.* gardener
jaune yellow

Verbs with spelling changes are explained on pp. 302–304.

Jeannot Johnnie
jeter (*irr. sp.* **F**) throw; **jeter les yeux**
  glance; **se jeter** throw oneself
jeu *m.* game; play; **jeu de mots** play on
  words, pun
jeudi *m.* Thursday
jeune young; **jeune fille** *f.* girl; **jeunes
  gens** *m.* young men; young people
jeunesse *f.* youth
joie *f.* joy
joindre (*conj. like* **craindre**) join; **joindre les deux bouts** make ends meet
joli pretty
joliment nicely
jouer (**de** + instrument; **à** + game)
  play; **jouer de** make use of; turn on
jouet *m.* toy
joueur *m.* player
jour *m.* day; **au jour le jour** day by day;
  from one day to the other; **dans les
  beaux jours** during the summer
  months; **de nos jours** in our days; in
  our time
journal *m.* newspaper; magazine; **journal de sport** sports magazine
journaliste *m.* newspaper man; journalist
journée *f.* day
jovial fun loving
joyeusement joyfully
juger (*irr. sp.* **B**) deem; judge; examine;
  scan; **juger bon** deem advisable
jurer swear; **je vous jure** (in a tone of
  exasperation) honestly!
jus *m.* juice
jusqu'à up to; as far as; to the point of
jusqu'à ce que (+ *subjunc.*) until
juste just
justice *f.* justice; **palais de justice** courthouse

K

kilo *m.* kilogram (2.2 pounds)

L

là there; here; **çà et là** here and there
là-bas over there
là-haut up there
lac *m.* lake
lacet *m.* lace; **lacet de bottine** boot lace

lâcher let go
laine *f.* wool
laisser (+ *inf.*) let; leave
lait *m.* milk
laiteux (*f.* **laiteuse**) milky; in milky foam
laitier *m.* milk dealer; milkman
lampe *f.* lamp
lancer (*irr. sp.* **A**) throw
langage *m.* manner of speech
langue *f.* language
lapidaire *m.* lapidary, cutter, polisher,
  or engraver of precious stones
lapin *m.* rabbit
large *m.* open sea; *adj.* wide
laver wash; **se laver** wash oneself
le, la, les (*definite article*) the; (*personal
  pron.*) him; her; it; them
leçon *f.* lesson; **leçon de danse** dancing
  lesson
lecteur *m.* reader
lecture *f.* reading
léger (*f.* **légère**) light; slight
lendemain *m.* next day; **le lendemain
  matin** the next morning
lent slow
lentement slowly
lequel (*f.* **laquelle**) (*interrog.*) which;
  which one; (*rel.*) whom; which
lettre *f.* letter; **faire une lettre** write a
  letter
leur (*pron.*) them, to them; (*adj.*) their;
  le leur, etc. theirs
lever (*irr. sp.* **D**) raise; lift; **se lever** get up
lèvre *f.* lip
lézard *m.* lizard
libérer free, liberate
liberté *f.* freedom
libraire *m.* bookseller
libre free; open
librement freely
lier link; tie; **se lier avec** form a friendship with
lieu *m.* place; spot; **s'il y a lieu** if
  necessary; **au lieu de** instead; **avoir
  lieu** take place
ligne *f.* line; **pilote de ligne** commercial
  air pilot
limite *f.* limit; threshold; **à la limite de
  la nuit** at nightfall
linge *m.* dirty clothes; linen; laundry
lire (**lisant, lu, je lis, je lus**) read

Irregular verbs are conjugated on pp. 284–301.

lisant (*pres. part. of* **lire**) reading
lisse smooth
lit *m.* bed
litre *m.* about 1.06 liquid quarts
livre *m.* book; *f.* pound
loge *f.* semi-public room at entrance of French *lycée* which adjoins the apartment of the *concierge*
loi *f.* law
loin far; **de loin** by far
lointain distant
Loire *f.* river in central France
Londres *m.* London
long (*f.* **longue**) long; **le long de** along
longuement at length
louer rent; reserve (a seat)
Louisiane *f.* Louisiana
loup *m.* wolf
lu, lus (*pp and sp of* **lire**) read
lucide lucid; clear
lui him, to him; to her; it, to it; **bien à lui** typical, characteristic; **lui parti** once he had gone (*lit.* he having left)
lumière *f.* light; **mettre en lumière** throw light on
lundi *m.* Monday
lune *f.* moon; **clair de lune** *m.* moonlight
lutte *f.* wrestling; struggle
luxe *m.* luxury
Lybie *f.* Lybia
lycée *m.* French secondary school equivalent to American high school and junior college
lyrique lyrical
lyrisme *m.* lyricism

M

machinalement mechanically
machine *f.* machine; **machine à écrire** typewriter; **taper à la machine** typewrite
madeleine *f.* a small cupcake; a small sponge-cake
magasin *m.* store
magicien *m.* magician
magnésien (*f.* **magnésienne**) with magnesia
magnétophone *m.* tape recorder
magnifique magnificent

maigre very thin, skinny; low (salary)
maigrir get thin
main *f.* hand; **porter la main à** put one's hand on; **se tenir par la main** hold hands
maintenant now
maire *m.* mayor
mais but; **mais non** why no; **mais oui** certainly; why yes
maïs *m.* corn
maison *f.* house; home; **maison de campagne** country home
maître *m.* teacher; master; leader; title given to lawyers
maîtriser control; master
majorité *f.* majority
mal *m.* evil; (*adv.*) badly; not well; **avoir mal** be sore; ache; **avoir mal au cœur** feel nauseated; **avoir mal à la tête** have a headache; **avoir un terrible mal de tête** have a terrible headache; **finir mal** end up badly; **mal élevé** ill-bred; **se sentir mal** feel sick; **se trouver mal** faint
malade *m. or f.* patient; sick person; (*adj.*) sick; **tomber malade** get sick
maladie *f.* sickness
maladroitement clumsily, awkwardly
malaise *m.* uneasiness; discomfort
malgré in spite of; **malgré lui** in spite of himself
malheureux (*f.* **malheureuse**) unhappy
manche *f.* sleeve
manger (*irr. sp.* **B**) eat
manie *f.* mania
manifeste obvious
manquer (*p.* 106) miss; lack
manteau *m.* overcoat
manuscrit *m.* manuscript
marchand *m.* merchant; storekeeper
marche *f.* walking; progress
marcher walk; run
mardi *m.* Tuesday
marée *f.* tide; flood
mari *m.* husband
mariage *m.* wedding; marriage
marier (*person* + **à** + *person*) marry; **se marier** (**avec** + *person*) marry; get married
Maroc *m.* Morocco
marquer mark; measure; indicate

Verbs with spelling changes are explained on pp. 302–304.

Mars Mars
mars March
Marseille *f.* Marseilles
massif (*f.* **massive**) massive; large and heavy
match *m.* game
mathématiques *f. pl.* mathematics
matin *m.* morning
Mauresque *f.* Moorish woman
mauvais bad
me me, to me
mécanicien *m.* mechanic
méchant mean, vicious; bad; naughty
médecin *m.* doctor
Méditerranée *f.* Mediterranean
méditerranéen (*f.* **méditerranéenne**) Mediterranean
méfier (se) (de + *n.*) mistrust; distrust
meilleur better; best; **meilleur marché** cheaper; **de meilleure heure** earlier
mélancolique melancholy
mélange *m.* mixture
mélanger (*irr. sp.* **B**) mix
mêlé mixed; involved in
mêler mix; **se mêler** be mixed; be blended; make oneself a part
même self; same; even; itself; mere; very; **quand même** even so, just the same; **tout de même** all the same; exactly as, just as
mémoire *f.* memory
mémoires *m. pl.* memoirs
menace *f.* threat
menacer (*irr. sp.* **A**) (de + *inf.*) threaten
ménage *m.* household; housework; **femme de ménage** *f.* cleaning woman
mener (*irr. sp.* **D**) lead, take (a person)
mensonge *m.* lie
menu small, tiny
menuisier *m.* carpenter
mer *f.* sea; **revenir de la mer** come back from the seaside
mercredi *m.* Wednesday
mère *f.* mother
mériter deserve
merveilleux *m.* marvelous quality; **ouvert à son merveilleux** aware of its marvelous qualities
merveilleux (*f.* **merveilleuse**) marvelous
messieurs (*pl. of* **monsieur**) gentlemen

mesure *f.* measure; **à mesure que** as; **au fur et à mesure** gradually
mesurer measure; look over
méthodique methodical
métier *m.* trade; type of work
mètre *m.* meter (39.37) inches)
métro (*abbreviation for* **métropolitain**) *m.* subway
mettre (**mettant, mis, je mets, je mis**) put, put on; **mettre à la poste** mail; **mettre en lumière** throw light on; **mettre en œuvre** apply; illustrate; **mettre la table** set the table; **se mettre** become; **se mettre à** begin; **se mettre au travail** set oneself to work; se **mettre en colère** get angry; **se mettre en quête** set out in search of
meuble *m.* (piece of) furniture
meubler furnish
Mexique *m.* Mexico
midi *m.* noon
miel *m.* honey
miette *f.* crumb
mieux better; best; **faire de son mieux** do one's best
milieu *m.* middle
milieu mondain high society
militaire *m.* soldier; (*adj.*) **militaire** military
militant militant
mille thousand
millier *m.* thousand
mimique *f.* mimic
mine *f.* looks, appearance
ministre *m.* minister
minute *f.* minute; **une minute** just a minute
minutie *f.* attention to minute detail
mis (*pp and sp of* **mettre**) put
Misanthrope, Le *The Misanthrope*, a play by Molière (1666)
misérable *m. or f.* scoundrel; unfortunate person
mode *f.* fashion; style
moderato (Italian) moderate; **moderato cantabile** musical term meaning that the piece is to be melodious and moderately paced
modéré moderate; subdued
moderne modern
modifier modify

Irregular verbs are conjugated on pp. 284–301.

moi me, to me; self; I

moindre least; slightest

moins less; **de moins en moins** less and less; **du moins** at least; **à moins que** (+ *subjunc.*) unless

moite damp, moist

Molière (1622–1673) French dramatist, writer of comedies

molle (*f. of* **mou**) soft; weak

mollet *m.* calf of the leg

moment *m.* moment; time; **ce n'est pas le moment** it isn't the proper time; **d'un moment à l'autre** from one minute to the next, at any time

monarque *m.* monarch

mondain fashionable; **milieu mondain** high society

monde *m.* world; people; **tout le monde** everybody

monsieur *m.* (*pl.* **messieurs**) sir, Mr.; gentleman

mont *m.* small mountain

Mont Blanc *m.* highest peak of the French Alps

montagne *f.* mountain

montée *f.* rise

monter go up; go up to; rise; climb; bring up; **monter dans une chambre** go to a room; **monter dans un train** get on a train

montre *f.* watch

montrer show; **se montrer** appear

moquer (**se**) (**de** + *n.*) make fun of; not care about

morceau *m.* piece

mordant *m.* pungency, sharpness

mordre bite

morne gloomy; drag

mort (*pp of* **mourir**) died; dead

mort *f.* death

mortel (*f.* **mortelle**) mortal

Moscou Moscow

mot *m.* word; **encore un mot** one more word; **jeu de mots** play on words, pun; **mots croisés** crossword puzzle; **mot de passe,** password

moto *f.* motorcycle; **en moto** on a motorcycle

motocyclette *f.* motorcycle

mou (*before vowel sound* **mol**; *f.* **molle**) weak; soft

moucher (**se**) blow one's nose

mouillé wet

mouiller wet, moisten; **se mouiller** get wet

mouler mold

moulu (*pp of* **mouler**) molded

mourir (**mourant, mort, je meurs, je mourus**) die

mouvement *m.* movement; **rentrer en mouvement** be on the move again

moyen *m.* means; way

m'sieur (*colloquial for* **monsieur**) sir; Mr.

muet (*f.* **muette**) silent

mur *m.* wall

musée *m.* museum

musicalité *f.* musical quality

musique *f.* music; **faire de la musique** play music

mystérieux (*f.* **mystérieuse**) mysterious

mythe *m.* myth

N

nager (*irr. sp.* **B**) swim

naïf (*f.* **naïve**) naïve

narrateur *m.* narrator

natif (*f.* **native**) native

nationalité *f.* nationality

natte *f.* braid of hair; pigtail

naturellement naturally

né (*pp of* **naître**) born

négatif *m.* negative

négliger (*irr. sp.* **B**) neglect

neige *f.* snow; **se battre à coups de boules de neige** have a snowball fight

neiger (*irr. sp.* **B**) snow

nerveusement nervously

netteté *f.* sharpness; clearness

nettoyage *m.* cleaning; **faire un grand nettoyage** do a thorough cleaning

nettoyer (*irr. sp.* **C**) clean

neuf nine

neuf (*f.* **neuve**) new

neutre neutral; impersonal

neuve (*f. of* **neuf**) new

neveu *m.* nephew

nez *m.* nose; **il saignait du nez** his nose was bleeding

ni neither; **ni... ni** neither ... nor

noblesse *f.* nobility; nobleness

Noël *m.* Christmas

Verbs with spelling changes are explained on pp. 302–304.

noir *m.* dark; darkness; night; (*adj.*) black

noircir blacken

nom *m.* name

nombreux (*f.* **nombreuse**) many; numerous; **famille nombreuse** large family

nord *m.* north

Normandie *f.* Normandy, a province in northwestern France

Norvège *f.* Norway

nos (*pl. of* **notre**) our

nostalgie *f.* nostalgia; longing

notaire *m.* notary

note *f.* check; grade; note

noter note; notice

notion *f.* idea; notion

notre (*possessive adj.*) our

nôtre (*possessive pron.*) ours

nourrissant nourishing

nourriture *f.* food

nouveau (*before vowel sound* **nouvel**; *f.* **nouvelle**) new; **à nouveau** again; **de nouveau** again, once more; **nouveau roman** school of writers, who, from 1950 on, searched for completely new forms for the novel

nouvel, nouvelle (*m. and f. of* **nouveau**) new

nouvelle *f.* a piece of news; **les nouvelles** *f. pl.* news; **nous avons de ses nouvelles** we've heard from him

Nouvelle-Orléans, la *f.* New Orleans

nu bare

nuage *m.* cloud

nuit *f.* night

nul (*pron.*) no one

nylon *m.* nylon

O

obéir (**à** + *n.*) obey

obéissant obedient

objet *m.* object

obligatoire compulsory

obliger (*irr. sp.* **B**) force; oblige

observation *f.* remark; observation

observer watch; observe

occasion *f.* opportunity

occupé busy

occuper (**s'**) (**de** + *n.*) take care of; turn one's attention to; take charge of; busy oneself with

odeur *f.* odor, smell

œil *m. sing.* (*m. pl.* **yeux**) eye; **coup d'œil** glance

œillet *m.* carnation

œuf *m.* egg

œuvre *f.* work; **mettre en œuvre** make use of

offenser offend

officier *m.* officer

offre *f.* offer

offrir (*conj. like* **ouvrir**) offer

oiseau *m.* bird; **oiseau de mer** sea bird

oisif (*f.* **oisive**) idle

olivier *m.* olive tree

ombrageux (*f.* **ombrageuse**) easily offended

ombre *f.* shade; shadow

omnibus *m.* local train; **les trains omnibus** local trains, that is, those which stop at every station. In Spain they are called *correos*

on (*indefinite pron.*) one; we; you; they; people

oncle *m.* uncle

ondulation *f.* ripple; wave

ongle *m.* nail

onirique dreamlike

opéra *m.* opera; opera house

opérer operate; work

opinion *f.* opinion, view

opposé opposite

or *m.* gold

oralement orally

oranger *m.* orange tree

ordinateur *m.* computer

ordonner (**à** + *person* + **de** + *inf.*) order

ordre *m.* order; **à vos ordres** at your orders

oreille *f.* ear

organiser organize; plan; utilize

orgueil *m.* pride

original original; odd, strange, eccentric

Orléans French city on Loire between Paris and Tours

oser (+ *inf.*) dare

où where; in which; when; **au moment où** at the time when; **où que** wherever

oublier (**de** + *inf.*) forget

Irregular verbs are conjugated on pp. 284–301

ouf! phew! (with a sigh of relief)
oui yes; **mais oui** certainly; why yes
ours [urs] *m.* bear
outre besides, in addition to
outre-tombe beyond the grave
ouvert open; exposed to; aware; **ouvert à son merveilleux** aware of its marvelous qualities
ouverture *f.* opening
ouvrage *m.* work
ouvrier *m.* worker, workingman
ouvrir (**ouvrant, ouvert, j'ouvre, j'ouvris**) open; **s'ouvrir** lay open one's heart; get open
ovale oval

P

paie, paient (**payer**) pay
paille *f.* straw
pain *m.* bread
paix *f.* peace
palais *m.* palate; palace; **palais de justice** courthouse
pâle pale
pâleur *f.* paleness
panier *m.* basket
panne *f.* breakdown; **panne d'électricité** power failure
papier *m.* paper
paquet *m.* package
par through; by; with; for; per; **par ce temps** in such weather; **par jour** per day, each day
paragraphe *m.* paragraph
paraître (*conj. like* **connaître**) look, seem; appear
parallèlement parallel
parcourir (*conj. like* **courir**) travel; go through
pardonner (**à** + *person* + **de** + *inf.*) pardon; forgive
pareil (*f.* **pareille**) same, identical; such a
pareillement similarly
parent *m.* parent; relative
parenthèse *f.* parenthesis
parfaitement perfectly
parfois sometimes
parfum *m.* perfume
Parisien *m.* Parisian

parler (**à** + *person;* **de** + *n.*) speak; talk
parmi among
parole *f.* (spoken) word
part *f.* part; **à part** except; **de ma part** for me, in my behalf
partager (*irr. sp.* **B**) share
parti *m.* party; **prendre le parti de** side with
participe *m.* participle
participer participate, take part
particulier (*f.* **particulière**) particular; peculiar; **rien de particulier** nothing particular
particulièrement particularly
partie *f.* part; **faire partie de** belong to, be a part of
partir (2) leave; go away; depart; **lui parti** once he had left (*lit.* he having left); **à partir de demain** from tomorrow on
partition *f.* (musical) score
paru, parus (*pp and sp of* **paraître**) seemed, looked, appeared
pas *m.* step; footstep; gait; **pas à pas** step by step; **s'attacher aux pas** follow closely
passage *m.* passage; passing
passant *m.* passer-by
passé *m.* past; **passé composé** compound past; (*adj.*) past
passeport *m.* passport
passer pass; pass by; give; spend (time); advance; **j'ai passé par là** I've gone through that; **passer** (**à** + *inf.*) spend time; **passer un examen** take an examination; **se passer** happen; take place; be done; **il se passe quelque chose** something is happening; **se passer de** do without
passif (*f.* **passive**) passive
passionnant fascinating
passionnel (*f.* **passionnelle**) of love; of passion; **drame passionnel** drama of passion
pasteur *m.* minister (in church)
Pasteur, Louis (1822–1895) French scientist
Patagonie *f.* Patagonia, region in the southern part of South America
patron *m.* boss
patte *f.* paw; foot

Verbs with spelling changes are explained on pp. 302–304.

paupière *f.* eyelid; **battre les paupières** blink

pauvre *m.* poor man; (*adj.*) poor

payer (*irr. sp.* **C**) pay; pay for

pays *m.* country

paysage *m.* countryside; landscape

peau *f.* skin

pêche *f.* fishing

peindre (**peignant, peint, je peins, je peignis**) paint; portray

peine *f.* trouble; difficulty; pain; grief; **à peine** slightly, scarcely; not very; **cela me fait de la peine** I am sorry; **valoir la peine** be worthwhile

peint (*pp of* **peindre**) painted

peintre *m.* painter

peinture *f.* painting; portrayal

pelouse *f.* lawn

pendant during; **pendant que** while

pendule *f.* clock

pénétrer fill

penser (**à** + *n.*) think; think of; believe; (+ *inf.*) intend; (**à** + *inf.*) consider; (**de** + *n.*) have an opinion of

pension *f.* boarding house; boarding school

pensionnaire *m. or f.* boarder

pente *f.* slope

perdre lose

père *m.* father

période *f.* period; **faire une période militaire** do a short tour of military duty

périodiquement periodically

permettre (*conj. like* **mettre**) (**à** + *person* + **de** + *inf.*) permit, allow

permis *m.* license; **permis de conduire** driver's license

Pérou *m.* Peru

perron *m.* porch

personnage *m.* character (in a literary work)

personne *f.* person

personne no one, nobody; **ne . . . personne** no one, nobody

perspective *f.* prospect

peser (*irr. sp.* **D**) weigh; **peser lourd** be heavy; be important

peseta *f.* Spanish monetary unit worth about 1½¢

petit *m.* baby; little boy; (*adj.*) small, little; **petit employé** minor office

clerk; **un petit cognac** a small glass of brandy; **petits pois** *m. pl.* peas

petit-fils *m.* grandson

peu little; **à peu près** about, approximately; **un peu** a little, a bit; **peu fréquenté** not very often visited

peuple *m.* people; masses

peur *f.* fear; **avoir peur** be afraid; **de peur** for fear; **faire peur** scare

peut, peuvent, peux (**pouvoir**) can

pharmacien *m.* druggist; pharmacist

philologue *m. or f.* philologist

philosophie *f.* philosophy; **faire sa philosophie** study philosophy, carry on one's studies in philosophy

philosophique philosophical

photo *f.* photograph; snapshot

photographier photograph

phrase *f.* sentence

physiologie *f.* physiology

physique physical

pianiste *m. or f.* pianist

piano *m.* piano

pièce *f.* play; room

pied *m.* foot

piège *m.* trap

pierre *f.* stone

Pierrot (*diminutive of* **Pierre**) little Peter

pilote *m.* pilot; **pilote de guerre** military pilot; **pilote de ligne** commercial air pilot

pilule *f.* pill

pionnier *m.* pioneer

pire (*comparative of* **mauvais**) worse

pisciculture *f.* pisciculture (fish raising)

piscine *f.* swimming pool

place *f.* seat; public square; place (space); spot; job; **sur place** on the spot

placer (*irr. sp.* **A**) place; find a home for

plage *f.* beach

plaindre (*conj. like* **craindre**) pity; feel sorry for; **se plaindre** (**de** + *n.*) complain

plaire (**plaisant, plu, je plais, je plus**) (**à** + *person*) please

plaisanter joke

plaisir *m.* pleasure; **faire plaisir à** please, give pleasure to

plaît (*pres. of* **plaire**) pleases: **s'il vous plaît** please; **si ça vous plaît** if you wish

Irregular verbs are conjugated on pp. 284–301.

plan *m.* plan; map (of a city)
planète *f.* planet
plante *f.* plant
planter plant
plat flat; **à plat ventre** on one's stomach
plein full; **en plein exotisme** in the middle of an exotic land; **en pleine poitrine** right in the chest, in the middle of the chest
pleurer cry
pleut (*pres. of* **pleuvoir**) it is raining; it rains
pleuvoir (**pleuvant, plu, il pleut, il plut**) rain
plonger (*irr. sp.* **B**) plunge
plu, plut (*pp and sp of* **pleuvoir**) rained
plu, plus (*pp and sp of* **plaire**) pleased
pluie *f.* rain
plupart *f.* majority
pluriel *m.* plural
plus more; most; **de plus en plus** more and more; **ne...plus** no more; no longer; **non plus** either; neither; not ...either
plusieurs several
plutôt rather
poche *f.* pocket
poème *m.* poem
poids *m.* weight
poignant gripping
point *m.* point; period; **point de vue** point of view; **être sur le point de** be about to; (*adv.*) **ne...point** not at all
pointu sharp
poire *f.* pear
pois *m.* pea; **petits pois** *m. pl.* peas
poisson *m.* fish
poitrine *f.* chest; **en pleine poitrine** right in the chest, in the middle of the chest
poli polite
policier *m.* policeman; **roman policier** *m.* detective story
politique *f.* politics
polonais Polish
pomme *f.* apple; **pomme de terre** potato
pommier *m.* apple tree
Pompéi Pompeii
pompeux (*f.* **pompeuse**) pompous
ponctuer punctuate; emphasize
pont *m.* bridge

populaire popular; well liked by the masses
population *f.* people
port *m.* seaport; port
Port-Bou the first Spanish seaport when one crosses the French-Spanish border at the eastern extremity of Spain, directly opposite Cerbère
porte *f.* door; doorway; **porte de derrière** back door; **prendre la porte** get out
portefeuille *m.* billfold
porte-monnaie *m.* pocket book
porte-plume *m.* penholder; pen
porter carry; bear; lift; raise; wear; **porter la main à** put one's hand on; **de ne porter aucun bijou** for not wearing any jewelry
portrait *m.* picture, portrait
portugais Portuguese
Portugal *m.* Portugal
posé resting
poser put; pose; put down; rest; **poser une question** ask a question; **un problème se pose** a problem presents itself
possible possible; **dès que possible** as soon as possible
poste *m.* position, job
poste *f.* post office; **mettre à la poste** mail
poudre *f.* powder
poulet *m.* chicken
poupée *f.* doll
pour for; in order to; **pour que** in order that
pourchasser pursue
pourquoi why
pourrai, pourrais (*fut. and cond. of* **pouvoir**) will be able to; would be able to
poursuivre (*conj. like* **suivre**) continue; pursue
pourtant however; yet
pourvu que provided that
pousser push; **pousser un cri** utter a cry
poussière *f.* dust
pouvoir (**pouvant, pu, je peux, je pus**) (+ *inf.*) can, be able to; may; **il se peut** it is possible; **puis-je** can I; may I; **sauve qui peut!** look out! run for your life!
pouvoir *m.* power

Verbs with spelling changes are explained on pp. 302–304.

pratiquant practicing

préalable: au préalable to begin with

précieux (*f.* **précieuse**) precious; exquisitely finished

précipité hasty

précipiter (**se**) rush

préféré favorite

préférence *f.* preference; **de préférence** preferably

préférer (*irr. sp.* **F**) prefer

premier (*f.* **première**) first; prime

prendre (**prenant, pris, je prends, je pris**) (+ *thing* + **à** [*from*] + *person*) take; have; catch; **prendre une décision** make a decision; **prendre le deuil** go into mourning; **prendre le parti de** side with; **prendre la porte** leave the room; get out; **prendre sa source** (of river) begin; **prendre ses responsabilités** assume some responsibility; **prendre un verre** have a drink

préparatif *m.* preparation

préparer prepare

près (**de** + *n.*) near; **à peu près** about, approximately

présent *m.* gift; (*adj.*) present

présenter (*person* + **à** + *person*) introduce

presque almost

presser press; weigh; rush; **se presser** crowd; peer

prêt (**à** + *inf.*) ready

prétendre claim

prêter lend

prévenir (*conj. like* **venir**) warn; inform; let someone know; call (the doctor)

prévoir (*conj. like* **voir** *except in fut. and conditional*) foresee

prier (*person* + **de** + *inf.*) pray; ask; beg; **je vous prie** please

printemps *m.* spring

pris (*pp and sp of* **prendre**) taken; took

prisonnier *m.* prisoner

priver (**de** + *n.*) deprive

prix *m.* price; prize

problème *m.* problem; **poser un problème** present a problem

procédé *m.* process

prochain next

proche near

producteur *m.* producer

produire (*conj. like* **conduire**) produce; create

produit *m.* product

professeur *m.* professor; teacher

profil *m.* profile; side; **de profil** in profile

profiler (**se**) be outlined

profiter (**de** + *n.*) take advantage of

profond deep

profondeur *f.* depth

programme *m.* program

progrès *m.* progress

progresser progress, advance

proie *f.* prey

projet *m.* plan; project

prolonger (**se**) (*irr. sp.* **B**) last

promenade *f.* walk; **faire une promenade** take a walk

promener (**se**) (*irr. sp.* **D**) take a walk

promeneur *m.* stroller

promettre (*conj. like* **mettre**) (**à** + *person* + **de** + *inf.*) promise

promis (*pp and sp of* **promettre**) promised

pronom *m.* pronoun

prononcer (*irr. sp.* **A**) pronounce

propos *m.* remark; **à propos de** concerning

proposer propose; suggest

proposition *f.* proposition; proposal

propriétaire *m. or f.* owner; landlord, landlady

protestant *m.* protestant

protestation *f.* protest

prouver prove

Provence *f.* a region of southern France

provoquer challenge; set into motion

prudence *f.* prudence, care

prudent cautious; prudent

psychanalyse *f.* psychoanalysis

psychologique psychological

pu, pus (*pp and sp of* **pouvoir**) could, was able

public *m.* audience

publier publish

puis then

puis, puisse (*pres. indic. and pres. subjunc. of* **pouvoir**) can, am able; may

puissant powerful; all-powerful, overwhelming

pull-over *m.* sweater

punir punish

Irregular verbs are conjugated on pp. 284–301.

pur pure
purger (*irr. sp.* **B**) purge
Pyrénées *f. pl.* Pyrenees

Q

quadrillé ruled in squares
quai *m.* wharf; quai; bank
quand when; **quand même** just the same, even so
quant à as for
quarante forty
quart *m.* quarter
quartier *m.* district
quartz *m.* quartz, a type of crystallized stone
quatorze fourteen
quatre four
que that; which; what; whom; how; when; **qu'on est bien!** how comfortable one is!
quel (*f.* **quelle**) which; what; **quel que soit** whatever is
quelconque some sort of
quelque some
quelque chose something
quelqu'un someone
quereller (**se**) (*irr. sp.* **F**) quarrel
question *f.* question; **poser une question** ask a question
questionner question; inquire
quête *f.* quest; **se mettre en quête** set out in quest of something
qui who; whom; that; which; **à qui le dites-vous!** you're telling me! **qui que ce soit** whoever he is
quinze fifteen
quitter (+ *n.*) leave; **ne pas quitter quelqu'un des yeux** not to take one's eyes off someone
quoi what; **de quoi** the money; the wherewithall; **n'importe quoi** anything, anything whatever; **quoi que** whatever; **quoi qu'il en soit** however that may be, however the case may be
quoique although

R

raconter tell
radio *f.* radio
Radio-Télévision française French na-

tional radio and television network
rafraîchir refresh
rage *f.* rabies
rainuré grooved
raison *f.* reason; **à plus forte raison** all the more
raisonnable reasonable
raisonner (**se**) reason with oneself; try to be reasonable
ramener (*irr. sp.* **D**) bring back
rang *m.* row; **au premier rang** of the first rank
ranger (*irr. sp.* **B**) put in order; arrange; put away
ranimer (**se**) regain consciousness, come to
rapide fast
rappeler (*irr. sp.* **F**) remind; call back **se rappeler** (+ *n.*) remember
rapport *m.* report
rapporter bring back
rapprocher (**se**) draw near
raser shave; **se raser** shave oneself
rassurant reassuring
rassurer reassure
raviser (**se**) change one's mind
rayon *m.* ray
rebord *m.* edge
recette *f.* recipe
recevoir (**recevant, reçu, je reçois, je reçus**) receive; entertain
réchauffer (**se**) warm oneself
recherché studied; refined; affected
récit *m.* story
récolter harvest
recommander recommend
recommencer (*irr. sp.* **A**) do over; begin again; resume; make a fresh start; **ça recommence** "here we go again"
récompenser reward
reconnaître (*conj. like* **connaître**) recognize
reconsidérer reconsider; take another long look at
recoucher (**se**) go back to bed
rectifier straighten
reçu, reçus (*pp and sp of* **recevoir**) received
recueillir gather
recul *m.* recoil, withdrawal, drawing back; **prendre du recul** withdraw

Verbs with spelling changes are explained on pp. 302–304.

redécouvrir discover again
redemander ask again
redescendre go down again; lower again
rédiger (*irr. sp.* **B**) write; compose
redonner give again
refermer close up
réfléchir think; reflect
refléter (se) (*irr. sp.* **E**) be reflected
réfrigérateur *m.* refrigerator
réfugié *m.* refugee
refuser (de + *inf.*) refuse
regagner regain
regard *m.* look; glance; observation;
  jeter un regard glance
regarder (+ *n.*) look; look at
régime *m.* regime; diet
règlement *m.* rule
régler (*irr. sp.* **E**) settle
réglisse *f.* licorice
régner (*irr. sp.* **E**) reign; exist
regret *m.* regret; grief
régulier (*f.* **régulière**) regular
régulièrement regularly
rejecter (*irr. sp.* **F**) reject
rejoindre (*conj. like* **craindre**) meet
  again; join
relatif (*f.* **relative**) relative
relativité *f.* relativity
relever (*irr. sp.* **D**) call attention to;
  point out
relire (*conj. like* **lire**) read again
relu, relus (*pp and sp of* **relire**) read again
remarier (se) marry again
remarquable remarkable
remarque *f.* remark
remarquer notice
rembourser pay back
remède *m.* remedy; medicine
remercier (*person* + **de** *or* **pour** + *thing;*
  person + **de** + *inf.*) thank
remettre (*conj. like* **mettre**) put back on
  again; hand in; turn in; put back;
  postpone
remis (*pp and sp of* **remettre**) put back
  on; handed in; postponed
remonter go up; go up again; raise
  again; **remonter la rue** go up the
  street
remplacer (*irr. sp.* **A**) replace
remplir fill; fill up; fill out; fulfill
renard *m.* fox
rencontrer meet (by chance)

rendez-vous *m.* date; appointment
rendormir (se) (2) go back to sleep
rendre return (something); (+ *adj.*)
  make; **rendre étranger** alienate; **se**
  rendre go; **se rendre compte** realize;
  se rendre malade make oneself sick
rêne *f.* rein
renifler sniff
renommé famous
renoncer (*irr. sp.* **A**) give up; renounce
renseignement *m.* information
renseigner give information; **se ren-**
  seigner ask for information: get information, inform oneself
rentrer return; come back home; go
  back home; come back in
renverser overthrow; tip over
renvoyer (*conj. like* **envoyer**) dismiss
répandre spread; **se répandre** spread
  out
répandu common
réparation *f.* repair
réparer repair, fix
repas *m.* meal
répéter (*irr. sp.* **E**) repeat
replonger (*irr. sp.* **B**) plunge again
répondre (à + *n.*) answer, reply to
reposer (se) rest
repousser push aside; push back
reprendre (*conj. like* **prendre**) resume;
  take again; regain; continue
représentation *f.* show; performance
repris (*pp and sp of* **reprendre**) resumed;
  regained; continued
république *f.* republic
réputé famous; well known
réserver reserve; make a reservation
résister (à + *n.*) resist
respirer breathe; take a breath; feel
  relieved
responsabilité *f.* responsibility; **prendre**
  ses responsabilités assume some responsibility
ressembler (à + *n.*) look like, resemble
ressource *f.* resource
ressusciter resuscitate; come to life again
reste *m.* remainder; **ne pas être en**
  reste be equal to the situation; not be
  backward
rester remain; stay; stand; **il me reste à**
  I'll have to; **il ne me reste rien** I have
  nothing left

Irregular verbs are conjugated on pp. 284–301.

résultat *m.* result

retard *m.* delay; **avoir du retard** be late; **être en retard** be late

retarder delay

retéléphoner telephone again

retenir (*conj. like* **tenir**) reserve

retirer (**se**) withdraw

retour *m.* return; **à ton retour** when you return

retourner return, go back; turn again; **se retourner** turn around; look back **s'en retourner** go back

retraite *f.* retreat; **prendre sa retraite** retire

retraverser cross again

retrouver find; discover; find once more; **j'ai retrouvé le calme** peace came over me again

réunion *f.* meeting

réussi successful

réussir (**à** + *n.*; **à** + *inf.*) succeed

revanche *f.* revenge; **en revanche** on the other hand

réveiller awaken; **se réveiller** wake up

révélateur (*f.* révélatrice) revealing

révéler (*irr. sp.* **E**) reveal; discover

revenir (*conj. like* **venir**) return; come back

revenu *m.* income

rêver (**de** + *n.*; **de** + *inf.*) dream

rêveur *m.* dreamer

reviendrai, reviendrais (*fut. and cond. of* **revenir**) will, would come back

revivre (*conj. like* **vivre**) live again; relive; come back to life

revoir (*conj. like* **voir**) see again; **se revoir** meet again; **au revoir** goodbye

revue *f.* magazine

rez-de-chaussée *m.* ground floor, first floor

Rhin *m.* Rhine

Rhône *m.* Rhone, a river whose source is in Switzerland, and which flows through France, and empties into the Mediterranean near Marseilles

rhume *m.* cold

ri, rit (*pp, pres., sp of* **rire**) laughed; laughs; laughed

riche rich; **riche de sens** rich in meaning

rideau *m.* curtain

rien nothing; **ne . . . rien** nothing; **servir à rien** be useless

rire (**riant, ri, je ris, je ris**) (**de** + *n.*) laugh; **rire de quelqu'un** make fun of someone

rivière *f.* river; stream; tributary

Robbe-Grillet, Alain (1922–) contemporary French writer

robe *f.* dress

roche *f.* rock

rôle *m.* role; part

roman *m.* novel; **roman policier** detective story; (*adj.*) Romance; **nouveau roman** school of writers who, from 1950 on, searched for completely new forms for the novel

romancier *m.* novelist

rompre break

rond *n.* circle; **tourner en rond** run around in circles; go round and round; (*adj.*) round

rosée *f.* dew

rosier *m.* rosebush

rôti *m.* roast beef; a roast; (*adj.*) roasted

roué sly; crafty

rouge red; **feu rouge** red light; traffic light

rougeole *f.* measles

rouleau *m.* roll

rouler drive; go; roll; move

route *f.* way; road; **en route** on the way; **se tromper de route** take the wrong road

roux (*f.* **rousse**) (referring to hair) red, reddish

ruche *f.* ruche (pleated strip of lace or ribbon); frilling

rue *f.* street

ruine *f.* ruin

ruiner (**se**) ruin oneself

ruisseau *m.* brook

rusé sly; tricky

russe Russian

Russie *f.* Russia

S

sa (*f. of* **son**) his; her; its

sable *m.* sand

sac *m.* bag; handbag

saccadé jerky

sachant (*pres. part. of* **savoir**) knowing

sache, sachiez (*pres. subjunctive of* **savoir**) know

Verbs with spelling changes are explained on pp. 302–304.

sacré sacred
sacrifier (se) sacrifice oneself
sage wise; (speaking of behavior) good, well-behaved
saigner bleed; il saignait du nez his nose was bleeding
Saint-Exupéry, Antoine de (1900–1944) twentieth century French novelist
sais, sait (*pres. of* savoir) know
saisir seize
saison *f.* season; la belle saison the summer months
sale dirty; (*fig.*) "lousy"
salé salted
salle *f.* room (for meetings); salle à manger dining room; salle de séjour living room
salon *m.* drawing room; living room
saluer greet
salut *m.* salute; salvation
samedi *m.* Saturday
San Antonio city of Argentina
sans without; sans doute probably
santé *f.* health
Sartre, Jean-Paul (1905–) famous French existentialist philosopher, playwright and novelist
satellite *m.* satellite
sauce *f.* sauce; gravy
sauf except; but
saurai, saurais (*fut. and cond. of* savoir) will know; would know
sauvage wild
sauver save; sauve qui peut! look out! run for your life!
savant *m.* scientist; (*adj.*) learned; Les Femmes savantes *The Learned Women*, a play by Molière (1672)
savoir (sachant, su, je sais, je sus) know; (+ *inf.*) know how to; savoir bien know very well
savourer enjoy
savoureux (*f.* savoureuse) tasty
scène *f.* scene; stage
scie *f.* saw
science *f.* science; homme de science scientist
scintiller sparkle
sec (*f.* sèche) dry
secondaire secondary
secrétaire *m. or f.* secretary
secrètement secretly

seigneur *m.* lord
sein *m.* breast
Seine *f.* French river which crosses Paris
séjour *m.* stay, sojourn; salle de séjour living room
sel *m.* salt
selon according to
semaine *f.* week
semblable similar
sembler (+ *inf.*) seem
sens [sãs] *m.* way; direct; meaning; riche de sens rich in meaning; dans un sens in a way
sensible sensitive
sensiblement more or less; perceptibly, noticeably
sentiment *m.* feeling; sensation
sentir (2) feel; smell; se sentir feel; se sentir mal feel sick
séparer separate
serai, serais (*fut. and cond. of* être) will be; would be
sérieux (*f.* sérieuse) serious; au sérieux seriously
serpentin snakelike
serrer shake; press; serrer les dents clench one's teeth
serrure *f.* lock
service *m.* service; silverware
serviette *f.* towel; briefcase
servir (2) serve; ne servir à rien be useless; se servir de use; make use of
seul alone; lonely; only; solely; single; être seul à be the only one to
sévère strict
si so; yes; si riches qu'ils soient however rich they are
siamoise *f.* cotton fabric
Sibérie *f.* Siberia
siècle *m.* century
sien (*f.* sienne) his; hers; its
sieste *f.* siesta
siffler whistle
signal (*pl.* signaux) signal
signaler point out
signe *m.* sign
signification *f.* signification, meaning
signifier mean
silence *m.* silence
silencieusement silently
silencieux (*f.* silencieuse) silent
simplement simply

Irregular verbs are conjugated on pp. 284–301.

singulier *m.* singular; (*adj.*) (*f.* **singu-lière**) singular; strange
sinon otherwise
sirène *f.* siren
six six
ski *m.* ski; **faire du ski** go skiing
socialisme *m.* socialism
société *f.* society; firm, company
sœur *f.* sister
soi oneself; **en soi** in itself; **ça va de soi** it goes without saying
soif *f.* thirst; **il a soif** he is thirsty
soigner take care of, care for; treat (a patient)
soigneusement carefully
soin *m.* task
soir *m.* evening
soirée *f.* evening; party
soixante sixty
soldat *m.* soldier
soleil *m.* sun
solidarité *f.* solidarity
sombre dark; **il fait sombre** it is dark
somme *f.* sum (of money)
sommeil *m.* sleep; **avoir sommeil** be sleepy
sommet *m.* peak; top
son, sa, ses his; her; its; one's
songer (*irr. sp.* **B**) think
sonner ring
sonnerie *f.* ring; doorbell
Sorbonne *f.* building which formerly housed the *Faculté des Lettres et des Sciences* of the University of Paris
sort *m.* fate
sorte *f.* sort; **de sorte que** so that, in such a way that
sortie *f.* exit; **à la sortie de l'école** after school
sortilège *m.* magic spell; charm
sortir (2) leave, go out
sot (*f.* **sotte**) foolish; silly
sottement foolishly; sheepishly
sou *m.* penny, cent
souci *m.* worry; care; **se faire du souci** worry
soucoupe *f.* saucer
soudain (*adj.*) sudden; (*adv.*) suddenly
souffrir (*conj. like* **ouvrir**) suffer
souhaiter wish
soulever raise
soulier *m.* shoe

souligner underline
soupçon *m.* suspicion
soupe *f.* soup
souper *m.* supper; evening meal
soupirer sigh
souple supple, pliant
source *f.* source; **prendre sa source** (of a river) begin
sourcil *m.* eyebrow
sourd deaf
souriant smiling
sourire (*conj. like* **rire**) (**à** + *n.*) smile; (*n.*) *m.* smile
souris *f.* mouse
sous-entendu *m.* secret understanding; implication
sous-sol *m.* basement
souvenir (**se**) (*conj. like* **venir**) (**de** + *n.*; **de** + *inf.*) remember; (*n.*) *m.* souvenir; memory; remembrance; recollection; keepsake
souvent often
soyeux (*f.* **soyeuse**) silky
spectacle *m.* show
spectateur *m.* spectator
splendide marvelous
spontané spontaneous
sport *m.* sport; **faire des sports** participate in sports; **journal de sport** sports magazine
sportif (*f.* **sportive**) sport loving; inclined toward sports
squelette *m.* skeleton
stationner park
statistique *f.* statistics
stéréotypé stereotyped
stopper stop
strictement strictly
strié streaked
stupéfait amazed
style *m.* style
stylo *m.* fountain pen
su, sus (*pp and sp of* **savoir**) known; knew; learned, found out
subjonctif *m.* subjunctive
subtil subtle
subtilement subtly
succéder (**à**) take the place of; inherit from
succès *m.* success
succomber succumb; die
sucer (*irr. sp.* **A**) suck

Verbs with spelling changes are explained on pp. 302–304.

sucre *m.* sugar
sucrerie *f.* candy
sud *m.* south
Suède *f.* Sweden
suédois Swedish
suffire (suffisant, suffi, je suffis, je suffis) suffice
suggérer (*irr. sp.* **E**) suggest
suis (*pres. of* **être**) I am; (*pres. of* **suivre**) I, you follow
Suisse *f.* Switzerland
suite *f.* continuation; aftermath, consequence; **à la suite** as a result; **à sa suite** after them, following them; **tout de suite** right now, right away, immediately; in succession
suivant (*adj.*) following; next; (*prep.*) according to
suivre (suivant, suivi, je suis, je suivis) follow; **suivre un cours** take a course
sujet *m.* subject; **au sujet de** about, concerning
superbe superb
superflu superfluous
supermarché *m.* supermarket
supplémentaire supplementary
supportable bearable
supporter put up with, stand for
sur on; out of
sûr sure
sûrement surely
surnaturel (*f.* **surnaturelle**) supernatural
surprenant surprising
surprise *f.* surprise, astonishment
surtout especially; above all; mostly
surveiller watch over; keep an eye on
suspens *m.* suspense; **en suspens** hanging
symbole *m.* symbol
symphonie *f.* symphony
système *m.* system

T

tabac *m.* tobacco; **bureau de tabac** tobacco shop
table *f.* table; **mettre la table** set the table; **table de nuit** night stand
tableau *m.* picture; painting; **tableau noir** blackboard
tache *f.* spot; **une tache de soleil** a bit of sun
tâche *f.* task; duty

tact *m.* tact
taille *f.* height
tailler cut
tandis que while, whereas
tant so much
tante *f.* aunt
taper type, typewrite; **taper à la machine** typewrite
tapis *m.* rug
tard late
tarder (**à** + *inf.*) be late; delay, put off
Tardieu, Jean (1903–) contemporary French poet and playwright
tari dried up
tasse *f.* cup
taudis *m.* slum; hovel, shack
taxi *m.* taxi, taxicab, cab
technique *f.* technique
téléphoner (**à** + *person*) telephone
télévision *f.* television; television set
tellement so; so much
témoignage *m.* testimony
témoigner show; witness
tempe *f.* temple (part of body)
temps *m.* time; weather; tense; **en même temps** at the same time; **il est grand temps** it is high time; **par ce temps** in this weather; **le temps de** long enough to
tendance *f.* tendency
tendre (*v.*) hold out; extend; give; stretch; **tendre la main** hold out one's hand; (*adj.*) tender
tendresse *f.* tenderness
tenez look here!
tenir (tenant, tenu, je tiens, je tins) hold; keep; **tenir à** insist on; be eager to; **tenir de** inherit from; **tenir ferme** hold fast; **se tenir** be; stand; **se tenir par la main** hold hands
tenue *f.* uniform
terminer finish
terrain *m.* ground; land; tract of land; field
terre *f.* earth; land; **pomme de terre** *f.* potato
terreur *f.* terror
testament *m.* will
tête *f.* head; **hocher la tête** nod one's head; **quelle tête** what a stubborn person
thé *m.* tea

Irregular verbs are conjugated on pp. 284–301.

théâtre *m.* theater
théologie *f.* theology
théorie *f.* theory
thèse *f.* thesis; dissertation
tiens look
tigre *m.* tiger
timbre *m.* stamp
timidité *f.* timidity
tire-lire *f.* piggy bank
tirer take out; pull; shoot; pull the trigger; (**sur** + *person*) shoot at
tiret *m.* dash
tiroir *m.* drawer
tituber stagger
toile *f.* linen; **toile cirée** oilcloth
toit *m.* roof
Tolède Toledo, a picturesque walled Spanish town some 50 miles south of Madrid, noted for the El Greco museum
tomber fall; **tomber malade** get sick
ton *m.* tone
tonnerre *m.* thunder; **coup de tonnerre** thunder clap
tôt early; soon
totalement completely
toucher touch
toujours always; still; continually
tour *m.* stroll; trip; trick; turn; **à son tour** in turn; **faire le tour du monde** take a trip around the world
touriste *m.| |f.* tourist; (*adj.*) tourist; for tourists
tourment *m.* torment
tourmenter torment; bother
tournemain *m.* turn of the hand; **en un tournemain** in the twinkling of an eye
tourner turn; **tourner en rond** turn around in circles
Tours French city southwest of Paris in Loire valley
tout (*m. pl.* **tous**) (*adj.*) all, every; whole; **tout le monde** everyone; **tous les samedis** every Saturday
tout (*pron.*) everything; **avant tout** above all; **une fois pour toutes** once and for all; **capable de tout** capable of anything; **tous deux** both
tout (*adv.*) very, quite; **tout à côté** right near; **tout à coup** all of a sudden; **tout à fait** quite, completely; **tout à l'heure** in a little while; a little while

ago; **tout bas** in a whisper; **tout d'abord** first of all; **tout droit** erect; straight ahead; **tout de même** all the same; exactly as, just as; **tout de suite** immediately, right now; **tout en lisant** while reading
traditionnel (*f.* **traditionnelle**) traditional
traduction *f.* translation
traduire (*conj. like* **conduire**) translate
trafiquant *m.* dealer; trafficker
train *m.* train; **en train de** in the act of
traité *m.* treaty
traiter treat
traître *m.* traitor
tranquille quiet, calm; **nous avons été tranquilles** we were in peace
tranquillement calmly
transatlantique *m.* ocean liner
transmettre (*conj. like* **mettre**) transmit
transport *m.* transportation
transporter carry
travail *m.* work; job; **se mettre au travail** set to work
travailleur (*f.* **travailleuse**) hard working; industrious
travers: à travers across; through
traversée *f.* crossing; **traversée en bateau** boat trip
traverser cross
treize thirteen
Trelew city in Argentina
tremblant shivering
trembler shake; tremble
tremper wet; soak; dunk
trente thirty
très very
trésor *m.* treasure
tressaillir start; give a start
tressé braided
trêve *f.* truce; solace
trimestre *m.* trimester; (school) quarter
trinquer clink glasses; toast
triste sad
tristesse *f.* sadness
trois three
tromper deceive; **se tromper de route** take the wrong road
trottoir *m.* sidewalk
trou *m.* hole
troubler trouble; move; **troubler** (**se**) become upset; become embarrassed

Verbs with spelling changes are explained on pp. 302–304.

troupe *f.* flock
trouver find; **comment trouvez-vous** what do you think of; **se trouver** be; be found, be located; lie; **se trouver mal** faint; **se trouver mieux** feel better
tue-tête: à tue-tête at the top of one's voice
tuer kill
Tunisie *f.* Tunisia
tutoyer (*irr. sp.* **C**) use the "tu" form in speaking to someone

U

un a, an; one
uniforme *m.* uniform; (*adj.*) uniform
universel (*f.* **universelle**) universal; versatile and universal
usé worn out
usine *f.* factory
utile useful

V

va (*pres. of* **aller**) goes; **ça va de soi** it goes without saying
vacances *f. pl.* vacation; **cours de vacances** summer courses; **en vacances** on a vacation
vaccin *m.* vaccine
vache *f.* cow
vague *f.* wave
vaille (*pres. subjunc. of* **valoir**) be worth
vaisselle *f.* dishes; **faire la vaisselle** do the dishes
valeur *f.* value
valide valid, good
valise *f.* suitcase; **faire une valise** pack a suitcase
valoir (**valant, valu, je vaux, je valus**) be worth; **il vaut mieux** it is better; **valoir la peine** be worth the trouble; **votre idée ne vaut pas grand-chose** your idea isn't worth much
valve *f.* valve (a half shell)
Vatican *m.* Vatican, papal headquarters in Rome
vaut (*pres. of* **valoir**) is worth
veau *m.* calf; veal
vécu, vécus (*pp and sp of* **vivre**) lived
veille *f.* watch

veiller watch; **veiller sur quelqu'un** watch over someone
velours *m.* velvet
vendeuse *f.* salesgirl; saleswoman
vendre sell
vendredi *m.* Friday
venir (**venant, venu, je viens, je vins**) come; **faire venir** send for; **venez me voir** come and see me; **venir de** have just (**il vient d'arriver** he has just arrived); **il en vint à conclure** he finally concluded
Venise Venice
vent *m.* wind
ventre *m.* belly; abdomen; stomach
verbe *m.* verb
verglas *m.* ice
véritable real
véritablement really; truly
vérité *f.* truth
Verlaine, Paul (1844–1896) French symbolist poet
verni varnished; shiny
verrai, verrais (*fut. and cond. of* **voir**) will see; would see
verre *m.* glass; **prendre un verre** have a drink
vers toward; around; about
vert green
vertu *f.* virtue
vestiaire *m.* cloak room
vétérinaire *m.* veterinary
veut (*pres. of* **vouloir**) wants, wishes
vexer vex; hurt
viande *f.* meat
victorieux (*f.* **victorieuse**) victorious
vider empty
vie *f.* life
vieillard *m.* old man; *m. pl.* old people
vieillir grow old
viens, vient, viennent (*pres. of* **venir**) comes; come
vierge *f.* virgin; (*adj.*) untouched
vieux (*before vowel sound* **vieil**; *f.* **vieille**) old
vif (*f.* **vive**) alert
ville *f.* city; town; **en ville** downtown; **hôtel de ville** city hall
vin *m.* wine
vingt twenty
vingtaine *f.* about twenty

Irregular verbs are conjugated on pp. 284–301.

violent violent; very strong

virtuose *m.* virtuoso

visage *m.* face; **avec des étoiles sur le visage** stars were shining on my face

vision *f.* vision; point of view

visiter visit (a place)

visiteur *m.* visitor

vit (*sp of* **voir**) saw; (*pres. of* **vivre**) lives

vite quick; quickly, fast

vitesse *f.* speed

vitre *f.* window pane

vitrine *f.* store window; show window

vivant living; merry; alive

vivre (**vivant, vécu, je vis, je vécus**) live

voici here is, here are; **et voici que** and now; **voici que** then

voilà there is, there are; here it is; **les voilà** here they come

voir (**voyant, vu, je vois, je vis**) see; notice; **aller voir** go and see; visit; **venez me voir** come and see me; **voir du pays** see places

voisin *m.* neighbor

voiture *f.* car

voix *f.* voice; **à haute voix** aloud; **à trois voix** between three people

vol *m.* flight; theft

volant flying

voler fly; rob

volet *m.* shutter

voleur *m.* thief

volontairement willingly; voluntarily

volonté *f.* will

volontiers willingly; with pleasure

Voltaire (1694–1778) eighteenth century writer of philosophical novels, essays, poems, and plays

vont (*pres. of* **aller**) go

vos (*pl. of* **votre**) your

votre (*pl.* **vos**) your

voudrai, voudrais (*fut. and cond. of* **vouloir**) will want; would like

vouloir (**voulant, voulu, je veux, je voulus**) want; wish; desire; **voulez-vous** will you please; **vouloir bien** be willing; **vouloir dire** mean

vous you; **vous deux** both of you

voyage *m.* trip; **faire un voyage** take a trip

voyager (*irr. sp.* **B**) travel

voyageur *m.* traveller; passenger

voyant (*pres. part. of* **voir**) seeing

voyons (**voir**) we see; come now; look here

vrai true; real

vraiment really; truly

vu (*pp of* **voir**) seen

vue *f.* view; sight

Y

y there; in it

yeux (*m.; pl. of* **œil**) eyes; **jeter les yeux** glance; **quitter quelqu'un des yeux** take one's eyes off someone

Z

zèle *m.* zeal

zoologique zoological; **jardin zoologique** zoo

Verbs with spelling changes are explained on pp. 302–304.

English-French Vocabulary

adj.	adjective	*irr. sp.*	irregular spelling	*pers.*	person
adv.	adverb	*m.*	masculine	*prep.*	preposition
cond.	conditional	*n.*	noun	*pres.*	present
conj.	conjugated	*obj.*	object	*pron.*	pronoun
conjunc.	conjunction	*p.*	page	*rel.*	relative
f.	feminine	*part.*	participle	*sing.*	singular
fut.	future	*pl.*	plural	*sp*	simple past
inf.	infinitive	*pp*	past participle	*subjunc.*	subjunctive
interrog.	interrogative			*v.*	verb

* aspirate *h*   (2) **-ir** verbs which do not insert **-iss-;** all other **-ir** verbs insert **-iss-.**

Page references immediately following the English word refer to explanations of the word in question.

Verbs whose principal parts are given are irregular, and their conjugations may be found on pp. 284–301. The use of the principal parts is explained on page 283. Verbs followed by (*conj. like* . . .) are irregular and follow the pattern of the verb indicated.

Verbs followed by (*irr. sp.* **A** to **F**) undergo a spelling change in certain forms. The letter refers to the appropriate type of change explained on pp. 302–304.

A

a un, une

able capable; be able pouvoir (pouvant, pu, je peux, je pus) (+ *inf.*)

about (p. 236) de; sur; environ; à peu près; vers; au sujet de; à propos de; about that à ce sujet; be about to être sur le point de; talk about parler de; tell about parler de

above (p. 237) sur; au-dessus de

abroad à l'étranger; from abroad de l'étranger

absence absence *f.*; in the absence en l'absence

absent absent

absolutely absolument

accent accent *m.*

accept accepter

accident accident *m.*

according to (p. 237) selon, suivant, d'après

accused (*n.*) accusé *m.*

accustomed: get accustomed to s'habituer (à + *inf.*)

ache (*v.*) faire mal; I have a headache j'ai mal à la tête

acquaintance connaissance *f.;* relation *f.*

across (p. 237) à travers; de l'autre côté de; run across traverser en courant; travel across traverser

act agir

action action *f.*

actress actrice *f.*

actually (p. 10) vraiment, réellement; en fait, à vrai dire

address adresse *f.*

admire admirer

admit admettre (*conj. like* mettre)

adopt adopter

adore adorer

adventure aventure *f.*

advice (p. 10) conseil *m.;* a piece of advice un conseil *m.*

advise conseiller (à + *person* + de + *inf.*); advise against déconseiller

affair affaire *f.*

afraid: be afraid avoir peur, craindre;

became afraid *compound past of* avoir peur, prendre peur; avoir peur

Africa Afrique *f.*

after (pp. 224, 231, 238) après; d'après; after hearing après avoir entendu

afternoon après-midi *m. or f.*

again (pp. 10–11) encore, encore une fois, de nouveau, à nouveau; re- + *verb*

against contre; advise against déconseiller

age âge *m.;* old age vieillesse *f.*, vieux jours *m. pl.*

ago il y a; a little while ago tout à l'heure; a month ago il y a un mois

agree (pp. 11–12) s'accorder; consentir (à + *inf.*); être d'accord

agreed d'accord, c'est entendu, entendu

aim but *m.*

air air *m.;* in the air en l'air

air conditioner climatiseur *m.*

airplane avion *m.*

airport aéroport *m.*

alarm clock réveil *m.*

Alexander Alexandre

all tout (*f.* toute, *m. pl.* tous); all the same quand même; all the while (p. 63) tout en; come out all right finir bien; not at all pas du tout

allow laisser (*person* + *inf.*); permettre (à + *person* + de + *inf.*); I was allowed j'ai pu

almost presque

alone seul; leave me alone laissez-moi tranquille

along (p. 238) le long de; get along se débrouiller; go along the road suivre le chemin

already déjà

although bien que, quoique

always toujours

amateur amateur *m.*

ambassador ambassadeur *m.*

ambitious ambitieux (*f.* ambitieuse)

America Amérique *f.*

American Américain *m.;* South American Sud-Américain *m.*

amuse amuser; amuse oneself s'amuser (à + *inf.*)

Irregular verbs are conjugated on pp. 284–301.

amusing amusant
Andrew André
anger colère *f.*
angry fâché; en colère; vexé; **get angry** se mettre en colère; se fâcher
animal animal *m.*
Anne Anne
anniversary anniversaire *m.*
announcement annonce *f.*
announcer speaker *m.*
annoying ennuyeux (*f.* ennuyeuse)
another encore un(e)
answer (*v.*) répondre (à + *n.*) (*n.*) réponse *f.*
any du, de la, des; quelque; (*obj. pron.*) en; **any at all** pas du tout; **in any case** en tout cas; **not any** pas de, ne . . . aucun; **not any more** ne . . . plus
anyone quelqu'un; **not . . . anyone** ne . . . personne
anything quelque chose; **not . . . anything** ne . . . rien
apartment appartement *m.*
approach approcher (de + *n.*); s'approcher (de + *n.*)
April avril
Arabic (*n.*) arabe *m.*
ardent ardent
are sont; se trouvent; **are to** doivent; **there are** il y a
area région *f.*
aren't you n'est-ce pas
arm bras *m.*
armchair fauteuil *m.*
army armée *f.*
around: get around se déplacer (*irr. sp.* **A**)
arrest arrêter
arrive arriver
art art *m.*
artist artiste *m. or f.*
as (pp. 19, 232) comme; **as . . . as** aussi . . . que; **as for** quant à; **as long as** tant que; **as soon as** dès que
ashamed: be ashamed avoir honte
ask demander (*thing* + à + *person;* à + *person* + de + *inf.*); **ask a question** poser une question; **ask for something** demander quelque chose; **ask of someone** demander à quelqu'un; **he asked my pardon** il m'a demandé pardon

asleep: be asleep dormir (2)
assistant assistant *m.*
astronaut astronaute *m. or f.*
at (pp. 210–211, 239) à; chez; **at length** longuement; **at once** tout de suite; **not at all** pas du tout
Athens Athènes
attend (p. 81) aller à; assister à
attention attention *f.*
attentively attentivement
attitude attitude *f.*
aunt tante *f.*
author auteur *m.*
automatically automatiquement
awaken réveiller; se réveiller
away: right away tout de suite

B

back (*n.*) dos *m.*
back: come back revenir; **come back home** rentrer; **go back** retourner
bad (*n.*) mauvais *m.* (*adj.*) mauvais
ball danse *f.*, bal *m.*
ball (point) pen stylo à bille *m.;* bic, *m.*
Balzac Balzac
bank banque *f.*
barber coiffeur *m.*
bare nu
bark aboyer (*irr. sp.* **C**)
bathe se baigner
be être (étant, été, je suis, je fus); **be able** pouvoir (pouvant, pu, je peux, je pus); **be asleep** dormir (2); **be better** aller mieux; être mieux; valoir mieux; **be bored** s'ennuyer (*irr. sp.* **C**); **be careful!** attention!; **be mistaken** se tromper; **be warm** avoir chaud; **be well** aller bien; **be willing** vouloir bien
beach plage *f.*
beautiful beau (*before vowel sound* bel; *f.* belle)
beauty beauté *f.*
because (p. 233) parce que; **because of** à cause de
become (pp. 24–25, 69) devenir (*conj. like* venir); **become afraid** prendre peur; **become frightened** s'effrayer; **become interested in** s'intéresser à; **it became cold** il a fait froid

Verbs with spelling changes are explained on pp. 302–304.

bed lit *m.*; **go to bed** se coucher

before (pp. 224, 232, 240) (**time**) avant (+ *n. or pron.*), avant de (+ *inf.*), avant que (+ *subjunc.*); (**place**) devant

begin commencer (à + *inf.*) (*irr. sp.* **A**), se mettre (à + *inf.*)

beginning commencement *m.*

believe croire (croyant, cru, je crois, je crus) (+ *inf.;* + *person;* à + *thing;* en + *person* [with the sense of *to have faith in*])

belong appartenir (*conj. like* tenir)

best (*adj.*) meilleur; (*adv.*) mieux

better (pp. 25–26) (*adj.*) meilleur; (*adv.*) mieux; **be better** valoir mieux, être mieux; (referring to health) aller mieux

between entre

big grand

billfold portefeuille *m.*

bird oiseau *m.*

bit: a bit un peu

blame blâmer

blanket couverture *f.*

blue bleu

boat bateau *m.;* **sailboat** bateau à voiles

book livre *m.;* **telephone book** annuaire *m.*

bored ennuyé; **be bored** s'ennuyer (*irr. sp.* **C**)

boring ennuyeux (*f.* ennuyeuse)

born: be born naître (naissant, né, je nais, je naquis); **he was born** il est né

boss patron *m.*

both les deux, tous les deux; **both of you** vous deux

bother déranger (*irr. sp.* **B**); ennuyer (*irr. sp.* **C**)

boy garçon *m.*

brave courageux (*f.* courageuse)

break casser; se casser; **break down** être en panne

bridge (*over river*) pont *m.;* (*game*) bridge *m.*

briefcase serviette *f.*

brilliantly brillamment

bring (p. 26) (*a thing*) apporter; (*a person*) amener (*irr. sp.* **D**)

brother frère *m.;* **brother-in-law** beau-frère *m.;* **oldest brother** aîné *m.*, frère aîné

brush brosser

Brussels Bruxelles

build construire (*conj. like* conduire)

building immeuble *m.;* bâtiment *m.*, édifice *m.*

bus (*within city*) autobus *m.;* (*between cities*) autocar *m.*

business affaire *f.;* les affaires *f. pl.;* **businessman** homme d'affaires *m.;* **talk business** parler affaires, parler des affaires

busy (pp. 64–65) occupé; **be busy** être en train de; **he was busy writing** il était occupé à écrire, il était en train d'écrire

but (p. 233) (*conjunc.*) mais; (*prep.*) sauf, excepté

buy acheter (*irr. sp.* **D**)

by par; de; en; **by falling** en tombant; **by plane** par avion, en avion; **by the time** quand; **go by** passer

C

café café *m.*

call appeler (*irr. sp.* **F**); téléphoner (à + *person*)

can (pp. 26–27) pouvoir (pouvant, pu, je peux, je pus); (*know how*) savoir (sachant, su, je sais, je sus)

Canada Canada *m.*

candidate candidat *m.*

capable capable

car voiture *f.*, auto *f.*, automobile *f.*

care soin *m.*, prudence *f.*

careful: be careful! attention!

carefully attentivement

careless négligent

carnation œillet *m.*

carol: Christmas carol cantique de Noël *m.*

carpenter menuisier *m.*

case cas *m.;* **in any case** en tout cas; **in case of** en cas de

cash (*a check*) toucher (un chèque)

cat chat *m.*

catastrophe catastrophe *f.*

catch attraper; **catch sight of** apercevoir (*conj. like* recevoir)

Catholic catholique

Irregular verbs are conjugated on pp. 284–301.

caught pris
celebrate célébrer
center: shopping center centre commercial *m.*
certain certain
chair chaise *f.*
change (pp. 36–38) (*v.*) (*irr. sp.* **B**) changer; **change one's mind** changer d'avis; (*m.*) changement *m.;* (*small*) **change** monnaie *f.*
character (p. 38) personnage *m.;* caractère *m.*
charge prendre (prenant, pris, je prends, je pris)
charm charme *m.*
charming charmant
chat bavarder
chauffeur chauffeur *m.*
cheap bon marché
check chèque *m.*
chess échecs *m. pl.*
child enfant *m. or f.*
Chinese chinois
Christmas Noël *m.;* **Christmas carol** cantique de Noël *m.*
church église *f.*
cider cidre *m.*
cigaret cigarette *f.*
city ville *f.;* **city hall** hôtel de ville *m.*, mairie *f.*
claim prétendre
class classe *f.;* **conversation class** classe de conversation *f.*
classmate camarade de classe *m. or f.*
cleaner teinturier *m.;* **to the cleaner's** à la teinturerie; chez le teinturier
cleaning woman femme de ménage *f.*
clear évident
clear the table débarrasser la table
climate climat *m.*
clock: alarm clock réveil *m.*
close (*v.*) fermer (*adj.*) proche; **a close friend** un ami intime *m.*
clothes habits *m. pl.;* vêtements *m. pl.*
club club *m.*, cercle *m.*
coat (*overcoat*) manteau *m.;* (*suitcoat*) veste *m.*
coffee café *m.*
cold (*n.*) rhume *m.;* (*adj.*) froid; **it became cold** il a fait froid; **it was cold** il faisait froid

colleague collègue *m. on f.*
collection collection *f.*
colonel colonel *m.*
come venir (venant, venu, je viens, je vins); **come back** revenir (*conj. like* venir); **come back home** rentrer; **come and see me** venez me voir; **come in** entrer; **come to dinner** venir dîner; **come out all right** finir bien
comfortable confortable
company compagnie *f.;* maison *f.;* société *f.*
completely complètement
computer ordinateur *m.*
concern: concern oneself with s'occuper (de + *n.*)
concerning (p. 236) au sujet de; sur; **concerning them** à leur sujet
concert concert *m.*
condemn condamner
condition condition *f.;* **on the condition that** à (la) condition que
conditioner: air conditioner climatiseur *m.*
confess avouer
considerable considérable
contest concours *m.*
continue continuer (à + *inf.*); **continue on our way** continuer notre route
convention congrès *m.*
conversation conversation *f.;* **a conversation class** une class de conversation *f.*
convince convaincre (*conj. like* vaincre)
cook faire la cuisine
cooky biscuit *m.*
copy copier; **copy again** recopier
correct (*v.*) corriger (*irr. sp.* **B**); (*adj.*) exact
corridor corridor *m.;* couloir *m.*
Corsica Corse *f.*
cost prix *m.*
count compter (+ *inf.*)
country pays *m.;* (*opposite of city*) campagne *f.*
courage courage *m.*
course cours *m.;* **take a course** suivre un cours; **course** (*of action*) démarche *f.;* **drop a course** abandonner un cours, laisser tomber un cours
cousin cousin *m.;* cousine *f.*

Verbs with spelling changes are explained on pp. 302–304.

cream crème *f.;* **ice cream** glace *f.*
crime crime *m.*
criminal criminel *m.*
criticize critiquer
cross traverser
crossword puzzle mots croisés *m. pl.*
crowd foule *f.*
cry pleurer
cultured cultivé
curious curieux (*f.* curieuse)
curtain rideau *m.*
cut couper
cute mignon (*f.* mignonne)

D

dance danse *f.;* bal *m.*
danger danger *m.*
dangerous dangereux (*f.* dangereuse)
dark brun; sombre
date rendez-vous *m.*
daughter fille *f.*
dawn aube *f.*
day (pp. 38–39) jour *m.;* journée *f.;* **the day after tomorrow** après-demain; **the next day** le lendemain, le jour suivant, le jour après
daylight jour *m.*
dead mort
deal: a great deal beaucoup
December décembre *m.*
decide décider (de + *inf.*), se décider (à + *inf.*)
decision décision *f.;* **make a decision** prendre une décision
decorator: interior decorator décorateur, *m.;* décoratrice *f.*
deep profond
deep-seated profond
defend défendre
defendant inculpé *m.*
delegate délégué *m.;* déléguée *f.*
delighted enchanté
demanding exigeant
democracy démocratie *f.*
Denmark Danemark *m.*
dentist dentiste *m.* on *f.*
describe décrire (*conj. like* écrire)
desk bureau *m.*
destiny destinée *f.*

detective inspecteur *m.;* **detective story** roman policier *m.*
diamond diamant *m.*
die mourir (mourant, mort, je meurs, je mourus)
difference différence *f.*
different différent
difficult difficile
difficulty difficulté *f.*
dinner dîner *m.;* **come to dinner** venir dîner; **have dinner** dîner
directly directement
director directeur *m.;* directrice *f.*
discuss discuter
discussion discussion *f.*
dishes vaisselle *f. sing.* **wash the dishes** faire la vaisselle
disillusion désillusion *f.*
distance distance *f.;* **in the distance** au loin
distribute distribuer
do faire (faisant, fait, je fais, je fis); **do without** se passer de; **do wrong** faire du tort
doctor docteur *m.*, médecin *m.*
doctorate doctorat *m.*
dog chien *m.*
dollar dollar *m.*
door porte *f.*
dormitory dortoir *m.*, résidence *f.*
doubt douter (de + *n.*)
doubtful douteux (*f.* douteuse)
down (p. 240) en bas; **go down** descendre; **slow down** ralentir
drawer tiroir *m.*
dream rêver (de + *n.;* de + *inf.*)
dress robe *f.*
drink boire (buvant, bu, je bois, je bus)
drive conduire (conduisant, conduit, je conduis, je conduisis)
drop (*a course*) abandonner, laisser tomber
duck canard *m.*
duty devoir *m.*

E

each chacun; **each other** se; l'un l'autre
earlier plus tôt; de meilleure heure
early (p. 52) tôt, de bonne heure; en avance

Irregular verbs are conjugated on pp. 284–301.

earn gagner
ease facilité *f.*
easily facilement
Easter Pâques *m.*
easy facile; **easy-going** indulgent
eat manger (*irr. sp.* **B**)
egg œuf *m.*
Egypt Egypte *f.*
eight huit
either non plus
elbow coude *m.*
election élection *f.*
elegant élégant
else: something else autre chose
elsewhere ailleurs, autre part
emergency urgence *f.*
encourage encourager (*irr. sp.* **B**)
end (pp. 52–53) fin *f.;* bout *m.*
energetically énergiquement
engineer ingénieur *m.*
England Angleterre *f.*
English (*n.*) Anglais *m.; (adj.)* anglais
enough assez
enter entrer (dans + *n.*)
entertaining amusant
erase effacer (*irr. sp.* **A**)
error erreur *f.*, faute *f.*
escape (pp. 53–54) échapper (à + *n.*);
   s'échapper (de + *n.*)
especially surtout
even même; **even though** bien que,
   quoique; tout en (+ *pres. participle*)
evening (pp. 38–39, 135) soir *m.;* soirée
   f.; **evening party** soirée *f.;* **last eve-**
   ning hier soir
event événement *m.*
ever jamais
every (p. 53) chaque; tous les; **every**
   other year tous les deux ans
everyone (p. 53) tout le monde
everything (pp. 54, 127) tout; n'importe
   quoi; **everything that** tout ce qui,
   tout ce que
everywhere partout
evident évident
examination examen *m.*
excellent excellent
except (p. 240) sauf, à part, excepté
exchange (p. 38) échanger (*irr. sp.* **B**)
exercise devoir *m.*, exercice *m.*
exist exister; régner

exotic exotique
expect (pp. 66–67) attendre (+ *n.*);
   s'attendre (à + *n.*); compter (+ *n.*)
   what do you expect que voulez-vous
expensive cher (*f.* chère); **be expensive**
   coûter cher
experience expérience *f.*
explain expliquer
explosion explosion *f.*
exterior extérieur *m.*
extraordinary extraordinaire
eye œil *m.* (*pl.*) yeux

F

face figure *f.*
factory usine *f.*
fail (pp. 67–68) manquer (de + *inf.*);
   échouer (à un examen); coller (quelqu'un)
fair exposition *f.*
fall tomber; **fall out** tomber de
family famille *f.*
famous célèbre, connu
far loin
farmer fermier *m.*
fast rapide; vite
fate sort *m.*
father père *m.*
father-in-law beau-père *m.*
faucet robinet *m.*
favorite préféré
feel (pp. 68–69) sentir; se sentir; **feel**
   well se sentir bien; **How do you feel?**
   Comment allez-vous?
few peu; **a few** quelques
field champ *m.;* domaine *m.*
fifty cinquante
fight se battre (battant, battu, je bats,
   je battis)
fill remplir (de + *n.*)
film film *m.*
finally enfin, finalement
find trouver; **find again** retrouver; **find**
   out découvrir (*conj. like* ouvrir), apprendre (*conj. like* prendre)
fine excellent; beau (*before vowel sound*
   bel; *f.* belle); **those fine people** ces
   braves gens *m. pl.*
finger doigt *m.*

Verbs with spelling changes are explained on pp. 302–304.

finish finir
fire incendie *m.*
first premier (*f.* première); **on the first floor** au rez-de-chaussée
fish poisson *m.*
five cinq
fix réparer
floor plancher *m.;* étage *m.;* **on the first floor** au rez-de-chaussée
Florida Floride *f.*
florist fleuriste *m.* or *f.*
flower fleur *f.*
fluently couramment
follow suivre (suivant, suivi, je suis, je suivis)
foolish stupide
foot pied *m.;* **on foot** à pied
football ballon *m.;* football *m.;* **football game** un match de football, une partie de football
for (pp. 233, 240) (*conjunc.*) car (*prep.*) pour; pendant; depuis, il y a . . . que, voilà . . . que
forbid défendre (à + *person* + de + *inf.*)
foreign étranger (*f.* étrangère)
foreigner étranger *m.* (*f.* étrangère)
forget oublier (de + *inf.*)
former ancien (*f.* ancienne); **the former** celui-là
formerly autrefois
fortune fortune *f.*
forty quarante
fountain pen stylo *m.*
four quatre
France France *f.*
Frances Françoise *f.*
Francis François *m.*
frankly franchement
Frederick Frédéric
free libre
French français; **French class** classe de français *f.*
Friday vendredi *m.*
friend ami *m.*, amie *f.;* **a close friend** un ami intime
frightened effrayé; **become frightened** s'effrayer (*irr. sp.* **C**)
frigidaire réfrigérateur *m.;* frigidaire *m.*
from de; **keep from** empêcher (+ *person* + de + *inf.*)
front: **in front of** devant
fruit fruit *m.*

full plein
fun: **make fun of** se moquer (de + *n.*)
funny amusant
fur fourrure *f.*
furious furieux (*f.* furieuse)

G

gain gagner; **gain ground** avancer (*irr. sp.* **A**)
game match *m.*, partie *f.;* **a football game** une partie de football, un match de football
garden jardin *m.*
general général *m.*
generous généreux (*f.* généreuse)
George Georges
German (*adj.*) allemand
Germany Allemagne *f.*
get (pp. 69–70) chercher; recevoir; prendre; faire; avoir; obtenir; atteindre; **get along** se débrouiller; **get angry** se fâcher; **get around** se déplacer; **get into** entrer dans; **get married** se marier; **get out of** sortir de; **get pale** pâlir; **get somewhere** arriver; **get tired** se fatiguer; **get up** se lever (*irr. sp.* **D**); **it got warm** il a fait chaud
gift cadeau *m.;* **give a gift** faire un cadeau
girl jeune fille *f.*
give donner; consacrer; **give a lecture** faire une conférence
glad content, heureux (*f.* heureuse)
glance regard *m.*
go (pp. 80–81, 245) aller (allant, allé, je vais, j'allai); **go and see** aller voir; **go away** partir (2), s'en aller; **go back** retourner; **go by** passer; **go down** descendre; **go for a walk** aller se promener; **go out** sortir (2); **go to bed** se coucher; **go through** passer par; **go up** monter; remonter
going: **easy-going** indulgent
golf golf *m.*
good (*n.*) bon *m.;* bien *m.* (*adj.*) bon; (*well-behaved*) sage; **good looks** beauté *f.;* **have a good time** s'amuser
goodbye au revoir
grandchild petit-fils *m.;* petite-fille *f.;* petits-enfants *m.* or *f. pl.*

Irregular verbs are conjugated on pp. 284–301.

grandmother grand-mère *f.*
grandparents grands-parents *m. pl.*
grapefruit pamplemousse *m.*
grave grave
great grand; **a great deal** beaucoup;
  a great many beaucoup
Greece Grèce *f.*
green vert
ground: gain ground avancer (*irr. sp.* **A**)
group groupe *m.*

H

hair cheveux *m. pl.*
hairdresser coiffeur *m.;* coiffeuse *f.*
half (*n.*) moitié *f.* (*adj.*) demi; **a half
  hour** une demi-heure
hall: city hall hôtel de ville *m.*, mairie *f.*
hand main *f.* **shake hands** se serrer la
  main
hand in remettre (*conj. like* mettre)
happen (pp. 81–82) se passer; arriver;
  se trouver; **it happened to me** cela
  m'est arrivé
happiness bonheur *m.*
happy heureux (*f.* heureuse), content;
  Happy New Year Bonne Année, une
  Bonne Nouvelle Année
hard (*adj.*) dur; difficile
hard (*adv.*) dur
hateful méchant
have avoir (ayant, eu, j'ai, j'eus); (pp.
  190–191, 192–202) (*causative*) faire
  (+ *inf.*) **have dinner** dîner; **have
  lunch** déjeuner; **have to** devoir,
  falloir, être obligé de
head tête *f.*
headache mal de tête *m.;* **have a headache** avoir mal à la tête
hear (p. 83) entendre; **hear of** entendre
  parler de; **hear that** entendre dire que
heartily de bon cœur
heaven ciel *m.*
heavy lourd
hell enfer *m.*
help (*v.*) aider (*person* + à + *inf.*); (*n.*)
  aide *f.*
her (*direct obj.*) la; (*indirect obj.*) lui;
  (*with prep.*) elle; (*adj.*) son, sa, ses
here ici; **here is, here are** voici
hero *héros *m.*
hesitate hésiter

high élevé; *haut
hill colline *f.*
him (*direct obj.*) le; (*indirect obj.*) lui;
  (*with prep.*) lui
hire engager (*irr. sp.* **B**)
his (*adj.*) son, sa, ses; (*pron.*) le sien, la
  sienne, etc.
history histoire *f.*
hold tenir (tenant, tenu, je tiens, je tins);
  avoir lieu
home maison *f.;* **at home** chez soi; chez
  nous; **be home** être chez soi; **come
  back home** rentrer; **return home**
  rentrer
homework devoir *m.*
honor honneur *m.*
hope espérer (+ *inf.*) (*irr. sp.* **E**); **hope
  for** espérer (+ *n.*)
horrified scandalisé
horseback: go horseback riding faire du
  cheval, faire une promenade à cheval
hostile hostile
hotel hôtel *m.*
hour heure *f.;* **a half hour** une demi-
  heure
house maison *f.;* **at your house** chez
  vous
housework ménage *m.*
how comment; **how often** tous les combien; **know how to do something**
  (p. 95) savoir faire quelque chose
however cependant, pourtant; si (+
  adj.); **however rich he is (may be)**
  si riche qu'il soit; **however that may
  be** quoi qu'il en soit
humble humble
hundred (*n.*) centaine *f.;* (*adj.*) cent
hurry se dépêcher (de + *inf.*)
hurt (*v.*) faire mal (à + *person*); **hurt
  oneself** se faire mal; (*adj.*) vexé
husband mari *m.*
hypothesis hypothèse *f.*

I

I je; moi
ice glace *f.;* **ice cream** glace *f.;* **ice
  water** eau glacée
idea idée *f.*
if si
illness maladie *f.*
illustrated illustré
imagine imaginer

Verbs with spelling changes are explained on pp. 302–304.

immediate immédiat
immediately immédiatement
import importer
important important
impression impression *f.*
in (pp. 210–212, 241–242) dans; en; à; de; **eight in the evening** huit heures du soir; **in that manner** de cette façon; **in the theater** au théâtre; **in two hours** dans deux heures; en deux heures
in spite of (p. 243) malgré
indifference indifférence *f.*
information information *f.;* renseignements *m. pl.*
initiative initiative *f.*
inquire se renseigner
inspect inspecter
instead of (p. 243) au lieu de
insult insulte *f.*
intelligence intelligence *f.*
intelligent intelligent
intend (p. 93) avoir l'intention de; compter (+ *inf.*); penser (+ *inf.*)
interest (*v.*) intéresser; s'intéresser (à + *n.*); (*n.*) intérêt *m.*, **take an interest in** s'intéresser (à + *n.*)
interested: become interested in s'intéresser (à + *n.*)
interesting intéressant
interior intérieur *m.;* **interior decorator** décorateur *m.;* décoratrice *f.*
interrupt interrompre
intervene intervenir (*conj. like* venir)
into dans; en
introduce (p. 93) présenter
invitation invitation *f.*
invite inviter (à + *inf.*)
Ireland Irlande *f.*
Irene Irène
is est
isn't it? n'est-ce pas?
it (*subject*) il; elle; ce; ça; (*direct obj.*) le, la
Italian (*n.*) Italien *m.* (*adj.*) italien (*f.* italienne)
Italy Italie *f.*

J

Jack Jacques

Japan Japon *m.*
Japanese japonais
Jean Jeanne
job (p. 168) place *f.;* travail *m.;* position *f.;* situation *f.*
Johnnie Jeannot
joy joie *f.*
Julia Julie
July juillet *m.*
June juin *m.*
just juste; **I have just done something** je viens de faire quelque chose

K

keep garder; **keep from** empêcher (*n.* + de + *inf.*)
key clé *f.*
kilometer kilomètre *m.* (⅝ of a mile)
kind aimable
kindness bonté *f.*
king roi *m.*
knife couteau *m.*
knock frapper; **there was a knock** (pp. 93–94) on a frappé
know (pp. 94–95) (*something*) savoir (sachant, su, je sais, je sus); (*be acquainted with someone or something*) connaître (connaissant, connu, je connais, je connus); **know how to** savoir (+ *inf.*)

L

laboratory laboratoire *m.*
lack (p. 106) manquer (de + *n.*)
ladder échelle *f.*
lady dame *f.;* femme *f.*
lake lac *m.*
lamp lampe *f.*
language langue *f.*
large grand; gros (*f.* grosse)
last dernier (*f.* dernière); **last evening** hier soir; **last night** (p. 107) cette nuit; la nuit dernière
late (p. 107) (*not early*) tard; (*not on time*) en retard
latter: the latter celui-ci; ce dernier
laugh (*v.*) rire (riant, ri, je ris, je ris) (de + *n.*); **laugh at** rire de, se moquer de; (*n.*) rire *m.*

Irregular verbs are conjugated on pp. 284–301.

Laura Laure
Lawrence Laurent
lawyer avocat *m.*
lazy paresseux (*f.* paresseuse)
learn apprendre (*conj. like* prendre)
leather cuir *m.*
leave (pp. 107–109) (*something somewhere*)
 laisser; (*a place*) quitter; partir (de +
 n.) (2); sortir (de + *n.*) (2); **leave me
 alone** laissez-moi tranquille
lecture conférence *f.*
leg jambe *f.*
lend prêter
length longueur *f.;* **at length** longuement
lesson leçon *f.*
letter lettre *f.*
library bibliothèque *f.*
lie mentir (2)
lieutenant lieutenant *m.*
life vie *f.*
light lumière *f.*
like (*v.*) aimer; vouloir; (*prep.*) comme
lip lèvre *f.*
listen écouter; **listen to** écouter (+ *n.*)
little (*adj.*) petit; (*adv.*) (p. 122) peu;
 un peu
live (p. 122) habiter (+ *n.* or, à + *n.*,
 or, dans + *n.*); vivre (vivant, vécu, je
 vis, je vécus)
living room salle de séjour *f.;* salon *m.*
lock fermer à clé
London Londres *m.*
long (p. 123) long (*f.* longue); **a long
 time** longtemps; **as long as** tant que;
 how long depuis quand, depuis combien de temps; combien de temps,
 pendant combien de temps
longer (time) plus longtemps; **no . . .
 longer** ne . . . plus
look regarder; **look after** s'occuper
 (de + *n.*); **look at** regarder (+ *n.*);
 look for chercher (+ *n.*); **look well
 on someone** aller bien à quelqu'un
looking: good looking joli; beau
looks: good looks beauté *f.*
lose perdre
lot: a lot beaucoup
loud fort
Louvre Louvre *m.*
love aimer

luck chance *f.*
Lucy Lucie
lunch déjeuner *m.;* **have lunch** déjeuner
Lyons Lyon

M

machine machine *f.*
magazine revue *f.;* magazine *m.*
mail mettre à la poste
main principal
majority plupart *f.;* majorité *f.*
make faire (faisant, fait, je fais, je fis);
 make + *adj.* (p. 124) rendre + *adj.;*
 make fun of se moquer de; **make a
 decision** prendre une décision; **make
 a trip** faire un voyage
man homme *m.;* **businessman** homme
 d'affaires; **old man** vieil homme *m.*,
 vieillard *m.;* homme âgé *m.;* (*adj. used
 as n.*) vieux *m.;* **young man** jeune
 homme (*pl.*) jeunes gens)
manage to s'arranger pour
manager gérant *m.*
many beaucoup; **a great many** beaucoup; énormément, des tas de; **many
 times** bien des fois
March mars *m.*
Margaret Marguerite
Mark Marc
marriage mariage *m.*
married marié; **get married** se marier
marry (p. 133) épouser; se marier avec;
 marier (quelqu'un à quelqu'un)
Martha Marthe
marvelous superbe; merveilleux (*f.* merveilleuse)
master maître *m.*
mathematics mathématiques *f. pl.*
matter: what is the matter with me ce
 que j'ai
mayor maire *m.*
me me, moi
meager maigre
meal repas *m.*
mean vouloir dire; signifier
meet (p. 94) (*by appointment*) retrouver;
 (*by chance*) rencontrer; (*make the acquaintance of*) faire la connaissance de,
 connaître

Verbs with spelling changes are explained on pp. 302–304.

meeting réunion *f.*
mention mentionner
Mexico Mexique *m.*
Michael Michel
Michelle Michelle
midnight minuit *m.*
military militaire
milk lait *m.*
milliner modiste *f.*
mind esprit *m.;* **change one's mind** changer d'avis
mine le mien, la mienne, etc.; à moi
minister (of the gospel) pasteur *m.*
minute minute *f.*
miss (pp. 133–134) manquer; regretter
mission mission *f.*
mistake faute *f.;* erreur *f.*
mistaken: be mistaken se tromper
model mannequin *m.*
modern moderne
money argent *m.*
monster monstre *m.*
month mois *m.*
moon lune *f.*
more (p. 134) plus; **more and more** de plus en plus; **the more . . . the more** plus . . . plus; **no longer** ne . . . plus; **not any more** ne . . . plus
morning (pp. 38–39) matin *m.;* matinée *f.;* **the next morning** le lendemain matin, le matin suivant; **yesterday morning** hier matin
most plus; le plus
mother mère *f.*
mother-in-law belle-mère *f.*
motorcycle motocyclette *f.*, moto *f.;* **on a motorcycle** en moto
mountain montagne *f.*
mouth bouche *f.*
move bouger (*irr. sp.* **B**); remuer; (*change dwellings*) déménager (*irr. sp.* **B**)
movie cinéma *m.;* film *m.;* **movies** cinéma *m.*
much beaucoup; **so much** tellement; tant; **very much** (p. 227) beaucoup
music musique *f.*
musical musicien (*f.* musicienne)
must (pp. 198–203) devoir (devant, dû, je dois, je dus) (+ *inf.*); falloir (—, fallu, il faut, il fallut) (+ *inf.*); être obligé (de + *inf.*)
my mon, ma, mes

N

nasty désagréable
native natal; (*language*) maternel (*f.* maternelle)
natural naturel (*f.* naturelle)
nature nature *f.*
near près de, à côté de
necessary nécessaire; **it is necessary** il faut
necklace collier *m.*
need (*v.*) avoir besoin de; (*n.*) besoin *m.*
neighbor voisin *m.;* (*biblical sense*) prochain *m.*
neither . . . nor ni . . . ni
nervous nerveux (*f.* nerveuse)
never jamais; ne . . . jamais
new nouveau (*before vowel sound* nouvel; *f.* nouvelle)
news nouvelles *f. pl.;* **piece of news** nouvelle *f.*
newscast informations *f. pl.*
newspaper journal *m.*
next (p. 135) prochain; suivant; **the next day** le lendemain, le jour suivant, le jour après; **the next morning** le lendemain matin, le matin suivant
nice (*of persons*) gentil; (*of things*) joli; beau; **he is nice to us** il est gentil avec nous; **it is nice of him** c'est gentil de sa part
niece nièce *f.*
night nuit *f.*
nine neuf
no (*adj.*) aucun; ne . . . aucun; **no longer** ne . . . plus; **no more** ne . . . plus; (*adv.*) non
no one personne; ne . . . personne
noise bruit *m.*
noon midi *m.*
not ne . . . pas; **not any** pas de
nothing rien; ne . . . rien
notice (p. 153) remarquer; voir; s'apercevoir (*conj. like* recevoir)
novel roman *m.*
now maintenant; **up to now** jusqu'à présent
number nombre *m.;* (*street, telephone*) numéro *m.*
numerous nombreux (*f.* nombreuses); beaucoup de
nylon nylon *m.*

Irregular verbs are conjugated on pp. 284–301.

O

P

obey obéir (à + *person*)

obliged obligé (de + *inf.*)

observe observer

o'clock heure *f.*

of de; **both of you** vous deux

office bureau *m.; (doctor's)* cabinet *m.*

often souvent; **how often** tous les combien

old vieux (*before vowel sound* vieil; *f.* vieille); âgé; **I was four years old** j'avais quatre ans; **old age** vieillesse *f.;* vieux jours *m. pl.;* **old man** vieil homme *m.,* vieillard *m.;* homme âgé *m.; (adj. used as n.)* vieux *m.*

oldest brother aîné *m.;* frère aîné

Oliver Olivier

on sur; dans; en; pour; à; **on the condition** à (la) condition; **on foot** à pied; **on a motorcycle** en moto; **on Saturdays** le samedi; **on the telephone** au téléphone; **on the way** en route; **try on** essayer (*irr. sp.* **C**)

once une fois; **at once** de suite; tout de suite

one un; on; **the one** celui qui; **no one** ne . . . personne

only seulement, ne . . . que

open (*v.*) ouvrir (ouvrant, ouvert, j'ouvre, j'ouvris); (*adj.*) ouvert

opera opéra *m.*

operation opération *f.*

opinion opinion *f.;* avis *m.*

opportunity (pp. 153–154) occasion *f.;* possibilité *f.*

optimistic optimiste

or ou

orange orange *f.*

order (*v.*) ordonner; (*meal*) commander; (*prep.*); **in order to** pour

other autre; **each other** se; l'un l'autre; **every other year** tous les deux ans; **others** (*pron.*) les autres

ought to (p. 201) devrais, devrait, etc. (*conditional form of verb* devoir)

out (pp. 252–253) dehors; **fall out** tomber de; **go out** sortir (2); **one out of three** un sur trois; **out of** hors de; **out of money** sans argent

overtake rattraper

pack one's suitcase faire sa valise

package colis *m.*

page page *f.*

paint peindre (peignant, peint, je peins, je peignis)

painter *m.* peintre

painting tableau *m.;* peinture *f.*

paper (p. 154) papier *m.;* copie *f.;* composition *f.; (newspaper)* journal *m.*

parade défilé *m.*

pardon pardon *m.;* **he asked my pardon** il m'a demandé pardon

parent parent *m.*

part partie *f.; (in a play)* rôle *m.*

partner associé *m.*

party soirée *f.*

pass passer; **pass an examination** réussir à un examen

passport passeport *m.*

past passé *m.*

patient *m.* patient; (*adj.*) patient

pay (*v.*) payer (*irr. sp.* **A**); (*n.*) salaire *m.;* paie *f.*

peace paix *f.;* **in peace** en paix; **Peace Street** rue de la Paix

peaceful tranquille, calme, paisible

pen plume *f.;* **fountain pen** stylo *m.*

pencil crayon *m.*

people (pp. 155–156) gens *m. pl.;* on; personnes *f. pl.; (nation)* peuple *m.;* **those fine people** ces braves gens; **young people** jeunes gens *m. pl.*

per par

percent pourcent *m.*

perfume parfum *m.*

perhaps peut-être

permit permettre (*conj. like* mettre) (à + *person* + de + *inf.*)

permission permission *f.*

person personne *f.*

piano piano *m.;* **play the piano** jouer du piano

pick up ramasser; cueillir

picture tableau *m.;* peinture *f.*

picturesque pittoresque

piece (p. 167) morceau *m.;* bout *m.; (of advice)* conseil *m.; (of paper)* feuille *f.*

pilot pilote *m.*

Verbs with spelling changes are explained on pp. 302–304.

place (pp. 167–168) endroit *m.;* lieu *m.;* place *f.;* espace *m.;* **at their place** chez eux

plain: in plain daylight en plein jour

plant plante *f.*

play (*v.*) jouer (de + *instrument;* à + *game*); (*n.*) pièce *f.*

pleasant agréable

please plaire (plaisant, plu, je plais, je plus) (à + *person*); faire plaisir à; s'il vous plaît

pleasure plaisir *m.*

pocket poche *f.*

poetry poésie *f.*

point point *m.*

poker poker *m.*

Poland Pologne *f.*

police police *f.*

policeman agent *m.;* agent de police *m.;* policier *m.*

polite poli

politics politique *f. sing.*

pool (**swimming**) piscine *f.*

poor pauvre

popular populaire

portrait portrait *m.*

Portugal Portugal *m.*

Portuguese portugais

position place *f.;* position *f.;* situation *f.*

possible possible

postcard carte postale *f.*

powerful puissant

practice pratique *f.*

preach prêcher

prefer préférer (*irr. sp.* **E**); aimer mieux

prepare préparer

present (*time*) présent *m.;* (*gift*) cadeau *m.*

president président *m.*

pressed together serré

pretty joli

prince prince *m.*

prison prison *f.*

prize prix *m.*

probable probable

probably probablement

problem problème *m.*

prodigy prodige *m.*

product produit *m.*

professor professeur *m.*

program programme *m.*

progress progrès *m.;* **make progress** faire des progrès

promise promettre (*conj. like* mettre) (à + *person* + de + *inf.*)

proud fier (*f.* fière)

prove prouver

provided that pourvu que (+ *subjunc.*)

public public, publique *f.*

publish publier

publisher éditeur *m.*

punish punir

pupil élève *m. or f.*

purple mauve

purse sac *m.*

put mettre (mettant, mis, je mets, je mis); **put down** baisser; **put on** mettre

puzzle: crossword puzzle les mots croisés *m. pl.*

Pyrenees Pyrénées *f. pl.*

Q

quality qualité *f.*

question (*v.*) questionner; interroger (*irr. sp.* **B**); (*n.*) question *f.;* **ask a question** poser une question

quickly vite

quiet tranquille, calme

R

radio radio *f.*

rain (*v.*) pleuvoir (pleuvant, plu, il pleut, il plut); (*n.*) la pluie (*f.*)

raise (*v.*) lever (*irr. sp.* **D**); (*n.*) augmentation *f.*

rapidly vite; rapidement

rare rare

rarely rarement

rather (p. 169) plutôt; plutôt que de; assez; aimer mieux; au lieu de

read lire (lisant, lu, je lis, je lus)

real vrai

realize se rendre compte

really vraiment

reason (pp. 169–170) raison *f.;* **the reason for** la raison de; **the reason that** la raison pour laquelle

reassure rassurer

Irregular verbs are conjugated on pp. 284–301.

reassured rassuré
receive recevoir (recevant, reçu, je reçois, je reçus)
recently récemment
reception réception *f.*
recognize reconnaître (*conj. like* connaître)
recommend recommander
recommendation recommandation *f.*
record disque *m.*
red rouge
refuse refuser (de + *inf.*)
regret (*v.*) regretter; (*n.*) regret *m.*
relate raconter
relative parent *m.*
religion religion *f.*
remain rester
remarkable remarquable
remember se souvenir (*conj. like* venir) (de + *n.;* de + *inf.*); se rappeler (*irr. sp.* **F**) (+ *n.*)
repair réparer
repent se repentir (2)
reply (*v.*) répondre (à + *n.*); (*n.*) réponse *f.*
Republic République *f.*
require exiger (*irr. sp.* **B**)
resemble ressembler (à + *n.*)
reserve réserver, louer
resignation démission *f.*
resist résister (à + *n.*)
rest se reposer
restaurant restaurant *m.*
restful reposant
result résultat *m.*
résumé résumé *m.*
retire prendre (sa) retraite
retirement retraite *f.*
return (*v.*) (pp. 179–180) (*come back*) revenir (*conj. like* venir); (*go back*) retourner; (*go back home*) rentrer; (*give back*) rendre; (*n.*) retour *m.*
reward récompenser
Rhone Rhône *m.*
rich riche
ridiculous ridicule
riding: go horseback riding faire du cheval, faire une promenade à cheval
right bon; juste; **right away** tout de suite; **be right** avoir raison
ring (*v.*) sonner; (*n.*) bague *f.*

river fleuve *m.;* rivière *f.*
Riviera Côte d'Azur *f.*
road route *f.;* chemin *m.;* **go along the road** suivre la route (le chemin)
roast rôti *m.*
roasted rôti
room (pp. 180–181) (*in general*) pièce *f.;* (*bedroom*) chambre *f.;* (*room for meetings*) salle *f.;* (*living room*) salle de séjour *f.;* salon *m.;* (*space*) place *f.*
rose rose *f.*
row rang *m.*
rub frotter
rule règle *f.*
rummage around fouiller
run courir (courant, couru, je cours, je courus); **run across** traverser en courant
rush se précipiter
Russia Russie *f.*
Russian russe

S

sad triste
sailboat bateau à voiles *m.*
salesman vendeur *m.;* représentant *m.*
same même; **all the same** quand même
sample échantillon *m.*
sandwich sandwich *m.*
satisfied content; satisfait
Saturday samedi *m.*
save (pp. 181–182) sauver; économiser; faire des économies; garder; mettre de côté
say dire (disant, dit, je dis, je dis) (à + *person* + de + *inf.*)
scarcely à peine
scarf écharpe *f.*
school école *f.;* **to, in, at school** à l'école
scientific scientifique
scientist savant *m.*
season saison *f.*
secretary secrétaire *m. or f.*
see voir (voyant, vu, je vois, je vis); **see again** revoir (*conj. like* voir); **come and see me** venez me voir
seem sembler (+ *inf.*); paraître (*conj. like* connaître) (+ *inf.*); avoir l'air (+ *adj.;* de + *inf.*)
sell vendre

Verbs with spelling changes are explained on pp. 302–304.

senator sénateur
send envoyer (envoyant, envoyé, j'envoie, j'envoyai)
sentence phrase *f.*
separate séparer
serious sérieux (*f.* sérieuse)
servant serviteur *m.;* domestique *m. or f.*
serve servir (2)
service service *m.*
set (*v.*) (*the sun*) se coucher; (*n.*) (*television*) télévision *f.*
seven sept
several plusieurs
shake secouer; serrer; **shake hands** se serrer la main
sharp: at one o'clock sharp à une heure précise
sheet drap *m.*
shirt chemise *f.*
shopping center centre commercial *m.*
short court, bref (*f.* brève); **short story** conte *m.*
shortcoming défaut *m.*
should (p. 201) devrais, devrait, etc.; *conditional form of verb*
shoulder épaule *f.*
show montrer
shrug hausser; **shrug one's shoulders** hausser les épaules
shut fermer
sick malade
sight vue *f.;* **catch sight of** apercevoir (*conj. like* recevoir) (+ *n.*)
sign signer
silk soie *f.*
silly bête; sot (*f.* sotte)
silver argent *m.*
silverware argenterie *f.*
since (pp. 111, 233–234) puisque; comme; depuis que; depuis
single seul
sister sœur *f.;* **sister-in-law** belle-sœur *f.*
sit, sit down (p. 182) s'asseoir (s'asseyant, assis, je m'assieds, je m'assis) (*imperative*) asseyez-vous; **sitting** assis
situate situer; **be situated** se trouver
situation situation *f.*
six six
sixteen seize
skin peau *f.*
sleep dormir (2)

sleepy: be sleepy avoir sommeil
slight léger (*f.* légère)
slightest moindre
slow down ralentir
small petit
smile sourire *m.*
smoke (*v.*) fumer; (*n.*) fumée *f.*
snapshot photo *f.;* photographie *f.*
snow (*v.*) neiger; (*irr. sp.* B) (*n.*) neige *f.*
so si; tant; tellement; le; **so much** tant, tellement; **so that** pour que
soap savon *m.*
sofa sofa *m.;* canapé *m.*
soft doux (*f.* douce)
solve résoudre; (*pp*) résolu
soldier soldat *m.;* militaire *m.*
somber sombre
some (*adj.*) du, de, la, de l', des; quelque; (*pron.*) quelques-uns; en
someone quelqu'un
something quelque chose; **something else** autre chose
sometimes quelquefois, parfois
somewhere quelque part
son fils *m.*
song chanson *f.*
soon (pp. 194–195) tôt; bientôt; **as soon as** dès que
sore douloureux (*f.* douloureuse); **I have a sore throat** j'ai mal à la gorge
sorrow chagrin *m.;* **to my great sorrow** à mon vif regret
sorry désolé; **be sorry** regretter; **I'm sorry** pardon
sort sorte *f.*
soundly profondément
south sud *m.*
South American Sud-Américain *m.*
Spain Espagne *f.*
Spanish espagnol
speak parler
special particulier (*f.* particulière); spécial
specialist spécialiste *m.*
spend (p. 195) (*money*) dépenser; (*time*) passer
spite: in spite of (p. 243) malgré
sport sport *m.*
spring printemps *m.*
spy espion *m.*
square place *f.*

Irregular verbs are conjugated on pp. 284–301.

stamp timbre *m.*

stand se tenir, se tenir debout; (*bear*) supporter

state état *m.*

station gare *f.*

stay rester

step (*course of action*) démarche *f.*

still encore; toujours

stocking bas *m.*

stop (pp. 195–196) cesser (de + *inf.*); arrêter (+ *n.*; de + *inf.*); s'arrêter (de + *inf.*) **without stopping** sans arrêt

store magasin *m.*

storm orage *m.*

story histoire *f.*; **detective story** roman policier *m.*; **short story** conte *m.*

strange étrange; curieux (*f.* curieuse)

stranger étranger *m.*

street rue *f.*; **on the street** dans la rue

stretch étendre; **stretched out** tendu; étendu

strict sévère

strong fort

stubborn entêté, têtu

student (*college*) étudiant *m.*, étudiante *f.*; (*grade and high school*) élève *m. or f.*

study (*v.*) travailler; étudier; (*n.*) étude *f.*

succeed réussir (à + *inf.*)

such (pp. 196–197) tel (*f.* telle); aussi; comme ça; pareil (*f.* pareille)

suddenly soudain; tout à coup; tout d'un coup

suffer souffrir (*conj. like* ouvrir)

sugar sucre *m.*

suit costume *m.*

suitcase valise *f.*; **pack one's suitcase** faire sa valise

sum somme *f.*; somme d'argent *f.*

summer été *m.*

sun soleil *m.*; **there is sun** il fait du soleil, il y a du soleil; **the sun set** le soleil s'est couché

Sunday dimanche *m.*

sunlight soleil *m.*

surprise étonner

surprised étonné

surprising étonnant

Susan Suzanne

suspect suspect *m.*

Sweden Suède *f.*

swim nager (*irr. sp.* **B**)

swimming pool piscine *f.*

T

table table *f.*; **clear the table** débarrasser la table

take (pp. 204–206) prendre (prenant, pris, je prends, je pris); mener (*irr. sp.* **D**); emmener (*irr. sp.* **D**); amener (*irr. sp.* **D**); apporter; (= *subscribe to*) s'abonner à, être abonné à; **take a course** suivre un cours; **take an interest in** s'intéresser (à + *n.*); **take a walk** se promener (*irr. sp.* **D**), faire une promenade

talent talent *m.*

talk (*v.*) parler; (*n.*) causerie *f.*; **give a talk** faire une causerie; **talk business** parler affaires, parler des affaires

taxi taxi *m.*

tea thé *m.*

teach (pp. 206–207) enseigner; apprendre (*conj. like* prendre)

teacher professeur *m.*; maître *m.*

team équipe *f.*

teen-agers les jeunes, les adolescents, les "teen-agers," les moins de vingt ans

telephone (*v.*) téléphoner (à + *person*); (*n.*) téléphone *m.*; **telephone book** annuaire *m.*; **telephone number** numéro de téléphone

television télévision *f.*, la télé, la TV; **television set** télévision *f.*

tell dire (disant, dit, je dis, je dis) (à + *person* + de + *inf.*); raconter; **tell about** parler de

ten dix

tender tendre

terrible terrible

than que; (*before numerals*) de

thank remercier (de *or* pour + *thing*; de + *inf.*)

that (*conjunc.*) que; **so that** pour que; (*demonstrative*) ce, cet, cette, ces; celui, etc.; cela; (*relative*) qui; que

the le, la, l', les

theater théâtre *m.*; **in the theater** au théâtre

Verbs with spelling changes are explained on pp. 302–304.

their leur
then ensuite, puis; alors
theory théorie *f.*
there y; là; **from there** en; de là; **there is, there are** il y a; voilà
these ces
they ils; on; eux
thief voleur *m.*
thing chose *f.*
think penser (à + *n.*); croire (croyant, cru, je crois, je crus)
third troisième
thirty trente
this ce, cet, cette
though bien que, quoique; **even though** quoique; bien que; tout en (+ *pres. participle*)
thought pensée *f.*
three trois
throat gorge *f.;* **I have a sore throat** j'ai mal à la gorge
through par; **go through** passer par; parcourir (*conj. like* écrire)
Thursday jeudi *m.*
tie cravate *f.*
tied up attaché
time (pp. 207–209) temps *m.;* fois *f.;* heure *f.;* époque *f.;* moment *m.;* **by the time** quand; **for a long time** longtemps; **from time to time** de temps en temps; **have a good time** s'amuser, bien s'amuser; **in time** à temps; **many times** bien des fois; **on time** à l'heure
tired fatigué
title titre *m.*
to à; chez; dans; en
today aujourd'hui
together ensemble; **pressed together** serré
tomorrow demain; **the day after tomorrow** après-demain
tonight ce soir
too trop
tool outil *m.*
top sommet *m.*
tourist touriste *m. on f.*
tournament tournoi *m.*
toward (p. 244) vers; envers
town ville *f.*
toy jouet *m.*
traffic (*adj.*) de la circulation

train train *m.;* **by train** en train, par le train
translate traduire (*conj. like* conduire)
travel (*v.*) voyager (*irr. sp.* **B**) (p. 211); **travel across** traverser; (*n.*) voyage *m.*
traveller voyageur *m.*
tray plateau *m.*
trip voyage *m.;* **take a trip** faire un voyage
troop troupe *f.*
trouble histoire *f.;* ennuis *m. pl.;* difficultés *f. pl.*
true vrai
truly vraiment
truth vérité *f.*
try essayer (*irr. sp.* **C**) (de + *inf.*); chercher (à + *inf.*); **try on** essayer
turn around se retourner
twelve douze
twenty vingt
twice deux fois
twist tordre
two deux
type taper à la machine, écrire à la machine
typewrite taper à la machine, écrire à la machine

U

ugly vilain
unbearable insupportable
under (p. 244) sous; au-dessous de
understand comprendre (*conj. like* prendre)
undeveloped sous-développé
uneasiness malaise *m.*
unfortunately malheureusement
United States Etats-Unis *m. pl.*
university université *f.*
unless à moins que (+ *subjunc.*)
until (p. 234) (*conjunc.*) jusqu'à ce que (+ *subjunc.*); (*prep.*) jusqu'à
up (pp. 244–245) dessus; sur; en haut; **go up** remonter; monter; **up to now** jusqu'à présent
use se servir (de + *n.*); employer (*irr. sp.* **C**); **used to** (pp. 87–88) *a form of the imperfect tense*
useful utile
useless inutile

Irregular verbs are conjugated on pp. 284–301.

V

vacation vacances *f. pl.*

valuable précieux (*f.* précieuse); de prix; de valeur

vase vase *m.*

very très; **very much** (p. 227) beaucoup beaucoup; énormément, un tas de; des tas de

vicious méchant

village village *m.*

violin violon *m.*

visit (pp. 227–228) (*a place*) visiter; (*a person*) aller voir; rendre visite à; faire une visite à

visitor visiteur *m.*

voice voix *f.*

W

wait attendre; **wait for** attendre (+ *n.*)

waiter garçon *m.*

wake up réveiller; se réveiller

walk (*v.*) marcher; se promener (*irr. sp.* **D**); (*n.*) promenade *f.;* **go for a walk, take a walk** aller se promener, faire une promenade, se promener (*irr. sp.* **D**)

want vouloir (voulant, voulu, je veux, je voulus) (+ *inf.*)

war guerre *f.;* **world war** guerre mondiale *f.*

warm chaud; **be warm** avoir chaud

wash laver; **wash the dishes** faire la vaisselle

waste perdre; gaspiller

watch (*v.*) regarder, observer; surveiller; (*n.*) montre *f.*

water eau *f.;* **ice water** eau glacée

way route *f.;* manière *f.;* façon *f.;* **continue on our way** continuer notre route; **in that way** de cette façon; **on the way** en route

wear porter

weather temps *m.;* **the weather is good** il fait beau

wedding mariage *m.*

week semaine *f.*

weekend week-end *m.*

well bien; **well known** connu, célèbre; bien connu

what (*interrog.*) qu'est-ce qui; que, qu'est-ce que; quoi; quel, quelle; comment; (*relative*) ce qui; ce que

whatever quoi que; quel que (*f.* quelle que)

when (p. 131) quand; où

where où

whereas tandis que

wherever où . . . que (+ *subjunc.*)

whether si

which (*interrog.*) quel, quelle; lequel, laquelle; (*rel.*) qui; que; lequel; quoi

while (pp. 63, 228) (*at the same time*) pendant que; (*whereas*) tandis que; **a little while ago** tout à l'heure; **all the while** tout en (+ *pres. participle*)

white blanc (*f.* blanche)

who (*interrog.*) qui; (*rel.*) qui; que

whoever qui que; quel que; **whoever he is (may be)** qui que ce soit; quel qu'il soit

whole tout (*m. pl.* tous)

why pourquoi

wife femme *f.*

willing: be willing vouloir bien

win gagner; remporter

window fenêtre *f.;* vitre *f.*

windowpane vitre *f.*

wine vin *m.*

winner gagnant *m.*

winter hiver *m.*

Wisconsin Wisconsin *m.*

wish (pp. 138–139, 229–230) vouloir (voulant, voulu, je veux, je voulus) (+ *inf.*); désirer (+ *inf.*); souhaiter

with (pp. 245–246) avec; sur; de; chez

without sans; **do without** se passer de

woman femme *f.;* **cleaning woman** femme de ménage *f.*

wonder se demander

wonderful merveilleux (*f.* merveilleuse)

won't ne pas vouloir (+ *inf.*)

wood bois *m.*

word mot *m.* (*spoken word*) parole *f.*

work (*v.*) travailler; (*n.*) travail *m.;* **out of work** sans travail

workman ouvrier *m.;* travailleur *m.*

world monde *m.;* **world war** guerre mondiale *f.*

worried inquiet (*f.* inquiète)

worry inquiéter; s'inquiéter (*irr. sp.* **E**)

Verbs with spelling changes are explained on pp. 302–304.

would (pp. 87–88, 118, 120, 247) vouloir; *as auxiliary verb: (in conditional) conditional of main verb;* (*= used to*) *imperfect of main verb*

write écrire (écrivant, écrit, j'écris j'écrivis)

writer écrivain *m.*

wrong faux (*f.* fausse); be wrong avoir tort; do wrong faire du tort

Y

yawn bailler

year (pp. 247–248) an *m.;* année *f.;* Happy New Year Bonne Année, Bonne Nouvelle Année; I was ten years old j'avais dix ans; twice a year deux fois par an; every year tous les ans; youthful years années de jeunesse *f. pl.*

yes (p. 248) oui; si

yesterday hier; yesterday evening hier soir; yesterday morning hier matin

you tu; vous; both of you vous deux

young jeune

young men (pp. 248–249) jeunes gens *m. pl.*

your votre, vos

yours le vôtre, la vôtre, etc.

yourself vous-même

youthful jeune; youthful years années de jeunesse *f. pl.*

Irregular verbs are conjugated on pp. 284–301.

Index

References are to pages [ex. 157] and, in the *Textes*, to pages and notes [ex. 276 (12)].

Problem words are normally indexed only under their English meaning.

à

à + **de** verbs 218–219
characteristic 246
with cities 210
with countries 211
être à to show possession 79
with expressions such as **à pied, à bicyclette** 166
à l'heure 165
before infinitive 216
à + infinitive where English uses present participle 275 (3)
à mesure que 232
meaning *with* 245
verbs requiring à before noun object 271 (9)

about 236
above 237
abstract nouns 158
according to 237
across 237
actually 10

adjectives
beau, nouveau, vieux, etc. 16–17
c'est + adjective + infinitive 222
comparison of equality 19
comparison of inequality 17–18
de + adjective + plural noun 172–173
demonstrative 96–97
descriptive 20–22
feminine 17–20
il est + adjective + infinitive 222–223
interrogative 1–2, 7
irregular 16
limiting 22, 264 (1)
of material 177
plural 13–17
position 20–24, 265 (9)
possessive 72–73

adverbs
à peine 31–32
aussi (meaning *therefore*) 32
formation 29–30
irregular 30
negative 33–36
peut-être 31–32

position 30–33
of quantity 175–176

advice 10
after
après vs. **après que** 231
d'après 238
+ verb + *-ing* 224–225

again 10
agent (with **par** and **de**) 185–186
agree 11–12

agreement
of past participle
with **en** 58
of **faire** followed by the infinitive 193
of **la plupart** with verb 272 (14), 278 (4)
of verb in passive voice 185
of verb in person and number with antecedent of its subject 268 (20)
of reflexive verbs 60–61
of verbs conjugated with **avoir** 57–58
of verbs of motion 59
with preceding **vous** 59
of possessive adjective 72
of present participle 62

-aine 237
along 238
an vs. **année** 247–248
apercevoir vs. **s'apercevoir** 275 (6)
apparaître vs. **paraître** 268 (2)
appositives 160–161

après
après vs. **après que** 231
après + compound infinitive 224–225

article (uses and omission)
with appositives 160–161
with cities 164
with countries and continents 163–164
with dates 159
with days of week 158
after **dont** 130
after **en** 161
forms of 157
with languages 159–160
with means of locomotion 166